International Perspectives on Violence

International Perspectives on Violence

Edited by
Leonore Loeb Adler
and
Florence L. Denmark

Foreword by Melvin Ember

 PRAEGER

Westport, Connecticut
London

Library of Congress Cataloging-in-Publication Data

International perspectives on violence / edited by Leonore Loeb Adler and
Florence L. Denmark; foreword by Melvin Ember.
    p. cm.
  Includes bibliographical references and index.
  ISBN 0–275–97498–7 (alk. paper)
    1. Violence—Cross-cultural studies. I. Adler, Leonore Loeb. II.
  Denmark, Florence. III. Title.
  HM886.I57 2002
  303.6—dc22   2002066339

British Library Cataloguing-in-Publication Data is available.

Library of Congress Catalog Card Number: 2002066339
ISBN: 0–275–97498–7

First published in 2004

Praeger Publishers, 88 Post Road West, Westport, CT 06881
An imprint of Greenwood Publishing Group, Inc.
www.praeger.com

Printed in the United States of America

The paper used in this book complies with the
Permanent Paper Standard issued by the National
Information Standards Organization (Z39.48–1984).

10 9 8 7 6 5 4 3 2

To the memory of Dr. Helmut E. Adler, who was professor emeritus of psychology at Yeshiva University.

Dr. H.E. Adler was opposed morally to the conflict and violence that exists around the world. He suggested to the editors (Leonore Loeb Adler and Florence L. Denmark) that they prepare a book with an international focus on this topic in order to provide a basis for the development of solutions worldwide. Dr. H.E. Adler understood the meaning of shalom and the concept of global peace.

Contents

Illustrations

FIGURES

Foreword

Melvin Ember

This book is full of interesting findings and suggestions about how and why violence varies in different cultures. Only by looking at other cultures can we find out what is universal and what is variable and why, with regard to violence or anything else. Cross-cultural studies are mainly of two types—investigations of other cultures, one or a few at a time (generally using data collected by the investigator) and investigations of samples of cultures worldwide (generally using data collected by others). Both types have their advantages and disadvantages with regard to the goals of generating and testing theory. Investigation of particular cultures may suggest the causes of variation, but we still have to find ways to test the generalizability of the suggested explanations. This is because the particular cases studied may not be representative of the world, and therefore our understandings may be biased in ways that may be difficult to uncover. Thus, case studies of other cultures must be supplemented by studies of samples of cultures to minimize the possibility of culture-bound explanations. This is why social and behavioral scientists first started using data from worldwide samples of cultures to test hypotheses.

Hypotheses can be generated in the same two ways. In case studies, different investigators examine different cultures, as in this book. Over time, with many such investigations by different people with different theoretical orientations, we eventually may realize what is generally cause and what is generally effect. The other way to come up with a generally valid understanding is by developing cross-cultural measures and deliberately testing hypotheses on cross-cultural samples. This is the quicker way to determine what regularly occurs along with the characteristics of interest to us, since we also will be examining cases in which those characteristics are absent and in which, therefore, the causes should also be absent. Even many independent single-case investigations are not as likely to come up with general understandings as deliberate as cross-cultural tests of hypotheses. Cross-cultural tests using worldwide samples will be more likely to produce not only a generally valid and reliable understanding, that will maximize the effectiveness of our attempts but also results from which we can base applications and policies to solve or reduce real world problems such as violence. How often could an explanation that is not universally valid (or nearly so) suggest an application or policy that would be generally effective, whatever the time or place?

As yet, while there are not that many worldwide cross-cultural studies of violence, a few general understandings have emerged. (For a brief review, see Marshall H. Segall, Carol R. Ember, and Melvin Ember "Aggression, Crime, and Warfare.") For example, we now know that many cultures exhibit what has been called a "culture of violence" (see Marc H. Ross, *The Culture of Conflict Interpretations and Interests in Comparative Perspective*). Some cultures are generally more violent than others, and many kinds of aggression go together; the higher the frequency of war, for example, the higher the rate of homicide and assault. What may explain this relationship between war and interpersonal violence? The mechanism seems to be socialization for aggression: Parents seem to want their sons to be courageous warriors if their societies have frequent warfare. Once people learn to kill an enemy, they may find it easier to hurt or kill anyone. Thus, a high rate of interpersonal aggression may be an inadvertent consequence of socialization for aggression due to the need to raise courageous warriors. This argument is supported by multiple regression and path analyses (see Carol R. Ember and Melvin Ember, "War, Socialization, and Interpersonal Violence: A Cross-Cultural Study").

Anthropologists and other social scientists started doing cross-cultural research when they realized that explanations could be culture-bound. If we studied only one society at a time, we might come up with explanations that fit that society but not others. What is worse, we couldn't know about generalizability unless we made a worldwide cross-cultural test. We face this hazard whenever we do a single-case study, even if it involves statistical hypothesis testing. No single case can give us general understanding. We could do a series of case studies to see if a general pattern exists and to seek comprehensive explanations. But the study cases would have to be selected in some random way if we were to generalize from them. Cross-cultural research, if it investigates a representative sample of the world, is the most efficient way to find out how generalizable an explanation is. Social science research is most explanatory, and potentially most useful, if it contributes to our understanding of human beings everywhere. Even if we derive a hypothesis from a theory, and even if we find that it is confirmed by one or a few single-case studies, we cannot be confident *in any measurable way* that it is generally true. Only a randomly selected worldwide sample can give us a p-value for the world.

To be sure, many, if not most, of our explanatory ideas come out of single-case studies. That is the way it is in much of social science, except where we have mathematical models from which explanatory hypotheses can be derived formally. Because the results of a single-case study are not generalizable by themselves, the relationship between cross-cultural research and the study of a particular culture is analogous to the relationship between epidemiology and the clinical practice of medicine. In ethnographic and other single-case studies, as in clinical practice, the primary focus is on the individual case (the culture, the patient), while in cross-cultural research (particularly the kind that investigates samples of cultures) the focus is on the sample as representative of some larger universe of cases. Epidemiologists look at the distribution of a disease across populations and try to understand the causes and effects of the disease, primarily through correlational and especially multivariate analyses of presumed causes and effects. Similarly, cross-cultural researchers who examine samples of cultures test for correlates and predictors of cultural variation.

This book of case studies invites us to make many cross-cultural tests of the ideas and explanations suggested. I want to invite the readers of these chapters to consider doing worldwide cross-cultural research to test the ideas and explanations contained therein. It is not hard to do worldwide cross-cultural research, that is, unless you try to go to each of your sample cases to collect primary data. You can collect secondary data for a sample of world cultures by arranging with colleagues in the sample cultures to collect the data needed. Or you can use the ethnographic texts in the HRAF Collection of Ethnography to measure the variables of interest to you. Either way, you will be able to attach a probability value to your results, which will tell you and others how likely your results are true for the world.

If you think you can find out what predicts or causes something, that is as likely to be a self-fulfilling prophecy as assuming that the world is indecipherable. You should not worry about not being able to measure a possible cause using HRAF or other secondary data, and you should not worry that you will not be able to discover how much effect it has. Just about anything you can think of can be measured (usually ordinally at least), and its effect estimated, using secondary data. Worldwide cross-cultural research is just another form of content analysis. I stand ready to help anyone who wants advice on how to design a cross-cultural study using secondary data. It is your best protection against being wrong.

REFERENCES

Ember, C.R., and Ember, M. (1994). War, socialization, and interpersonal violence: A cross-cultural study. *Journal of Conflict Resolution, 38*, 620–646.

Ross, M.H. (1993). *The culture of conflict interpretations and interests in comparative perspective.* New Haven, CT: Yale University Press.

Segall, M.H., Ember, C.R., and Ember, M. (1997). Aggression, crime, and warfare. In John W. Berry et al. (Eds.), *Handbook of cross-cultural psychology* (Vol. 3, pp. 213–254). 2nd ed. Needham Heights, MA: Allyn & Bacon.

Introduction

Leonore Loeb Adler and Florence L. Denmark

The terrorist attacks against the United States on September 11, 2001, confronted individuals from around the globe with the inescapable reality that violence in our world is all too real. While violent acts of this magnitude are rare in occurrence, they serve as a chilling reminder that issues of violence in our world are far from solved. Many questions linger in our minds: What are the root causes of violence? How are violent acts implemented? And, most important, how can violence be eradicated? With its focus on violence in many countries around the world, this text offers a comprehensive picture of a timely topic of international concern.

While terrorist acts of violence seem particularly salient in the aftermath of September 11, it is important to note that violence takes many different forms. It can occur between single individuals, gangs, military soldiers, or other large groups of people. Acts of violence can be facilitated with the use of weapons, including guns, knives, missiles, bombs, and biological or chemical agents, among many others. As we have seen recently, some perpetrators of violence sacrifice their own lives to carry out acts of violence.

Violence ranges along a continuum from a scuffle between two individuals to a grand-scale war among nations. The nature and scope of violent acts can vary dramatically, but all acts of violence share certain key components. Generally, violence is associated with aggression, brute force, and the intention of causing harm. However, what constitutes an act of violence may be a point of debate. For example, the practice of female genital mutilation (FGM) that is carried out routinely in various African countries is viewed by those in power in those nations as standard cultural practice, while others view FGM as a cruel act of violence. When an act of violence is embedded in a nation's culture, it is much more difficult to challenge such customs and traditions while remaining respectful of cultural diversity.

The causes of violence are often multifaceted, and there are countless motives underlying violent acts. Some of the broadest driving forces into which violent acts are categorized are political, social, religious, economic, criminal, and personal. On a political level, governments sanction violence for many reasons. For example, they use violent measures to protect the rights of their citizens or as a defensive maneuver when attacked by outside forces. Racial and ethnic groups use violence in their fight against oppression and discrimination. Violence has been perpetuated along gender lines; there are many examples of violent acts against women, including rape and female infanticide. Conflicts in Northern Ireland demonstrate violence that is driven by religious fervor. Criminal activities, including assault, robbery, and homicide, necessarily require acts of violence. Fights that erupt among individuals can be prompted by a host of personal issues and disagreements. Emotions can also be a trigger for violence, as is seen in crimes of passion. While it is nearly impossible to catalog the many motivations beneath violent acts, the division of violent acts into broad categories can offer some insight into the reasons why violence occurs.

There is not one country or corner of the earth that is immune to violence. It is a universal phenomenon that has existed throughout our history. In this text, we have selected carefully a wide variety of countries around the world, representing the majority of the continents, to examine in detail. Among the countries covered in this volume are Australia, Brazil, Great Britain, Israel, Japan, Russia, South Africa, and the United States of America.

The foreword was written by an eminent anthropologist, Melvin Ember, and the epilogue was written by Kay C. Greene, a nongovernmental organization (NGO) representative at the United Nations who has had extensive contact with countries around the world. Each chapter in this text was written by an expert on the topic of violence. The authors were given the freedom to organize their chapters according to their own views of violence in that particular country. Some chose to present an overview of violence, while others focused their chapters around one particular theme of violence. For example, chapter 11 investigates the many forms of violence against women in Nigeria and Africa. Violence against children is a focal point of chapters on violence in Brazil and in the Philippines.

One interesting departure from the traditional chapter format is chapter 10, entitled "Peace and Violence: A Comparison of Buddhist Ladakh and the United States." This chapter offers a refreshing glimpse into a peaceful way of life as illustrated by the Buddhist Ladakh, a predominantly Tibetan society in northwest India. The philosophies of Buddhism are contrasted with the Western philosophy adopted by the United States.

It is our hope that this volume will enable the reader not only to learn about the many different forms of violence around the world, but also to gain a foundation of knowledge upon which to draw comparisons and make distinctions among nations. This type of cross-cultural comparison will contribute to a more general understanding of the degree of the universal phenomenon of violence. It is important to compare not only the ways that violence occurs in various countries, but also the aftermath of violence in these nations. In particular, successful attempts to reduce violence are worthy of study. As we gain an increased understanding of violence, we can use these insights to inform programs directed at violence reduction.

The authors wish to express appreciation to the following graduate students who assisted in preparation of this volume: Rachele Flora, Scott Gallagher, Erica I. Heitner, Michelle Kessous, Sara Shenker, and Lani Sherman.

International Perspectives on Violence

1

A Critical Review of Arab Research Studies on Violence/Aggression and Extreme Behavior

Ramadan A. Ahmed

THE ARAB WORLD, LAND, AND PEOPLE: AN OVERVIEW

The Arab world—the territory extending from Morocco to Iran inside Asia, and from Turkey between the Black and Mediterranean Seas to Somalia—is a vast realm of enormous historical and cultural complexity. It lies at the crossroads where Europe, Asia, and Africa meet, and is part of all three; throughout history, its influences have radiated through these continents and to practically every other part of the world. This is one of humankind's primary source areas. On the Mesopotamian Plain between the Tigris and Euphrates Rivers (Iraq) and on the banks of the Egyptian Nile arose civilizations that must have been among the very earliest. In this territory walked prophets whose religious teachings are still followed by hundreds of millions of people. And, in the twentieth century, this area is the setting for the most bitter and dangerous conflicts on earth—ones that could still provoke a wide-armed confrontation.

Violence/aggression and extreme behavior constitute a very old phenomenon that started with the beginnings of human history. Many writers consider violence (aggression and extreme behavior) as one of the main aspects of human beings. Forms of violence changed according to social, economic, political, and cultural circumstances (Berkowitz, 1993; Gelles, 1999; Ohlin and Tonry, 1989). Currently, the common forms of violence are (1) domestic violence (such as marital violence; violence against women; child, sexual, and physical abuse; and violence against the elderly), (2) demonstrations, (3) strikes, (4) riots, (5) mutiny events, (6) assassinations and assassination attempts, and (7) coup d'état or attempted coup d'état (Ismail, 1988, 1996; Seiam, 1994; El-Matewally, 1995).

In the Arab world, as in other parts of the world, violence became a common phenomenon due to many social, economic, political, and cultural factors (Jalabi, 1998). For example, Egyptian society has witnessed, especially during the last two decades, a marked increase in violent events which have caused a huge amount of psychological, social, physical, and economic damage. Since 1981, Egyptian society has been the subject of a great number of political and religious violent accidents, resulting in more than a thousand deaths and thousands of wounded (Ahmed and Khalil, 1998). In Algeria, the picture is even worse. Since the early 1990s, the daily violent political events have left more than a hundred thousand dead and an equal number wounded (Sidaoui, 2000; Al-Otaibi, 2000). Violence also has been manifest in other Arab countries. For example, Lebanon—during the civil war period (1975–1990)—and Yemen—in the early 1990s—both witnessed a long and wide series of violent actions. Regrettably, people in the Palestinian territory are living under extreme circumstances of concern and uncertainty. Daily violent actions and counteractions feed an endless cycle of violence. It is hoped that such conflicts would find a peaceful end.

Several Arab research studies, books, and articles have been conducted and written during the last three or four decades to investigate violence/aggression and extremist behavior (Nasr, 1994; Safwet and El-Douseki, 1993; Ghalab and El-Dousseki, 1994; Hegazy, 1986; Ismail, 1988, 1996; Ghanem, 1998; Ahmed and Khalil, 1998).

This review of Arab research studies on violence/aggression and extreme behavior in the Arab world, may be classified in relation to

1. demographic variables (such as gender, age, socioeconomic status, religious backgrounds, family size, place of residence, and educational and vocational levels),
2. socialization practices,
3. personality traits,
4. juvenile delinquency and criminal behavior,
5. family,
6. school and university students,
7. the sociocultural context
8. clinical studies,
9. factorial studies,
10. experimental and laboratorial studies,
11. politics, and
12. general conclusions.

VIOLENCE/AGGRESSION AND EXTREME BEHAVIOR IN RELATION TO DEMOGRAPHIC VARIABLES

The first study in this context was Soueif's (1958) pioneer study on the extreme responses of tension in different gender, age, social, and religious groups in Egypt, which used a scale for friendship to assess the extreme behavior. The subjects included 1,028 Muslim and Christian male and female adolescents and adults between the ages of 12 and 46 years old. Results showed that both Muslim and Christian male adolescents scored significantly higher on extreme responses than their adult counterparts. However, female Christian adolescents and adult scored significantly higher on extreme responses than did either their Muslim or their male counterparts. Finally, it was found that lower middle-class subjects showed significantly higher levels of extreme behavior than did the higher middle-class subjects.

In one of the early studies of the Egyptian national character, Nasr and Soliman (1989, cited in Ghanem, 1998) investigated violence and aggressive behavior as possible traits of this character. Results indicated a high level of violence/aggression in the majority of the subjects. However, males outnumbered their female counterparts in both violence and aggression.

In 1976, the National Center for Sociological and Criminal Research in Cairo, Egypt, conducted a study (cited in Safwet and El-Douseki, 1993) on the relationship between violence, rebellion against authority, and several demographic variables. The results indicated that lower socioeconomic status, accompanied with awareness of deprivation, was the influential factor in the subjects' tendencies toward violent actions in Egypt.

In a more recent study (Seiam, 1994), it was found that members of fundamental groups in Egypt who had acted violently during the last three decades stemmed from populations of lower middle-class educated youth residing in remote or suburban areas who had faced a great deal of social and economic frustration during their early years.

Another study, conducted in 1979 by the police academy in Egypt (cited in Safwet and El-Douseki, 1993), of 325 adolescents who participated in the violent actions that occurred in Egypt on January 18 and 19, 1977, reported that the intellectual levels of most subjects did not surpass the average, and that the subjects had normal aggressive tendencies.

To test the impact of place of residence on violence and aggressive behavior, Al-Fangery (1987) carried out a study using a local scale to assess aggressive manifestations in urban and rural Egyptian children. Results showed that rural children were more aggressive than urban children. Urban male children were forced to perform significantly higher in terms of aggressive behavior than their female counterparts. However, such differences have not been found in rural children. Some other Egyptian studies (Abdel-Hamid, 1990; El-Sheribini, 1991; Lutfy, 1992; Abouel-Kheir, 1995; Abdel-Kader, 2000), however, found that urban subjects had significantly higher tendencies toward violence and aggression than rural subjects.

El-Gamil (1988) conducted a study on fifth and sixth graders in Egypt, who were between the ages of 10 to 12 years old. It was found that violence correlated positively with watching violent television programs. Another study, this one of urban and rural male and female university students in Egypt and conducted by Abdel-Mokhtar (1992) cited in Abdel-Mokhtar, 1998), found that males were more prone to violence than were females and that, the more violent television these models watched, the greater this tendency was.

As for the development of the aggressive behavior in children, Al-Fakherani (1989, cited in Nasr, 1994) applied Eysenck and Wilson's scale for assessing aggressive behavior to a sample of male and female nursery and primary school children. Results showed that aggressive behavior correlated negatively with age and that nursery school children were higher in instrumental (functional), or actual, aggression, while primary school children were higher in verbal aggression.

Shehata (1990, cited in Faied, 1996) studied the relationship between aggression and gender in a sample of male and female secondary school students and found that aggression was higher among males than females. Males showed clearly more manifestations of direct aggression and, to a lesser extent, verbal aggression, while females showed more manifestations of indirect aggression.

In 1996, Faied, using Buss and Perry's scale of aggressive behavior, conducted a factorial study in Egypt to investigate the dimensions of aggressive behavior in regard to gender, place of residence, and academic specialization with urban and rural university students. Results revealed that dimensions of aggressive behavior included hostility, anger, physical aggression, and verbal aggression, in that order. Results also showed that, while males were significantly more likely to engage in physical and verbal aggression, females had significantly more anger. Physical and verbal aggression were more common among rural subjects as compared to their urban counterparts, and actual college students (e.g., arts, social sciences, law, etc.) proved to be significantly more prone to physical aggression than those studying applied science (e.g., engineering, medicine, etc.).

Abdel-Mokhtar (1998) studied the relationship between alienation and violence in different male groups of farmers (peasants), skilled workers, teachers, working or non-working individuals, university graduates, and students from urban and rural areas in Egypt. Results showed a positive relationship between alienation and violence. This relationship was stronger among working, well-educated urban subjects and those of higher socioeconomic status. Results also indicated that education, socioeconomic status, work, and place of residence have an effect on the relationship between alienation and violence.

Hafez's 1989 (cited in Safwet and El-Douseki, 1993) cross-sectional study on Egyptian women's criminal behaviors reported that violent crimes (murders) committed by women increased markedly in the 20- to 40-year-old age group, while women pushing women to commit violent crimes increased in the 20- to 30-year-old age group.

Family relations in two samples of female convicted murderers and drug dealers were investigated by El-Khashab (1983). Results showed that social relations, communication styles, and affectionate feelings were higher and stronger among drug dealers' families than murderers' families. However, no significant difference has been found between families of murderers and drug dealers concerning power and decision making.

Several Egyptian research studies have focused on the relationship between parental behavior and family size on the one hand and violence/aggression and extreme behavior on the other hand: Nasr (1983); Hashem (1991, cited in Safwet and El-Douseki, 1993); Mahmoud (1988, cited in Abou-Sheba, 1992); Boanka (1989, cited in Nasr, 1994); Al-Kamel and Soliman (1990); Salama (1990, cited in El-Deeb, 1996); El-Deeb 1995 (cited in El-Deeb, 1996); Habib, (1995, cited in El-Deeb, 1996). The following sections briefly discuss examples of these studies.

One of the first studies on the relationship between family size and violence/aggression was conducted by Salama (1990, cited in El-Deeb, 1996), who found positive correlations between levels of violent/aggressive behavior and family size. Small families provided their children with a healthy atmosphere for sufficient communication between parents and children, especially in tense situations. Similar results were found in an Algerian study by Boanka (1989, cited in Nasr, 1994), who found that violence and aggressive behavior correlated positively with larger family size, lower educational level, and lower socioeconomic status. In 1995, El-Deeb (cited in El-Deeb, 1996) conducted a cross-cultural study aimed at investigating the impact of parental behaviors (e.g., support, responsibility, punishment, control, and dominance) on producing trust or aggression in children in Egypt and the sultanate of Oman. Results revealed a positive relationship between family size and aggression in children.

In addition, Habib (1995, cited in El-Deeb, 1996) investigated the relationship between perceived parental behavior and family size in samples of extreme and non-extreme university students from different academic specializations in Egypt. Results showed that extreme subjects perceived their parents as having more control, being more rejecting, wielding more aggressive control, and being more self-centered and more inconsistent. In addition, results revealed that 66 percent of the extreme subjects and 41 percent of the non-extreme subjects came from large families.

A recent Saudi study (Al-Garni, 2001) explored the function factors that could increase the likelihood of deviant behavior in male high school students by examining the relationship between family structure and deviant behavior, school truancy, and academic performance. Results showed that family size, parent-child attachment, sponsorship, and parents' educational level were the most important factors influencing the behavior.

It was hypothesized that the layout of certain spaces affects the ability of inhabitants to establish behavior control. To test this hypothesis,

Naceur (2001) examined rates of vandalism and design variations in two residential areas in Batna City, Algeria. Findings suggested that physical characteristics of the areas were particularly relevant to the patterns of the antisocial behavior observed.

Instigators of aggressive behavior in Iraq have been studied by Hasan (1998) who used a sample consisting of thirty-one men convicted of murder in Baghdad. The results revealed that murderers tended to live in slums and suburban areas; lack necessary requirements of life; have insufficient income, little or no education, low self-image; and are between 18 and 30 years old.

Several Arab studies (Abdalla, 1992; El-Sayed, 1996; Ahmed, 2003 and in press) showed that factors such as father absence and weak family influence were associated with increases in levels of or tendencies toward violent or aggressive behavior or delinquency.

Finally, a few Arab research studies have focused on the relationship between unemployment and violence/aggression and extreme behavior (Mustapha, 1993; Mourad, 1997). Results of these studies revealed positive correlations between unemployment (and its effects such as alienation and frustration) and tendencies toward violence and aggressive and extreme behavior.

VIOLENCE/AGGRESSION AND EXTREME BEHAVIOR IN RELATION TO SOCIALIZATION PRACTICES

In Arab countries, the conservative and traditional socialization practices are dominant. Parental behaviors in most cases are strict and authoritative. Several Arab research studies have shown that parents tend to use strictness, neglect, and physical and verbal aggression (as forms of punishment) in raising their children.

In an early Lebanese study, Diab (1965) reported a significant positive relationship between traditional socialization practices and authoritative behavior in children. Results showed that such practices produced a tendency for children to be not only submissive to more powerful individuals, but also dominant and authoritative to individuals weaker than themselves. Similarly, Meleikan (1965) investigated authoritarianism and its relation with some variables in two Lebanese subcultural groups (Muslims and Christians) and found a positive relationship between authoritarianism in familial atmosphere and both aggression and submission in children. In 1983, Nasr found a positive correlation between parents' authoritarian and aggressive behaviors and children's levels of violence, aggression, and extreme behaviors. Moreover, results showed that children, especially boys, who were raised by authoritarian parents had higher aggression and neuroticism. Hussein and his associates (1983, cited in Nasr, 1994) focused on the relationship between socialization practices followed by Egyptian families raising daughters in college and these daughters' aggressive behaviors and authoritative attitudes. Results showed that aggression, hostility, and authoritarianism among daughters correlated positively with their parents' aggression and inconsistency in raising their children. In the same context, Hashem (1991, cited in Safwet and El-Douseki, 1993) reported positive correlations between parental authoritarianism, rejection, and inconsistency and children's levels of aggression, resistance of authorities, and extreme behavior. Hashem's results were in line with the results of a previous study conducted by El-Douseki (1989, cited in Safwet and El-Douseki, 1993), which reported that parental behaviors characterized by authoritarianism, frustration, and guilt are the main sources of extreme behavior in violent individuals, neurotics, and paranoid people. In 1990, Al-Kamel and Soliman investigated samples of male and female university students between 17 and 25 in the sultanate of Oman and found that authoritarianism and neglect will lead to both spontaneous and defensive aggression. Results revealed no significant difference between male and female students with regard to aggressive behavior.

In addition, Mahmoud (1988, cited in Abou-Sheba, 1992) studied five wives and five husbands who had been convicted of murdering their spouses and found that all subjects had been exposed to long and continuous violent and aggressive parental behaviors during childhood.

VIOLENCE/AGGRESSION AND EXTREME BEHAVIOR AND PERSONALITY TRAITS

Several Arab research studies have been conducted to assess the relationship between violent/aggressive/extreme behavior and personality traits. One of the first studies on violence and personality was conducted by Hannourah (1969, cited in Nasr, 1994) and focused on psychological tension in a sample of convicted murderers in Egypt. It was revealed that a significant relationship between the maximum level of aggression and psychological tension existed. A later study by Hannourah (1982, cited in Nasr, 1994) assessed personality traits in two samples of male murderers and non-violent criminals between 32 to 48 years old. Results showed no significant difference between murderers and non-violent criminals except that the murderers were significantly higher on extreme response sets than were the non-violent criminals.

In 1982, El-Shernoubi (cited in Abou-Sheba, 1992) applied the Thematic Apperception Test (TAT) and the Projective Hand Test on ninety women, including thirty convicted murderers. She found that female murderers were characterized by higher levels of neuroticism, aggression, and theoretical values and by greater needs for familial, marital, and other sexual belonging, social acceptance, and independence. In a later study, Abdel-

All (1987) investigated the psychological factors and personality traits of a sample of female Egyptians convicted of murders and compared them to a similar sample of non-murderers. Results showed that murderers had higher levels of paranoia, dominancy, liberal tendencies, tension, and self-sufficiency, while non-murderers were found to have greater emotional stability, ego-strength, sensitivity, insight, result expectancy, and ability to forgive. The researcher pointed out that higher scores of sadism in murderers were related to using direct ways of executing their crimes, while their higher degrees of maschuvitism correlated positively with indirect ways of committing crimes. Impulsivity was correlated positively with both direct and indirect criminal acts. The study by Mahmoud and Mekaway (1989) on the characteristics of criminals' personality traits, intellectual levels, and electroencephalogram (EEG), reported that criminals were significantly more likely to suffer from depression, hysteria, schizophrenia, and psychopathic deviations than were the controls, and they performed worse on both verbal and non-verbal intelligence measures. Finally, 90 percent of the criminals showed evidence of slowing brain activity.

Few Arab studies have focused on the characteristics of criminal prostitutes and rapists. Abdalla (1984) compared convicted prostitutes and non-offending women with regards to personality dynamics, intelligence, family milieu, and lifestyle. Both groups were similar in levels of education, religion, marital status, age, and socioeconomic status. Results showed that prostitutes scored significantly lower than controls on the Wechsler Bellevue Intelligence Scale for adults, which indicates that they were adapted to reality less efficiently. Also, prostitutes were significantly more suggestible, fearful, and anxious and less religious than controls. They were also more likely to have broken families than their non-prostitute counterparts. In a similar project, Tawifik (1994) studied tendencies toward rape in convicted male rapists as compared to non-rapist controls. Results indicated that rapists had significantly greater levels of neuroticism, psychosis, hysteria, aggression, and psychopathic deviations, but lower in levels of satisfaction. Rapists reported that they experienced long periods of drug and alcohol abuse and were affected negatively by the mass media.

Shoukry (1993) compared personality characteristics in two samples of convicted male murdering (rapists) and economy criminals (forgers) between 23 and 52 years old. The forgery sample was significantly more likely to have phobias, psychosis, and criminal tendencies, while rapists were more likely to be anxious. A general factor for criminality/psychosis emerged in both criminal samples. Tawifik (1994) studied the social and psychological factors related to rape in an a sample of forty convicted male rapists and a similar sample of university students between the ages of 25 and 35. Results revealed that unhealthy family structures and atmospheres were common in the rape sample. Rapists displayed significantly higher levels of extroversion, neuroticism, psychosis, and hostility than did the controls.

El-Mestkaway (1981, cited in Safwet and El-Douseki, 1993) investigated personality traits in 372 university students in Egypt and found that extreme subjects, compared to non-extreme ones, were mentally more rigid and had less insight into the demands and requirements of social reality.

Members of extreme groups (e.g., fundamentalists and militants) in Egypt were studied by El-Sheikh (1993, cited in Ghanem, 1998. Results showed that fundamentalists had a high need for order and change, while non-extremists had higher scores for submission to authority, interpersonal dominance, self-blame, sympathy, and aggression. Another study (Al-Taib, 1985) showed that aggression toward others was associated with neuroticism.

Hasan and Shehata (1991, cited in Ghalab and El-Douseki, 1994) studied personality traits in forty Muslim male adults who had been arrested repeatedly for extreme religious actions and compared them to those of forty fundamental Christians (who have a wide range of religious activities), thirty-three police officers (who were assigned to stop violent activities), and forty-two non-religious Muslim adults. Results showed that police officers showed greater rigidity and intolerance of ambiguity than any of the other three groups.

In 1989, El-Douseki (cited in Safwet and El-Douseki, 1993) carried out a study aimed at determining the different personality dimensions and attitudes toward authorities and systems in three male samples: eighty convicted rebels (militants), eighty psychopathic convicted criminals, and eighty controls. Results indicated that the rebels had significantly more neuroticism than the other two groups. However, psychopathics' attitudes toward authorities and systems were more negative than the rebels'.

In the same context, El-Douseki (1992, cited in Safwet and El-Douseki, 1993) compared personality traits of religious fanatics, neurotics, psychotics, and control adults. Comparisons showed similarities between fanatics and neurotics in regard to rigidity, dominancy, fear, passivism, and aggression and similarities between fanatics, paranoids, and schizophrenics on great illusion. Fanatics were significantly higher than controls with regard to rigidity, anxiety, schizophrenia, and paranoia. El-Douseki's (1989, 1992, cited in Safwet and El-Douseki, 1993) results received support from Al-Tai's (1992, cited in Ghalab and El-Douseki, 1994) study of a sample of Kuwaiti university students found significant negative correlations between psychopathic deviations and religious attitudes and between religiosity and neuroticism. By using case studies, Shalaby and El-Douseki (1993) investigated one of the fanatic group's members and collected information about rigidity, dominancy, independence, aggression, religious extremeness, and daily activities. Results were in line with the results of El-Douseki's 1992 (cited in Safwet and El-Douseki, 1993) study, and showed that fanatics score higher on scales of rigidity, anxiety, passivism, schizophrenia, and paranoia. As for reasons for violent actions, results revealed that social schema, self-schema, political schema, and religious schema, in that order are the responsible motives.

Other Arab studies focused on different aspects of personality, motivation, and values. It is worth noting that most of these studies have been carried out in Egypt. Examples include those of Soliman and Abdel-Hamid (1994) on the relationship between aggression, self-esteem, and locus of control; Ghalab and El-Douseki (1994), on the differences between intrinsic and extrinsic religiously oriented individuals in both their attitudes toward aggression and other personality traits; and Abdalla (1997) on the relationship between prejudiced attitudes and personality traits and value systems. In the following sections, the above-mentioned studies will be reviewed briefly.

In the study carried out by Soliman and Abdel-Hamid (1994), which used a sample of Saudi male university students, it was hypothesized that there would be both a positive correlation between external locus of control and hostility and a negative correlation between hostility and positive self-esteem. Results showed (1) a significant and positive relationship between external locus of control and implicit aggression, latent aggression, and tendency toward aggression and (2) a significant negative relationship between positive self-esteem and each of these dimensions of aggression.

In recent years, many writers, especially those in mass media, have concluded that a link exists between violence/aggression or extreme behavior and religiosity or religious attitudes. Ghalab and El-Douseki (1994) conducted their study to test this so-called link by comparing attitudes toward violence and personality traits in a sample of intrinsically religious-oriented individuals and a sample of extrinsically religious-oriented individuals. Subjects included 454 Muslim and Christian university students between 18 and 22 years old. Subjects were administered scales assessing religious orientation and attitudes toward violence, dominance, and self-assertiveness. Results showed significant differences between higher intrinsic and higher extrinsic religious orientations in that higher extrinsic religious orientation resulted in more positive attitudes toward violence, neuroticism, rigidity, and anxiety. Extrinsic Muslim and Christian male subjects alike had higher rates of neuroticism, rigidity, and anxiety, while intrinsic subjects had higher self-assertiveness. Muslim extrinsic females showed more neuroticism, rigidity, and dominancy than their Christian counterparts.

As a conclusion, an unproved relationship between violent actions and religion has been assumed, especially in the mass media. In this context, Ibrahim (1989, cited in Ghalab and El-Douseki, 1994) investigated a sample of Kuwaiti adults and found a negative correlation between psychopathic deviation and religious attitudes and a similar correlation between religiosity and extroversion.

Very few Arab studies have focused on the relationship between violence, prejudicial attitudes, values, and personality traits. One of these, the study by Abdalla (1997), investigated eight hundred male and female secondary school and university students in Egypt. Results showed significant differences between males and females, and between adolescents and youth in terms of prejudicial attitudes. Females and adolescents were found to have more prejudicial attitudes than males and adults. In addition, positive correlations were found between measures of prejudicial attitudes and measures of liberalism, conservatism, and selectivity.

VIOLENCE/AGGRESSION AND EXTREME BEHAVIOR IN RELATION TO JUVENILE DELINQUENCY AND CRIMINAL BEHAVIOR

The Egyptian psychologist M.I. Soueif is considered an Arab and Egyptian pioneer in studies on extreme responses. In the late 1950s he developed the Personal Friendship Scale (PFS), in which the extreme is considered a response style, not a response content. The scale measures general extremeness, positive and negative extreme responses, carelessness, and ego-strength. Soueif (1958, 1968) has conducted a series of studies using the PFS on Muslim juvenile delinquents and non-delinquents between 15 and 21 years old. While no difference between delinquents and non-delinquents on general extremeness were found, delinquents were found to possess more positive and negative extremes. Soueif's studies were replicated by Morsi and Hannourah (1996, cited in Soueif, 1968) and by Farag (1975), who used the same scale and similar subjects. The following conclusions could be drawn from Soueif's, Morsi and Hannourah's, and Farag's studies:

1. no significant differences in general extremeness were reported between delinquents and non-delinquents,

2. positive extreme responses outnumbered the negative extreme responses among delinquents, and

3. delinquents were significantly more likely than non-delinquents to score high on measures of positive and negative extreme behaviors.

Another Egyptian study on risk, behavior, and intelligence in juvenile delinquents revealed that delinquents, as compared to non-delinquents, showed significantly more risk-taking behavior and lower levels of intelligence (Sabry, 1989).

El-Kadem (1995) studied a small number of male and female delinquents between the ages of 7 and 18 in Qatar. Results showed a 21 percent increase in juvenile delinquency in Qatar between 1976 and 1995. Unhealthy family atmosphere, lower socioeconomic status, and rapid modernization seemed to be responsible for this increase.

Al-Musallam (2001) investigated the effects of the mother/father relationship and the family atmosphere on juvenile delinquency in a sample of institutionalized Kuwaiti males and females between 15 and 18 years old. It was found that the relationship between the parents has the greatest effect on juveniles. Parents who live together have a positive effect on their children. Younger fathers and fathers with good work status were correlated negatively with juvenile delinquency in children, while the presence of older-aged and non-working fathers correlated positively with juvenile delinquency. Mothers' age and work status had no effect.

Some Arab research studies investigated juvenile delinquency cross-culturally. One of these studies was conducted by Morsi (1986) and investigated the differences in perception of harmful experiences in six samples of male delinquents and non-delinquents between 14 and 19 years old from three Arab countries: Egypt, Kuwait, and Saudi Arabia. Results revealed significant differences between the three nation-samples, where delinquents perceived experiences to be more harmful. It was also concluded that exposing children in their early age to harmful experiences will lead to the development of delinquent tendencies later.

VIOLENCE/AGGRESSION AND EXTREME BEHAVIOR WITHIN THE FAMILY

There is no doubt that acts of violence and willful neglect within families have been occurring for as long as there have been families (Helmy, 1999; Berkowitz, 1993; Ohlin and Tonry, 1989; Gelles, 1999). While family violence has been a subject of public concern for a decade or two, the recognition of family violence as a subject for social science research is much more recent. The rapid increase in public awareness of child abuse, sexual abuse, incest, spousal abuse, and other forms of family violence has led some Arab professionals and many lay people to conclude that family violence is a new phenomenon that has increased to epidemic proportions in the last decade. For example, recent statistics (*Al-Ahram*, 2001) showed that 60 percent of the murders in Egypt were committed among family members. An increase also was noticed in the number of incest crimes (Tawifik, 1994; Helmy, 1999).

Research on family violence in the Arab countries has focused on many forms of violence: spousal assault, child (sexual and physical) abuse, and abuse of the elderly, of adolescents, and between siblings.

In this context, several studies have been conducted in some Arab countries during the last ten years. In the following section, examples of these studies will be discussed briefly.

Farag and Al-Naser (1999) tried to identify violence against women through the victims' views. Two hundred and nine 23-year-old Kuwaiti female university students who were either single, married, or divorced completed a battery of tests that included scale rating, self-concept, locus of control, and experience of violence. Forcing a young girl to marry an old man, was the top form of violence reported, followed by husbands' violent threats, sexual provocations, and female genital mutilation (FGM), in that order. The lowest rated form of violence was restriction from leaving the house.

Differences between battered and non-battered women have been investigated in Kuwait by El-Sheikh (2001). This sample consisted of 242 female university students whose mean age was 19. Among them, twenty-eight were married and 214 unmarried. Results showed that battered women had significantly higher levels of depression, compulsive obsessions, sleep disorders, and post-traumatic disorders and lower self-concepts than non-battered women.

Some Egyptian studies have focused on the impact of family atmosphere and structure on women's violence and criminality. Among these studies are those cited in Nasr (1994)—Abdel-Wahab (1992), Ragab (1992), and El-Sayed (1992)—and that of Abdel-Wahab (1994). In a sociological study, Abdel-Wahab (1992, cited in Nasr, 1994) investigated ten wives who were convicted of murdering their husbands. The subjects were uneducated working class women and had been forced by their parents to marry at an early age (between 14 and 16 years old). Interviews revealed that the convicted wives had been subjected to continued forms of physical abuse by their husbands. The second study, carried out by Ragab (1992, cited in Nasr, 1994), investigated women's criminality and attitudes toward violence. This sample consisted of 229 women who were convicted for committing violent acts such as beating or hurting others. Results show that insufficient income, broken homes, and weaker religious attitudes correlated positively with attitudes toward violence. The third study, conducted by El-Sayed (1992, cited in Nasr, 1994), was on female university students' attitudes toward women's criminality and women's violence, and showed that, in most cases, women's criminality and violence were associated with social and economic factors. In the fourth Egyptian study, Abdel-Wahab (1994) studied husbands who hurt their wives and found that these men had lower educational and vocational achievement and lower socioeconomic status. Urban husbands tended to use more violence against their wives than rural husbands.

Some Arab studies dealt with child abuse and related social and psychological variables. Among these is a study by Ismail (2000), who investigated anxiety in a sample of begger children between the ages of 9 and 13 in Cairo. Demographic data revealed that these children came from lower socioeconomic families with little or no education. Results showed a high level of anxiety and negative self-image among begging children. Children reported that they continually were subjected to different forms of physical abuse conducted by their parents.

VIOLENCE/AGGRESSION AND EXTREME BEHAVIOR AMONG SCHOOL AND UNIVERSITY STUDENTS

As a response to the gradual increase of violent and aggressive behavior among school and university students, a number of Arab research studies have been conducted over the last ten years to determine reasons for and correlated variables of this phenomenon.

Farag (1992, cited in Nasr, 1994) investigated societal factors related to violent behavior among male university students in Egypt. Results showed that violent behavior among students correlated positively with an unhealthy family atmosphere, including parent unemployment, lack of or weak family control, lack of the students' participation in the decision-making process, negative influences of mass media, and a lack of absence of religious awareness.

Saleh (1998) observed and interviewed two samples of male secondary school students in Cairo between the ages of 16 and 19 to assess the impact of the family's socioeconomic status (SES) and place of residence on children's violent behavior in school. Results revealed a significant negative correlation between family's SES and place of residence to children's violent behavior in school.

In Kuwait, Al-Naser (2000) used a scale measuring antisocial behavior to investigate aspects of violent behavior and actions toward self and others with relation to the influences of age, sex, and place of residence in a sample of 2,385 14- to 18-year-old secondary school students. Results revealed that violent behavior and violent actions did exist among male and female subjects. However, males and older subjects scored significantly higher than females and younger subjects in terms of violent behavior and actions. No significant difference has been found concerning the influence of place of residence on violent behavior and actions.

VIOLENCE/AGGRESSION AND EXTREME BEHAVIOR IN THE SOCIOCULTURAL CONTEXT

It is well known that the sociocultural context (including law, religion, traditions, customs, schooling, etc.) of a society plays a crucial role in controlling the individual society members' behavior. In this context, Ahmed (1971, cited in Abdel-Hamid, 1990) conducted a study in Egypt and found that law, religion, and customs, in that order, are the main sources that control individuals' behavior.

In another study, Saliem (1985, cited in Abdel-Hamid, 1990) reported that religion, along with habits and social customs, have an important part in the socialization process, especially in rural and suburban areas. Abdel-Hamid's (1990) study on Egyptian rural and urban school students showed that schooling systems are responsible for producing social differentiation (discrepancies).

Studies by Saad (1980, cited in Abdel-Hamid, 1990), El-Gamil (1988), and Abdel-Mokhtar (1992, cited in Abdel-Mokhtar, 1998) on the influence of watching violent television programs and action or sex in movies reported positive correlations between watching aggressive models and increased violent attitudes among youth. This result was noted repeatedly in many other later studies (*Al-Ahram*, 2000b).

In another study, Helmy (1986, cited in Abdel-Hamid, 1990) focused on the order of violent deviations among Egyptian youth. It was found that the order of alcoholism, stealing, robbery, gambling, and then drug abuse was the common path of violent deviations.

CLINICAL STUDIES ON VIOLENCE/AGGRESSION AND EXTREME BEHAVIOR

Several Egyptian and Arab studies have been carried out to diagnose violent aggression and extreme behavior. Other studies were interested in assessing the efficiency of some psychological therapeutic approaches to reducing violence/aggression and extremeness. In the following section, examples of these two categories of studies will be discussed briefly.

Diagnostic Studies

In 1971, Sadek (cited in Abou-Sheba, 1992) conducted a psychiatric study on fifty Egyptian male and female convicted criminals and hospitalized mental patients by using the Wechsler Bellevue Intelligence Scale for Adults, TAT, the Projective Hand Test, and an EEG. Results indicated that the sample had a high incidence of neurosis, psychological disturbances, psychoses, psychopathic tendencies, thought disturbances, and depression during their childhood years. Abou-Sheba's (1992) study, which analyzed the responses to the Rorschach Ink Blot Test for thirty-three women who were convicted of killing their husbands, revealed that the basic motives behind the murders were sexual and aggressive in nature. Subjects had high rates of schizophrenia, neurosis, depression, and psychopathic deviations. By using clinical interviews, Abou-Sheba (1992) found that overprotective parents, as a socialization practice, played an important role in the development of violent and aggressive behavior in children. Reshad (1992, cited in Safwet and El-Douseki, 1993) compared violent behavior in three clinical neurotic samples: those with conversion hysteria, those with compulsive neurosis, and those with neurotic depression. No differences were found between the three samples in the level of violent behavior. However, verbal violence was significantly higher in the compulsive neurotics as compared to the other two samples. Al-Fakherani (1993), focusing on assessing psychological conflicts, stress, pressures, neurotic disturbances, and illusions that accompanied violent actions and behaviors, used the case-study method to investigate an 18-year-old fanatical male. Results showed that the subject was suffering from acute anxiety, neurotic depression, hysteria, social introversion, guilt, and feelings of homosexuality.

Therapeutic Studies

Few studies have been conducted paticularly to assess the efficient therapeutic approaches to reducing violent/aggressive and extreme behavior. Al-Fakherani (1993) was interested in using the Rational-Emotive Approach to reduce extreme behavior in a member of a fanatic group. Results indicated a marked decline in the subject's clinically violent symptoms. In addition, Gebrial (1994) found that Gestalt Therapy Approach had a positive impact in reducing hostility levels.

FACTORIAL STUDIES ON VIOLENCE/AGGRESSION AND EXTREME BEHAVIOR

Some Arab research studies during the last twenty years have been aimed at determining the factorial components of violence/aggression and extreme behavior. In the following section examples of such studies will be reviewed briefly.

Hussein (1983, cited in Nasr, 1994) assessed aggressive behavior in a sample of Egyptian female students by using a local scale for aggressive behavior. Five factors emerged through factor analysis, general aggression, outside overt active aggression/inside covert negative aggression, direct/indirect aggression, aggressive tension, and verbal/physical aggression. In a later study (Shoukry, 1993) on personality traits in samples of convicted male rapists and forgery criminals, a general factor for criminality/psychosis was extracted.

In Saudi Arabia, Debais (1997) examined the differences between age and place of residence in dimensions of aggressive behavior in 503 institutionalized and non-institutionalized mildly retarded children between 7 and 16 years old. Subjects were classified into three age groups (7–9; 9–12; and 12–16 years, respectively) and into two residence groups (children who resided in institutes for the mentally retarded and children who resided with their families). While no significant differences in aggressive dimensions among the three age groups were found, children who resided in institutes had significantly higher aggressive behavior dimensions than the children who resided with their families.

Abdalla and Abou-Abaa (1995) conducted a study to investigate the intercorrelations between four dimensions of aggression: anger, hostility, verbal aggression, and physical aggression. They administered Buss and Perry's scale for aggressive behavior to 573 male intermediate, secondary school, and university students, ages 15, 17, and 22, respectively, who lived in Saudi Arabia. The results supported the idea that aggressive behavior is a general domain that includes anger, hostility, verbal aggression, and physical aggression. The four dimensions of aggressive behavior intercorrelated positively in all three age subgroups, especially among university students. While anger correlated positively with physical aggression in the three subgroups, its correlation was weaker than expected in regard to verbal aggression, especially among secondary school and university students. Finally, it was reported that the factorial components of aggressive behavior differ with age.

In Kuwait, Farag and Al-Naser (1999) administered a scale to assess violence against women to a sample of female university students in Kuwait. Twelve factors have been extracted from the data, eight of which were defined as marital violence, sexual violence, male dominance, social violence, verbal violence (both inside and outside the home), traditional violence, threatening of/psychological violence, and expected violence resulting from reaction.

In another Kuwaiti study (Al-Naser, 2000) on violent behaviors and actions among secondary school students between 14 and 18 years old, eight factors have emerged, including stealing and destruction, rejection of the social context, hostility, self-assertiveness, self-destruction, rudeness, avoiding the elderly, and academic carelessness.

A third Kuwaiti study (El-Sheikh, 2001) on battered and non-battered married and unmarried female university students extracted three more factors. These were (1) negative self-concept/depression, (2) psychological disturbances (e.g., depression, compulsive obsession, sleep disorders, and post-traumatic stress disorder (PTSD]), and (3) moral and social self-concept/verbal and physical violence.

EXPERIMENTAL AND LABORATORIAL STUDIES ON VIOLENCE/AGGRESSION AND EXTREME BEHAVIOR

Very few Arab studies have been carried out to investigate violence/aggression and extreme behavior experimentally or in labs. Among this small number of studies are the studies of Farghli (1979, cited in Nasr, 1994) and the study of Mahmoud (1990).

An early attempt to assess psychological factors related to aggression and the impact of a program of athletic activity in reducing aggression in a sample of male and female adults was carried out by Farghli (1979, cited in Nasr, 1994). Results showed that males were more violent than females. It was reported also that an athletic activity program produced a significant reduction in paranoia, illusion and delusion, depression, and social introversion.

Using the Bernreuter Personality Inventory, Mahmoud's (1990) study in Iraq on one hundred male and female psychology students assessed the relationship between knowledge of the experimenter's authority on producing aggressive behavior in subjects, and the subjects' personality traits. The experiment showed that individuals learned both submission to the more powerful persons through a socialization process and to be aggressive with less powerful persons. These two characteristics influence the individuals' lives and become salient in everyday situations, especially when an opportunity to manifest aggression toward those weaker than they became available.

VIOLENCE/AGGRESSION AND EXTREME BEHAVIOR IN RELATION TO POLITICS

Several Arab psychological and sociological research studies have been conducted during the last three decades, especially in Egypt. Hefny (1980, cited in Ghanem, 1998) analyzed the contents of 393 violent actions against Egyptian authorities that took place between 1966 and 1974. Hefny concluded that a denial mechanism was a common tool or method used by people while they confronted the authorities.

Hegazy (1986) studied three acts of group violence that took place in Egypt between 1977 and 1986. It was found that group violence was not a systematic phenomenon. It reflected aggressive acts toward other groups that represented a threat. This phenomenon has two components: physical aggression and destruction. In addition, members of the violent groups were not connected through strongly attached or bonded relationships.

In a later study, Safwet (1990, cited in Safwet and El-Douseki, 1993) investigated riots that occurred in one of Cairo's suburbs in August 1988. It was found that violent groups basically consisted of adolescents and youth who generally were not connected with the fundamental groups. Yet these adolescents and youth had found such violent activities a good opportunity to express their anger and frustration.

Other studies (Al-Taib, 1993, cited in Ghanem, 1998); Abdel-Quei, 1994; Ibrahim, 1996; Mourad, 1997; Taha, 1998; Ghanem, 1998; Jalabi, 1998; Sidaoui, 2000; Al-Otaibi, 2000: and Naceur, 2001) have focused on social, economic, and political structures and their relationships with violence/aggression and extreme behavior. Results of these studies gener-

ally revealed that violence/aggression and extreme behavior are the ultimate outcomes of several conditions, such as lack of democracy; social and
psychological frustration (as a result of the gap between the goals and the
reality); gradual and continued increase of prices (which creates hardships, especially for the poorer); lack of housing, for youth in particular;
administrative and political corruption; lack of ideals; insufficient schools;
and insufficient transportation. In this context, some writers (*Al-Akhbar*,
2001) emphasized the role of family, schooling system, and society in controlling violence and aggressive behavior.

Al-Otaibi's (2000) study aimed at determining the origins and implications of political violence as well as the causes of its diffusion in Algeria between 1976 and 1998. The study revealed that violence in Algeria—which
has historical, political, economic, and social dimensions—is a politically,
economically, militarily, and socially complicated issue and comes about as
a result of internal and external factors. Al-Otaibi concluded that eradication of political violence in Algeria could not be achieved by exercising military power. It was suggested that political and economic reforms should
be considered as necessary measures for checking violence.

Egyptian intellectuals' outlook on violence has been studied by
Ghanem (1998). The main results of this study are

1. a proper and exact definition for violence should be presented, and differences between violence, extremism, terrorism, anger, assault, hostility, aggression, and criminality should be pointed out clearly;
2. violence in Egypt, as in other countries, has many forms, yet the media only
   concentrate on violent acts committed by religious groups (fundamentalists
   or militants);
3. violence's instigators are typically local;
4. reasons for violence are political, economic, social, religious, and psychological, in that order.

Adult attitudes toward extremism and fanaticism have been studied by
Ismail (1996) in Kuwait. Results revealed no significant difference in attitudes due to sex (gender), age, or level of education. However, female, mature, and married subjects showed more negative attitudes toward
extremism and fanaticism than did their male, younger, and unmarried
counterparts.

GENERAL CONCLUSIONS

1. Reviewing Arab research studies on violence/aggression revealed
that most of these studies have been conducted in Egypt. To a lesser extent, such research also has been conducted in countries such as Kuwait,
Saudi Arabia, Algeria, Qatar, Iraq, and Lebanon.

2. Arab research studies on violence/aggression and extreme behavior are still small in number and suffer from many methodological problems, such as lack of theoretical framework, insufficient tools, and small numbers of subjects (Helmy, 1999). Another problem is that the literature on violence (and especially family and political violence) traditionally has been fragmented.

3. Most of the Arab research studies on violence/aggression and extreme behavior have tended to concentrate on the relationship between violence/aggression and extreme behavior on the one side, and on personality traits and parental behaviors on the other, leaving some other important aspects, such as socioeconomic and cultural contexts, uncovered.

Violence/aggression and extreme behavior could not be investigated without considering the social structure, as Hasan (1990), Bayyumi (1992), and Helmy (1999) have noted.

In addition, some writers (Seiam, 1994; Al-Otaibi, 2000) have noticed that most Arab research studies on violence have focused on acts committed by individuals. Not enough attention has been given to violence conducted by the authorities who are sent to deal with violent actions (or what could be called *official violence*). It was concluded that the increased level of violence in the Middle East is a form of social conflict.

4. The differences in the tools used, means of evaluation, and methods of data analysis preclude running an exact comparison regarding the results of Arab research studies on violence/aggression and extreme behavior.

5. In reviewing the Arab research studies on violence/aggression and extreme behavior, it was noted that, researchers have used the terms *violence, aggression*, and *extreme* differently, which could yield a great amount of ambiguity on the obtained results.

6. Until now, no Arab research study has investigated violence, aggression, or extreme behavior developmentally. It was also noted that Arab research studies on violence/aggression and extreme behavior have been conducted by either psychologists or sociologists, and, as yet, no cross-disciplinary study has been carried out.

7. Almost all of the Arab studies on violence, aggression, and extreme behavior have focused on the diagnosis of correlations between violence, aggression, and/or extreme behavior and some other variables. Arab research studies should move a step forward to develop and design programs and techniques aimed at the prevention of violence, aggression, and extreme behavior, especially for youth.

8. From previous Arab studies on violence/aggression and extreme behavior, it can be concluded that violence, aggression, and extreme behavior are manifested in a small section of the population and could not be considered a common phenomenon (Bayyumi, 1992).

Also, results of the previous studies pointed out that violence, aggression, and extreme behavior are due to serious dysfunctions and weak influences of the family, school system, university education, and rapidly changed values and to the negative impact of the media (Ahmed, in press, a and b; *Al-Akhbar*, 2001).

9. Hypothetically, some researchers made a link between religion (Islam, in particular) and violence/aggression and extreme behavior. They concluded that religious orientation and attitudes are responsible for violence and aggressive behavior, at least in part (*Al-Ahram*, 2000a). Yet the results of the previous Arab research studies (Ghalab and El-Douseki, 1994) clearly showed that violence/aggression and extreme behavior correlated negatively with intrinsic (true) religious orientation, which indicates that religion could be used as a way to control violence and aggression.

10. Investigating violence, aggression, and extreme behavior, especially in the Third World, needs a full and sincere collaboration. Without this collaboration, results of such research will be faulty at best.

REFERENCES

Abdalla, J. (1992). Hostility as a function of father absence. *Psychological Studies* (Egypt), 2(2), 351–369 (in Arabic).

Abdalla, M.S. (1997). *Prejudice: A psychosocial study.* 2nd ed. Cairo: Dar Ghreeb for Printing, Publishing and Distribution (in Arabic).

Abdalla, M.S., and Abou-Abaa, S.A. (1995). Dimensions of aggressive behavior: A comparative factor analytic study. *Psychological Studies* (Egypt), 5(3), 521–580 (in Arabic).

Abdalla, N.A. (1984). *Psychology of prostitution.* Cairo: El-Khangy Library (in Arabic).

Abdel-All, G. (1987). A study of psychological factors lead to committing murder in Egyptian female murders. *Journal of Psychology* (Egypt), 1(2), 81–89 (in Arabic).

Abdel-Hamid, T. (1990). *Producing compelling: A study in education and social control.* Cairo: Sinai for Publishing (in Arabic).

Abdel-Kader, A.A. (2000). Assertiveness between submission and hostility (aggression) toward authority: A comparative study of adolescents in rural and urban areas. *Proceedings of the 7th International Conference of the Center of Psychological Counseling* (pp. 313–348) Ain Shams University, Cairo, Egypt (in Arabic).

Abdel-Mokhtar, M.Kh. (1998). *Alienation and [the] extreme toward violence: A psychological study.* Cairo: Dar Ghreeb for Printing, Publishing and Distribution (in Arabic).

Abdel-Quei, S. (1994). Terrorism in the eye of youth: A psychological pilot study. *Journal of Psychology* (Egypt), 8(31), 48–77 (in Arabic).

Abdel-Wahab, L. (1994). *Family violence: Crime and violence against women.* Beirut, Lebanon: Dar-el-Mada for Culture and Publishing (in Arabic).

Abou-el-Kheir, M.M.S. (1995). *Physical punishment and patterns of parental control and their relation with psychological characteristics in children and adolescents.* Unpublished Ph.D. thesis, Faculty of Arts, Zagazig University (Egypt) (in Arabic).

Abou-Sheba, H. (1992). Clinical meanings of husband murderers responses: A case study by using Rorschach Ink Blot Test. *Journal of Psychology* (Egypt), 5(21), 38–47 (in Arabic).

Ahmed, R.A. (in press, a). Egyptian families. In J. Roopnarine and U.P. Gielen (Eds.), *Families in global perspective*. Boston: Allyn & Bacon.

Ahmed, R.A. (2003). Egyptian migrations. In L.L. Adler and U.P. Gielen (Eds.), *Migration: Immigration and emigration in international perspective*. Westport, CT: Praeger.

Ahmed, R.A., and Khalil, E.A. (1998). A critical review on the Arab research studies on aggression/violence and extreme behavior with particular emphasis on the Egyptian research. *Proceedings of the International Conference on Social Sciences and their Roles in Eradication of Violence and Extreme Crimes in Islamic Societies* (Vol. 4, pp. 61–105). Saleh Kamel Center for Islamic Economy, Al-Azhar University, Cairo, Egypt, June 28–30 (in Arabic).

Al-Ahram (2000a). An Egyptian daily newspaper (in Arabic). Sun., Aug., 20.

Al-Ahram (2000b). An Egyptian daily newspaper (in Arabic). Mon., Sept., 11.

Al-Ahram (2001). An Egyptian daily newspaper (in Arabic). Mon., Mar., 12.

Al-Akhbar (2001). An Egyptian daily newspaper (in Arabic). Thu., July, 3.

Al-Fakherani, Kh.I. (1993). Efficacy of the relational emotive therapy in facing some psychological disturbances among extremism: A case study. *Journal of Counseling* (Egypt), 1(1), 257–281 (in Arabic).

Al-Fangery, H.A.H. (1987). *Aggression among rural and urban children: A comparative study*. Unpublished M.A. thesis, Institute for Higher Studies on Childhood, Ain Shams University (Egypt) (in Arabic).

Al-Garni, M.M. (2001). The impact of family structure and family function factors on the deviant behaviors of high school students in Makkah City, Saudi Arabia. Paper presented at *The First International Conference on Social Sciences & the Development of Society*, College of the Social Sciences, Kuwait University, Kuwait, April 10–12.

Al-Kamel, H.M., and Soliman, A.E. (1990). Aggressive behavior and students' perception of parental attitudes toward socialization: A predictive study. *Proceedings of the 6th Annual Convention on Psychology in Egypt* (Part 2, pp. 763–788). Egyptian Association for Psychological Studies, Cairo, Egypt, January 22–24 (in Arabic).

Al-Musallam, B.Kh. (2001). The effects of parents-child relationships on juvenile delinquency: A comparative study. *Journal of the Social Sciences* (Kuwait), 29(1), 71–107 (in Arabic).

Al-Naser, F.A. (2000). Aspects of violent behavior among secondary school students. *Annals of Arts and Social Sciences*, Kuwait University, Kuwait, Monograph 146, Vol. 20 (in Arabic).

Al-Otaibi, S.D. (2000). Political violence in Algeria: A comparative and analytical study, 1976–1998. *Journal of the Social Sciences* (Kuwait), 28(4), 7–57 (in Arabic).

Al-Taib, M.A. (1985). A comparative study on the hostility levels in male and female neurotics and normals. In F.A. Abou-Hatab (Ed.), *Yearbook in Psychology* (Vol. 4, pp. 399–416). Cairo: Anglo-Egyptian Bookshop (in Arabic).

Bayyumi, M.A. (1992). *Violence phenomenon: Reasons and treatment.* Alexandria, Egypt: Dar el-Maarefa al-Gamiaa (in Arabic).

Berkowitz, L. (1993). *Aggression: Its causes, consequences, and control.* Philadelphia: Temple University Press.

Debais, S.A. (1997). Dimensions of aggressive behavior in children with mild mental retardation in terms of age and place of residence. *Psychological Studies* (Egypt), 7(3), 353–385 (in Arabic).

Diab, L. (1965). Authoritarianism and prejudice in Near Eastern students attending American universities. In. L.K. Meleikan (Ed.), *Readings in social psychology in the Arab countries* (Vol. 1, pp. 220–229). Cairo: National House for Printing and Publishing (in Arabic).

El-Deeb, A.M. (1996). Learning transfer, socialization and family size and their relationship with self-esteem and hostility as learned behavior in Egyptians and Omanis: A factorial and comparative study. In A.M. El-Deeb (Ed.), *Research in psychology* (Vol. 2, pp. 285–322). Cairo: General Egyptian Book Organization.

El-Gamil, S.S. (1988). *Watching violence in TV programs and their relation to some aspects of aggressive behavior while watching children.* Unpublished M.A. thesis, Faculty of Arts, Zagazig University (Egypt) (in Arabic).

El-Kadem, A.A. (1995). Juvenile delinquency in Qatari society: A pilot study of the manifestations and factors. *Bulletin of the Faculty of Humanities and Social Sciences, University of Qatar* (Qatar), 18, 109–141 (in Arabic).

El-Khashab, S.M. (1983). *Woman and crime: A field sociological study.* Cairo: Anglo-Egyptian Bookshop (in Arabic).

El-Matewally, M. (1995). *Violence and legality in Egypt: A legal study.* Cairo: General Egyptian Book Organization (in Arabic).

El-Sayed, A.A. (1996). *Father image in addicts.* Unpublished Ph.D. thesis, Faculty of Arts, Ain Shams University (Egypt) (in Arabic).

El-Sheikh, A. (2001). *Differences between battered and non-battered women in some personality and clinical variables.* Unpublished M.A. thesis, College of Social Science, Kuwait University (Kuwait) (in Arabic).

El-Sheribini, E.K. (1991). *A comparative study in attitude towards violence in rural and urban settings.* Unpublished M.A. thesis, Faculty of Arts, Ain Shams University (Egypt) (in Arabic).

Faied, H.A. (1996). Dimensions of the aggressive behavior among university students. *Proceedings of the 3rd International Conference of the Center of Psychological Counseling* (pp. 135–182). Ain Shams University, Cairo, Egypt (in Arabic).

Farag, M.F. (1975). Response sets among delinquents and non-delinquents. In S. Fahmy (Ed.), *Yearbook on psychology* (Vol. 3, pp. 149–161). Cairo: General Egyptian Book Organization (in Arabic).

Farag, S.E., and Al-Naser, H.A. (1999). Violence against women. *Psychological Studies* (Egypt), 9(3), 321–354 (in Arabic).

Gebrial, T.H. (1994). Hostility (aggression) among university students and the impact of Gestalt therapy in reducing it. *Proceeding of the First International Conference of the Center of Psychological Counseling* (pp. 615–655). Ain Shams University, Egypt, November 28–December 2 (in Arabic).

Gelles, R.J. (1999). Family violence. In R.L. Hampton (Ed.), *Family violence: Prevention and treatment: Vol. 1. Issues in children's and families' lives* 2nd ed. (pp. 1–32). Thousand Oaks, CA: Sage Publications.

Ghalab, M.A., and El-Douseki, M. (1994). A comparative psychological study between extrinsic religious orientations and intrinsic religious orientations in attitudes toward violence and some personality traits. *Psychological Studies* (Egypt), 4(15), 327–374 (in Arabic).

Ghanem, M.H. (1998). Violence phenomenon in the eyes of a sample of Egyptian intellectuals. *Journal of Psychology* (Egypt), 12(45), 80–90 (in Arabic).

Hegazy, E. (1986). Mass violence: A preliminary observation. In F.A. Abou-Hatab (Ed.), *Yearbook in psychology* (Vol. 5, pp. 279–296). Cairo: Anglo-Egyptian Bookshop (in Arabic).

Hasan, H.A. (1990). Conformity and non-conformity to norms of Egyptian society. *Journal of the Social Sciences* (Kuwait), 18(2), 109–128 (in Arabic).

Hasan, M.S. (1998). Instigators of the aggressive behavior. *Journal of Social Affairs* (U.A.E.), 15(59), 123–136 (in Arabic).

Helmy, I.I. (1999). *Familial (marital) violence.* Cairo: Dar Kabaa for Printing, Publishing and Distribution (in Arabic).

Ibrahim, M.A.M. (1996). The societal factors leading to violence in some schools in greater Cairo. *Educational and Social Studies, Faculty of Education, Helwan University* (Egypt), 2(3,4), 1–35 (in Arabic).

Ismail, E.M.S. (1988). *Psychology of terrorism and violent crime.* Kuwait: That el-Selasal (in Arabic).

Ismail, E.M.S. (1996). The psychology of extremism and terrorism. *Annals of the Faculty of Arts, Kuwait University,* Kuwait, Monograph 110, Vol. 16 (in Arabic).

Ismail, E.M.S. (2000). Child abuse: A pilot study on begging children. *Journal of Psychology* (Egypt), 14(53), 24–52 (in Arabic).

Jalabi, Kh. (1998). *Violence psychology and peace process strategy.* Beirut, Lebanon: Dar al-Fikr (in Arabic).

Lutfy, T.I. (1992). Socialization and violent behavior in children: A field study of a sample of primary school children in Beni Soueif, Egypt. In A. Shukry (Ed.), *Family and childhood* (pp. 177–231). Alexandria, Egypt: Dar el-Maarefa al-Gamiaa (in Arabic).

Mahmoud, M.H., and Mekaway, H.A. (1989). Characteristics of criminals: A psychobiological study. *Journal of Psychology* (Egypt), 3(9), 19–28 (in Arabic).

Mahmoud, M.M. (1990). The effect of authority on aggression and its relationship with personality. *Journal of the Social Sciences* (Kuwait), 18(2), 83–107 (in Arabic).

Meleikan, L.H. (1965). Authoritarianism and some related variables in two different cultural groups. In L.K. Meleikan (Ed.), *Readings in social psychology in the Arab countries* (Vol. 1, pp. 572–589). Cairo: National House for Printing and Publishing (in Arabic).

Morsi, K.I. (1986). Differences between delinquents and non-delinquents in perception of harmful childhood experiences: An empirical study in three Arab societies. *The Educational Journal* (Kuwait), 2(8), 9–32 (in Arabic).

Mourad, W.F. (1997). *Manifestations of frustration as a result of unemployment among well-educated youth.* Unpublished M.A. thesis, Faculty of Arts, Ain Shams University (Egypt) (in Arabic).

Mustapha, S.A. (1993). *Unemployment and its relation with alienation among univer-sity graduates.* Unpublished Ph.D. thesis, Faculty of Arts, Assiut University (Egypt) (in Arabic).

Naceur, F. (2001). Built environment and antisocial behavior: Case study of Batna City, Algeria. Paper presented at *The First International Conference on Social Sciences & the Development of Society,* College of the Social Sciences, Kuwait University, Kuwait, April 10–12.

Nasr, S. (1983). *Aggressive personality and its relation with socialization.* Unpublished M.A. thesis. Faculty of Arts, Ain Shams University (Egypt) (in Arabic).

Nasr, S. (1994). *Violence in Egyptian society: A bibliography of Arab studies on violence* (Vol. 1). Cairo: National Center for Sociological and Criminal Research (in Arabic).

Ohlin, L., and Tonry, M. (1989). Family violence in perspective. In L. Ohlin and M. Tonry (Eds.), *Family violence* (pp. 1–18). Chicago: University of Chicago Press.

Sabry, Y.E. (1989). Risk behavior among juvenile delinquents and its relation to in-telligence. *Contemporary Education* (Egypt), *13,* 133–149 (in Arabic).

Safwet, A., and El-Douseki, M. (1993). The contributions of Egyptian psychological research studies in investigating prejudice. *Psychological Studies* (Egypt), *3*(4), 429–477 (in Arabic).

Saleh, S.Kh. (1998). *A strategy for eradication of violence among secondary school stu-dents: A critical view and field study.* Cairo: Dar Ghreeb for Printing, Publish-ing and Distribution (in Arabic).

Seiam, S. (1994). *Violence and religious speech in Egypt.* 2nd ed. Cairo: Sinai for Pub-lishing (in Arabic).

Shalaby, M.A., and El-Douseki, M.I. (1993). Cognitive components of extremity: A case study. *Psychological Studies* (Egypt), *3*(1), 11–32 (in Arabic).

Shoukry, M.M. (1993). A comparison between personality characteristics of homi-cide criminals (rapists) and economy criminals (forgers). *Psychological Studies* (Egypt), *3*(2), 101–126 (in Arabic).

Sidaoui, R. (2000). Sociology of violence: Discourse and action. *Arab Studies* (Lebanon), *36*(3–4), 75–92 (in Arabic).

Soliman, A.E., and Abdel-Hamid, M.N. (1994). Hostility and its relation with locus of control and self-esteem in a sample of Imam Mohammed Ibn Saud Is-lamic University male students, Saudi Arabia. *Journal of Psychology* (Egypt), *9*(3), 28–59 (in Arabic).

Soueif, M.I. (1958). Extreme response sets and delinquency. *The National Review of Criminal Science* (Egypt), *1*(3), 24–38 (in Arabic).

Soueif, M.I. (1968). *Extreme as a response style.* 3rd ed. Cairo: Anglo-Egyptian Book-shop (in Arabic).

Taha, F.A. (1998). An important and objective test in the psychology of terrorism and peace. *Psychological Studies* (Egypt), *8*(2), 3–11 (in Arabic).

Tawifik, T.A. (1994). *The psychology of raping.* Alexandria, Egypt: Dar el-Fikr al-Arabi (in Arabic).

2

Violence in Australia

Diane Bretherton

The image of Australia, promoted in television serials and tourist advertisements around the world, is of faraway sun-drenched landscapes, he-
donistic lifestyles, and good mates. In this easy-going setting there does
not seem to be a place for violence. The media image has some truth to it.
Indeed, most Australians do enjoy a level of security that, by world standards, is enviable. However, the public relations picture can only be maintained through denial: denial of the violence in Australian history and
denial of "everyday" violence that is unreported, or inadequately responded to, in the present. A literature survey of violence in Australia un-
covers a rich body of information amid a bewildering variety of issues and
topics. Homicide, assault, aggravated assault, community violence, violence against women, date rape, stalking, road rage, children witnessing
violence, gangs, violence in and around licensed premises, mandatory
sentencing—these are but a few of the topics that could be explored in a
survey of violence in Australia.

There are, as the Social Development Committee (SPC, 1998) noted,
problems in reaching a consensus on a working definition of violence. A
submission to the *Inquiry into Strategies to Deal with the Issue of Community
Violence* from Suzanne E. Hatty defines *violence* narrowly as "the use of
unlawful or unacceptable physical force against another person, often culminating in injury and involving the exertion of physical strength or the
use of weapons" (p. 12), while that provided by Wendy Weeks and Kate
Gilmore describes *violence* broadly as "any action that diminishes another
person" (p. 10).

Rather than skimming over a smorgasbord of topics, this chapter aims
to survey violence in Australia by considering a smaller number of examples at each of the three levels of violence described below.

The first and most obvious level of violence matches Hatty's definition and will be termed *community violence*. This violence is public, overt, and consists of discrete observable physical action toward another with the likelihood of observable physical harm to the victim. It is criminal in nature and has been appraised by courts in light of contextual factors, such as the perpetrator's intention to cause harm as well as the amount of damage done. Factors such as the degree of premeditation and the level of provocation are taken into account to mitigate the severity of jail sentences.

Women's groups have pointed out, though, that the most obvious forms of violence may not be the most damaging in the long run. They point to the debilitating effect of more subtle forms of emotional abuse within the family over a long period of time. This second level of violence, "everyday" covert violence, comes closer to the Weeks and Gilmore definition. It is less observable because not only is it emotional, rather than physical, but also it takes place in the privacy of the home. Even if it escalates to a physical level, it is less likely to come to the attention of or be taken seriously by the law. Because of the network of relationships between family members, violence is less likely to be reported to the police. When it is, it is often dismissed as "just a domestic."

At a third and even deeper level is violence that is not marked by an obvious physical act but is built into the institutions of a society. Its manifestations, considered separately, may seem small and innocuous, but may have devastating consequences for the victims. An example is the South African laws that were tools for implementing the system of apartheid. This type of violence does not show up in national crime statistics because it is not criminal violence. The state not only condoned violence, but also perpetrated it.

COMMUNITY VIOLENCE

The story related to me by my student, Emmanuel, is both true and true to the prototype. It not only gives a profile of such incidents, but also illustrates the inadequacy of our methods of responding to violence. The VVCAV found that, while it is believed widely that the best way to prevent violence in and around licensed venues is to use force in the form of tough bouncers, employing tough bouncers can itself lead to more violence. The anecdote also illustrates the complex interplay of variables. Because Emmanuel and Peter had been drinking, their credibility as complainants was reduced. Their weaker status as visiting students with foreign accents, their lack of knowledge of services, and their fear that, even now, the bouncer might figure out who they are and come back to get them, all combine to lower the likelihood of justice being done. Their names have been changed, here, to protect their identity. Their story also illustrates the fact that violence is patterned. Rather than being something that breaks out at random, violence is often perpetrated in a patterned and systematic way. For example, there was calculation behind the bouncer's leading Peter out of the range of the security camera before assaulting him.

The time is just after 4:00 A.M. early Sunday morning. The place is a club. Emmanuel goes back to the bench, where he had been sitting, to collect his jacket before leaving. A young woman is seated on the bench, and apologizing for the interruption, he asks her to please get up so that he can retrieve his jacket and leave. As he turns to go, a young man comes up to Emmanuel and challenges him for "messing with" his girlfriend. The young man and his friends then start hitting Emmanuel. Emmanuel's friend Peter runs downstairs to ask security staff for help. The bouncer is outside and tells Peter to follow him down the road to the side door of the venue. Once outside the range of the security videotape camera, the bouncer turns on Peter and punches him in the face. Meanwhile, Emmanuel manages to escape from his attackers and come to the aid of his friend.

In terms of the damage done, Peter is more badly hurt. He has a fractured skull and impaired vision, which may heal over time, or may require surgery. The police are called but are not particularly sympathetic, suggesting that such incidents are commonplace and there is "not much you can do."

Media reports of community violence in the newspapers in Australia highlight and hark back to a pivotal incident. In 1987, a young man, Julian Knight, went on a shooting rampage on Hoddle Street in Melbourne and killed seven people and wounded nineteen others. This deeply shocked Australians, myself among them. Until this time, the idea of a gunman on a rampage was foreign to us. We had thought that this type of dramatic shooting spree was something that happened elsewhere, perhaps in America, not something that could happen here in Australia, as if our remote location could keep us safe from such events.

Hoddle Street is close to where I live: I used to drive it most days on my commute between home and work. Some friends reported actually having driven through the shootings (though this may be an urban myth, and other friends knew the families of the victims. Perhaps the strongest connection for me was as a parent, since, some years earlier, my son had attended school with the shooter. I became involved in the community-healing process that followed, a process that was personally challenging and deeply moving. Being a local psychologist and having a long-standing interest in nonviolence, I often was asked to give public talks. But who would be in the audience? How does one speak about such tragedy with sufficient sensitivity when the families and neighbors of the victims might be listening? How does one speak with sufficient compassion when family, friends, neighbors, and teachers of the killer might be in attendance? How does one speak with sufficient courage when members of the gun lobby surely would be there as well?

Melbourne is a multicultural city, and the families of the victims were given a new tolerance, a space to grieve in their own ways. Customs, such as building small shrines and placing wreaths on the places where people died, were honoured. A ceremony was performed at the local park, where the community planted new trees, patting down dirt, as if onto a grave. This degree of ritual might have been treated with some mockery or derision at another time, but, in 1987 a deep spirit of love drew the community together. Policemen, mothers in mourning, tough-looking teenage skinheads, members of the clergy, politicians, and children joined together in placing the sod. There was almost a biblical feeling as such diversity was drawn together in shared grief.

During a meeting at the school for members of the community, a drunken lad—perhaps from the local school, perhaps Julian's peer—began to taunt a policeman. It was hot, and feelings were running high. The hall was very overcrowded, and the audience had spread up into the area normally reserved for speakers. Members of the press had been excluded and, anxious for action, were hovering outside the hall. How would the situation be resolved? To reprimand the boy might lead to a split in the community. Sending him outside would start a public incident. Heckling the police in this context seemed unforgivable, but no one knew what to do. It seemed, though, that the spirit of reconciliation was present. And, after a while, the alcohol and the heat began to take effect on the boy, who started to nod off to sleep and whose head gradually began to droop until it came to rest on the shoulder of the policeman. He awoke with a start when the audience, having realized what had happened, began to laugh.

A number of features of the case of Julian Knight illustrated issues that were of concern to psychologists: the link between watching violence on television and committing violence in real life, the impact of guns and violent toys on child development, and the relationship between fantasy and reality. Newspaper reports indicated that Julian was isolated socially and estranged from his family and had a militarized imagination. He attended school wearing army fatigues and insisted on being called "SOF," short for *soldier of fortune*. He obsessively collected military magazines and videos and slept with an arsenal of military-style weapons under his bed. The reason given for committing his act of violence was, reportedly, to make his father proud of him for "killing communists."

This incident soon was to be followed, in December of the same year, by another multiple shooting in Melbourne. Nine people died and an additional five were injured when a young man went on a shooting spree on an office block on Queen Street. These shootings became a spur, mobilizing the public and the governmental bodies to inquire into the causes of violence and the means by which it could be prevented. The stories of these dramatic multiple shootings enthralled the media and made exciting narratives that continue to provide copy for newspapers. Fourteen years after the killings, Knight has become less of a real person and more of a television character. On June 15, 2001, the headline on the *Herald Sun* newspaper read, "Hoddle St. Killer's Jail List of Fear: Knight's Secret Files." The article begins, "Mass murderer Julian Knight has been compiling secret files with the personal details of his prison guards and judges. The Hoddle St. killer used a computer at his maximum security jail to keep his chilling lists" (p. 6C). The next day the same newspaper carried a headline that harked back to another multiple shooting: "Young Guns: Shooter Ranks Grow as Sport Regains its Glory Image." This article explains that the number of shooters had risen for the first time since the Port Arthur massacre, in which thirty-five people were gunned down in Tasmania in 1996. My point here is that these dramatic multiple shootings not only sold newspapers at the time they occurred, but constantly are recalled and revisited in the present.

The newspaper headlines dramatized the killings with headlines such as, "Year of the Gun Makes Us All Recoil," "Rise in Killings Blamed on Lack of Deterrent," "58 Murders and Four Months to Go," and "I am 15 and I am Scared." Actually, the homicide rate in Victoria had remained fairly constant and, even including these shootings, was not high by international standards. The homicide rate in the 1999–2000 fiscal year was 1.8 per 100,000 of the population. "The mundane reality of homicide," Neal (1989) notes, is "that the vast majority of cases arise from disputes between people with existing relationships. . . . The horror of incidents like Hoddle and Queen Street should not be minimized, but Victoria has twice as many people killed annually in domestic homicides as died in those two incidents, to say nothing of the physical injury and psychological trauma of non-fatal domestic violence" (p. 12).

As a response to the Hoddle Street killings in Melbourne, the state government established the Victorian Community Council Against Violence (VCCAV). I served on the council, first as a member, then as the chair of the Task Force on Violence against Women, and later as chair of the council. And, as a federal response to the killings, a National Conference on Violence was held in Canberra in 1989. This was an important event, bringing together a number of criminologists and other experts, politicians, and law enforcement officials from the various states in Australia. The conference not only was a step forward in giving a national overview of the field, but also demonstrated how the federal structure of Australia can make the implementation of reforms difficult. The prevention of violence is a concern of all levels of government: local councils, states and territories, as well as the federal government. Because uniformity is needed to ensure effectiveness, as in the case of gun control, agreement must be reached across local loyalties, state rivalries, and party divisions. It was not until 1996, after the shooting at Port Arthur in Tasmania, that Prime Minister John Howard introduced gun control legislation.

While homicide rates in Australia have remained fairly constant, there has been a concerning rise in serious assaults. At first glance it may seem that there is not a clear difference between serious assaults and homicides, that the latter are assaults that have escalated to the point of fatality. The VCCAV (1992) cites a study by Polk and Ranson that found that the first and most predominant theme of homicide is an intimate link between the victim and offender. In over half of the homicides studied, the victim and the offender had known each other through family relations, friendship, or sexual partnership. An Australian study of nationwide homicide data for 1989–1991 found that, of 150 killings between adults in intimate relationships, 121 victims were female. Of the perpetrators of domestic homicides, around 80 percent were male (Easteal, 1993). A second theme was a confrontational homicide, which can be seen as an assault that escalated out of control. This dynamic interaction is one of challenge and counterchallenge. In these cases there is no strong relationship between the participants, except within the conflict itself, and there is no motive to kill the victim. In each of these cases, which comprised 21 percent of the total cases in the study, both the offender and victim were male, and the incident occurred in a leisure setting. In the majority of cases alcohol played a significant role. The third type of homicide took place during the commission of other crimes, such as robbery. These accounted for 18 percent of the cases.

"If you had to sum up the nature of serious assaults reported to police in recent years," notes Robb (1989), "the common notion that it involves young men in their twenties and thirties fighting each other for no particular reason in and around pubs, or at home, after closing time on Friday and Saturday nights is not far off the mark" (p. 3).

In 1990 the VCCAV was asked by the Australian government to investigate violence in and around licensed premises, clubs, hotels, and venues for young people's entertainment; to collect, analyze, and verify current methods of measuring violence related to these areas, and to develop and recommend practical strategies to reduce or eliminate such problems. The council adopted a comprehensive approach that included the collection of statistics, the conduct of surveys and consultation with community groups and stakeholders, and the examination of trends. The resulting 1990 report notes that council members "saw thousands of relaxed people having a good time, local bands with large followings and well designed and well cared for interiors. We saw some door and security staff handling difficult situations very successfully. We also witnessed aggression and fights, extreme drunkenness, violence videos and dangerous overcrowding and dirty interiors" (p. 7).

An analysis of a sample of serious assaults for the years 1987–1989 was undertaken by the Ministry of Police and Emergency services. It found that 19.2 percent of these assaults took place in licensed venues, 31.6 percent occurred in residential areas, and 27.5 percent took place on the street or in other public areas. Twenty-one percent of the incidents relating to licensed premises involved bouncers, either as alleged perpetrators or victims. These figures are consistent with trends in other Australian states and in Britain. A much lower number of assaults were reported to the Liquor Licensing Bureau. A submission from a member of the public in the VCCAV (1990) report says to "Listen to any person who frequents these places or stand outside any from 1 A.M. onwards. Then go inside after closing time and listen to the bouncers brag to each other about the faces they invested with their boots and fists. The fact is there are dozens of unnecessary incidents on any given night in any major city" (p. 26).

The link between violent assaults and the consumption of alcohol is not understood clearly. A number of studies have suggested that there is an association. Robb (cited in VCCAV, 1990) concludes that the predictors for trouble were "groups of male strangers, low comfort, high boredom, high-drunkenness and aggressive unreasonable bouncers" (p. 32). There is also a link between violence and victim's alcohol consumption. Their intoxication not only makes them more vulnerable to attack, but also undermines their credibility in, and likelihood of, reporting the attack.

To sum up, then, while dramatic multiple homicides have captured public attention and spurred the nation to action, most instances of community violence in Australia do not involve killing or guns. Rather, most involve assaults between males, in and around pubs and clubs. Such tales are so commonplace that it is difficult to get the police and others to take them seriously or respond to them.

VIOLENCE IN THE FAMILY

My story, perhaps, is not that much different from others. A girl who replaced her mother in bed as she replaced her around the home. Mum joined an organization to get out of the house. Seven children, six surviving. I don't think she wanted to get pregnant again, so she got out. That way she could honestly say she was too tired. I was left with the cooking, the cleaning and looking after my younger brothers and sisters and my dad. I grew up hurt and confused, not knowing what love was, because the only type of love I knew was what my father taught me. Other women, also incest victims, to whom I have spoken, also grow up with the precept that love is sex. The other week, in the city, I noticed a sermon for Father's Day outside a church, "Daddy, how do you spell love?" and I cried. I came back to the group blathering about it being a great title for a play, but I cried.

During improvisation for this show many memories I thought were safely buried away have emerged, ones that I thought I'd never have to face again. Mum and I, talking. Mum told me the facts of life when I was around 12 (in those days a child was allowed innocence until puberty) and me saying "But Mummy, Daddy does that to me all the time" Mum smacked me in the mouth—hard—abusing me and calling me a liar, then, as she began to believe me, a whore. (Somebody's Daughter Theatre, n.d., (36)

This extract was taken from Gloria's story in the play *Tell Her that I Love Her*. Former women prisoners, who use theater to narrate their stories of abuse and healing, formed Somebody's Daughter Theatre. A large proportion of the prisoners have had experiences of violence and abuse and end up in jail for drug-related offenses or defrauding social security.

While crime statistics indicate that most victims of crime are male, findings of studies based on victims' reports suggest that the official figures seriously underestimate the amount of violence against women in society. Men are more likely to be victims of crime in public places, but women are most vulnerable to violence in the privacy of their own homes. Alder (1989) points out that violent assaults against women are marginalized and trivialized within the legal system and that a good deal of the violence against women never is recorded in the official statistics, in part because the women themselves have been reluctant to define violent interactions as "criminal." Some of the factors that inhibit victims from disclosing domestic violence are their feelings of shame, their fear of retribution from the perpetrator, and the pressures of negative community attitudes toward victims. Also, because domestic violence often occurs in the privacy of the home, there are few outside witnesses. Furthermore, surveys often require fluency in English, which means that the experiences of people from non–English speaking backgrounds may not be represented adequately. Statistics from public agencies such as police, courts, counseling, and accommodation services can provide only information about people who come to the public's attention, and many victims never contact such agencies. Some agencies do not collect statistics on domestic violence, and those that do define and record domestic violence in different ways. According to a recent survey on domestic violence, "the information that is available reveals that hundreds of thousands of Australian women are subjected to violence within their relationships. Studies consistently indicate that such violence occurs in all social classes, races and cultures, and that women constitute the majority of victims, while men are the majority of perpetrators" (Australian Statistics on Domestic Violence, 2001).

Cuthbert (1989) surveyed attendance at a hospital emergency service and contrasted male and female victims. "Males of any age were more likely to be victims of violence and to be under the influence of drugs at the time, which was frequently after 9 pm at night. The drug influence was usually alcohol. Male victims were more likely to be involved in an assault that involved two or more people and not know the assailant. The assault was most likely to have occurred in the street or near a hotel or club and was not likely to be reported to the police by a male victim. In contrast, the female victim was less likely to have been under the influence of drugs and was more likely to have been the victim of an assault with one assailant who was known to her and who was more likely to have been her partner. Females were more likely to have been victims of assault in their own homes and this usually occurred earlier in the evening than the male assaults" (p. 11).

Australian Bureau of Statistics (ABS) conducted the *Women's Safety Survey* in 1996. Approximately 6,300 Australian women were asked about their experiences of actual or threatened physical and sexual violence. The ABS estimated that, in the twelve months prior to completing the survey,

> 7.1 percent of the adult female population (or 490,400 women) experienced violence,
>
> 6.2 percent of women experienced violence perpetrated by a male,
>
> 1.6 percent of women experienced violence perpetuated by a female,
>
> 2.61 percent of women who were married or in a de facto relationship (111,000) had experienced violence perpetrated by their current partner, and
>
> 4.8 percent of unmarried women had experienced violence by their previous partner in the last twelve months.

Of women who had been assaulted physically in the twelve-month period, 58 percent spoke to a friend or neighbor, 53 percent spoke to a family member, 19 percent reported the incident to police, 12 percent spoke to a counselor, 4.5 percent spoke to a crisis service organization, and 18 percent never had told anyone about the incident. Women who experienced violence by a current partner were the least likely to have reported the assault, while women who were assaulted by a stranger were more likely to report the incident to police.

The survey also recorded women's experience with violence during their lifetime. From the results it was estimated that 2.6 million women (or 38% of the adult female population) had experienced one or more incidents of physical or sexual violence since the age of 15, 1.2 million women had experienced sexual violence, 2.2 million women experienced physical violence, and 345,400 women (8% of women currently in a marital or de facto relationship had experienced an incident of physical or sexual violence at the hands of their partner at some time during their relationship. Of the women who had been in a previous relationship, 1.1 million (42%) had experienced an incident of physical violence by their previous partner (ABS, 1996).

In 1995, a national telephone survey of 2,004 Australian adults found that there was a greater community understanding of domestic violence, as compared to a similar survey in 1987. In the 1995 survey, more people identified psychological abuse as a form of domestic violence (e.g., in 1995, 77% classified "yelling abuse" as a form of domestic violence, compared to only 48% in 1987) and more people understood that domestic violence is a criminal offense (in 1995, 93% agreed that it was compared to 79% in 1987). However, there was still a lack of understanding of the victims needs in 1995: 77 percent of respondents reported that it was difficult to understand why women do not leave situations of domestic violence (Commonwealth Office of the Status of Women, 1995).

The work of the Task Force on Violence against Women tended to focus on the provision of services to victims, rather than the prevention of violence. The task force monitored the issuing and policing of intervention orders that aimed to prevent violent partners from approaching women and children. It provided shelter and accommodations for the victims of family violence. It also conducted public campaigns to raise awareness of family violence.

An important issue, one that divided the committee, was the question of men's groups. Women had set up refuges with their own money and worked many hours without pay, so, naturally, they resented the new development of men's groups moving in on the scarce resource pool. However, I felt that, from a theoretical perspective, violence is tied so closely to notions of masculinity that it was important to work with men, that a women-only approach would lock us into providing for victims and fail to tackle the root causes of violence. Laing (2000), in her excellent overview of Australian responses to domestic violence, notes that "the value of programs for men who use violence has been the subject of vigorous debate," but that "the debate has shifted from whether such programs should be offered to the conditions under which they should be offered" (p. 10).

As Gloria's story suggests, one of the key issues is how to stop women from being blamed for being victims and from blaming themselves for their abuse. Even service providers may encourage women not to take matters to court lest they find retraumatization rather than justice. The person who speaks up and breaks the silence risks a smack in the mouth.

INSTITUTIONAL VIOLENCE

> My father and his father, his grandfather pass stories on y'know and runs in that family, old stories like that. Oh, it just hurts, even when you just read about it y'even got tears an' everythin', you're just readin' about it, and thinking about it. It still hurts mate, y'know? You can never take away the pain. Give us land, get our land back, whatever, still won't take away the pain. The oldies still feeling it today mate. They, they've been there and done that, 'n' trapped an' seen all the other people die. Their stories are, they tell 'em on down to the young people, Y'know like today. See with my kids, I'll tell 'em too. Y'know? Still keeps goin'. (P. 173)

In this way one Aborigine described to Mellor (1998) his sense of loss and dispossession. Before white people arrived in Australia, the continent was occupied by as many as 754,000 indigenous people who lived in approximately seven hundred different groups. Each group had its own territory, political system, laws, and dialect. However, when the continent of

Australia was claimed for the British two hundred years ago, it was regarded as being empty. It was seen as having no law, no culture, and no system of ownership. There followed a long history of frontier wars between white settlers and Aborigines, with many large-scale massacres occurring. The settlers considered themselves superior to the indigenous population, and behaved accordingly. Such massacres continued into the twentieth century, with, for example, fifteen people being killed by police at the Forrest River Mission in western Australia in 1928 after some cattle "disappeared" from an adjoining property. A history of these wars is given by Yarwood and Knowling (1982).

After the turn of the century, a phase of forced, but limited, assimilation and "protection" of Aboriginal people commenced. In various states, Native Welfare departments were established to supervise the lives of the indigenous population. Such supervision also consisted of exclusion, as Aboriginal people were denied access to many facilities within the community, suffered numerous restrictions in their activities, and were not even recognized as citizens or included in the census.

One of the most significant aspects of this period was the removal of Aboriginal children from their parents in order to "better" care for them. The outcome of this policy was that many Aboriginal people born before 1960 lost contact with their families of origin, as they were raised on missions or in the homes of "kind-hearted" city-dwelling whites.

The present-day disadvantaged position of Aboriginal people is reflected in a range of statistics relating to employment, health, and the judicial system. The unemployment rate for Aborigines is four times the national average. Indigenous families earn only two-thirds the amount that white families earn. Infant mortality rates for Aboriginal groups are twice the rate of the national population. Death from circulatory and respiratory disease occurs at 2.5 times the rate of the national population. Ten percent of the Aborigines suffer from diabetes. In addition, people of Aboriginal descent still experience pervasive racism in their daily lives as they struggle to affirm their place as the original inhabitants of Australia with their own complex culture and relationship to the land, of which they largely have been dispossessed. Although they make up less than 2 percent of the population, 29 percent of those in police custody are Aborigines.

Mellor, Bretherton, and Firth (2000) have suggested that it is useful to conceptualize the state of Australian society in terms of institutions, which Johnson (1992) describes as "sets of habits, routines, rules, norms and laws, which regulate the relations between people and shape human interaction" (p. 26). These institutions are the fundamental building blocks in all societies and act as signposts for the relationships between people. Institutions mediate the relationships between black and white Australia. According to McQueen (1986), racism has been the most important single component of Australian nationalism. Cultural norms and the institution of racism allowed for the settlement, rather than the invasion, of Australia (as it was seen as empty); the massacres of Aborigines; the removal of Aboriginal children from their families; and the refusal to recognize Aboriginal people as citizens until 1967. To argue Hatty's definition (SDC, 1998, 12) this violence against Aborigines was neither unlawful nor unacceptable to the state.

The racism that is experienced by Aboriginal people is in contrast to the racism experienced by more recent immigrant groups, such as the Vietnamese. Many groups that come to Australia have a history of conflict and animosity, but are expected to leave it behind when they come. They are often only too happy to agree to this arrangement, as they have come to make a new start. For example, in seeking testimonies of rape as a war crime for The Hague in the former Yugoslavia, interviewers found that no volunteers came forward. While fear of reprisal was one factor, the given reason for silence was the wish to make a new beginning and leave behind the past. In Australia, diverse groups are expected, if not to play together, to at least work together in harmony. Serbians, Croatians, Arabs, Jews, Turks, Greeks, Tamils, and Sinhalas are expected to get along, and, to a surprising extent, they do just that. There are critics who suggest that trouble is being stored up and will break out one day, but many are more optimistic. Multiculturalism is not based on denial. Australia is tolerant of people maintaining their old identities, as well as taking on new ones. Many children attend Saturday schools in their own language, belong to ethnospecific clubs (such as Croatian clubs), and maintain contacts with relatives in the "old country" without being considered any less Australian.

However, the new (multicultural) settlers, for all their diversity, accept the claims of the dominant culture in Australia, and settle down to the business of becoming "Aussies." They bring with them a leavening of the dominant culture, new foods, and different customs, but they do not challenge the right of the earlier (British) settlers to be there. The claims of Aborigines are far more threatening to the white Australian's sense of self.

The manifestation of institutional violence is subtler than criminal violence and is harder for others to see and appreciate. It may be experienced as numerous pinpricks, every day, all the time. One example is the requirement to possess official documentation of citizenship. In enrolling an Aboriginal person in a university, I tried to get the administration of the institution to waive the requirement to show a birth certificate. The reason for my wish was political. It is insensitive for institutions to ask the original inhabitants of this land for a piece of paper to prove they exist, especially when the existence of the original population was denied for so long. My reason was also practical. Because Aboriginal people were not granted citizenship until 1967, many do not have birth certificates (which require parents to be citizens). I reasoned with the administration: What was the birth certificate needed for? Is it needed to prove residency? Wouldn't a passport or a license to drive a car or some other form of identification suffice? Wouldn't the university's own records be a sufficient form of proof? In the end, no, the enrollment was contingent on the production of a birth certificate. In this case it was possible to obtain a certificate, but only because the father had been a bit of a troublemaker and had been issued a birth certificate by the government to facilitate taking him to court. The mother, being of a more compliant temperament, was denied legal existence. Subsequently, the university regulation was amended and now states that some other means of identification is acceptable, and most students are not asked specifically for a birth certificate.

The disjunctions in our vision are obvious when we consider the violence the Aboriginal people have suffered, and yet, that the Port Arthur massacre—the shooting of thirty-five tourists April 28, 1996—is described as the biggest massacre of all time (as if there is some *Guinness Book of Records for Violent Crimes*, and Australia takes the prize). Tasmania possibly does have a claim to being the site of the biggest massacre, but not for this incident. The most successful genocide of all time was the systematic extermination of all the full-blooded Tasmanian Aboriginal people by the early settlers.

RESPONDING TO VIOLENCE

> The window portrays our lives of order and unity, shown by the circle, contrasting with the surrounding chaos and fragmentation. The circle is pierced by the tragedy of the shootings. The circle seeks to close again, the figures to reunite, representing the start of the healing process and the support given, each for the other.
>
> The circle represents the community of families, of the workforce and of the city, but it is also our earth, a symbol of our ultimate reliance on each other for meaning and comfort in our lives. Within the circle, figures are linked in a network of lines, the communication that binds us.

Such is how Melbourne artist David Wright describes the window he designed in memory of the victims of the Queen Street shootings. The window is pictured on the cover of Creamer, Burgess, Buckingham, and Pattison's book (1989)

Weatherburn (1989) notes that the problem in responding to violence is "how to steer a safe passage between the Scylla of unwarranted public anxiety and the Charybolis of public indifference" (p. 3). There tends to be a strong reaction when dramatic violent events occur and the media stirs up fears of violence. But, after some time passes, other issues are seen as more important, and it is difficult to maintain commitment to the consistent hard work needed to implement policy changes necessary for the reduction of violence in society. The three multiple shootings referred to in this chapter served to draw public attention to the issue of violence and to bring about changes both in individual behaviors and in government policy. At the time, I joined the rush to exploit public concern in order to pressure for reform. But is this the best way forward?

The problem with this approach is that it is driven by fear. Unfortunately, while fear is useful in situations needing rapid response, chronic fear can distort our perceptions and views of reality. Fear can be limiting, reining in our imagination and impairing our power to act effectively.

Perhaps the first step in responding effectively to violence is to get a clear view of what is happening. Given the variety of definitions of violence, the number of different approaches, the wealth of statistics, and the gap between common perceptions and fears of violence and the actuality of its occurrence, this is not an easy task. The popular understanding of violence is that it is random, that it is a product of anger or psychopathology, and that it is inevitable. The VCCAV (1992) report suggests that "Violent offenders can be and generally are rational people who choose their opportunities and are selective about whom, where and what they exploit to achieve their violent ends" (p. 51). Our responses to violence, on the other hand, are not rational. Reports of violence tend to be followed by calls for greater punishments, the reintroduction of the death penalty, zero tolerance, mandatory sentencing, or other tough measures, despite evidence that these measures rebound on the weakest and most vulnerable members of society. Nowhere is the mismatch between the problem of violence and the suggested solution more evident than in the issue of violence against women. Advice includes installing better locks or more sophisticated security systems, arming oneself or learning self-defense, carrying mace, getting home before dark, and so on. All of these measures are about protection from "stranger danger," attack from outside. However, the figures show women are much more at risk from people they know in their own homes than from strangers outside the home.

Perhaps the key to a more effective approach to violence is to recognize that violence is not a thing in itself, but rather a quality of relationships. Feminists argue that violence maintains gender inequality. Violence and the fear of violence act to restrain women and keep them in the "safety" of the home. Daly and Wilson (1988) argue that disputes between males are just as much about gender as is violence against women. At one level, tiffs between men may seem trivial, as they begin with insults or jostling. But such a minor affront is not an isolated stimulus. Rather, it must be understood in the larger social context. "Men are known by their fellows as the 'sort who can't be pushed around' or the 'sort who won't take any shit' as guys whose girlfriends you can't chat up without impunity, or guys you don't want to mess with. In most social settings, a man's reputation depends, in part, on the maintenance of a credible threat of violence" (p. 128). Male-to-male violence, then, is founded in testing and establishing power in relation to other males. Alder (1989) stresses that there are multiple masculinities and multiple forms of violence, and a complex analysis of the relationship between gender and violence is needed. In society, some violence is accepted, normalized, and legitimated to the extent that it becomes invisible, for example, corporal punishment in schools and homes.

Over the last decade the issue of violence in Aboriginal communities was seen as situational and culturally dependent. At a forum conducted by the Task Force on Violence against Women, it was noted that women from women's groups and services sat themselves on the right side of the hall; men from the emerging men's group movement sat separately, on the left-hand side of the hall; and Aboriginal people, with men and women interspersed and refusing to separate, formed a block across the back of the hall. The Aboriginal people argued that violence is a community issue that needs to be handled by Aboriginal men and women themselves.

More recently, stories of abuse of Aboriginal women by Aboriginal men have come to the fore. A prominent Aboriginal leader had been accused of rape, and shocking stories of abuse in remote Aboriginal communities make headlines. "Shameful: Women Blinded and Disfigured as Violence Grips a Community," read the *Herald Sun* on June 29, 2001 (p. 7C). The story includes a story of a woman who was blinded with a broom handle by her partner and who is permanently endangered by her reduced visibility. She loves to fish but is now less able to see approaching crocodiles.

Recent times have seen an upsurge of support for Aboriginal people. The Aboriginal opening to the Year 2000 Olympic Games in Sydney is a source of pride, and reconciliation walks and functions have been attended very well. It is probably only in the context of improved relationships between Aboriginal and white Australia that the issue of violence between Aboriginal people can be examined. In the past, the experience of racism has been so salient to Aboriginal people it has made gender relations seem trivial by comparison.

If violence is a patterned and systematic feature of social relationships, then it should be possible to develop long-term and sustained approaches to its prevention and containment and the care of its victims. While dramatic events get the maximum commitment, our focus needs to be on building a secure social fabric. This will be based on resolving problems through dialogue and communication. Dialogue can only occur within a framework of equality and respect for human rights. Although local contexts are important, the problem of violence is a global issue. In an increasingly globalized world, Australia needs to join the international community in efforts to build more harmonious relationships. We can no longer be complacent in our belief that "it doesn't happen here."

REFERENCES

Alder, C. (1989). Socio-economic determinants of violence. Paper presented at the Australian Institute of Criminology's National Conference on Violence, Canberra, October 1–13.

Australian Bureau of Statistics (ABS). (1996). *Women's safety survey* (Catalogue No. 4128.0). Canberra: Author.

Australian Statistics on Domestic Violence. (2001). <http://home.vicnet.au/~dvirc/statistics.htm>.

Commonwealth Office of the Status of Women. (1995). Commonwealth of Australia: Can Print Communications.

Creamer, M., Burgess, P., Buckingham, W., and Pattison, P. (1989). *The psychological aftermath of the Queen Street shootings*. Parkville, Victoria: Department of Psychology, University of Melbourne.

Cuthbert, M. (1989). Investigation of the incidence and analysis of cases of alleged violence reporting to the accident and emergency centre, St. Vincent's Hospital. Paper presented at the Australian Institute of Criminology's National Conference on Violence, Canberra, October 1–13.

Daly, M., and Wilson, M. (1988). *Homicide*. New York: Aldine De Gruyter.

Easteal, P. (1993). Killing the beloved: Homicide between adult sexual intimates. *Australian Studies in Law, Crime and Justice*. Australian Institute of Criminology, Canberra.

Johnson, B. (1992). Institutional learning. In B.A. Lundvall (Ed.), *National systems of innovation: Towards a theory of innovation and interactive learning*. London: Pinter Publisher.

Laing, L. (2001). Progress, trends and challenges in Australian responses to domestic violence (Issue Paper 1). Melbourne: Australian Domestic and Family Violence Clearinghouse.

McQueen, H. (1986). *A new Britannia*. Melbourne: Penguin Books.

Mellor, D. (1998). *Experiences of racism by Aboriginal Australians and Vietnamese immigrants*. Unpublished Ph.D. thesis, University of Melbourne.

Mellor, D., Bretherton, D., and Firth, L. (2000). Everyday racism in Australia: The experience of Aboriginal Australians. Paper presented at the *XXVII International Congress of Psychology*, Stockholm, July 23–28.

Neal, D. (1989). Violence and public policy: Information needs. Paper presented at the Australian Institute of Criminology's National Conference on Violence, Canberra, October 1–13.

Robb, T. (1989). Patterns of reported serious assault. Paper presented at the Australian Institute of Criminology's National Conference on Violence, Canberra, October 1–13.

Social Development Committee (SDC). (1988). *Inquiry into strategies to deal with the issue of community violence* (Report No. 1). Melbourne: Jean Gordon Government Printer.

Somebody's Daughter Theatre. (1999). *Tell her that I love her*. Sydney: Author unknown.

Victorian Community Council Against Violence. (VCCAC). (1990). *Violence in and around licensed premises*. Melbourne: Author.

Victorian Community Council Against Violence (VCCAV). (1992). *Public violence*. Melbourne: Author.

Weatherburn, D. (1989). Sources of confusion in the alcohol and crime debate. Alcohol and Crime Proceeding of a conference, April 4–6. Australian Institute of Criminology, Canberra.

Weatherburn, D., and Devery, C. (1989). How violent is Australia. Paper presented at the Australian Institute of Criminology's National Conference on Violence, Canberra, October 1–13.

Yarwood, A.T., and Knowling, M.J. (1982). *Race relations in Australia: A history.* Sydney: Methuen Australia Pty Ltd.

3

The Phases of Violence in Brazil

Clary Milnitsky-Sapiro

The task of narrating and analyzing contextual forms of violence in Brazil constituted a challenge due to the cultural complexity of the social interactions that convey hidden and explicit configurations of harmful acts. It is important to remember that Brazil was a colony from its "discovery" by Portugal in 1500 until its independence in 1822. During this period—and up until 1888, when slavery was abolished by Princess Isabel (the Brazilian emperor's daughter)—violence against native Indians and Africans was not only accepted, but also regulated, by law. The people's demands lead to the change from an imperial Portuguese colony to a republic nation in November of 1889, although this very political act has controversial interpretations.

Nevertheless, these minority ethnic and cultural groups continue to suffer discrimination, prejudice, and exclusion in regard to the exercise of the most basic rights of citizenship, such as health care, housing, and education. Simon, Aufderheide, and Kampmeter (2001) remind us that *minority* is the common term for oppressed groups, even when they represent a larger proportion of the population in terms of their numbers. The concept of majority relates to criteria such as social status or power among others. The Afro-Brazilians, mulattos, and poor people are "minorities" that include the majority of members of the Brazilian population—especially in the northeastern and northern states of Brazil. According to Simon, Aufderheide, and Kampmeter (2001), this means that the greatest part of the Brazilian population continues to be denied basic human rights.

As Véras (1999) states, social exclusion is not a new theme in Brazilian culture. Since Brazilian colonial times, exclusionary social processes have been present in Brazilian history, from Imperial Brazil to the republics. In fact, the exploitation and violation of human rights has characterized the history and social structure since Brazil's beginning as a colony. This was especially true during the period of military dictatorship that followed the coup d'état of 1964, which lasted until 1984. Censorship, prison, and torture had an impact on all forms of cultural expression, namely, music, theater, literature, and academics. Major scholars of human sciences and artists were also expelled or imprisoned. This chapter never would have been written under those circumstances.

Yet, as a reaction to oppression and as a form of unconscious collective resistance to the control of political and financial oligarchy, Brazilians have developed informal ways of protecting their intergroup interactions and interests in different segments of the official social structure. These informal manners—blended with a multiethnic creativity, rhythm, and sense of humor—gave us the image of the *malandro*, the light-footed people of samba and soccer and of a joyful adaptive style (*jogo de cintura*[1]).

Furthermore, the need to improvise under complex and ill-structured situations granted the cultural cognitive apparatus to figure out alternatives to solve contextual problems and to take advantage of situations from an in-group perspective. All these features together conferred a peculiar representation of Brazil that is obviously an oversimplification in the comprehension of its cultural diversity.

On the other hand, sharp social contrasts between social classes exposed the violence that always was rooted deeply in the Brazilians' daily life, underlying the corresponding optimistic image. Although violence has cultural roots, it is essential that the reader be immersed in the contemporary Brazilian context further than colonization for the circumstances and grounds of violence in this country to be understood.

Therefore, to aid the reader's comprehension, this chapter will focus on the groups classified as minorities and will conclude with analyses of contemporary forms of violence in Brazilian society in general, including:

1. Violence against children and adolescents
2. Violence against Afro-Brazilians
3. Violence against native Indians
4. Violence against the "landless people"
5. Violence against the human body in Brazilian society

FORMS OF VIOLENCE AGAINST CHILDREN AND ADOLESCENTS

Exclusion from the Educational System

A hideous form of violence against children involves the deprivation of their basic rights such as health care and education; and this happens among those who belong to minority groups in various regions of Brazil.

Their exclusion from the educational system starts early on when working-class mothers need to enroll their infants in public *crèches* (community nurseries for poor families) or preschools. There are very few municipal public *crèches* and preschools in urban centers, and even fewer in the slums (*favelas*) of urban centers and rural areas. To these women, who are mostly single, the lack of adequate day-care facilities is of crucial importance, since they can neither pay for caretakers nor provide meals for their children at home.

The most frequent solution to this problem is for women to collect money to pay an informal caretaker, usually a neighbor, to look after their children in a tiny *barraco* (the precarious huts in the slums) while they are working. The children often end up coming down with many types of diseases due to lack of hygienic care, and this will increase the number of children who are excluded permanently from the educational system. This factor becomes one among many of the important "levers" that increases the number of children living on the street, and all forms of child abuse.

Another form of violence against poor children is imposed labor in urban or rural centers. In the cities, the mothers or other adults may send the children into the streets to sell "candies" or to beg in order to increase the family's budget. There are many forms of children's labor exploitations in rural areas, and these children are forbidden to return home without the right profit. In order to avoid physical punishment and abuse, children in the urban centers usually spend two or more days on the street until they make the stipulated amount of money. Sadly, it quickly becomes increasingly easier for the children to remain on the streets as they establish affective ties and begin to integrate into the society of excluded and abandoned children.

Official data from the Brazilian Institute of Geography and Statistics (IBGE) [2] includes follow-up studies depicting the dramatic effects of this situation upon children. For example, a study conducted by the Institute of Economy and Applied Research (IPEA) found that children who have access to preschool later have less discontinuity in their schooling. They get to higher school levels and get better occupations in the future. The same research data shows that a lack of access to schooling has an indirect influence on many other factors that escalate other elements of inequity.[3]

The low income of the majority of the Brazilian people deeply affects the quality of life of children and, consequently, determines their exclusion from school. The children of deprived families are very limited in their ability to have a traditional childhood with time for play and education, while the middle-and upper-class children are able to attend private schools.

In Brazil, 4 million families with children 6 years old or younger earn less than half of the yearly minimum wage (the minimum wage is equivalent to $8,000). This figure constitutes one-third of Brazilian families with children of this age. In Maranhão (a northern state of Brazil), the percentage is of 63.9 percent, twice as much as the national average. According to data recorded by the Department of Population and Social Indicators of the IBGE, this situation is serious because these children live in extremely vulnerable situations.

In the northeast, if a mother of a child under 5 years old has completed up to four years of schooling, her child's chances of dying before reaching 5 years of age is 124.7 out of thousand. This percentage is six times higher than a mother and child in southern Brazil, where people have greater access to education.

Another consequence of poverty that affects children as well as adults is illiteracy. In 1992, 35.6 percent of the population of Alagoas (located in northern Brazil) was illiterate. In 1997, this figure went up to 36.2 percent, and, in 1999, the percentage fell to 32.8 percent.[4] Illiteracy is a disguised form of violence against Brazilian children because it can endanger their future and their very survival.

The unequal distribution of resources separates children who have the right to education from the ones who do not. Forty-two million citizens are illiterate or have not attended school, and 8 million school-age children are in the streets. "The major symbol of our society is the inequity, and the Brazilian life agenda should emphasize the mechanisms of distribution, not of income only, but for correcting the regional inequities, the inequity between men and women, and between blacks and whites," stated the president of IBGE, Sergio Besserman, during the presentation of the synthesis of Brazilian Social Index of 2000.[5]

Some criticize isolated actions that help only a few children, asserting that these actions deal only with the symptoms of poverty and do not address the primary causes. Contrary to this statement, James P. Grant (cited in Caverson, 1993), executive-director of United Nations Children's Fund (UNICEF), replied very emphatically: "This argument doesn't acknowledge that many diseases, malnourishment, deficient physical development, and illiteracy are some of the primary causes that lead to poverty. It does not consider also, that the rhythm of economic development goes backwards when the deprivation of physical and mental development strikes millions of children. The march on direction of equal opportunities slows down when children of the poorest population drop out of school, and the perspectives of salary, savings, and profit are impaired by physical and mental incapacitation provoked by inevitable diseases."

Street-Children: Children without Childhood

The patterns of Brazilian social classes lead to the perpetuation of exclusionary practices and involve a portion of the population that is characterized by Souza Martins (1991) as "the children without childhood, because they are born at the societal fringes having no room for play and fantasy." The street-child's profile is one of a human being who sleeps and wakes in the public space. This child is afforded no right to privacy and, at the same time, remains invisible to others unless he commits an infraction. The cement slab, among the garbage and rats, is his home. He is likely to become a murderer or a murder victim, a pickpocket, and a drug addict. Most street-children will never know what it is like to play with real toys or to wake up in a clean and warm bed. The street-kids are children who stay in the streets not because they do not know what to do, but it is a condition inflicted upon them, and it is also a way to assure their own survival.

Research conducted in 1993 and 1995 by Milnitsky-Sapiro, Dutra, Coelho, and Correa (1995) found that street-children, if they had a choice, would rather be studying and playing like others of their age. In Brazil, street-children have a peculiar way of interacting with people in cars and with peasants; they call them "aunt" or "uncle." Psychologists can interpret the use of these terms as a survival strategy, as it establishes some kind of emotional tie or affection.

Considering the cognitive-developmental prerequisites for attachment development, Flavell (1971) states "there is a mutually facilitating, reciprocally meditative developmental relationship between cognitive (perceptual and conceptual) processes and social behavior. This is true during infancy, and it is also true at later periods of development." Flavell also maintains that it is difficult to conceive any significant cognitive development at all, if the infant's social relations with other human beings has fallen below some unknown minimum. In agreeing with Flavell concerning the development of attachment, one needs to ask the question: What can we expect from children who are exposed to all sorts of inhumane conditions of social arrangements, besides the very adaptation to an imposed violence?

Camata (1992) termed the Brazilian people's and authorities' lack of consciousness about abandoned children *the Brazilian fascism*. At that time, as a federal deputy, she stated that, like the Germans in the Holocaust, Brazilians are ignoring the deaths of eight hundred children per day, or 24,000 per month. These figures have not changed significantly until the present year.

Milnitsky-Sapiro and Santos (1993) reported that, in the urban centers, violence against children and adolescents is brutal and frequent. All of the victims are abandoned in the streets and struggle for survival. Once they reach adolescence, these children end up reproducing the violence that was imposed on them, making the issue of public safety even more complex. Zalvar's (1998) data shows that the homicide rate before the age of 17 is the highest in São Paulo. The increase of violence is provoked mainly by the deterioration of the quality of life in the urban centers and the action of juvenile gangs, policemen, and ex-policemen.

In 1998 the Brazilian Information Center on Psychotropic Drugs (CE-BRID) published its *IV Survey on Children and Adolescents Drug Users who Live in the Streets of the Six Brazilian Larger Cities*. The demographic data indicates that there is a great percentage of drug users among street-boys and-girls and also suggest that there are qualitative differences in the patterns of drug use in the different state capitals (Noto, Nappo, Galduróz, Mattei, Carlini, 1998). Kuchenbecker (2000) explains that the most common drug used by street-children is *loló* which is a solvent originally intended to be used as a shoemaking glue. As an inhalant drug, its chemical components depress the central nervous system. It is very common to see street-children clenching a dirty cloth (*paninho*) soaked with *loló* against their noses and mouths. In addition, marijuana and cocaine are used. Cocaine is more popular than marijuana and is used mostly by sharing needles, which increases the risk of HIV contamination.

As soon as these adolescents become drug-addicted, they also become and feel more excluded socially—from school, family, and work. They get closer to violence and organized crime, drug dealing, and prostitution. They expose themselves to some kind of violent death, while, at the same time, they are paradoxically "socially invisible" (Dimenstein, 1998). The drug users are the ones who make more explicit the feeling of futility in fighting the battle of exclusion. For homeless adolescents, the public space has become their own space in which all sorts of social and private interactions take place. Moreover, although these children and adolescents are living near shopping malls, at stoplights, and in downtown streets, most of the time they are invisible to the rest of the population (Kuchenbecker, 2000).

VIOLENCE AGAINST AFRO-BRAZILIANS

The last demographic census indicated that there are 167 million inhabitants of Brazil. Only 15 percent of the population retains 17.3 percent of the national profit, while the poorest 10 percent (6.6 million) keep only 0.6 percent of the national income (IBGE, 1989). Fifteen million people in Brazil age 15 or more are illiterate (equivalent to the population of Chile or three times the population of Israel).

The Afro-Brazilians and Mulattos

As mentioned before, prejudice and social discrimination against Afro-Brazilians remains the same. The Brazilian society generalizes the "people of color" for the purpose of tacit discrimination. According to data collected by the IBGE, even when Afro-Brazilians and mulattos reach higher levels of education, they have more difficulty improving their income and life standards than white people do. For the white (Caucasian) people, each year of study means an income increase of 1.25 percent of the minimum wage, while for the Afro-Brazilians and mulattos the increase is 0.53 percent of the minimum wage.

According to data of the National Research Sample of Housing (PNAD) of 1999,[6] 54 percent of the 167 million Brazilians declared themselves as "whites," 5.4 percent declared themselves as "blacks" (official terminology of the IBGE), and 39.9 percent classified themselves as mulattos (pardos). The study compared data between 1992 and 1999, and showed that the rate of illiteracy decreased in all groups of color; however, the rate of illiteracy among Afro-Brazilians and mulattos was still three times higher than that of Caucasians. In 1999, 8.3 percent of whites, 21 percent of Afro-Brazilians ("blacks," according to the official data of IBGE), and 19.6 percent of mulattos were illiterate.

In Brazil, the inequity of rights is present among those excluded by virtue not only of their social condition, but also of their ethnicity. Research done by Magalhães at the University of Brasilia in 1993 points out that, in Brazil, prejudice against Afro-Brazilians is a fact. Data showed that among 503 federal deputies, there are less than ten black men. There are 357 bishops in the hierarchy of the Catholic Church (the main religion of Brazilians), but only five of them are black men. The pattern of beauty depicted on Brazilian television is Caucasian, and, in soap operas, Afro-Brazilians perform only secondary roles, such as servants, slaves, chauffeurs, and so on. White is the "official color" in Brazil, in spite of the fact that Brazil has the largest population of black people after Nigeria.

According to the IBGE (2000), social statistical data of this last decade (1990–2000) shows that all Brazilians had more access to schools, lowering the rate of illiteracy and increasing the family income. However, the great socioeconomic gap between Afro-Brazilians and white Brazilians remained the same during the nineties.

VIOLENCE AGAINST NATIVE INDIANS

Brazilian Indians are classified according to the cultural areas to which they belong and the language they speak. The three main linguistic roots of Brazilian Indians are the Tupi, the Macro-jê, and the Aruaque. This classification system takes into account the homogeneity of customs. There are ten Indian cultural regions in Brazil: the North Amazon, the Juruá-Purus, the Guaporé, the Tapajós-Madeira, the Alto Xingu, the Pindaré-Gurupi, the Paraguai, the Paraná, the Tietê-Uruguai, and the Northeastern.

During the Portuguese colonization, it was estimated that the population of Indian people was between 2 and 5 million. According to the National Foundation of Indian (FUNAI), the current Indian-Brazilian population is limited to about 220,000 habitants, concentrated mainly in the North Amazon and Northeastern regions of Brazil, although a few tribes still can be found in other regions of the country. Another 330,000 live in isolated communities. Their reserves, or nation-states, designate them a group of people linked by a sense of historical community, religion, language, or race, making them a nation within the geographic limits governed by a state. However, the invasion and presence of peasants and landlords in the reserves mark the fragmentation and destruction of these people.

When Pedro Alvares Cabral dropped anchor in Brazil in 1500, the native Indians occupied the entire geographic area. Today, 503 years later, they still fight to maintain their cultures and nations. On April 19, 1940, the first Indigene Inter-American Congress was organized in Patzcuaro City, Mexico. Since then, this day has been celebrated as National Indian's Day, marking the day the Brazilian congress allowed the native Indians' participation.

On April 19, 2001, congress received a group of native Indian representatives who asked them not to approve the Indian Statute. According to the native Indians, the statute does not respect "real Indian rights." In fact, the proposal calls for the exploration of mineral, wood, and water resources and harms the biodiversity. The Indians no longer wish these precious resources to be extracted from their territories. The government defends the privatization of services in the areas of health and education. The Indians disagree, arguing that this proposal is unconstitutional, since the federal government is responsible for the assistance to Indian peoples.[7]

VIOLENCE AGAINST THE "LANDLESS PEOPLE"

The peasants without land, or the "landless" population, also constitute an important minority group in Brazil. Poor people are victims of individual and organized violence in both the cities and the country. Today, the modernization of Brazilian agriculture has resulted in selective technological developments. The modern techniques have not solved the problem of hunger affecting most of the Brazilian population, but have intensified the exploitation of the soil without respecting its social function.

Milnitsky-Sapiro and Tavares dos Santos (1993) pointed out that the other side of modernization is the transference of rural populations to the Amazon's programs of colonization, of which the ecological irrationality adds to the inefficacy of the state agencies. The most significant result of this selective model of modernization has been the increase of the "landless peasants." Moreover, the major conflict is that these people resist multiplying the marginal urban population, and still fight for the right to have a lot of land.

In addition, land reform has long been a social and political battle.

Landlords evidently opposed the ambitious reforms that were planned for the expropriation of approximately 107 million acres, an area the size of Spain, and for the settlement of 1.4 million families (7 million people) (Harvey, 1987).

On April 17, 1996, nineteen peasants, or landless people, were massacred; while another sixty were wounded in Eldorado do Carajás (state of Pará) by 150 military policemen. The police were under the orders of the governor of Pará to liberate a road that had been blocked as a protest by the landless peasants. To date, no one involved in the massacre had been condemned for their actions.

Tavares dos Santos in Milnitsky-Sapiro and Tavares dos Santos (1993) emphasizes that the land is a primary means for production and a source of appropriation of capital. The land can be local or regional, and it is the foundation of political power. The ownership of large areas of land means a guarantee of domination and clientelism maneuvered by politics. Landownership constitutes one of the basic forms of social prestige and the exercise of domination. Thus, different segments of the rural bourgeoisie hold a relationship of symbolic and material appropriation with the land, which fosters the social reproduction of classes even at the present time. The exercise of power through landownership and oligarchies goes back to the colonization times of Brazil and, in most cases, reflects political power.

VIOLENCE AGAINST THE HUMAN BODY
IN BRAZILIAN SOCIETY

Brazilian society exposes the permanent abuse and maltreatment of the human body; peoples' laceration is constant. Human life is viewed as disposable, and cruel and painful punishment is used as retaliation against the very existence of anonymous individuals. This denotes an explicit form of the contemporary human condition. As a facet of postmodern life, the "deconstruction" of values is transformed into physical destruction. Moreover, those violent acts are extensive and affect not only the objects that symbolize inclusion in a specific group, but also the human lives and bodies who own the objects.

Physical violence underlies every act of violence and is a central area of focus oriented toward the logic of social coercion. Forms of physical violence performed against the human body are intended to submit people to inhuman conditions. This technology of power operates through the anatomy of pain; it is a common practice in Brazilian prisons to use physical violence to obtain confessions of crimes that were not committed. The exercise of violence over men, women, and children is used to make people into demonstrations so that "witnesses" and social groups are more submissive. It is a political act intended to maintain the silence of the living ones. This is the technology of omnipresence and of impunity (Foucault, 1975). During the military dictatorship, the Brazilian prisons became the very concrete examples of the terrifying history of violence against the human body.

Recently, a permanent commission named Torture Never More was established. The members of this group are either relatives of executed political prisoners or survivors who had been exiled and then allowed to come back to Brazil by the political amnesty in 1984. These people made the commitment to keep the consequences of authoritarianism and military dictatorship alive in Brazil's collective memory.

Unfortunately, the situation remains the same in the prisons for the "ordinary" and nonpolitical criminals. Concerning the participation and influence of Brazilian press and media in general, the advertisement of pain constitutes a tragic spectacle that fosters the dehumanization and detachment of individuals in the community.

Youth and adolescents obviously are affected by these factors, since they have to adapt to new social roles and enter into the world of adulthood. The hypothesis of uncontrolled "identity rescuers" is based on evidence from general parental acceptance that they are seeing their children turn into "unknown people for an unknown world" in regard to their unpredictability and crisis of values. Just as the crisis in the transmission of values is evident, the same difficulty brings about the question of boundaries. Lacking clear rules, the adolescent seems to look for them through tortuous ways, including turning to delinquent behavior (Rassial, 1997).

Considering the high occurrence of adolescent delinquency, Sennet (1970) mentioned the importance of some ecological characteristics such as life in a city, material deterioration or the architecture of the environment, and the poverty of the population.

CONCLUSION

To introduce the study of human development, we need to acknowledge that the process of socialization plays a crucial role throughout the lifespan. The potential to develop and to become a healthy and productive individual is related directly to one's quality of life. The development of a sense of belonging to a social group also requires adaptation to societal norms, rules, and dynamics.

Freud (1930) stated that civilization serves two main purposes: to protect men against nature and to adjust their mutual relationships. Collective human life is possible only when the whole group is stronger than any isolated individual and joins together against all isolated individuals. Most of the conflicts in human society are the result of trying to recreate a satisfactory accommodation between individual claims and cultural claims of the social group. In addition, one of the major problems to solve is how such accommodations can be reached: through a specific form of civilization, or whether this is an irreconcilable conflict.

Following Freud's ideas, humans are inclined to act aggressively, as we can detect these feelings ourselves and assume others share them as well. This fact disturbs the relationships between individuals and constrains the civilization to such critical expenditure of energy. Therefore, Freud adopted the perspective that the inclination toward aggressiveness constitutes an instinctive and original disposition that is self-maintained, and it is a great impediment to the development of civilization.

In *Civilization and its Discontents* (1930), Freud states that the power of the community is established as a "right" that is in opposition to the power of the individual, which he condemns as a "brutal force." The first requirement, then, is justice, the warranty that once a law is established, it cannot be changed to favor any person. On the other hand, in order to fulfill the needs of the whole group, a legal jurisdiction may call on any party to forgo his instincts, without leaving anybody at the mercy of the "brutal force."

The main issue in this context is that the minorities are exceptions, and are left to the mercy of the "brutal force." Therefore, they recreate and reproduce forms of violence against the community from which they are excluded. Furthermore, they are not the exceptions anymore. They are the individuals who are lead instinctively into the struggle for the recognition by the social group and for the right to have their rights.

The Human Rights Commission was created to protect all human beings, and every society should respect it. Due to the inequity of social organization in Brazil, the inequity of rights was established. To diminish the problem, an educational system that promotes true civic consciousness is necessary.

The Brazilian society appears to have reached a stage of the fragmentation of its urban space. The incriminated population faces society through the middle- and upper-class jails of the "closed condominiums" and through the formation of ghettos. Besides the social and spacial segregation of the population, there are also applications of first-hand "solutions," such as lynching, that became common in high-risk locations as a result of the discredit in the police apparatus.

Bourdieu and Wacquant (1992) reminded us how easy it is to interpret the collective violence that comes from the most destitute social classes as a symptom of a moral crisis. It is interpreted, according to Freud (1930), as something like "breaking the established order." The real violence, I argue, comes from the top and is institutionalized and imposed through a set of economic and political transformations which reinforce one another. The increased rate of unemployment, hostility to the marginalized people, and restriction of residential areas to the poor are major factors that led to the present violence.

Now that Brazil has become a democracy, it is imperative to discriminate in the societal praxis the real dimensions of personal prerogatives from the intrusion and damage on rights and boundaries of "the other." Brazilian society has exhausted all the alternatives of "growing older" without a commitment to its citizenship. It has ignored the moral values that must underlie the practice of democracy.

It is the duty of educators and developmentalists to review the moral principles that explain why it is impossible for a nation to be well developed without structural equity and an ethical paradigm. The people have to exercise the distinction of fundamental values and instrumental ones through an educational system to which everyone has access and which promotes the perpetual questioning and critical reasoning about social actions for achieving solidarity.

As Tavares dos Santos mentioned in Milnitsky-Sapiro and Tavares dos Santos (1993), it is well known that violence is a widespread social phenomenon whose manifestations strike the global society at all levels. It varies, however, from one society to another, as do its causes, symptoms, and means of eradication. There is no agreement on its proper definition or about the spatial-temporal and cultural-historical relativity of its meaning. The point of convergence is that violence is a complex social phenomenon, which discards any simplistic, deterministic, or unilateral approach. In the face of this upheaval, developmental psychologists, sociologists, and researchers of related fields of knowledge must confront the theoretical limits of academy and engage in the advancement of the social knowledge about the structure of violence.

What is the relationship between violence and the characteristics of Brazilian society? How can we explain the paradox between the progressive Brazilian democratization and the expansion of violence at micro and macro social levels? This question is striking the whole Brazilian society, although it is known tacitly that the sharp social contrasts that result from poverty and deprivation provoke various forms of social violence. However, institutional or individual acts of violence have a complex set of dynamics whose contours require multidisciplinary and multifactorial explanations. The social origins of urban violence have been afflicting people daily for more than a decade in practically all Brazilian cities.

The striking historical character of these facts cannot paralyze our faculty of being real social *human* beings, because, as Sennet (1970) states, "The eruption of social tension becomes a situation in which the ultimate methods of aggression, violent force and reprisal, become not only justified, but life-preserving. There is an intrinsic paradox concerning the escalation of conflict into violence in these communities, and the means by which 'law and order' should be maintained."

On the other hand, how can we reach an understanding of the various manifestations of violence in order to propose social measures to control it, and maybe eradicate it from our social milieu? If we agree that violence implies the destruction of our citizenship, we must build a democratic society that respects the diversity of rights and the contemporary life, including civil and political rights; social rights, such as the right to work; human rights; and environmental rights. There is a claim to conceive a social space in which the right to life and respect to have different opinions can be assured in a way.

NOTES

1. The expression means the skill of "dribbling obstacles" in order to pursue an achievement.
2. Data obtained in the *Folha de São Paulo* archives, March 27, 2001.
3. Data obtained in the *Folha de São Paulo* archives, April 5, 2001.
4. Ibid.
5. IBGE information includes data between 1992–1999 in the *Folha de São Paulo* archives, April 5, 2001.
6. Data obtained in the *Folha de São Paulo archives*, March 27, 2001.
7. This information was obtained at the Agency for Protection of Indians.

REFERENCES

Bourdieu, P., and Wacquant, L.J.D. (1992). *An invitation to reflexive sociology*. Chicago: University of Chicago Press.

Camata, R. (1992, December 10). A miséria do menor. *Folha de São Paulo*.

Caverson, L. (1993, May 13). Crianças primeiro. *Folha de São Paulo*.

Dimenstein, G. (1998). *O cidadão de papel, a infância, a adolescência e os direitos humanos no Brasil*. São Paulo: Ática.

Flavell, J.H. (1971). Stage related properties of cognitive development. *Cognitive Psychology, 2*, 237–259.

Foucault, M. (1975). *Surveiller et punir*. Paris: Gallimard.

Freud, S. (1930). *O mal estar na civilização*. São Paulo: Imago.

Harvey, R. (1987, April 25). Brazil unstoppable: A survey of Brazil. *The Economist*, 1–26.

IBGE. (2000). *Censo demográfico* [Demographic census]. Brasil: Ministério do Plane; amento, Orçamento e Gestão.

Instituto Brasileiro de Geografia e Estatística (IBGE). (1989). <http://www.ibge. gov.br/>.

Kuchenbecker, A. (2000). *Uso de drogas entre meninos e meninas de rua no centro de Pôrto Alegre*. Unpublished Master's thesis, Institute of Psychology, UFRGS Pôrto Alegre.

Magalhães, J.B. (1993, May). Matar criança custa $10,000 no Rio. *Folha de São Paulo*.

Milnitsky-Sapiro, C., Dutra, L., Coelho, S., Correa, C. (1995). *Domains' distinction of social knowledge among "street-kids."* Report presented at AERA, Department of Psychology, Universidade Federal do Rio Grande do Sul, Pôrto Alegre.

Milnitsky-Sapiro, C., and Kuchenbecker, A. (2000). The exclusion and invisibility of adolescents who live in the streets of Pôrto Alegre (Poster). In *Society for Research on Identity Formation*. Seventh Annual conference, Chicago.

Milnitsky-Sapiro, C., and Tavares dos J.V. Santos, (1993). A violência urbana e rural contra a crianca no Brasil: Uma perspectiva interdisciplinar. *Humanas Revista do Instituto de Filosofia e Ciências Humanas*, 16(2), 91–107.

Noto, A.R., Nappo, S., Galduróz, J.C.F., Mattei, R., and Carlini, E.A. (1998). *IV levantamento sobre o uso de drogas entre meninas em situação de rua de seis capitais brasileiras—1997*. Centro Brasileiro de Informações sobre Droga Psicotrópicas—Departamento de Psicobiologia da Escola Paulista de Medicina.

Rassial, J.J. (1997). A adolescência como conceito psicanalític. In *Adolescência: Entre o passado e o futuro* (p. 52). Pôrto Alegre, R.S.: Aneseofficio, Appoa.

Sennet, R. (1970). *The uses of disorder: Personal identity and city life*. York: Vintage Books.

Simon, B., Aufderheide, B., and Kampmeter, C. (2001). The social psychology of minority-majority relations. In Rupert Brown and Samuel L. Gaertner (Eds.), *Blackwell handbook of social psychology: Intergroup processes*. Oxford: Blackwell Publishers.

Souza Martins, José de. (1991). *O massacre dos inocentes: a criança sem infância no Brasil*. São Paulo: Hucitec.

Véras, M. Pardini Bicudo (Ed.). (1999). *Por uma sociologia da exclusão social*. São Paulo: Educ.

Zalvar, Alba. (1998). Violence related to illegal drugs, "easy money," and justice in Brazil: 1980–1995. UNESCO Discussion Paper No. 35. Management of Social Transformations Programme (MOST).

4

Violence in Colombia: Social and Psychological Aspects

Ruben Ardila

INTRODUCTION

Colombia has been considered one of the most violent countries in the world. The violence—political violence; economic violence; family violence; violence against children, the spouses, and the elderly; and violence against "undesirable" people ("social cleansing")—embraces all aspects of life. Colombia is one of the countries that the U.S. State Department has recommended that people not visit or, do so "at your own risk." This warning is echoed by other countries, especially in Europe. The negative image of Colombia has hurt tourism, foreign investment in Colombia, and scientific and academic exchange; for example, it has decreased the possibility of organizing international congresses in the country.

The official statistics indicate an approximate number of thirty thousand violent deaths a year in Colombia. Additional acts of violence include kidnappings, disappearances, extortion, and civil rights abuses. The history of political violence in Colombia is more than fifty years old. It has been concentrated in the rural zones, which have small populations and where the state does not make itself known. In many of these regions the "law of the jungle" or the "law of the strongest" rules and the empire of weapons continues to be very important. This covers an immense territory, including not only the eastern plains and the jungles of the country, but also the agricultural and cattle regions where there are important developments in industry and crops.

The violence began at the end of the 1940s, although it probably had roots in previous epochs. Later, it developed into a war against the "establishment," against the government, supposedly in favor of social justice. This period, in the 1960s and 1970s, was inspired by the Cuban Revolution. The left-wing guerrillas were inspired to fight against social injustice and to establish a communist (or socialist) government in Colombia similar to that of Fidel Castro in Cuba.

The next step was the association of the guerrillas with the drug dealers and the drug cartels. The guerrillas lost their ideals of social justice and associated themselves with the narcotics traffickers (first marijuana, then cocaine, and later heroin). The association between guerrillas and drug traffickers has been complex, and has resulted in the loss of prestige of the insurgents among the intellectual population and within the international context. As we begin the twenty-first century, it appears that the guerrilla fighters (FARC [Revolutionary Armed Forces of Columbia] and ELN [National Liberation Army]) are no longer interested in mounting a social revolution similar to the Cuban Revolution of the 1960s. Very few people believe that their goal is social change and the construction of a more just society in Colombia. The majority of Colombians think that the guerrillas are just criminals, and that the social and philosophical ideals previously associated with their movement are a thing of the past.

Paramilitary defense groups, such as AUC (United Autodefenses of Colombia) and others, have arisen. These groups have served to perpetuate the vicious circle of violence that begins with death and vengeance, and leads to more deaths and more vengeance. The Colombian Army, as the representative of legitimacy and the law of the country, is an important force, and its credibility has been on the increase in recent years. In other words, the authors of the armed conflict are the guerrilla fighters, the paramilitary groups, and the national army. In the background can be found the action of drug traffickers, the search for easy money, a lack of state presence, institutional weakness, and the creation of a culture of violence that has been perpetuated for many decades.

This complex panorama of violence in Colombia, is presented below and the psychological, social, and historical factors that sustain it are outlined with references to political violence as well as social and family violence. Some basic information in this context is found below so that the reader may better understand these problems.

BASIC INFORMATION

Colombia possesses an extension of 1,338,000 square kilometers, and is one of the largest countries of Latin America (after Brazil, Mexico, and Argentina). It has a population of 38 million people. It is a country of Roman Catholic ancestry. Its official language is Spanish, although small groups of people speak Indian languages. The life expectancy is seventy-two years, and 90.9 percent of the people are literate.

Table 4.1 shows demographic information for the year 2000, comparing

Table 4.1
Demographic Indicators, 2000

	Colombia	World
Population	38 million	6,000 million
Life Expectancy	Total, 72 years	Total, 67 years
	Males, 70 years	Males, 62 years
	Females, 75 years	Females, 69 years
Average Age	25 years	22 years
Fertility Rate per Woman	2.8 children	3.3 children
Per Capita Income	US $1,600 annually	US $3,610 annually
Literacy Rate	90.9%	87%
Percent Urban	71%	44%
Percent of Population Older Than 65	5%	7%

Human Development Index: Colombia is 57 among 174 countries.

Colombia with the rest of the world. In some parameters, Colombia is above the world average; in others it is not. Colombia possesses the oldest democracy of Latin America and does not have the tradition of dictators that has been so frequent in Latin America. There is a great respect for knowledge, literature, the arts, philosophy, and politics. Colombians are proud to be "cultured," much more so than their neighbors. Seventy-one percent of the population is urban. The Human Development Index places Colombia in fifty-seventh place among 174 countries.

Colombia (like the rest of Latin America) is a mixture of cultures that have brought different philosophies to the country. These cultures include indigenous Americans, Spanish, Africans, and recent immigrants from the rest of Europe and from the Orient (e.g., Lebanese and Chinese people). Colombia is a heterogeneous, multicultural country, but it has a clear predominance of Spanish culture.

Social values are traditional and center on the family, cooperation, altruism, education, tolerance of frustration, humor, and passive coping (Ardila, 1996, 2001). However, Colombia is an individualistic and not a collectivistic culture. The process of modernization has been very rapid, particularly after 1960, with growing industrialization and urbanization. The pace of social change is different in various parts of the country, and the difference between generations is marked. Among the social factors that have changed in the last few decades are the role of women in society, economic development, urbanization, illiteracy rates, ease of overseas travel, marked differentiation between social classes, role of the Catholic Church, internationalization, globalization of the economy, and others. Drug trafficking, guerrilla warfare, and rural violence are also relevant social factors. The complexity of the panorama indicates that no easy solutions to Colombia's social problems can be found.

On the other hand, Colombia is a country with a highly educated elite. It has top-level economists, administrators, scientists, and politicians. These elite people usually are educated abroad (previously in Europe and, at the present time, in the United States). They aspire to gain the material benefits of a modern lifestyle, defend the advantages of the globalization of economic processes, have a technological and futuristic outlook of life, and are in clear contrast with the large segments of society that want to preserve the traditional values and systems.

This elite minority lives in the main cities (Bogotá, Medellín, Cali, and Barranquilla), travel abroad, and are active participants in international affairs. For many years, the problem of Colombian violence was something that did not affect them directly. At the present time, however, the elite have recognized the importance of the problem of violence in Colombian society and the central role that the solution to these kinds of problems will play for the future of the country.

VIOLENCE IN SOCIETY

Endemic violence is one of the main facets of Colombian society at the beginning of the twenty-first century. The public image of Colombia is that of a violent country that is very unstable and very dangerous, and whose pressing needs are unmet. The recent governmental administration centered all its energies in understanding and solving this problem. The peace program of the Pastrana administration (1998–2002); the Plan Colombia, which is supported financially and technically by the United States; and all the analysis of Colombia and its future perspectives are centered on the issue of violence.

It is important to point out that violence is not a set of phenomena restricted to one sector of society. Violence can be found in both rural and urban areas, including all towns, cities, and regions of the country. This includes political violence, social-economic violence, family violence, violence against children, and so on.

Violence is defined as "a physical, biological or spiritual pressure, directly or indirectly exercised by a person on someone else, which, when exceeding a certain threshold, reduces or annuls that person's potential for performance, both at an individual and group level in the society in which this takes place" (Rupesinghe and Rubio, 1994, 3). This general definition of violence applies to Colombia, and includes all the aspects of violence that are present in the country at this time.

The modernization and industrialization (of the 1950s and 1960s) has had a mixed effect on Colombia. While vastly increasing the potential for human understanding and cooperation, they accelerated the disintegration of traditional cultures, widened the actual and perceived chasms between advanced technological societies and developing ones struggling to provide just the basic necessities of life. For Colombians, modernization and industrialization raised expectations to a level that was unattainable. As is seen in research, frustration is correlated with aggression in a large number of cases.

Governmental institutions lost their credibility because of a lack of efficiency. The Colombian legal system, police, and army were not able to guarantee a functional and efficient state. Turmoil in society increased, and the lack of credible state institutions in vast areas of the country spread later to urban centers, where the population had increased dramatically while economic opportunities were declining. It is surprising to find that rural guerrilla movements sought to fill the institutional vacuum by providing security and some social services.

Paramilitary groups (or self-defense groups) were formed by local landowners and peasants who wanted to defend their lives and property from the armed guerrilla groups. Drug traffickers, particularly important in the 1980s and 1990s, joined forces with the local armies and with mercenaries to fight the guerrillas. At the present time, the guerrilla groups (in particular FARC and ELN), the drug traffickers, the Colombian Army, and the paramilitary groups form a complex system. There are some known alliances between some of these groups (i.e., guerrilla and drug traffickers), and other alliances that are denied and not accepted by the possible participants (e.g., between the Colombian Army and the paramilitary). In this complicated matrix, the civilian population—which includes the peasants, the poorest members of society—are always the victims.

FAMILY VIOLENCE

Violence exists within the family: against the spouse (above all the wife), against the children, and against the elderly. The family is not a "rose garden," and, in many cases, poor conditions exist for the development of children and for conjugal harmony.

This is not exclusive to Colombia, nor is it exclusive to Latin America. It exists in all societies and in all cultures, in varying degrees. However, it is strange that a society that values the children and the family as much as Colombia does would contain this class of abuse and this class of violence.

Psychologists and other professionals have become aware of these problems and, in recent years, have turned their attention to family violence, child sexual abuse, and physical mistreatment. The violent conflicts within the family have been a topic of great concern (Grupo Familia, Cultura y Sociedad, 1998). Officials in charge of public policies relating to the family, wives, and children (e.g., the Colombian Institute of Family Welfare) have worked a lot on these problems.

Following are the explanations that have been proposed to try to understand Colombian violence, especially at the macro social level and political level. We will examine the role of "genetic determinism" on frustration-aggression, on social learning, and on friction between groups.

SCIENTIFIC INVESTIGATION

A problem of this magnitude could not have been ignored by the social scientists. On the contrary, there is a very large body of research investigating the topic of violence in Colombia. The first book examining this topic was written by Guzmán Campos, Fals Borda, and Umaña Luna (1964) and entitled *Violence in Colombia.* More recent works have investigated the psychological aspects of the violence in Colombia (Ardila, 1994) and the impact of drug trafficking on Colombian culture (De Roux, 1994).

The theme has been investigated amply by sociologists, anthropologists, psychologists, historians, political scientists, and economists. A new social science called *violentology*, whose specific objective is the study of violence, has been proposed. There has been talk about the "culture of violence," which is a conceptualization based on the fact that Colombians have adapted to live in situations of violence, to solve their conflicts in a violent form, to think that violence and destruction are inevitable, and to believe that there is no light at the end of the tunnel. Many Columbians assume that violence is an integral part of the culture and that it is never going to change. Unfortunately, this position of "learned helplessness," in the manner of Seligman (1975), is very widespread in Colombia.

The explanations of violence that the social scientists have proposed can be summarized in this form:

Genetic Determinism

It has been said that the primitive inhabitants of the territory of present-day Colombia were violent and aggressive warriors, and that so are their descendents. According to this theory, the primitive indigenous people possessed genetic tendencies toward violence and aggression, which were passed on to future generations. Hence, violent and aggressive individuals exist in contemporary society, in spite of the influences of Western civilization, religion, industrial society, and so forth.

This explanation completely lacks foundation. The majority of the indigenous groups that populated the territory that is now Colombia were peaceful, not aggressive. The Spanish dominated them easily and imposed their culture, language, religion, and philosophy of life on them. The few aggressive groups that resisted the Spanish conquest lived in the regions of the country where violence does not exist (like the Caribbean coast). Their present-day descendents are not violent, as their ancestors were. Therefore, saying that today's violence is due to Colombians' descending from violent indigenous groups is false.

Frustration-Aggression Theory

This theory affirms that frustration always leads to some form of aggression and that aggression always emerges from frustration. In its recent form, this theory proposes that frustration instigates several different responses, and one of those is aggression.

As it relates to Colombia, this theory suggests that Colombians are people with many frustrations, which causes them to act in aggressive ways. Their frustrations probably would be centered around social issues: overcoming economic limitations, barriers against social advancement, the stratification of the social classes, the rigidity of institutions, authoritarian education, the lack of political participation, the lack of empowerment, and the marginalization of great segments of the population. These frustrated groups (which comprise a very large part of Colombian society) would be aggressive groups and, as a last resort, they could become violent groups.

Social Learning Theory

It has been suggested by Albert Bandura that human beings are social animals who base their behavior on the imitation of others. Behavior is learned vicariously by following the conduct of role models. We learn adaptive and prosocial behaviors, as well as nonadaptive and antisocial ones, by imitation.

Violence and aggression are learned from models in the family, in the classroom, on the street, and on television. Colombian children and adults observe many episodes of violence from their peers in daily life, in school, and in the mass media. In this context of the "culture of violence," Colombians must have learned how to face problems in a nonadaptive form, namely, by force and by violence. In this form the cycle of violence perpetuates.

Friction between Groups

Violence, war, and aggression are exclusively social products. One fights for power, for the possession of material resources, for the imposition of ideologies. One who has a different ideology from ours is considered an "enemy," and one who has our same ideology is considered a "friend."

Colombia is a heterogeneous country, with much friction between groups. Those who possess power seek to maintain their privileges and their status quo, while those without it seek to obtain it and to change the status quo. There is the struggle between ideologies—between policies, social classes, ethnos, religious positions—and there is the desire of the marginal groups to destroy the foundations of the powerful groups; all this leads to the presence of violence.

The imbalance of power, the anomie, the marginality, the lack of partic-ipation, and the necessity of empowerment are at the base of violence in Colombia.

CONCLUSIONS

The previous explanations are partly true, especially the ones that refer to social learning, to the culture of violence, and to the friction between groups. Nevertheless, it is probably also true that all the explanations are incomplete, due to the complexity of the problem of violence in Colombia.

The traditional position, which is based on poverty, lacks foundation since there are countries far poorer than Colombia that do not suffer from an endemic violence of more than fifty years duration. Besides, the coun-try possesses the immense natural, biological, and water resources, plus the well-known resources of biodiversity and raw materials. It is also a widely known fact that Colombia possesses human resources of great quality, education of the highest quality, excellent schools and universities, and a great intellectual tradition. With physical and human resources of that level, Colombia is not a "poor" country under any standard that is considered.

The cause of violence is more social in origin, stemming from an un-equal allocation of resources, rather then from the inexistence of such re-sources. It is more one of the culture of violence, of having learned to try to solve problems and difficulties in a violent form. A lack of the presence of the state in the isolated parts of the country is also a problem. Colombia is a centralist nation, and the sources of power, the resources, and the in-stitutions have been concentrated in Bogotá and other main cities where important decisions that effect all the country are made. Many people lack power and do not have control over their own destiny.

When the problems of Colombian violence end, when we solve these conflicts, the next great step is to try to heal the wounds. A lot of rancor, scars, resentment, and an entire history of violence and revenge will re-main. The reconciliation, forgiveness, and the search for sustainable peace and human development will be the great task for psychologists and other professionals.

Psychologists had to face similar tasks in South Africa, Chile, and Ar-gentina. They were called upon to heal the wounds of violence and to achieve national reconciliation. The "day after" in Colombia will be a challenge of enormous importance. Those in charge must construct a society without violence and try to prevent the reappearance of the chaotic and painful experiences that have existed in Colombia for more than fifty years.

REFERENCES

Ardila, R. (1994). La violencia en Colombia: Parametros psicologicos (Violence in Colombia: Psychological parameters). *Psicologia Contemporanea* (Mexico), *1*, 22–28.

Ardila, R. (1996). Ethnopsychology and social values in Colombia. *Interamerican Journal of Psychology, 30*, 127–139.

Ardila, R. (2001). *La psicologia de los Colombianos* (The psychology of the Colombian people). Bogotá: Editorial Panamericana.

De Roux, F.J. (1994). The impact of drug trafficking on Colombian culture. In K. Rupesinghe and M. Rubio, (Eds.), *The culture of violence* (pp. 92–118). Tokyo: United Nations University Press.

Grupo Familia, Cultura y Sociedad. Centro de Investigaciones. Sociales y Humanas. (Family, Culture and Society Notebook, Central Investigations, Social and Human). (1998). University of Antioquia, CIHS.

Guzmán Campos, G., Fals Borda, O., and Umaña Luna, E. (1964). *La violencia en Colombia* (Violence in Colombia). Bogotá: Tercer Mundo Ediciones.

Palacios, M. (1995). *Entre la legitimidad y la violencia: Colombia 1875–1994* (Between legitimity and violence: Colombia 1875–1994). Bogotá: Editorial Norma.

Rupesinghe, K. and Rubio, M. (Eds.). (1994). *The culture of violence*. Tokyo: United Nations University Press.

Seligman, M.E.P. (1975). *Helplessness*. San Francisco: Freeman.

Wesslles, M.G. (2000). Contributions of psychology to peace and nonviolent conflict resolution. In K. Pawlik and M.R. Rosenzweig (Eds.), *International handbook of psychology* (pp. 526–533). London: Sage Publications.

5

Violence in Great Britain

Ludwig F. Lowenstein

INTRODUCTION

Violence in Great Britain is of great concern to the general population. As we begin the twenty-first century, there is the feeling that violence may be increasing rather than decreasing in various areas of society. The perceived increasing violence may well be due to the fact that violent acts are more likely to be reported today as compared to the Victorian or Elizabethan periods. However, comparing one generation or era with another is likely to lead to uncertain results.

It should be noted that the author of this chapter has been involved in the area of violence through running a therapeutic center for adolescents with severe personality problems, including violent behavior and, in many cases, delinquent demeanor. Despite the interrelationships between various aspects of violence in society, efforts are made to attempt to distinguish between these different areas. Only the most recent research is being considered here. In some cases, comparisons are made between violent activities in Great Britain and other parts of the world, including the United States. Psychological problems frequently have been associated with violence and, in the extreme, turn individuals to criminal acts, including rape, murder, arson, and so on. The targets of violent acts in Great Britain frequently have been the more vulnerable members of society, including women and children, as well as the aged.

The British press, as well as the mass media on the whole, frequently reports acts of violence. Newspaper articles published between January 1 and December 31, 1995, in eight British newspapers were analyzed and evaluated for content. The theme of the articles was the amount of violence on television and its effects on children. Comparisons were made with similar studies in other countries (Gunter and Ward, 1997). Lowenstein (1979b) studied the effect of television violence on children and found there to be a correlation between that and the violent acts of children, providing they already had the tendency to be violent through watching violent scenes on television.

SOCIETY AND VIOLENCE AND CRIME

Although the predominant acts of crime and violence are committed by males, females are also increasingly coming into the limelight by committing serious acts of violence, including murder (Lowenstein, 1984b).

Williams and Dickinson (1993) conducted a three-stage study of the relationship between newspaper reporting of crime and fear of crime. The first stage involved measuring the amount of space and prominence given to reports of crime, particularly violent crime, in ten British daily newspapers. The second stage of the study involved a questionnaire survey of 290 readers on the relationship between newspaper reporting of crime and fear of a crime. A significant positive correlation was found, which appeared to be independent of the demographic factors associated with readership. In the third stage, seventeen of the readers surveyed in the second stage examined qualitative aspects of reporting styles in these newspapers. Consistent differences were found between newspapers. Those newspapers classified as "broadsheets" carried proportionally fewer crime reports and reported those crimes in a less sensational fashion than the "tabloids," particularly the low-market ones. The conflict in Northern Ireland has long been in the news in Great Britain, at some times more than others. Benson (1995) argues that the prospect of resolving the conflict in Northern Ireland (Ulster) was illusory unless the Ulster situation was considered to be a violent expression of separation-individuation dynamics in the whole of the British Isles. The war was discussed in the context of relational separatist impulses and their repression by an archaic grandiose self-structure in the centralist political psyche, especially as viewed by the Irish Republican Army (IRA). Some of the particular psychological features of the conflict were elaborated by reference to a group session that occurred immediately after the October 1993 Shankhill Road, Belfast bomb explosion. It was asserted that a dream presented by one of the group members provided insight into the psychological anxieties and preoccupations structured into the Ulster state at its inception and which continued to fuel the violence.

Interpersonal violence in adults, adolescents, and children in Great Britain has also received much attention (Mezey and Kaplan, 1997). This includes violence on the football field, something that is apparently typical to Great Britain and common areas throughout Europe and the world. It has been argued that, at football games, male fans create imaginary masculine and national boundaries by which they have affirmed identities, and that, by fighting, they have sought to breach these boundaries in a postmodern fashion (King, 1997).

The impasse in Northern Ireland was studied by Lowenstein (1997a), who emphasized the destruction of distrust before disarmament. At the time this chapter was written, violence has continued due to the fact that none of the combatants are eager to demilitarize or disarm.

Needless to say, many acts of violence, especially those between ethnic groups, are due to prejudices, which lay claim to the young and which they pass on as they become adults (Lowenstein, 1985). This has led to the development of informal social controls and violence such as the use of vigilantes, which is common in Northern Ireland (Brewer, Lockhart, and Rodgers, 1998).

Ethnic minorities are a particular target due to their relative vulnerability upon which the majority vents violent acts. However, these acts often are reciprocated (Gunter, 1998). Gunter examined the portrayal of different ethnic groups (majority and minority) as aggressors or victims on British Television, focusing on violence depicted in made-for-television drama series and serials. Data was comprised of a content analysis of 1,161 drama programs monitored on ten channels. The results indicated that the overall ratio of aggressors to victims for all white characters and for all black characters revealed a greater likelihood of victimization for whites and blacks, both of whom were targeted mostly by white aggressors. However, Asian victims of violence on British Television were, more often than not, attacked by members of their own ethnic group.

STATISTICAL INFORMATION ON VIOLENT CRIMES IN GREAT BRITAIN

As is noted in Table 5.1, the extent of crime in 1997, the last year for which information was available, showed that the British crime rate was estimated to be 16,437,000 crimes against people.

The most common offenses involved some type of theft (62% of the total), as can be seen in Figure 5.1, vandalism against vehicles and other household and personal property made up a further 18 percent of offenses covered by the British Crime Survey (BCS, 1998). A minority of crimes were categorized as violent offenses (20%), and the majority of these were common assaults that involved minimal injury (14%). Only 4 percent involved significant injury (wounding), and 2 percent were muggings (robbery and snatch thefts).

Figure 5.2 shows the number of violent crimes experienced by men and women in 1997. Six out of ten incidents of violence in 1997 were against men (2,043,000 in total). Stranger assaults were particularly likely to be aimed at men: over eight in ten. Women were the victims of 70 percent of domestic incidents (582,000).

Table 5.1
Number of Crimes Estimated by the British Crime Survey, 1997

	Number of crimes in thousands
Vandalism (against vehicles and other private property)	**2,917**
All property thefts	**10,134**
Burglary (actual and attempted)	1,639
Vehicle related thefts (thefts of, from, and attempts)	3,483
Bicycle thefts	549
Other household thefts	2,067
Other personal thefts (including stealth thefts)	2,397
All violence	**3,381**
Mugging (robbery and snatch thefts)	390
Wounding	714
Common assault	2,276
All BCS crime	**16,437**

Note: Subtotals do not add to total due to rounding.

Source: BCS, 1998.

Figure 5.1
British Crime Survey, All Crimes

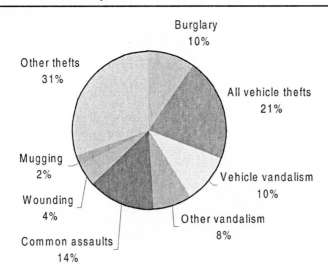

Source: BCS, 1998.

Fig. 5.2
Number of Violent Crimes against Men and Women, 1997

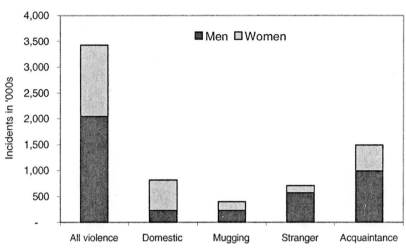

Source: BCS, 1998.

VIOLENT CRIME

Figure 5.3 shows that all violent crime categories decreased between 1995 and 1997, except for mugging. Figure 5.4 shows the trend of British crimes from 1981, up to and including 1997. As may be noted, there was a significant increase in crimes from 1981 and 1991, then a sharp increase until 1993, followed by a leveling off between 1993 and 1995. The fall between 1995 and 1997 equates to a 7.4 percent annual fall. In total, there were 49 percent more crimes in 1997 than in 1981.

All violent acts included in the BCS (1998) fall by 17 percent between 1995 and 1997, as noted in Figure 5.5. This followed a rise between 1981 and 1995 of some 88 percent. The overall rise between 1981 and 1997 was 56 percent.

The decrease between 1995 and 1997 was evident for all types of crime except mugging, which remained at the same level. Domestic violence fell by 16 percent between 1995 and 1997, while stranger violence fell by 28 percent and acquaintance violence by 15 percent.

Figure 5.6 indicates various fluctuations in violence depending on its form. Acquaintance violence rose by 89 percent, and domestic violence by 187 percent during the period from 1981 to 1997. Stranger violence, however, fell by a fifth (–19%). Mugging, which nearly always involved strangers, rose by 55 percent during the same period.

Figure 5.7 shows crime recorded by the police versus unrecorded crime.

Figure 5.3
Percentage Change in British Crime Survey Violent Crimes,
1995–1997

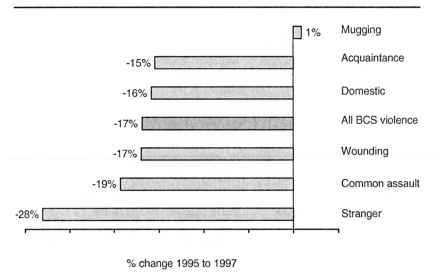

% change 1995 to 1997

Source: BCS, 1998.

Figure 5.4
Trends in British Crime Survey Crime, 1981–1997

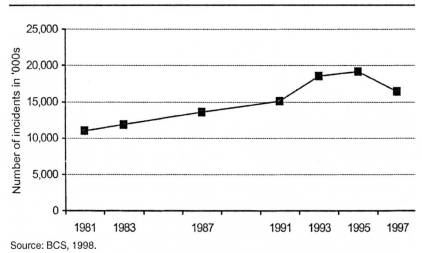

Source: BCS, 1998.

Figure 5.5
Trends in Violence, 1981–1997

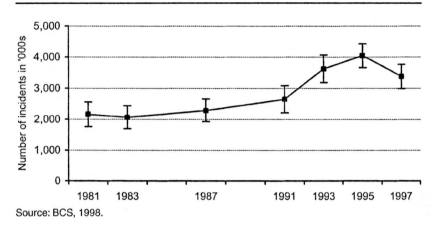

Source: BCS, 1998.

Figure 5.6
Trends in British Crime Survey Violence Typology, 1981–1997

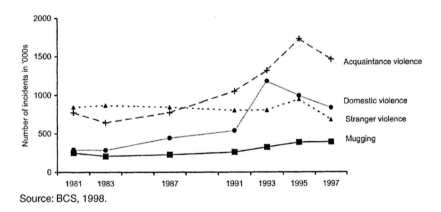

Source: BCS, 1998.

It may be noted that, in virtually every case, unrecorded crime exceeds recorded crime levels.

Figure 5.8 indicates the proportion of offenses reported to the police in 1997. It may be noted that the most commonly reported offense was the theft of vehicles, followed by burglary with loss, bicycle theft, robbery, burglary with no loss, wounding, and so on.

In 1997, 4.7 percent of adults nationally were victims of some type of violence (wounding, common assault, robbery, and snatch theft) once or more times. Again, there was considerable variation in the risk of violence.

Figure 5.7
Comparison of British Crime Survey and Police Counts of Crime, 1997

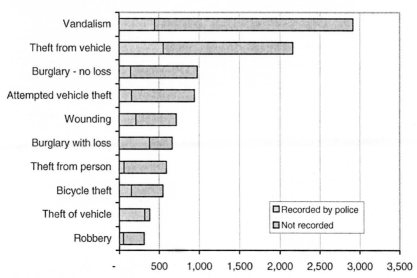

Source: BCS, 1998.

Figure 5.8
Proportion of Offenses Reported to the Police, 1997

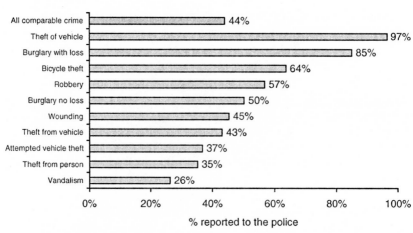

Source: BCS, 1998.

Table 5.2
Proportion of Adult Victims of Violence by Personal Characteristics, 1997

	% victims once or more		% victims once or more
Men	**6.1**	**Tenure**	
16-24	20.9	Owner occupiers	3.2
25-44	7.0	Social renters	6.3
45-64	3.0	Private renters	9.4
65-74	0.2		
75+	1.0		
		Accommodation type	
Women	**3.6**	Detached house	3.1
16-24	8.8	Semi-detached house	4.1
25-44	4.6	Mid terrace	5.9
45-64	2.0	End terrace	6.3
65-74	0.8	Flats/maisonettes	6.4
75+	0.2		
Living arrangements		**Hours out average week**	
Married	2.7	**day**	
Cohabiting	6.4	< 3 hours	2.0
Single	11.3	3 < 5 hours	3.6
Separated	8.4	5 hours +	6.3
Divorced	6.0		
Widowed	0.6		
		Evenings out in last	
Head of household under 60		**week**	
Single adult & child(ren)	11.9	None	3.0
Adults & child(ren)	5.6	One	4.1
No children	6.0	Two/three	5.7
Head of household over 60	1.2	Four/five	7.2
		Six/seven	12.8
Employment status			
In employment	5.6		
Unemployed	11.8	**Evening pub/wine bar**	
Economically inactive	5.9	**visits in last month**	
		None	2.9
Household income		Less than three times	
<£5k	6.6	a week	5.6
£5k to <£10k	2.9	Three or more times	10.6
£10k to <£20k	4.1		
£20k to <£30k	4.7		
£30k +	5.1	**All adults**	**4.7**

Source: BCS, 1998.

Risks differed markedly among adults, depending on their personal characteristics and those of the household to which they belonged. Those at higher risk were young men and young women, single adults, adults living alone with children (i.e., single parents), unemployed adults, adults in low income households (earning under £5,000 per annum [approximately $7,862.54 as of April 2003]), adults in accommodations rented privately or from a council or housing association, adults in flats or terraced properties, and adults who went out into the street more often. Table 5.2 indicates the age, gender, living arrangement, and other pertinent details in connection with when and to whom violence occurs.

Table 5.3
Proportion of Adult Victims of Violence by Locality, 1997

	% victims once or more		% victims once or more
Area type		**Region**	
Inner city	6.8	North	5.2
Urban	4.9	Midlands	4.5
Rural	3.3	Eastern	3.9
		London	5.6
Council estate area	5.9	South	4.4
Non-council estate area	4.5	Wales	4.2
Physical disorder in area			
Low	4.3		
High	7.6	**All adults**	**4.7**

Source: BCS, 1998.

Figure 5.9
The Risks of Violence for Selected Groups of Adults

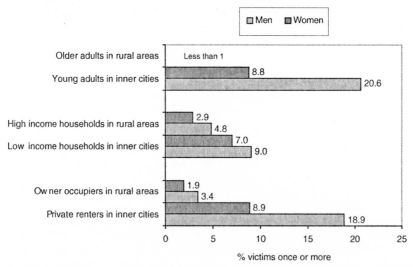

Source: BCS, 1998.

Table 5.3 indicates the proportion of adult victims of violence by location. Violent cuts are categorized into the type of environment in which they occurred, be it the inner city or the urban or rural area. The region in Britain is also indicated. It may be noted that violence occured predominantly in the inner-city areas, with levels being much lower in the rural areas. According to this data, violence is also more likely to occur in council estate areas—that is, cheaper housing—than in noncouncil estate areas, and in those areas where there is a high level of physical disorder. Few vi-

Table 5.4
Number of British Crime Survey Incidents of Crime, 1981–1997 (in thousands)

	1981	1983	1987	1991	1993	1995	1997	% change 1981 to 1997	% change 1995 to 1997
PROPERTY									
Vandalism	2,715	2,795	2,947	2,746	3,402	3,419	2,917	7	-15
Vehicle vandalism	1,558	1,708	1,629	1,678	1,801	1,854	1,616	4	-13
Other vandalism	1,155	1,089	1,317	1,069	1,601	1,565	1,301	13	-17
Burglary	750	914	1,186	1,372	1,776	1,756	1,639	119	-7
Attempts	275	383	533	508	756	758	761	177	0
Attempts and no loss	376	461	668	664	957	977	976	160	0
With entry	473	532	655	864	1,020	998	878	86	-12
With loss	374	454	517	708	818	780	664	77	-15
All vehicle thefts	1,753	2,115	2,916	3,827	4,345	4,317	3,483	99	-19
Theft from vehicle	1,287	1,537	2,098	2,412	2,565	2,525	2,164	68	-14
Theft of vehicles	286	284	387	520	544	500	375	31	-25
Attempts of & from	180	294	430	895	1,236	1,292	943	425	-27
Bicycle theft	216	288	389	567	602	661	549	154	-17
Other household theft	1,518	1,543	1,515	1,848	2,368	2,269	2,067	36	-9
Stealth theft from person	349	443	269	363	516	597	507	45	-15
Other thefts of personal property	1,588	1,732	1,797	1,750	1,919	2,075	1,890	19	-9
VIOLENCE									
Common assault	1,402	1,430	1,496	1,762	2,550	2,820	2,276	62	-19
Robbery & wounding	670	568	744	812	999	1,173	1,022	53	-13
Robbery	163	145	177	184	237	313	307	89	-2
Wounding	507	423	567	628	761	860	714	41	-17
Snatch theft from person	85	63	52	78	86	74	83	-2	12
All BCS violence	2,161	2,061	2,292	2,652	3,634	4,067	3,381	56	-17
Domestic violence	290	286	442	538	1,179	992	835	187	-16
Mugging	252	208	229	261	323	387	390	55	1
Stranger	844	866	840	803	806	947	681	-19	-28
Acquaintance	774	642	780	1,050	1,318	1,729	1,462	89	-15
All comparable crime	6,538	7,187	8,676	9,764	11,725	11,997	10,199	56	-15
All BCS crime	11,045	11,891	13,311	15,129	18,561	19,161	16,437	49	-14

Source: BCS, 1998.

olations were found across regions, but the area with the highest rate of violence appears to be London, the capital itself.

Figure 5.9 shows the risks of violence in regard to selected groups of adults. Here again it may be noted that the predominant targets of violence were young adults in the inner cities or from low-income households, as well as private renters in inner cities. The predominant targets were males rather than females. Repeat victimization—the experience of more than one act of violence—is fairly common.

Table 5.4 concerns the number, in thousands, of incidents of crime be-

Table 5.5
Range of British Crime Survey Estimates of Number of Crimes, (in thousands) 1997

	Best estimate	Lower estimate	Higher estimate
PROPERTY			
Vandalism	2,917	2,609	3,225
Vehicle vandalism	1,616	1,458	1,773
Other vandalism	1,301	1,151	1,451
Burglary	1,639	1,470	1,809
Attempts	761	667	855
Attempts and no loss	976	856	1,096
With entry	878	752	1,005
With loss	664	567	760
All vehicle thefts	3,483	3,294	3,675
Theft from vehicle	2,164	2,010	2,318
Theft of vehicles	375	327	424
Attempts of & from	943	857	1,029
Bicycle theft	549	476	621
Other household theft	2,067	1,845	2,289
Stealth theft from person	507	416	597
Other thefts of personal property	1,890	1,689	2,091
VIOLENCE			
Common assault	2,276	1,950	2,602
Robbery and wounding	1,022	793	1,259
Robbery	307	211	404
Wounding	714	551	878
Snatch theft from the person	83	48	118
All BCS violence	3,381	2,987	3,784
Domestic violence	835	617	1,053
Mugging	390	296	485
Stranger	681	546	816
Acquaintance	1,462	1,199	1,726
All comparable crime	10,199	-	-
All BCS crime	16,437	-	-

Source: BCS, 1998.

tween 1981 and 1997. The type of crime is divided into crimes of property and violence. The figures are self-explanatory, especially in regard to violence, of which there was a reduction between 1995 and 1997 in common assault, robbery, and wounding. There was an increase in snatch theft from 1995 to 1997 but an overall decrease in general crime.

Table 5.5 indicates the range on BCS (1998) estimates of the number (in thousands) of crimes in 1997. Since not all crimes are reported, the table that follows show estimates including the best estimate, lowest estimate, and highest estimate of actual crimes and violence that occurred.

Table 5.6
Number of Violent Incidents against Men and Women, 1997

	Number of incidents, in 000's			% of all incidents	% against men and women, within violence type	
	All	Men	Women	All	Men	Women
All violence	**3,381**	**2,043**	**1,382**	**100**	**60**	**41**
Domestic	835	234	582	25	28	70
Mugging	390	232	164	12	60	42
Stranger	681	568	139	20	83	20
Acquaintance	1,462	992	499	43	68	34

Source: BCS, 1998.

Table 5.6 deals with the number of violent incidents against men and women in 1997. Here again it is shown that men were more likely to become victims of crime, especially of acquaintances and strangers. However, women were more than twice as likely to be the target of domestic violence.

Table 5.7 describes the proportion of BCS (1998) incidents reported to the police between 1981 and 1997. It may be noted that there was a gradual decrease in crime in the interval between 1995 and 1997, with the exception of robbery, stranger violence, and wounding.

Finally, Table 5.8 shows the proportion of incidents recorded by the police from 1981 to 1997, reported in the BCS (1998). Robberies involving wounding appeared to increase, while robberies alone decreased between 1983 and 1997.

FAMILY AND DOMESTIC VIOLENCE

In most cases, the victims of domestic violence are either women or children. However, there has also been an increase in the amount of violence directed toward men by their wives. This may be attributed to changes in the social and cultural attitudes of individuals in Great Britain. Ussher and Dewberry (1995) surveyed 775 British women (aged 25–44 years) who were survivors of childhood sexual abuse. Eighty percent of the women reported interfamilial abuse, and 46 percent reported sexual abuse (involving intercourse). On average, the abuse began when they were 8.5 years old and lasted 5.2 years. Verbal coercion (blaming the child or saying disclosure would split the family) and the presence of threats or violence followed by repeated or prolonged abuse, were the most important predictors of long-term effects. Long-term abuse effects also were predicted by the age of the child at the onset of the abuse. Sexual abuse was more devastating when it commenced at a younger age. In addition, long-term effects were predicted by abuse involving sexual intercourse or con-

Table 5.7
Proportion of British Crime Survey Incidents Reported to the Police, 1981–1997

	1981	1983	1987	1991	1993	1995	1997
PROPERTY							
Vandalism	**22.2**	**22.0**	**23.7**	**27.0**	**26.5**	**29.0**	**26.3**
Vehicle vandalism	10.3	16.1	21.7	24.5	22.5	25.0	23.1
Other vandalism	36.4	31.6	26.2	30.9	31.0	33.7	30.3
Burglary	**66.2**	**67.8**	**62.8**	**73.0**	**67.8**	**66.3**	**64.3**
Attempts	42.0	48.1	37.9	48.1	47.5	45.8	47.6
Attempts and no loss	48.4	50.2	43.7	53.0	51.6	52.1	50.2
With entry	81.2	82.3	81.9	87.9	82.9	82.0	79.0
With loss	84.7	86.6	86.3	92.2	86.8	84.2	85.0
All vehicle thefts	**40.8**	**43.1**	**46.4**	**55.9**	**53.1**	**51.2**	**47.1**
Theft from vehicle	30.0	38.2	39.9	52.6	50.3	50.0	43.1
Theft of vehicle	94.9	96.4	94.9	98.6	96.2	97.5	96.5
Attempts of/from	30.7	18.0	33.9	41.2	40.0	35.7	36.8
Bicycle theft	**63.9**	**68.2**	**62.4**	**69.0**	**72.1**	**62.8**	**63.6**
Other household theft	**25.2**	**21.8**	**23.8**	**29.2**	**31.9**	**30.2**	**32.9**
Stealth thefts from the person	**32.9**	**28.8**	**31.3**	**33.9**	**23.0**	**36.6**	**32.8**
Other thefts of personal property	**22.7**	**29.8**	**31.2**	**38.0**	**30.3**	**29.6**	**33.2**
VIOLENCE							
Common assault	**25.1**	**30.5**	**32.5**	**25.5**	**23.1**	**34.3**	**31.2**
Robbery and wounding	**41.5**	**54.7**	**43.4**	**47.6**	**52.0**	**43.9**	**48.8**
Robbery	46.5	39.0	43.9	47.2	48.3	56.6	56.8
Wounding	40.2	59.6	43.3	47.7	53.2	39.2	45.3
Snatch theft from person	**24.1**	**47.2**	**48.8**	**37.5**	**38.1**	**77.8**	**50.0**
All BCS violence	**29.7**	**37.8**	**35.0**	**32.4**	**31.5**	**37.8**	**36.9**
Domestic violence	19.6	13.3	46.3	23.4	23.0	29.9	26.4
Mugging	37.8	41.6	44.9	47.2	45.0	59.6	55.3
Stranger	35.2	46.8	30.3	37.5	36.9	38.7	45.1
Acquaintance	25.2	35.3	34.0	29.1	29.7	36.7	34.4
All comparable crime	**36.0**	**38.7**	**41.1**	**49.4**	**47.1**	**46.4**	**44.3**
All BCS crime	**31.2**	**34.2**	**36.7**	**43.0**	**40.1**	**40.9**	**39.8**

Source: BCS, 1998.

tact perpetuated by a father or stepfather. Except for the fact that disclosure predicted the report of anger-related emotions, victim disclosure and reactions to disclosure were unrelated to reports of negative effects. This was contrary to the hypothesis that consequences of disclosure, such as parental reactions, have a negative effect on the victim. It was actually found that professional interventions were the main causes of negative sexual abuse effects.

A comparison of domestic violence in Great Britain with that of the United States was carried out and studied between 1974 and 1993 by Dwyer (1995). The hypothesis was that Britain's stronger feminist move-

Table 5.8
Proportion of British Crime Survey Reported Incidents Recorded by the Police, 1981–1997

	1981	1983	1987	1991	1993	1995	1997
PROPERTY							
Vandalism	33	37	44	56	51	46	58
Burglary	70	70	65	62	60	55	49
Attempts and no loss	41	39	37	41	38	33	29
With loss	87	87	84	74	76	72	67
All vehicle thefts	91	75	71	65	60	55	62
Theft from vehicle	88	64	68	61	59	52	59
Theft of vehicle	[100]	[100]	89	95	94	83	87
Attempts of/from	51	54	47	34	27	32	44
Bicycle theft	91	73	55	59	48	44	43
Theft from the person	26	21	37	26	32	23	29
VIOLENCE							
Robbery and wounding	37	37	46	51	42	45	51
Robbery	24	35	38	47	44	33	30
Wounding	41	37	48	52	42	51	63
All comparable crime	62	59	59	60	55	50	54

Source: BCS, 1998.

ment and much lower level of stranger-to-stranger violence may have lessened the public's willingness to engage in domestic violence and may have made the British criminal justice system more progressive in its response. The prevalence of domestic violence in Great Britain was found to be similar to that of the United States. Incidents of domestic violence did not come to public attention in all cases, and, when they did, they were trivialized or even ignored. Further, statistics showed that the prosecution rate in Great Britain was lower than that in the United States, and that there were no victim assistance units in the Crown Prosecution Services. At best, the response of the British criminal justice system was only *as* progressive as that of the United States, rather than more.

Doyle (1996) provided an overview of the current debate and concerns in child protection work, as reflected in current, mainly British, academic and professional journals. Some of the concerns that were expressed during the past twenty years are still part of the contemporary discourse. These include the divide between physical punishment and abuse, child fatalities, assessments, procedures, intervention, and prevention. More recent themes also have emerged: ritual abuse, links between domestic violence and child maltreatment, children as witnesses, and the plight of children with disabilities and young caregivers. Perhaps the most prominent feature of the current literature is the overwhelming preeminence of child sexual abuse. Physical neglect remains on the sidelines, while emotional abuse seems to merit barely a mention.

In *Pedophilia* (Lowenstein, 1998), it is stressed that many accusations of sexual abuse are false and stem from parental alienation. Hence, a three-part psychodiagnostic inventory was developed to identify and differentiate true and false allegations of sexual abuse.

One of the most extreme forms of violence in society is infanticide. This is considered to be a crime of desperation (Lowenstein, 1997b). Marks (1996) surveyed infanticide in Great Britain and found it to be a contributory factor in infant mortality. It was also an extreme indicator of more widespread but unrecognized infant abuse. Using data from epidemiological studies, he describes the features of the parents who killed their infants and characterizes the victims. Marks discusses the extent to which infant homicides were attributed to mental illness and social problems. Evidence suggested that another probable causative factor was a relationship pattern that was predominantly disorganized and violent and that was transmitted from generation to generation. There are needs for further systematic and qualitative research into the precursors and circumstances surrounding the homicide of infants so that appropriate preventative strategies can be developed.

Domestic violence against the elderly was studied by Glendenning (1997). The main thrust of research concerning this topic has come from the United States and Canada and, to a lesser degree, Great Britain. Topics addressed include the definition of *domestic abuse*, typologies of domestic abuse, the prevalence of abuse and neglect, and characteristics of the victims and the perpetrators. Also studied were the indicators of abuse, which aided in establishing a theory, the situational model, the social exchange theory, the symbolic interactionism, the role of the physician, and the legislative developments in America, Canada, and Great Britain. Lowenstein (1981a) found that many families were in turmoil due to the lack of appropriate role-playing by each member of the family and the fact that the controlling aspect of religion have lessened over the decades. This has resulted in a lack of socialization of young persons within families (Lowenstein, 1984a). Domestic violence has been portrayed from time to time through the phenomenon of hostage taking followed by sieges (Lipsedge and Littlewood, 1997). The protagonists in the fifty-eight cases were generally young men, and the majority of the sieges occurred in urban settings. Sieges with a domestic motivation were more likely to result in death or violence to the principle and the hostage than those of criminal motivation, that is, occurring in the course of a crime. In contrast, domestic sieges were to be understood as primarily expressive rather than instrumental, more so than were other Western culture-specific patterns or criminal sieges.

Marital violence in Great Britain was studied by Painter and Farrington (1996). The National Survey of Wives in Great Britain was carried out to estimate the prevalence of the rape of wives inside and outside of marriage. A sample of 1,007 wives, drawn from each of the ten standard regions of

Great Britain, were interviewed. The results showed that 28 percent of the wives had been hit by their husbands, while 13 percent had been forced to have sexual intercourse with their husbands. Wives from the lower class and those who were separated or divorced were particularly likely to have been assaulted. The assaulted wives were also disproportionately more likely to have been raped as well. In addition, 13 percent of the wives had been forced to have sex by someone other than their husband. All together, 22 percent had been raped inside or outside marriage.

Finally, in connection with domestic violence, seasonal patterns were revealed, with consistent increases found between July and August and decreases in February and March of each year. Over a three-year period, there was an estimated 30,740 repeat calls reporting abuse within five weeks of a prior domestic-dispute call. This was in one area of Great Britain, Merseyside (Farrell and Pease, 1994).

VIOLENCE AGAINST WOMEN

As already mentioned, the more vulnerable members of society, including women and children, appear to suffer a considerable amount of undeserved violence. This sometimes occurs in the form of rape (Lowenstein, 1977a, 1977c). Since Great Britain admits immigrants from Africa and elsewhere, female mutilation is another manifestation of violence practiced against some women in Great Britain (Lowenstein, 1981b). In an earlier article (Lowenstein, 1977c), a description is provided as to the causes of infanticide. All this has led to women being warned about the dangers that they may face, especially at night and in certain areas of cities and the country (Stanko, 1996).

THE USE OF ALCOHOL AND DRUGS LEADING TO VIOLENCE

It has long been recognized that the reduction of inhibitions through the use of drugs and alcohol lead to a greater likelihood of violent behavior. Leather and Lawrence (1995) explored how specific social and environmental characteristics of public houses (i.e., bars) influence the perceptions of some violence-prone individuals and lead them to become aggressive. Although a great deal of research literature suggests a regular connection between drinking and violence, as well as social disorder, much doubt remains as to the actual nature and significance of this link (Tomsen, 1997). Some strong insights into this were provided by a dual consideration of the tie between masculine social identity and heavy group drinking and the importance of the issues of male honor in the social interactions that lead to violent behavior. In addition, information from Tomsen's 1997 ethnographic study of assaults in public-drinking venues over a twelve-month period illuminates the subjective experience of participation in acts of disorder and violence. Although masculinist and frequently destructive, this violence was interpreted by many drinkers as providing a liberating and attractive sense of release, group pleasure, and carnival.

Five hundred and five reports of violent incidents in British pubs and bars were studied by using logical pathway modeling to provide information on the processes underlying work-related violence (Beale, Cox, Clarke, Lawrence, and Leather, 1998). This revealed the most common pathways of the misbehavior by customers, intervention by staff (before any physical violent act), physical attack on staff, and injury to staff. The data also highlighted the likelihood of further action after assailants had exited the pubs.

The link between alcohol and crime, especially violent crime, has also been well established (Touhig, 1998). The All-Party Group on Alcohol Misuse developed a cross-party forum for members of Parliament and House of Lords peers. The objective was to link alcohol and crime. Evidence was received from a wide range of organizations, including criminal justice agencies. The group drew up a report that summarized evidence received and put forward a range of recommendations aimed at battling alcohol-related crime, especially crimes of violence.

VIOLENCE TOWARD SOCIAL SERVICE WORKERS

In recent years there has been an increase in violence against those who are meant to protect and monitor society by working with children, the aged, and those with a variety of psychological problems. Leadbetter (1993) reported on the research initiative on violence against social work staff in 1990 within a single social work department. This study used four distinct methods. The first was a review of the initiatives under development within Scottish local authority social work departments gathered through written correspondence. Second, the reactions and perceptions of a sample of assaulted departmental employees were investigated. Third, reports submitted under the departmental violent-incident report procedure over a three-year period from the social work departments were analyzed. Fourth, a diary study with staff in three adolescent residential units was conducted to examine the issue of underreporting and the relationship between official perceptions of violence based on formal reports and the reality of staff experience. The results suggest that the exposure of social work staff to assaults and abuse by service users in the departments studied was increasing.

A review of such violence against social workers in the United States and Great Britain was carried out by Newhill (1995). The ways in which such violence was manifested was studied, as were risk factors for violent behavior and the ways in which incidents affected clinicians, both psychologically and physically. Systematic information to guide constructive action on the issue is lacking and there is a critical need for a large-scale investigation of the incidence, prevalence, and nature of violence toward social workers. Three case vignettes, which illustrated verbal threats, intimidation, and physical assault, were provided. Several recommended strategies and policies that social workers and agencies were capable of instituting to protect frontline workers from violence were considered. Strategies for preventing violence included education and in-service training, safety precautions, and philosophy.

Balloch, Pahl, and McLean (1998) reported the results from the first wave of interviews conducted during a major survey that examined sources of job satisfaction and the incidence of stress and violence in the social service workforce in England. Interviews were conducted with 1,276 individuals selected from four groups of staff: managers, social work staff, home care workers, and residential staff. The results suggested that those who worked in the statutory social services did experience more stress and violence than workers in other parts of the health and welfare services. However, different jobs presented different hazards. In general, home care workers were the most satisfied with their jobs and were also the group least likely to be stressed or to experience violence in the course of their work. By contrast, residential workers, especially those with management responsibilities, were most at risk of both violence and stress. Men were more likely than women to experience violence, while other groups with a higher-than-average risk of stress included the younger members of staff and the managers and social work staff responsible for elderly people.

VIOLENCE WITHIN SCHOOLS AND THE EDUCATIONAL SYSTEM

There have been manifestations of disruptive and violent behavior in schools in Great Britain, but not on the scale of the United States, as is noted in newspaper headlines. The present author was responsible for the first study ever carried out through teachers in Great Britain on the subject of violence and disruptive behavior in British schools (Lowenstein, 1972, 1975). This led eventually to the author writing further on the subject of bullying from the point of views of both the perpetrator (i.e., the bully) and the victim (Lowenstein, 1977b, 1978). A later study by the same author examined the treatment of bullying carried out at his own therapeutic center for disturbed adolescents (Lowenstein, 1991, 1997b).

The author suggested strongly that discipline problems should be identified early and hence prevented. When this is not possible, support should be given by outside agencies to teachers facing this problem. There should be greater support for teachers who are faced with difficult children. This support needs to come in the form of psychological services, among others. Without this support, there will be a need to isolate or remove exceptionally difficult children from regular classrooms or school in order to attend to their special needs and prevent disturbance in other youngsters.

It was also suggested that more curriculum changes are needed to educate special-needs youngsters who may not be academically inclined and could benefit from more vocational-type training. In addition, there should be better teaching ratios and more individualized education. Also proposed was a total-school program that would emphasize the need to discover the traumatic effects of bullying and to deal with these effects with the cooperation of parents, teachers, and society as a whole.

Blyth and Milner (1993) analyzed the existing evidence and identified difficult behavior in the classroom that often led to expulsion from school. This was seen by the authors as the first step in excluding such children from society as a whole. In recent years there has been increasing concerns expressed about the behavior of young people in Great Britain and how best to respond to it. Within schools, this concern focused on the nature and incidence of violent and disruptive behavior displayed by children and the levels of exclusion that resulted. Perceptions that too many youngsters were excluded from school have prompted inquiries by the government, professional teaching associations, and independent researchers. The authors argued that an adequate understanding of exclusion from school could be achieved by studying it within the wider field concerning social control and civic exclusion.

The importance of schools providing a proper education for not merely academic knowledge, but also for civic responsibility and socialization was emphasized by the author in numerous articles (Lowenstein, 1982). The articles, written for teachers and parents, also provide treatments for aggressive behavior in maladjusted children.

Great Britain has had its own share of extreme behavior in children. This includes the case of children inflicting pain and suffering on the elderly and younger children reported in a highly controversial article, "Born or Made to Kill?" (Lowenstein, 1995). It was also deemed necessary by the author (Lowenstein, 1979a) to find alternative ways of dealing with severely disturbed youngsters currently being sentenced and imprisoned.

Violence frequently occurs not merely against other individuals within society, but also toward material objects, as in the case of vandalism and arson. Violence against the self, such as suicide, has been well noted to occur very frequently among young persons.

DEALING WITH VIOLENCE IN SOCIETY

The subject of violence in society is a complex one. As may have been noted, it has been addressed in a segmented manner even more than before. It can be approached from many different directions. For instance, it may be approached by differentiating violence from assertive behavior or from courage. We can give clear examples of violence and counterviolence, including such behavior as bullying, vandalism, verbal aggression, and military aggression: behaviors that all have occurred throughout history. There is certainly a role for the psychologist in helping to reduce conflict and to promote peace. Three areas in which it can work are mental health, understanding the causes of conflict, and conflict reduction. In addition, psychologists may aid in the discovery of the causes of the authoritarian personality (Cairns, 1999).

Violence is often associated with mental illness and, additionally, with alcohol. Wessely (1997) examined the association between schizophrenia and the increased risk and higher rate of committing crimes. The author reviewed findings that society believed mentally ill people were likely to be violent. Data from every first-episode case of schizophrenia in the Camberwell case register (1964–1984) was reviewed. This data was compared with information from nonschizophrenic mental health patients in regard to criminal behavior, including theft, assault and serious violence, criminal damage, alcohol and drug-related crimes, and sexual crimes. Schizophrenic and nonschizophrenic groups were further divided by ethnicity, gender, employment status, and socioeconomic status. The findings showed that men with schizophrenia did not have an increased risk of criminality compared with other mental disorders, but their risk for being convicted for violent offenses was twice that of men with other disorders. Women with schizophrenia had an overall increased rate of convictions compared with women with other mental illnesses.

CURRENT VIEWPOINTS ON VIOLENCE

We can approach violence from a theoretical perspective by delineating the following five explanations for such behavior: (1) ethological, biological, or genetic aspects (including instinct); (2) psychodynamic processes that lead to aggression; (3) drive theory; (4) social learning theories; and (5) social alienation and the development of attitudes that lead to violent behaviors. It can also be approached in the study of developmental aggression, first within the child, adolescent, and adult; then by violence in society by group, by nation, and groups of nations. We can suggest how violence and aggression develop through religious beliefs or nationalism despite the fact that many religions or nations preach tolerance.

To complicate matters further, we can see violence as an evil and we can see counterviolence measures as the only means of controlling aggression, as was the case during many wars, including World War II, when Hitler and the fascists were destroyed by the more powerful acts of counterviolence of Western democracies. Finally, we must view violence and how to remedy it for the benefit of mankind. There are those who believe that evil is inherent in mankind and that its presence is a threat to all individuals and to all societies. There are those who believe that violence should be met only with kindness and compassion, while others who consider themselves to be more realistic believe punishment is the way to deal with violence. Those who feel that aggression is inborn or instinctive blame our genes, while others denigrate the influence of genetics. The idea that frustration leads to aggression is favored by many and has fostered support for the frustration-aggression hypothesis. Others view violence and aggression as learned behaviors when such is reinforced and maintained both by success in learning that behavior and by sheer habit. This is perhaps why violence in the early stages of development in children never should be reinforced or praised but, rather, corrected and replaced.

There is the role of models both in reality and in films and television. The screen frequently portrays individuals with high social status who act aggressively but go unpunished. These images serve as models for people of all ages. Punishment in any form can both decrease and increase aggression, depending on the manner in which it is applied and the context in which it is administered. Violent films on television are said to lead to two reactions. The first reaction is a form of catharsis; watching violence actually leads to the release of aggression. The second possible reaction is that these behaviors are encouraged through imitation and violent demeanor.

There are the "soft" and the "hard" approaches to dealing with violence. Both can lead to good as well as poor results, the poor being the continuation or increase of the violent behavior.

It is almost certain that good, strong models eventually tend to help in reducing aggression, and softness and gentleness frequently encourage further violence rather than its reduction. Therefore, anyone seeking to inculcate nonviolent behavior must be tolerant, caring, and strong. Unfortunately, there is often no other way of controlling or dealing with aggression and violence than with greater force.

Violence on the international scene is well documented frequently with conflicts between ethnic groups. As in the case of Saddam Hussein, the powers that favor peace and harmony between ethnic groups have been required to use violence in order to curtail the initial violence. It is unfortunate that violent conflicts frequently require violent solutions. With more violent and destructive weapons available than ever before, there is always the likelihood that self-annihilation will result unless mankind can come to terms with the dangers of violence toward their neighbors. Where the answer to this unfortunate situation lies is uncertain.

After many years of practical work dealing at the grassroots level with violent individuals at his own therapeutic community and school, the author has come to the conclusion that much of the violence in society, both nationally and internationally, is due to the attitudes and philosophies adopted by individuals. In Northern Ireland, for example, the concern appears to be whether one is judged as Catholic or Protestant and whether one is, therefore, in the in-group or out-group. It is the failure to judge *individuals*, rather than *groups*, that is at fault and is sustained by a leadership that capitalizes on such divisions. The answer in Great Britain could well be to involve the educational system as well as the mass media in dealing with aggression and violence at every level in society and to develop the capacity to talk to, rather than to terrorize, one's adversary. Individuals feel hopeless and helpless in regard to violence that occurs within the society in which they live, but there is hope that one day violence can be controlled through reason, as well as through compassion.

REFERENCES

Balloch, S., Pahl, J., and McLean, J. (1998). Working the social services: Job satisfaction, stress and violence. *British Journal of Social Work*, 26(3), 329–350.

Beale, D., Cox, T., Clarke, D., Lawrence, C., and Leather, P. (1998). Temporal architecture of violent incidents. *Journal of Occupational Health Psychology*, 3(1), 65–82.

Benson, J.F. (1995). The secret war in the dis-United Kingdom: Psychological aspects of the Ulster conflict. *Group Analysis*, 28(1), 47–62.

Blyth, E., and Milner, J. (1993). Exclusion from school: A first step in exclusion from society? *Children and Society*, 7(3), 255–268.

Brewer, D., Lockhart, E., and Rodgers, P. (1998). Informal social control and crime management in Belfast. *British Journal of Sociology*, 49(4), 570–585.

British Crime Survey (BCS), England and Wales. (1998). *Home Office Statistical Bulletin* (Issue 21/98). Comp. C. Mirnees-Black, T. Budd, S. Partridge and P. Mayhew.

Cairns, E. (1999). Diversity and division: Daunting challenge. *The Psychologist*, 12, 296–298.

Doyle, C. (1996). Current issues in child protection: An overview of the debates in contemporary journals. *British Journal of Social Work*, 26(4), 565–576.

Dwyer, D.C. (1995). Response to the victims of domestic violence: Analysis and implications of the British experience. *Crime and Delinquency*, 41(4), 526–540.

Elliot, M. (Ed.). (1997). *Bullying: A practical guide for coping in schools*. Harlow: Longman.

Farrell, G., and Pease, K. (1994). Crime seasonality: Domestic disputes and residential burglary in Merseyside 1988–90. *British Journal of Criminology*, 34(4), 487–498.

Glendenning, F. (1997). What is elder abuse and neglect? In P. Decalmer and F. Glendenning (Eds.), *The mistreatment of elderly people* (pp. 13–41). London: Sage Publications.

Gunter, B. (1998). Ethnicity and involvement in violence on television: Nature and context of on-screen portrayals. *Journal of Black Studies*, 26(6), 683–703.

Gunter, B., and Ward, K. (1997). New reporting of television violence in the British press. *Medienpsychologie: Zeitechrift fuer Individual and Massenkommikation*, 9(4), 253–270.

King, A. (1997). The postmodernity of football hooliganism. *British Journal of Sociology*, *48*(4), 576–593.

Leadbetter, D. (1993). Trends in assaults on social work staff: The experience of one Scottish department. *British Journal of Social Work*, *23*(6), 613–626.

Leather, P., and Lawrence, C. (1995). Perceiving pub violence: Influence of social and environmental factors. *British Journal of Social Psychology*, *34*(4), 395–407.

Lipsedge, M., and Littlewood, R. (1997). Psychopathology and its public sources: From a provisional typology to a dramaturgy of domestic sieges. *Anthropology and Medicine*, *4*(1), 25–43.

Lowenstein, L.F. (1972). *Violence in schools*. London: National Association of Schoolmasters.

Lowenstein, L.F. (1975). *Violence and disruptive behavior in British schools*. London: National Association of Schoolmasters.

Lowenstein, L.F. (1977a). The psychology of rape. *New Law Journal*, *127*, 220–222.

Lowenstein, L.F. (1977b). Who is the bully? *Home and school*, *11*, 3–4.

Lowenstein, L.F. (1977c). Who is the rapist? *Journal of Criminal Law*, *162*, 137–146.

Lowenstein, L.F. (1978). The bullied and non-bullied child, Part 1. *Home and School*, *12*, 3–5.

Lowenstein, L.F. (1979a). Are there and should there be alternatives to present forms of sentencing and imprisonment? *Journal of Criminal Law*, *171*, 165–180.

Lowenstein, L.F. (1979b). Television violence. *Home and School*, *15*, 220–222.

Lowenstein, L.F. (1981a). Families in turmoil. *Links Association*, 33–47.

Lowenstein, L.F. (1981b). Attitudes and attitude differences to female mutilation in the Sudan: Is there a change on the horizon? *Acta Ethographica Academiae Scientiarum Hugaricae*, *29*, 216–223.

Lowenstein, L.F. (1982). *The treatment of aggressive behavior in maladjusted children*. (Bulletin). London: National Council for Educational Standards.

Lowenstein, L.F. (1984a). Developing socialization in the young. *School Psychology International*, *5*(3), 175–180.

Lowenstein, L.F. (1984b). A probing study and intensive treatment of a potential murderess. *The Police Journal*, *LVII*(4), 360–373.

Lowenstein, L.F. (1985). Investigating ethnic prejudices among boys and girls in a therapeutic community for maladjusted children and modifying some prejudices: Can basic prejudices be changed? *School Psychology International*, *6*(4), 239–241.

Lowenstein, L.F. (1991). In M. Elliot (Ed.), *Bullying: A practical guide for coping in schools*. Harlow: Longman.

Lowenstein, L.F. (1995). Born or made to kill? *The Police Journal*, *LXVIII*(2), 159–167.

Lowenstein, L.F. (1997a). Impasse in Ireland: Destroying distrust before disarmament. *International Minds*, *7*(3), 15–16.

Lowenstein, L.F. (1997b). The study, diagnosis and treatment of bullying in a therapeutic community. In M. Elliot (Ed.), *Bullying: A practical guide for coping in schools* (pp. 181–192). Harlow: Longman.

Lowenstein, L.F. (1998). *Pedophilia: The sexual abuse of children, its occurrence, diagnosis and treatment*, Knebworth, UK: Able Publishing.

Marks, N. (1996). Characteristics and causes of infanticide in Britain. *International Review of Psychiatry*, *8*(1), 99–106.

Mezey, G.C., and Kaplan, T. (1997). Psychological responses to interpersonal violence. In D. Black et al. (Eds.), *Psychological trauma: A developmental approach* (pp. 176–198). London: Gaskell Publications.

Newhill, C.E. (1995). Client violence toward social workers: A practice and policy concern for the 1990s. *Social Work*, *40*(5), 631–636.

Painter, K. and Farrington, D.P. (1996). Marital violence in Great Britain and its relationship to marital and non-marital rape. *International Review of Victimology*, *5*(4), 257–276.

Stanko, E.A. (1996). Warning to women: Police advice and women's safety in Britain. In S.L. Miller (Ed)., *Crime control and women: Feminist implications of criminal justice policy* (pp. 52–71). Thousand Oaks, Calif.: Sage Publications.

Tomsen, S. (1997). A top night: Social protest, masculinity and the culture of drinking violence. *British Journal of Criminology*, *37*(1), 90–102.

Touhig, D. (1998). A British All-Party committee view on alcohol and violence. *Alcohol and Alcoholism*, *33*(1), 89–91.

Ussher, J.M., and Dewberry, C. (1995). The nature and long-term effects of childhood sexual abuse: A survey of adult women survivors in Britain. *British Journal of Clinical Psychology*, *34*(2), 177–192.

Wessely, S. (1997). The epidemiology of crime, violence and schizophrenia. *British Journal of Psychiatry*, *170*, 8–11.

Williams, P., and Dickinson, J. (1993). Fear of crime: Read all about it? The relationship between newspaper crime reporting and fear of crime. *British Journal of Criminology*, *33*(1), 33–56.

6

Violence in Indonesia

Sarlito Wirawan Sarwono

Indonesia (located in Southeast Asia) is a country comprised of 220 million people, hailing from hundreds of different ethnic groups, and was once famous for its friendly and peaceful people. The term *friendliness* had been used frequently and repeatedly in slogans and advertisements for many Indonesian restaurants, hotels, and airlines throughout the republic.

However, violence is not unknown in this country. Its history has been marked by territorial wars between ancient kingdoms, anticolonial wars against the Dutch and the Japanese, and a number of internal wars since its independence was declared on August 17, 1945. There are also cases of traditional ethnic and religious conflicts, child abuse, domestic violence, and street fighting, all of which can be found in almost any country in the world. However, the frequency of the violence in Indonesia increased significantly in 1996 (a few years before the momentary and political crisis occurred) and peaked around 1998 and the fall of President Suharto. New types of violence emerged, including guerrilla warfare, lynchings, and, most recently, terrorism. For example, when this chapter was written, on December 24, 2000, fifteen bombs exploded on Christmas Eve (December 25) in nine cities in Indonesia, killing approximately a dozen people and wounding over 100 more. Seventeen more bombs were found by the police before they exploded. Every bomb was located near a church, indicating the attacks were motivated by religion.

Considering the friendly and peaceful image of Indonesia, the question is how such violence could happen here. This chapter will explore and analyze some of the more common forms of violence, such as child abuse, as well as more extreme ones, such as acts of terrorism and lynching mobs.

REVIEW OF LITERATURE

For many Indonesians, America (U.S.) represents the most democratic country. Despite its Western way of life (which allows for sexual freedom, secularism, substance abuse, etc., which most Indonesians do not like), America is admired for the freedom to express oneself in the middle of a heterogeneous and multiethnic population. Most Indonesians also see America as a prosperous and peaceful country, which is, of course, not correct. In reality, Americans have much more experience with violence, but they are no closer to understanding it or knowing how to control it (Toch, 1992).

According to Freud, there are three types of violence, namely, primitive bloodthirstiness, traumatic experience, and deficient ego control. All violence, then, can be divided into two types according to its function: (1) instrumental, if it is deployed for gain, or (2) hostile, if it is intended as revenge or to destroy (Toch, 1992). According to Toch (1992), there are actually ten categories of violence, which can be grouped into two main categories: self-preserving violence and dehumanization. Self-preserving violence is meant to bolster one's ego in the eyes of oneself or others. There are six types of violence included under this subheading:

1. Rep-defending: A person commits violence because of his social position, physical size, or group status
2. Norm-enforcing: Violence is used to enforce norms that the violent person sees as universal
3. Self-image–compensating: Violence is used to defend one's self-image
4. Self-image–compensating: Violence is used to promote one's self-image
5. Self-defending: Violence is used to neutralize those who pose a threat
6. Pressure-removing: Violence occurs during situations one is unable to handle

Dehumanization is observed when people see only their wants and needs as socially relevant. Others are viewed only as means to an end. There are four types of violence included under dehumanization:

7. Bullying
8. Exploiting
9. Self-indulging: Other people are used to satisfy one's needs, with violence as the penalty for noncompliance
10. Catharsis: Violence is used to discharge accumulated internal pressure

Some will be described in the following sections, all ten types of violence occur in Indonesia.

Some authors hypothesize that violence is related to individual person-ality and social attitudes such as authoritarianism, conservatism, dogma-tism, intolerance, and rigidity (Eckhart and Newcombe, 1969), while others believe that there are violent subcultures within any culture, or that violence is contagious (Polansky, Lippitt, and Redl, 1950; Govea and West, 1981). An Indonesian anthropologist, Suparlan (2000), argues that inter-group violence might stem from poor interactions, where each group con-siders the others to be less than human and, therefore, not entitled to humane treatment. For example, in Sambas (West Kalimantan), the Man-durese kill the Dayak and Melayu people because the Mandurese see the Dayak people as *kafir* (sinful non-Moslems) and the Melayu people as lazy, hollow creatures. Similarly, the Dayak people see the Mandurese as dirty wild boars, and the Melayu people see the Mandurese as dirty dogs, and so they respond in kind.

In any case, there is no evidence that proves that friendliness automati-cally means the absence of violence. On the other hand, the reality is that violence has existed throughout history in almost every country and na-tion in the world, Indonesia included.

DOMESTIC AND GENDER VIOLENCE AND CHILD ABUSE

The most well-known case of child abuse in Indonesia is the case of Ar-rie Hanggara, a 10-year-old boy who died after being tortured by his fa-ther in the early 1980s. The boy's mother did not help him, and the neighbors (who had heard Arrie's scream for days) did not intervene be-cause they considered it to be a domestic concern. When interrogated by the police, the father said that he intended only to discipline his son, not an uncommon event. In Toch's (1997) terminology, the father's treatment to his son can be categorized as rep-defending, norm-enforcing, and self-indulging violence. Another famous case of child abuse in Indonesia in the 1980s was the case of R. Gedek, who was then a psychotic and homo-sexual street youth. He was sentenced to life imprisonment after being ar-rested for molesting and killing a number of street boys. In Toch's terminology, Gedek's acts of violence can be categorized as exploiting, self-indulging, and possibly cathartic.

Although these two cases involved people from the lower classes, this does not mean that violence only occurs among the poor. Acts of domestic (husband-wife) and gender violence occur without regard to level of edu-cation or economical condition. Some Indonesian authors argue that the law in Indonesia has failed to protect women from sexual abuse (ranging from verbal to physical abuse) because of the phallo-centric culture that is still dominant in the country. Munti (2000) revealed how a team of judges and attorneys asked humiliating questions to a rape victim when trying to determine the defendant's guilt or innocence. When the judges found the defendant not guilty, the whole story of defending women's rights and dignity ended. Another consequence of a phallo-centric culture is that most traditional women in the culture are not used to expressing their own will, making it difficult to differentiate voluntary intimacy and rape. Some studies show that most of the women who had been battered or sexually abused were those who accepted traditional sex roles (Wetzel and Ross, 1983), and most of the men who battered or abused women also endorsed more traditional gender roles (Truman, Tokar, and Fischer, 1996).

Cases of child abuse such as those of Hanggara and Gedek are certainly underreported in Indonesia. This is partly because familial child abuse is considered to be a private affair, not subject to outside intervention. Also, most cases occur among the lower classes, which generally do not receive social work services. In addition, most caregivers fail to identify the children as being abused when they see the abused mothers (Tomkins, Mohamed, Steinman, et al., 1994). Many physicians also have barriers in the assessment of assault violence (Acierno, Resnick, and Kilpatrick, 1997), especially since medical services are hardly available to most lower-class people. On the other hand, the occurrence or child abuse and intrafamily violence are much lower among the upper and middle classes, not because of the above mentioned factors, but because of more effective family functioning (Kratcoski, 1984; Margolin and Gordis, 2000).

CRIMINAL VIOLENCE

According to Kunarto (1999a), many murders in Indonesia are committed by someone close to them (friends, family, lovers, etc.) of the victims. In September 1998, for example, Katirah (age 24), a servant of the Adnan family, was stabbed to death by Mr. Adnan's cousin, an unemployed, delinquent substance abuser who was trying to rob the Adnans when he was caught in the act by Katirah. Another example is that of Mrs. Sibarani (age 81), who was killed in March 1998 by her own son, who presumably was intending to rob her. The next case, described by Kunarto (1999a), is that of A.L. (age 18), a high school student in Magelang (Central Java) who killed H.S., just to get his motorcycle. However, Kunarto (1999a) does not imply that Indonesia is free from ordinary crimes. In his compilation of crimes in Indonesia, he recorded cases of robbery, shootings, and hijacking. Kunarto (1999a) also wrote about street gangsters around the Tanah Abang Market in Central Jakarta. The gang leader, Hercules (whose body is much smaller and thinner than that of the real Hercules), is not different from other gang leaders in the West. His intelligence, courage, strength, and connections are extraordinary compared to those of his subordinates. However, in addition, as any other gang leader in Indonesia, Hercules is believed by his friends to be invulnerable to weapons and bullets, to have divine power and to be able to give amulets to his followers to make them invulnerable as well.

POLICE BRUTALITY

As any other country, Indonesia is not free from police brutality. In his list, Kunarto (1999a) reported such cases as six police officers in Kudus (Central Java) who were sentenced to four months imprisonment for torturing a suspected burglar as they interrogated him (August 1997); two police officers in Pontianak (West Kalimantan) were interrogated by the military police for torturing the suspected murderer of a local journalist (September 1997); and the police shot a man to death because he tried to run when being arrested as a suspect in a robbery. Kunarto (1999a) also recorded incidents of police brutality in handling riots. For example, ninety female students were treated roughly while being arrested by antiriot police when they were demonstrating in front of United Nations office in Central Jakarta (March 1999); eight workers were wounded after a clash with the police following a peaceful demonstration in Surabaya (February 1999); 200 demonstrating students were chased and beaten by the antiriot police, even though their demonstration had been registered legally by the Metropolitan Police Headquarters (April 1999); and eight workers in the village of Moroejo, Kendal (Central Java) were wounded by bullets as police tried to control their demonstration (April 1999). Other cases might be added to the already long lists.

There are general factors influencing police brutality—such as individual stress levels, personality, racial and social attitudes, situational hazards, and so on (Babovic, 2000; Loo, 1986; Inn, Wheeler, and Sparling, 1977; Inn and Wheeler, 1977)—that are pertinent in any country. However, there are other factors in Indonesia that are not very common in developed Western countries. First, the officers receive poor training, particularly those of the lower ranks, who were recruited directly from high school and received only eleven months of training. Most of them rely on the experience of their superiors. Second, the ratio between the police and the general population is also poor (1:1,200), making the provision of proper police services very difficult. Third, the salary of the officers is quite low. For example, a sergeant makes approximately Rupiah (Rp.) 700,000 per year, which is equivalent to $74 (January 2001 exchange rate). A police colonel takes home around Rp. 1,400,000, or $148. Fourth, the facilities provided by the government are very limited. For example, there are only a handful of helicopters to serve a country that is as big as the mainland United States, no patrol ships, very limited communication facilities, and so on. The two last factors make police officers very vulnerable to corruption and to wanting just to get their jobs done as soon as possible, using any means. Violence has been a common practice in the police force since it was merged into the Indonesian Armed Forces in the early 1960s. It has been only very recently (1999) that the police force was decreed by President Habibie as an independent law enforcer responsible directly to the president and, therefore, eligible for separate and bigger funds from the government to enable it to perform more properly. However, it will be some years (maybe generations) before the police can improve its image fully.

MASS VIOLENCE

In Indonesia, a country with modern mass communication infrastructures, the frequency of mass violence is relatively high. In Jakarta, the capital and the most modern and metropolitan city of Indonesia, there has been chronic inter-*kampung* (urban village) mass fighting going on since the late 1960s. In the last ten or fifteen years there have been more than 200 areas (*basis*) in Jakarta where groups of high school students fight each other (*tawuran* [fighting between those who are similar]). These incidents are due mostly to group dynamics (group identity, solidarity, and prejudices) on the street, rather than personal factors (religion, social-economical status, types of personality, personal hostility, etc.) (Mansur, 2000).

The frequency of mass violence has increased significantly during the last few years of economical and political crisis. Inter-*kampung* fighting and *tawuran* have spread outside Jakarta, in cities and towns as well as in rural areas. In the islands of Ambon and North Maluku, it has developed into religious conflicts, and in Sambas into ethnic violence. In Aceh and Papua it has lead to political violence in the pursuit of independence from Indonesia. In spite of the influence of the media, the main reason for this violence is the political reformation that has given people the feeling of euphoria, which leads into anarchy.

RELIGIOUS VIOLENCE

January 19, 1999, was Idul Fitri day, the end of Moslem fasting month. Moslems around the world, including in Indonesia, celebrated it with joy. But in Ambon it was a beginning of prolonged religious conflict. On that day, a fight between a local Christian Ambonese taxi driver and a migrant Bugese street gangster evolved into a violent clash between the two religious and ethnic groups. This was considered to be very unusual, as individuals of different ethnic and religious backgrounds fought every day, without further complication. On that particular day, however, a rumor was spread that the Central Mosque of Al Fetah had been burnt by the Christians. The violence continued until 1999, taking hundreds of lives and causing thousands of dollars' worth of damage. At first, people thought that the fighting was interethnic (indigenous Ambonese vs. migrant Bugese), but after all the migrants (Bugese and other Moslem ethnics coming from Sulawesi island) left Ambon, the fighting continued between religious groups (Islam vs. Christian). A few months later, the religious conflict had failed with a similar outburst on the island of Halmahera (North Maluku).

The religious populations of the two religions on the two islands (Ambon and Halmahera) are almost the same (50:50), which is not the case on the western island of the country (80:20). The balanced proportion of the two groups made it more possible to develop ingroup feelings and prejudices toward each other, leading to competition between the two groups, particularly political (want for authority or power) and economical (need for control of economic resources). In other words, at some point, religions were used only as means to achieve political and economical objectives (Williams, 1956).

In other areas outside Ambon and Halmahera, religious conflicts have been a chronic problem for a long time. For instance, on December 26, 1996, three people died and many shops, schools, churches, and vehicles were damaged or burnt in a religious riot between Moslems and Christians in the once peaceful town of Tasikmalaya (West Java). Originally the violence was triggered by a nonreligious personal dispute between a police corporal and an *ustadz* (teacher of Islam), because the policeman's son was beaten by the *ustadz*. There was a rumor that the *ustadz* was tortured while being interrogated, which made other *santris* (students of the *ustadz*) angry, leading them to attack the police office. The situation grew out of control when unidentified mobs came from neighboring villages.

Another example happened in the small town of Situbondo on October 10, 1996. An act of religious violence was triggered by the local court's decision to sentence Saleh (a Moslem) to five years imprisonment in his case against the late K.H. As'ad Syamsul Arifin's. Followers were not satisfied with the verdict and attacked the courthouse. Soon the violence shifted to other government offices and to Chinese and Christian properties, because it was rumored that the attorney who charged Saleh was a Christian. Five people died and some churches, Christian schools, and shops were damaged badly (Kunarto, 1999a).

The cases of Ambon, Halmahera, Tasikmalaya, and Situbondo, among others, reveal the fact that religions in Indonesia are conflict prone. According to Colemen (1956), the criteria for conflict-prone religions involve (1) its private-personal characteristics, (2) the high status and power of its leaders, (3) its function in providing alternative sets of values to those of the secular society, (4) the feelings of identity within it, and (5) the intergenerational continuation of its values.

Coleman's criteria fit the Indonesian situation well. In places where most of the criteria apply, religious violence becomes intensive and long lasting. In other places, where only a few of them apply, violence is controlled more easily.

In any case, religious conflicts cannot be solved only by social changes such as modernization, secularization, or economic improvement. The Indonesian experience indicates that religious conflicts occurred in both developed areas of Java and underdeveloped ones outside Java, in multiethnic areas, such as Ambon, and monoethnic areas like Halmahera. Some authors argue that there must be an explicit political action to reduce religious conflict (McAllister and Rose, 1983).

ETHNIC CONFLICT

An area where Coleman's criteria for religious conflict hardly exist is Sambas. In this *kabupaten* (county) there are several different ethnicities and religions. The East Coast primarily consists of the Moslem Melayu people. The West is inhabited by the animist and Christian Dayak people. In the West is also a large population of Chinese-Confusian and Christian people, as well as a number of migrants, mostly Moslem, from the islands of Java, Sulawesi, and Madura.

Since 1933 there have been eleven incidents of violent bloodshed between the Dayak people and the Madurese, involving the deaths of hundreds of people. One of the most violent of these occurred between the Melayu people and the Madurese. In the end, almost all the Madurese in Sambas either were killed or left the country to live as refugees in other areas, creating a lot of new problems in these areas (the refugees occupy public facilities and live in very poor conditions, lacking clean water, jobs, education for the children, health facilities, etc.) (Kunarto, 1999b; Sihbudi, 2000).

The government and the police failed to prevent more serious conflicts, although after each incident they managed to convince the conflicting parties to sign peace agreements. In reality, each agreement was violated by the Madurese, causing another conflict. The Madurese (particularly in Sambas) would do this because of their violent way of life and their tendency to solve problems by force. They also isolate themselves from the rest of the community, creating exclusive living areas, mosques, and religious schools using the Madurese language instead of Bahasa Indonesia. As it mentioned earlier, the Dayak and the Malayu peoples see the Madurese people as wild boars or dogs, and the Madurese perceive the Dayak people as *kafir* and the Melayu people as hollow chips. It is, then, logical that the Dayak and the Melayu peoples do not see the Madurese as human. By seeing each other less than human, violence against each other becomes possible. Some third parties' (e.g., Jakarta politicians, Moslem fundamentalists, Madurese organizations, etc.) efforts to intervene and shift the conflicts into religious ones have not succeeded, as the core issue involves ethnicity, not religion (Suparlan, 2000).

Another example of ethnic violence happened in Java, on January 30, 1997, in the middle of the Moslem fasting month. Some youths had been hitting the drums of a nearby mosque to wake people up for a predawn (3:00 A.M.) breakfast (*sahur*). One elderly Chinese lady was awakened by the noise and yelled at the drummers. This small incident lead to acts of violence against Chinese properties when neighboring villagers became involved at 6:00 A.M. The situation was under control again after additional police personnel were summoned to back up the local police (Kunarto, 1999b).

In Sulawesi, one case of the ethnic violence took place in Makassar (the capital of South Sulawesi) on September 15, 1997, when a 9-year-old girl was stabbed to death in front of her own house by a schizophrenic Chinese youth. The girl and the youth had been neighbors and knew each other very well. The youth later was killed when the police and other neighbors tried to arrest him. The whole city of Makassar exploded in ethnic riots for three days after the incident, involving a lot of damage to Chinese properties (Kunarto, 1999b).

Comparing cases (Sambas and Makassar) confirms the theory that ethnic conflicts can happen anywhere and that they may be based on economic competition, but will be more intense if the main concerns are politics, prestige (Williams, 1956), unfairness, and interethnic independency (Belanger and Pinard, 1991). The Sambas case particularly confirms another theory: the majority living in enclaves (e.g., the Dayak and Melayu) will be more intolerant than those who do not. On the other hand, an oppressed minority living in enclaves (e.g., the Madurese) also will be more intolerant than those who are scattered in small numbers among other ethnic groups (Massey, Hodson, and Sekulic, 1999). In any case, although economic factors are important, violence can be minimized if the ethnic conflict is reduced (Dion, 1997).

POLITICAL VIOLENCE AND TERRORISM

Beside Ambon, Halmahera, and Sambas, there are two other provinces in Indonesia that are known for their violence, namely, Aceh and Papua. The conflicts in those provinces are not horizontal between ethnicities or religions, but vertical between local groups and the central government, as some local organizations demand independence for Indonesia. Most of the victims are members of the police and military personnel on the government's side and members of the rebel's military organizations. But there are also Javanese who came to the provinces years ago as participants of a government-sponsored transmigration program and who were killed, injured, or forced to leave their properties because they were viewed by the locals as representing the central government in Java.

Two reasons of minority politicalization in relation to the conflict with authorities are importation and race consciousness. In the cases of Aceh and Papua, both reasons apply. They are both distinct ethnicities, living in their own provinces and having different cultures and physical character-istics from the people in Java. They also have rich natural resources in their provinces. Among others, Aceh has natural gas, and Papua is rich with copper and gold.

The importation and race consciousness are found also in other ethnici-ties, such as the Melayu people in the province of Riau, which is very rich with natural oil. There are also political movements demanding indepen-dence from Indonesia, but the population of the indigenous people (the Melayu) is not sufficient to build a majority in the providence (only 34%), while the rest of the population, who work in the oil mines and farms or as professionals, is made up of mostly migrants from North Sumatera, West Sumatera, and Java. That is why the independence movement in Riau didn't develop into a big revolution against the central government of Indonesia.

In Aceh and Papua, the violence has increased sharply despite the ef-forts of the Indonesian government under President Habibie (1998–1999) and President Abdurrahman Wahid (1999–) to build dialog with the rebels (Dharma and Eda, 1999). The deadlock is caused most probably by the inability of all parties concerned to accept the not-understanding situ-ation among them and focus only on the efforts to achieve agreement based on a common understanding (Gurevitch, 1989).

However, the violence in the two provinces was rooted in the history several decades ago. The people have been deprived relatively since the central government took most of the income from their natural resources to Jakarta (Gurr, 1970), making it difficult for the provinces to develop, while Jakarta develops very fast using the provinces' money. Following the relative deprivation, the other criteria of collective violent behavior emerged gradually: structural conduciveness, structural strain, general-ized belief, precipitating factors, and mobilization for action (Smelser, 1963). The decentralization and autonomous local government policies of-fered by President Abdurrahman Wahid's government (commencing Jan-uary 1, 2001) hardly can maintain the internal peace because the central government in Jakarta has failed in maintaining the transforming system and behavior (Benson and Kugler, 1998). The central government, due to its own internal problems, has prolonged uncertainty too much to en-hance the opposition's will to liberalize and ask for independence. Al-though the opposition didn't change any violence, violence may be unavoidable with any liberalization movement (Crescenzi, 1999). Most frequently, the violence takes place when the social control from the government is at its weakest point (Smelser, 1963). But it will not stop before the people in the provinces gain back their confidence that the economy will improve so that and their fear of loosing the ground they have gained through great effort will be eliminated (Muller and Weede, 1990).

Another form of political violence in Indonesia is terrorism. On May 13–14, 1998, just a few days before the fall of President Suharto, there were big riots in Jakarta and in Solo (Central Java), killing hundreds of people (mostly Chinese Indonesians) and destroying a lot of properties (looted, burned), mostly located in business areas. It is believed that the riots were planned and executed deliberately by a group of members of a special troop of the army that was commanded by Lieutenant General Prabowo, the son-in-law of President Suharto. Speculation says that Prabowo would show that the price of letting Suharto down could lead to a totally uncontrollable and chaotic situation.

Local terrorism of local politicians took place in the counties of Banyuwangi and Jember (East Java) in 1999, when fifty ulama and *ustadz* (Islamic leaders and teachers) were killed after being raided, by groups of masked man (locally called the *ninja*) in the middle of the nights. The rumors were that those who had been killed were men and women practicing black magic (*santet*) to kill or hurt other people. In fact, the victims were affiliated only to a religious organization called Nahdlatul Ulama (NU), which had been chaired at one time by President Abdurrahman Wahid. When the killings happened, NU was going into politics, and it was speculated that the killings were due to internal conflict within NU itself. Other speculation said that the victims spoke too much against the local governments, which were backed up by the military. Even today, the real motivation behind the serial killing is covered.

At the time this chapter was written, the most recent terrorist attack was a bombing that occurred on Christmas Eve, 2000 (see above). Some suspects were arrested, but four of them died when the workshop where they make the bombs (Bandung, West Java) exploded. Another two suspects were wounded seriously, and the police had to wait until they recovered before interrogating them. During that time, it was speculated that the bombings were intended to trigger conflicts between the Moslems and the Christians, leading to more chaos and providing further reason to replace President Abdurrahman Wahid's government.

Theorists say that terrorism is a rational method of action that employs acts of extraordinary violence against selected physical victims, deliberately creating psychological effects and thereby influencing political behavior and attitudes. The attractiveness of terrorism derives from the combination of economy and facility of means with high psychological and political effectiveness. The risks of the strategy are controllable, and the results are predictable. In other words, terrorism combines low cost with potentially high yield (Hutchinson, 1972).

To counter terrorism, a government has to do two things. First, it must counter the terrorist propaganda and explain and justify the political, judicial, and enforcement measures it adopts (Reinares, 1998). Second, terrorism can be repressed only by strong antiterrorist policies and actions. This strategy has been practiced successfully by Ayatullah Khomeini in controlling left-wing extremists, the Italian government in repressing victims the *Brigado Russo* (Red Brigade), and the British government in reducing victims of Irish Republican Army (IRA) terrorism. On the other hand, it is recorded in history that terrorism in Germany increased in the democratic era after World War II, not in the era of the monarchy and Hitler, and in Spain it grew after the death of Franco (Sabadan and Kunarto, 1999).

In Indonesia it is very obvious that terrorism has been on the rise since the fall of Suharto, as the nation tries to restore its democracy. In this situation, the government position is at its weakest, and the police and other security institutions are loosing their power to enforce the law because they are loosing the trust and support of the people. If not handled properly and quickly, this situation might endanger the existence of the Indonesian nation since it has been forecasted that in the future there will be more terrorism globally, which will be motivated mainly by religion and no longer constrained by limits of violence (Roy, Paz, Simon, and Benjamin, 2000; Simon and Benjamin, 2000).

OTHER VIOLENCE

On January 27, 1997, street vendors of Tanah Abang market violently damaged the local government (*kecamatan*) office after they were forced to leave their illegal places on the street to clear it for the traffic. Nobody was injured in this incident (Kunarto, 1999a). On January 14, 1996, thousands of Iwan Fals (an Indonesian rock singer) fans ran amok after his show in Bandung, leaving damaged property and vehicles. The riot exploded after the show had been delayed an hour and a half, and the fans had been waiting already for four hours, and then the show, frustratingly, went only for one hour. Nobody was injured (Kunarto, 1999a).

Soccer fans also ran amok after some soccer matches. Usually the fans of the loosing party are the ones who spontaneously become violent. Their usual targets are public property and public utilities such as traffic lights, train stations, trains, buses, and so on. Usually the hooligans (locally called *Abonek*) come from their original cities by public transportation (buses, trains) to support their favorite team, and get frustrated when their team loses. Although this kind of violence rarely takes casualties, sometimes it does cause injuries or even the death of some hooligans, usually due to traffic accidents or physical conflict with the police.

Another form of mass violence happening more frequently in Indonesia is that of the lynching mobs. Herman (age 30), who was caught trying to steal a bird from someone's garden in Pabauran (West Java), was lynched to death in April 1999 by the mass who arrested him. Another victim of a lynching mob was Asmat (age 35), a bus driver assistant who was lynched to death by a mob of junior high school students. The students got angry and suddenly attacked Asmat violently because one of them fell from the overcrowded bus and was lightly injured. Another example of this never-ending list of victims of lynching is Handoyo (age 29), who was captured when stealing a motorcycle and burned to death by an angry mob of people who were frustrated with the chronic high criminality in Jakarta (Kunarto, 1999a).

In Toch's theory, the spontaneous violence mentioned above might be categorized as cathartic violence. However, further studies are needed to identify the real motivation and social dynamic behind these cases, particularly because lynching mobs have become more and more frequent in the last years.

CONCLUSIONS

In many instances, Indonesians can be as violent as, or even more violent than, any other people of any nation of the world. The intensity of violence ranges between the ones that took only material loss to the ones that took casualties. The types vary from spontaneous violence to domestic violence to political violence and terrorism.

What is special in Indonesia is that this violence happens in a country that used to enjoy a very good image of its friendly and peaceful people, and that it has been happening more frequently during the last few years. Obviously, it is due partly to the economic and political crisis, but most probably the main problem lies in the weakness of the present government, which, despite its efforts to restore democracy, is not supported politically by all people, political parties, and interest groups.

REFERENCES

Acierno, R., Resnick, H.S., and Kilpatrick, D.G. (1997). Health impact of interpersonal violence: Prevalence rates, case identification, and risk factors for sexual assault, physical assault, and domestic violence in men and women. *Behavioral Medicine*, 23(2), 53–64.

Babovic, B. (2000). Police brutality or police torture. *Policing: An International Journal of Police Strategies & Management*, 3(7), 374–380.

Belanger, S., and Pinard, M. (1991). Ethnic movements and the competition model: Some missing links. *American Sociological Review*, 56(4), 446–457.

Benson, M., and Kugler, J. (1998). Power parity, democracy, and the severity of internal violence. *Journal of Conflict Resolution*, 42(2), 196–209.

Coleman, J.S. (1956). Social cleavage and religious conflict. *Journal of Social Issues*, 12(3), 44–56.

Coley, S.M., and Beckett, J.O. (1988). Black battered women: A review of empirical literature. *Journal of Counseling & Development*, 66(6), 266–270.

Crescenzi, M.J.C. (1999). Violence and uncertainty in transitions. *Journal of Conflict Resolution*, 44(2), 192–212.

Davies, J.C. (1962). Toward a theory of revolution. *American Sociological Review*, 27, 5–19.

Dharma, S.S., and Eda, F.W. (1999). *Aceh menggugatl* [The protesting Aceh]. Jakarta: Pustaka Sinar Harapan.

DiLalla, L.F., and Gottesman, L. (1991). Biological and genetic contributors to violence: Widom's untold tale. *Psychological Bulletin*, 109(1), 125–129.

Dion, D. (1997). Competition and conflict artifactual. *Journal of Conflict Resolution*, 41(5), 638–648.

Eckhardt, W., and Newcombe, A.G. (1969). Militarism, personality and other social attitudes. *Journal of Conflict Resolution*, 13(2), 210–219.

Erez, E. (1986). Intimacy, violence, and the police. *Human Relations*, 39(3), 265–281.

Feather, N.T. (1980). Value systems and social interaction: A field study in newly independent nations. *Journal of Applied Social Psychology*, 10(1), 1–19.

Fieldman, M.D. (2000). *Mass hysteria*. <http://www.imk.bubl.ac.uk/psychology>.

Firestone, J.M. (1974). Continuities in the theory of violence. *Journal of Conflict Resolution*, 18(1), 117–142.

Govea, R.M., and West, G.T. (1981). Riot contagion in Latin America. *Journal of Conflict Resolution*, 25(2), 349–368.

Gurevitch, Z.D. (1989). The power of not understanding the meeting of conflict identities. *Journal of Applied Behavioral Science*, 25(2), 161–173.

Gurr, T.R. (1970). *Why men rebel*. Princeton: Princeton University Press.

Haritos-Fatouros, M. (1988). The official torturer: A learning model for obedience to the authority of violence. *Journal of Applied Social Psychology*, 18(13), 1107–1120.

Hill, F. (1995). *A delusion of Satan: The full story of the Salem witch trials*. New York: De Capo Press.

Howitt, D., and Dembo, R. (1974). A subcultural account of media effects. *Human Relations*, 27(1), 25–41.

Hutchinson, M.C. (1972). The concept of revolutionary terrorism. *Journal of Conflict Resolution*, 16(3), 383–396.

Inn, A., and Wheeler, A.C. (1977). Individual differences, situational constraints, and police shooting incidents. *Journal of Applied Social Psychology*, 7(1), 19–26.

Inn, A., Wheeler, A.C., and Sparling, C.L. (1977). The effects of suspect race and situation hazard on police officer shooting behavior. *Journal of Applied Social Psychology*, 7(1), 27–37.

Kratcoski, P.C. (1984). Perspectives on intrafamily violence. *Human Relations*, 37(9), 443–453.

Krulewitz, J.E., and Payne, E.J. (1978). Attributions about rape: Effects of rapist force, observer sex and sex role attitudes. *Journal of Applied Social Psychology*, 8(4), 291–305.

Kunarto, A. (1999a). *Merenungi kiprah polri delam menangani berbagai kerusuhan* [Reflection of the Indonesian police's action in handling riots]. Jakarta: Cipta Manunggal.

Kunarto, D. (1999b). *Merenungi kiprah polri terhadap kejahatan menonjol: Bunuh, preman, rampok* [Retrospecting the Indonesian police action against salient crimes: Homicide, gangsterism, robbery]. Jakarta: Cipta Manunggal.

Lang, G.E., and Lang, K. (1972). Some pertinent questions on collective violence and the news media. *Journal of Social Issues, 28*(1), 93–110.

Leger, C., and Robert, G. (1983). Race, class, and conflict in a custodial setting: Toward the development of a theory of minority-group politicalization. *Human Relations, 36*(9), 841–863.

Loo, R. (1986). Post shooting stress reactions among police officers. *Journal of Human Stress, 12*(1), 27–31.

Lorenz, K. (1968). *On Aggression,* New York: Harcourt, Brace & World.

Mansur, W.D. (2000). *Participation of high school students in Tawuran.* Unpublished doctoral dissertation, Graduate School of Education, University of Queensland, Brisbane.

Margolin, G., and Gordis, E.B. (2000). The effects of family and community violence on children. *Annual Review Psychology, 51,* 445–479.

Marshall, L.L., and Rose, P. (1988). Family of origin violence and courtship abuse. *Journal of Counseling & Development, 66*(9), 414–418.

Massey, G., Hodson, R., and Sekulic, D. (1999). Ethnic enclaves and intolerance: The case of Yugoslavia. *Social Forces, 78*(2), 669.

McAllister, I., and Rose, R. (1983). Can political conflict be resolved by social change? Northern Ireland as a test case. *Journal of Conflict Resolution, 27*(3), 533–557.

Muller, E.N., and Weede, E. (1990). Cross-national variation in political violence: A rational action approach. *Journal of Conflict Resolution, 34*(4), 624–651.

Munti, R.B. (2000). Kekerasan Seksual: Mitos dan Realities; Kelemahan Aturan dan proses Hukum, serta Strategi Mencapai keadilan. In K. Purwandari and R.S. Hiudayat (Eds.), *Perempuan Indonesia dalam mayyarakat yang sedang berubah* (pp. 377–408). Jakarta: Program Studi Kajian Wanita, Program pasca Sarjana Universitas Indonesia.

Polanski, N., Lippitt, R., and Redl, F. (1950). An investigation of behavioral contagion in groups. *Human Relations, 3,* 319–348.

Reinares, F. (1998). Democratic regimes, internal security policy and the threat of terrorism. *Australian Journal of Politics and History, 44*(21), 351–371.

Roy, O., Paz, B.H.R., Simon, S., and Benjamin, D. (2000). America and the new terrorism. *Survival, 42,* 156–172.

Sabadan, D., and Kunarto, K. (1999). *Kejahatan berdimensi baru* [Crime's new dimension]. Jakarta: Cipta Manunggal.

Sarwono, S.W. (1999). Hasil penelitian kerusuhan di Ambon [Report of study on riots in Ambon]. In Parsudi Suparlan (Ed.), *Kerusuhan Ambon dn rekomendasi: Penanganannya.* Unpublished document, National Police Headquarters, Jakarta.

Sigelman, C.K., Berry, C.J., and Wiles, K.A. (1984). Violence in college student's dating relationships. *Journal of Applied Social Psychology, 14*(6), 530–548.

Sihbudi, R. (2000). *Studi tentang daerah rawan konflik: Kerusuhan Kuupang (NTT), Mataram (NTB) dan Sambas (Kal-Bar)* [Studies on conflict-proof areas: The riot cases in Kuupang (East Nusa Tengara), Mataram (West Nusa Tengara) and Sambas (West Kalimantan)]. Unpublished report, Lembaga Ilmu Pengetahuan Indonesia (LIPI, Indonesian Institute of Science), Jakarta.

Simon, S., and Benjamin, D. (2000). America and the new terriorism. *Survival, 42,* 59–75.

Smelser, N. (1963). *Theory of collective behavior.* New York: Free Press.

Soham, S.G., Ben-David, S., and Rahav, G. (1974). Interaction in violence. *Human Relations, 27*(5), 417–430.

Suparlan, P. (2000). Kerusuhan Sambas [Sambas riot]. *Jumal Polisi Indonesia, 2,* 71–85.

Toch, H. (1992). *Violent men: An Inquiry into the psychology of violence.* Washington, DC: American Psychological Association.

Tompins, A.J., Mohamed, S., Steinman, M., et al. (1994). The plight of children who witness women battering: Psychological knowledge and policy implications. *Law and Psychology Review, 18,* 137–187.

Truman, D.M., Tokar, D.M., and Fischer, A.R. (1996). Dimensions of masculinity: Relations to date rape, supportive attitudes and sexual aggression in dating situations. *Journal of Counseling & Development, 74*(6), 555–562.

Waller, J.A., and Whorton, E.B. (1973). Unintentional shootings: Highway crashes and acts of violence: A behavior paradigm. *Accident Analysis & Prevention, 5*(4), 351–356.

Wetzel, L., and Ross, M.A. (1983). Psychological and social ramifications of battering: Observations leading to a counseling methodology for victims of domestic violence. *Personnel & Guidance Journal, 61*(7), 423–428.

Williams, R.M., Jr. (1956). Religion, value orientation and intergroup conflict. *Journal of Social Issues, 12*(3), 12–20.

Wood, W., Wong, F.Y., and Chachere, J.G. (1991). Effects of media violence on viewers' aggression in unconstrained social interaction. *Psychological Bulletin, 109*(3), 371–383.

Zillman, D., and Weaver, J.B., III. (1999). Effects of prolonged exposure to gratuitous media violence on provoked and unprovoked hostile behavior. *Journal of Applied Social Psychology, 29*(1), 145–165.

7

Northern Ireland Violence: A Possible End

Joseph O'Donoghue

Acts of violence in Northern Ireland have resulted in an estimated 3,700 deaths and approximately 3,500 serious injuries within a thirty-two-year period, from 1969 to 2001 (NISRA, 2001). Northern Ireland is a division of the United Kingdom with a population of 1.7 million. The extent of damage to this society from these acts of violence can be understood contextually if the rate of killing and violent personal injuries over the last three decades were to be applied to U.S. society. A proportional level of violence in the United States would have produced approximately 400 violent deaths and 3,300 violence-related injuries *each week* for the past thirty-two years.

The immediate source of this violence is the coexistence of two groups with diametrically opposed political preferences: continued political existence as a division of the United Kingdom, and political reunification with the Republic of Ireland. Northern Ireland is believed to be 55 percent Protestant and 40 percent Catholic, with 5 percent of the population citing either no religious preference or affiliation with religions other than Protestant or Catholic. Public opinion polls consistently have indicated a clear majority of support for United Kingdom membership among Protestants, while Catholics overwhelmingly support some form of affiliation with the Republic of Ireland (Gallagher, 2001).

Acts of violence in Northern Ireland often appear to be random and senseless acts of brutality involving guns, bombs, or burning gasoline. With few notable exceptions, deaths and injuries occur in small numbers at the hands of quick-strike terrorists. The terrorists are either invisible, as in the case of bomb blasts, or visible only for a few moments, as in acts of direct assault on civilian or police targets.

In reality, however, the vast majority of violent acts are carefully orchestrated events (Alonso, 2001). In most cases, the specific acts of violence can be traced to groups that can be categorized as paramilitary, that is, relatively small units of voluntary militia acting independently of any formal line of control in the larger society. As will be noted later, there are three paramilitary groups claiming an association with the Protestant majority and three paramilitary groups that cite a relationship to the Catholic minority. Three decades of public opinion polls constantly have indicated that the Protestant community and the Catholic community overwhelmingly oppose the pattern of deaths and injuries imposed by paramilitaries on the victims they select (Crotty, 2000).

An understanding of the roots of the current violence in Northern Ireland requires some familiarity with the earlier development of Ireland and its partition into two distinct political units at the beginning of the twentieth century. Ireland emerged during the Middle Ages, basically as a colony of what was to become the British Empire. The sixteenth-century Protestant Reformation in Europe created a division between colony and empire, which had enormous political consequences in the development of both political units over the next four centuries (McAllister, 2000).

Post-Reformation Britain gradually evolved into a global power with a set of Reformation-derived Protestant values that were destined to become very different from the Roman Catholic–oriented values of the Irish colony, which it dominated militarily and economically. This domination was solidified with the defeat of the English King James II and his Catholic allies at the Battle of the Boyne in 1690.

The defeat of the Catholic forces by William of Orange, the first of a new line of British monarchs, became a defining event in both the political and cultural evolutions of Ireland. External observers are sometimes surprised at the fervor and the intensity with which Protestant groups in Northern Ireland annually celebrate a battle that occurred 300 years earlier between two absolute monarchs who fought each other to preserve their royal privileges. From the perspective of a large portion of today's Protestant population, the defeat of Catholic forces three centuries earlier, and the subsequent subordination of Catholics in the economic and political order of Northern Ireland, are the basis of an in-your-face celebration involving marches deliberately directed into Catholic neighborhoods.

World War I, from 1914 to 1918, dramatically altered the power relationship between Ireland as a colony and the United Kingdom as a declining empire after the disastrous losses of life and national assets it sustained in the four years of warfare. In the period immediately preceding World War I there had been a steadily rising popular opposition to Ireland's colonial status, particularly in the southern and western sections, where Catholicism had long been the near-total belief system of the population. Many observers in Ireland and in the United Kingdom believed that there eventually would be an orderly transfer of power. That transition would end Ireland's colonial status and possibly substitute a commonwealth arrangement similar to Canada's relationship to the United Kingdom (Coogan, 1996; Rose, 1999).

In the opening years of the twentieth century, Ireland had experienced a grassroots movement that advocated an immediate and complete end to any form of political relationship with the United Kingdom. These advocates, who became identified as "republicans" because of their support for an independent Republic of Ireland, initially appeared to lack widespread public support throughout Ireland. However, a small group of independence-seeking revolutionaries amazed public opinion in Ireland and England by proclaiming the birth of an independent Ireland in 1914 and by seizing the main post office in Dublin as their rallying point in a war of liberation.

The Irish population did not rally behind the revolutionaries. However, the response of the British government overcame the revolutionaries by cannon fire and executed most of the survivors. This radically altered public opinion within the Catholic population of Ireland. Total independence for Ireland, and the use of military force if necessary to achieve that independence, became acceptable goals. These goals replaced the earlier reliance on an evolutionary approach toward some form of federation or commonwealth relationship with the United Kingdom (Smith and von Tanzen, 2000).

The formation of the Irish Republican Army (IRA) in 1918 provided the beginnings for a military effort by clandestine guerrilla forces to gain independence from a war-devastated United Kingdom. The IRA revolutionaries were organized loosely into small units that harassed and attacked isolated British government positions. A major problem for the IRA was the absence of support for their movement in the predominantly Protestant area of Northern Ireland. That section of Ireland was the only barely industrialized area in an overwhelmingly rural and agriculture-focused country. The predominantly Protestant northeastern section of Ireland was the one area of Ireland with the promise of economic benefit to the United Kingdom if it were to be retained under its control.

The Anglo-Irish Agreement of 1921 ended a three-year guerrilla war characterized by a rising effectiveness of IRA forces. This agreement was a political compromise that achieved the United Kingdom's goal of retaining industrial power while forfeiting the non/unindustrial areas in Ireland (Dunn, 1995). Twenty-six counties in predominantly rural Ireland were granted independence, but six counties of Protestant majority in the marginally industrialized northeast were to remain under British control. This political unit, later to be known as Northern Ireland, was retained as a division of the United Kingdom with its own parliament. The British Parliament held ultimate control at Westminster.

Within a two-year period following the agreement, the British Parliament at Westminster passed legislation that discriminated against the

Catholic minority (33 %) in Northern Ireland in terms of housing, property, and voting rights. Disenfranchisement of Catholics was achieved
through the gerrymandering of voting districts to insure dominance by
Protestant candidates, and through their systematic elimination from consideration as candidates for positions in government bureaus, local administration, courts, and the police system (Reynolds, 2000; Rose, 1999).

Resistance to this structured and systematic denial of basic rights to
Catholics eventually served as the stimulus to a civil rights movement,
which began in Northern Ireland in the 1960s. This movement also, as will
be noted later, closely paralleled a contemporary civil rights movement in
the United States. In the four decades preceding this civil rights movement, a pattern of discrimination against the Catholic minority had been
sanctioned by the British government. This took place because of its benefits as a tool in retaining the loyalty of the Protestant majority. Protestants
rewarded with economic and political privileges in a state with very limited assets could be expected to oppose vigorously any loss of power
through a minority-led reunification with the Republic of Ireland.

As noted earlier, public opinion polls have demonstrated repeatedly
that Northern Ireland's Protestants have a very clear preference for remaining a division within the United Kingdom. The Protestant majority
owns most of the property and controls almost all of the domestic industries in Northern Ireland. The police forces, which are over 90 percent
Protestant and have a long-established pattern of discrimination against
hiring Catholics, can be relied upon to give preferential treatment to
Protestants in all aspects of law enforcement. The court system, solidly
dominated by Protestants in a similar pattern of discrimination against
Catholics, is understood by all involved to perform the role of a preserver
of the status quo (Brewer, Lockhart, and Rodgers, 1998).

The British government had believed that Northern Ireland would
evolve into an industrial asset benefiting the British economy. It annually
provides $8 billion in subsidies to Northern Ireland, with most of these
funds directed to the maintenance of an inefficient bureaucracy (Getso,
2001). An estimated 90 percent of these bureaucratic positions are held by
Protestants, a result of discrimination in hiring. The British government
has indicated its reluctance to continue its subsidies since they are an
enormous drain on the economy of the United Kingdom (Rose, 1999).

The "Troubles" is the comprehensive term frequently used to label the
thirty-two years of civil disorder and paramilitary violence that began in
Northern Ireland in 1969. This was the emergence of a very successful
Protestant backlash to the civil rights movement supported by the
Catholic community. The Northern Ireland civil rights movement of the
1960s bears a strong resemblance to the civil rights movement that took
place in the United States during the same decade. A minority in both
cases had experienced a long period of clearly evidenced discrimination

in voting, housing, and economic advancement. In the case of the United States, the pattern of discrimination had endured for a ninety-five–year period, extending back to the post–Civil War imposition of majority privileges. For Northern Ireland, the period of discrimination had been the forty years following the partition of Ireland into two political groups.

In both the U.S. and the Northern Ireland civil rights movements, a definite stimulus to an initially peaceful stage of lawful demonstrations had been the close proximity of a region where discrimination was not a dominant component of the political system. This encompasses the northern states in the United States and the Republic of Ireland as a border state to Northern Ireland.

The Catholic community supplied the leadership and the membership for the demonstrations for civil rights in Northern Ireland. These demonstrations mounted in intensity and numbers toward the end of the 1960s. The Protestant majority increased its opposition to the movement by opposing any form of meaningful social and economic change. This form of alignment initially gave the impression to the international media that the movement for civil rights, and the conflict that subsequently emerged when the civil rights protesters were denied their requests, was basically a sectarian battle between Catholics and Protestants. The British press described the demonstrations in terms of a resumption of century-old hostilities based on religious differences between Protestants and Catholics (Darby, 1997).

The reality is that religion has never been a defining source of the conflict over civil rights, nor has religion been a source of the violence that followed the rejection of the civil rights movement by a majority of the population of Northern Ireland. With the exception of a relatively small group of Protestant believers headed by the vitriolic Reverend Ian Paisley, the leaders and mainstream members of both religious communities routinely have repudiated every act of paramilitary violence in Northern Ireland. Paisley, who regards the conflict as part of an international conspiracy led by the pope as Antichrist, has the media advantage of a pulpit in a fundamentalist parish in Belfast.

Many analysts have pointed out that an early response to the civil rights reforms sought by Catholics in the late 1960s would have averted the subsequent three decades of violence that followed the majority's rejection of the civil rights movement (Crotty, 2000; Getso, 2001; Mulcahy, 1999). The British government in London, which is the ultimate control point for major issues involving Northern Ireland, basically adopted the position of the British media by regarding emerging hostilities as merely a short-term reappearance of a religion-based enmity from the past.

The failure of any meaningful response by the British government had the effect of entrenching the Protestant authorities in their belief that total resistance to the civil rights movement would quickly end the demonstrations. This pattern of behavior was similar to that of southern governors in the United States when responding to the initial phase of the civil rights movement. Local officials and local police forces were entrusted with the task of eliminating the protests and the protesters with whatever means they chose.

The parallel between the two civil rights movements continues in further ways. In both cases, the prejudice was brought about the by local authorities' errors of judgment. It eventually necessitated the introduction of military forces by a national leadership alarmed at the steady escalation of violence of the local officials against civil rights protesters. The parallel ends, however, when the outcome of military intervention is compared. British authorities eventually responded with a military overkill by suddenly inundating a relatively small region with a total force of over 15,000 regular troops intended to serve as a temporary peacekeeping force. These troops were destined to remain in place for over thirty years. Young recruits in the British army, with no expertise in civil control or police techniques, were given brief assignments in Northern Ireland and then returned to England at the end of their enlistment period.

British troops brought into Ireland in 1969 were opposed immediately by the Protestant majority. Their presence prevented a continuation of the crushing of the civil rights movement through direct violence by a majority with the power of the police and the courts on its side. The Catholic population initially welcomed the troops as a potential source of support in peaceful demonstrations. However, the lack of crowd control training on the part of young soldiers unhappy with their assignment, along with the arrogance of British officers who privately rebelled at being asked to perform police work on behalf of a minority, produced a steady buildup of hostility between soldiers and the Catholics whose civil rights were supposedly being protected by the military (Coogan, 1996).

Within a few months of their arrival, the British forces began to use their weapons and their armored vehicles as control mechanisms directed toward unarmed Catholics demonstrating for civil rights. The international press provided extensive Television coverage of the use of military force against Catholic victims, including the late 1972 unprovoked massacre of fourteen unarmed Catholic civil rights demonstrators in Derry. The emergence of British troops using advanced military hardware to eliminate lawful dissent by Catholics was the triggering device that reignited the IRA and its brand of guerrilla warfare. The original IRA of the early 1920s was regarded widely as the effective military force that had attained limited success in the liberation of part of Ireland from British control through a clandestine military operation against British personnel. The new IRA adopted a similar goal of forcing British troops out of Northern Ireland through carefully staged surprise attacks on military posts and on military personnel (Alonso, 2001).

The reappearance of the IRA as a pro-independence and pro-Catholic paramilitary group was countered by the creation of pro-union (with the United Kingdom) and pro-Protestant paramilitary groups. The pro-Protestant forces immediately encountered a major problem. Pro-Catholic paramilitaries could focus their attacks on the very visible British forces. Pro-Protestant paramilitaries, however, could not as easily identify a target for attack, since IRA members were generally successful in hiding their identities. This problem was solved tragically when Protestant paramilitaries adopted the technique of randomly killing Catholic civilians wherever they were most vulnerable to attack. The main units of the IRA continued to focus their attacks on British troops and domestic security forces. However, splinter groups of the IRA broke ranks with the leadership. They began a campaign of attacking those Protestants believed to be either active in pro-Protestant paramilitary groups or supportive through the provision of funds for their purchase of guns and explosives.

Thus began a pattern of personal executions and bombings by one group of paramilitaries, followed by retaliatory executions and bombings by an opposing paramilitary group. The resulting pattern of constant guerrilla warfare engulfed the relatively small region of Northern Ireland in a pattern of violence repugnant to both the Protestant and Catholic communities (Ruane and Todd, 1996). Slightly more than half of the previously cited 3,700 deaths in three decades were civilians who had no affiliation to any of the paramilitary groups or to the occupying British army. The British forces were acting ostensibly as reinforcements for domestic security purposes. But with the passing of decades of civil warfare, and the absence of any clearly defined success of the military operation, the British army found itself in a position of being opposed by all of the paramilitary groups. It was seen as an occupying force that was basically powerless to achieve any peace-related goal.

British military and local police forces sustained approximately 30 percent of all deaths due to civil strife over three decades. Paramilitaries experienced a relatively low loss of life in this same time period, and this factor inevitably sustained the conflict. The terrorists on both sides did not need to recruit replacements, and their chain of command remained intact year after year. Protestant paramilitaries, who referred to themselves as "loyalists," experienced a fatality rate of only 3 percent of all those killed. They had a total of less than 100 members dying in their terrorists attacks over thirty-two years. Catholic paramilitaries, adopting the name of "republicans," experienced a death rate four times that of their Protestant counterparts, with an estimated death count of almost 400 members (Bloomfield, 1998). This larger casualty rate can be attributed to the primary focus which Catholic paramilitaries placed on frontal attacks on British posts and personnel, as opposed to the basically civilian-focused attacks of the major Protestant paramilitary groups.

Ninety-seven percent of all individuals successfully targeted for death by Protestant paramilitaries were innocent civilians, both Catholic and Protestant. They had been selected deliberately for death as part of a symbolic killing designed to produce an impression of power held by those dedicated to the preservation of the status quo (McGarry and O'Leary, 1995). Only twenty-nine of the over 1,000 individuals whom Protestant paramilitaries claim to have killed had links to the IRA. In contrast, over half of all deaths claimed by the IRA were members of the British armed forces, military auxiliaries, or local police. IRA leaders also claimed responsibility for 119 deaths in Great Britain over three decades. This claim was part of its campaign to pressure British authorities into a negotiated departure of troops from Northern Ireland. Those violently killed by both sides in Ireland were predominantly male (91%), with over half of them being under 30 years old (Bloomfield, 1998).

Paramilitaries on both sides frequently have found it necessary to kill their own members in order to enforce authority within their chain of command (Dunn, 1995). The IRA has admitted to killing 149 of its own members when it suspected them of continuing disloyalty to the cause. Protestant paramilitaries claim that the number of their membership killed on order by their top command (because of doubts about their willingness to continue as terrorists) exceeds the total number of deaths they have experienced due to IRA actions against them.

A basic constant in IRA strategy, as stated repeatedly by its leadership, has been the necessity to drive all British military out of Northern Ireland. This has been seen as the key step in the eventual reunification of Ireland into a single nation. The assumption behind this strategy is that Northern Ireland would choose union with the Republic of Ireland without the presence of British troops. This would take place either through an IRA–led revolution, or a democratically selected process. The main obstacle impeding the attainment of this IRA goal has been a very strong conviction held by Protestants. The Protestants believe that the retention of the British army, however demeaning it might be to local self-esteem, is an absolute necessity in preserving the status quo with the Protestant domination of the economy, the courts, and the policing system. An immediate result of this conviction, expressed through political pressure on British legislators, has been the retention of almost 15,000 British military. These military exist in what is basically a war zone for these troops, and it is a constant military expense with no obvious benefit to the United Kingdom relative to the size of the expenditure.

From the beginning of the hostility the IRA leadership has asserted that a constant loss of British military lives, along with an unending stream of British expenditures in a war perceived as endless, eventually would bring enough public pressure within Britain to force the government into negotiating with the IRA (O'Donoghue and O'Donoghue, 1981). That process of negotiation between the IRA and the British government, fiercely resisted by the British authorities for twenty-four years of the conflict in Northern Ireland, finally began in 1993. A major goal of British negotiators was the attainment of some sort of face-saving withdrawal from a situation that had become too expensive to maintain. British officials sought, but did not attain, a concession whereby the IRA would agree to surrender its arsenal of weapons and explosives in return for a staged withdrawal of British forces (Reynolds, 2000). IRA leaders succeeded in obtaining an agreement that its political wing, then the splinter Sinn Fein Party, would be guaranteed direct participation in all future negotiations over the status of Northern Ireland. The agreement allowed them also to become eligible for direct political participation in a future Northern Ireland assembly. This assembly would be selected by a proportional voting system, which would ensure minority involvement.

As would be expected, this agreement between the British government and the IRA, which was regarded as a terrorist organization, aroused a storm of opposition from the Protestant community in Northern Ireland. A majority cf the Ulster Unionist Party (UUP), the political party that represents most of the Protestants in Northern Ireland, announced a refusal to participate in the agreement. This took place despite the fact that its party leaders had played a role in the negotiating process. Their opposition was based on the fear that this type of agreement inevitably would lead to a loss of Protestant political dominance and ultimately to some form of political union with the Republic of Ireland. This is due to the fact that the agreement would introduce effective political power to militant Catholics, including IRA leaders who could be expected to become legislators in their role as Sinn Fein–elected representatives.

The agreement probably would have collapsed if the IRA had not unilaterally declared a cease-fire in August, 1994. They stated their goal as attaining peace through the mechanism of their political party, rather than through continued violence. The IRA's announcement of the cease-fire, on its own and without a promise of a cease-fire by the opposing Protestant paramilitaries, was a bold move designed to gain support for the first serious and credible breakthrough in peace negotiations over the duration of the conflict. As anticipated by the IRA, public opinion placed extensive pressure on Protestant paramilitaries to agree to their own cease-fire (Wilson, 2000). The two major Protestant paramilitary groups, the Ulster Defense Association (UDA) and the Ulster Volunteer Force (UVF), agreed to a cease-fire two months after the IRA cease-fire had become effective.

This 1994 cease-fire did not bring an end to all forms of paramilitary violence. Each of the two major competing paramilitary groups had break away splinter groups that refused to honor the cease-fire proclaimed by the two largest paramilitary groups. The IRA, however, succeeded in advancing its image as peacemaker by controlling the acts of violence by its mainline members. The IRA simultaneously condemned the sporadic violence now continued by its splinter groups, known as the "Real IRA" and the "Continuing IRA" (Getso, 2001). The UNP was not as successful in its efforts to maintain a cease-fire from Protestant paramilitaries, which further enhanced the new and surprising role of the IRA as peacemaker. That image received an additional boost in the years following the cease-fire. At this time, the IRA demonstrated that it could control the violence of its mainstream members and provide assistance in securing a diminishment of violence by now declining splinter groups.

The resulting four years of diminished levels of violence from 1994 to 1998 produced a growing impetus toward a peaceful resolution of conflict in Northern Ireland. The number of major participants in the peace process steadily increased. For almost seventy-five years British authorities had shunned completely any form of contact with the IRA. They now accepted a situation whereby IRA leaders, acting as Sinn Fein political leaders, would become a constant part of negotiations toward peace.

In 1994 the U.S. government reversed a three-decade long policy of avoiding involvement in the civil strife of Northern Ireland on the basis that the conflict and the violence should be regarded as purely internal affairs to be managed by the United Kingdom (O'Donoghue, 2002). During his Belfast visit in 1994, President Bill Clinton announced his intention to provide personal assistance. This included help from U.S. government officials in advancing the peace process. Over the next four years Clinton became a constant and highly effective force in a successful effort to drive down unemployment rates by securing new investments by U.S. firms in Northern Ireland. Clinton also succeeded in bringing to the White House the key leaders in the conflict. Sometimes the leaders came as individual guests, but, more frequently, they came as group guests, joining otherwise hostile opponents in discussion at a neutral site and under the pressure of a president skilled in negotiations (Wilson, 2000).

A steadily increasing level of involvement by the leadership of the Republic of Ireland also provided a major impetus in the peace process. The Republic has been the recipient of $28 billion in development subsidies from the European Union in the twenty-five years following its decision to join that trade group. In the second half of the 1990s it was becoming very clear that those development funds, together with a well-educated and highly skilled labor force serving as a magnet in attracting multinational firms to Ireland, were transforming a formerly agriculture-focused nation into an economic powerhouse with the fastest growing economy in Europe.

Protestant participants in the peace process initially were alarmed by the expanding role played by the Republic in the negotiations as a consequence of its newly achieved trading power with business in Northern Ireland. These Protestants began to believe that closer business links with the Republic could produce an economic benefit far exceeding the ineffective subsidies that Northern Ireland received each year from the United Kingdom. For the first time in almost a century, Protestant leaders began to think the unthinkable: Some form of political union with the Republic of Ireland could quickly produce greater economic benefits than continued political ties with the United Kingdom.

Peace prospects were further enhanced in Northern Ireland as a result of the startling advance in the region's economic condition in the second half of the 1990s (Birnie and Hitchens, 1999). At the beginning of the 1990s, the unemployment rate in Northern Ireland had been almost 20 percent. A system of regionwide discrimination against Catholic workers was responsible for a Catholic unemployment rate twice that of the Protestant rate. The 1994 agreement produced a peace dividend when multinational firms, contacted and encouraged by President Clinton, turned to Northern Ireland as a relatively cheap source of English-speaking employees. These employees could work at new production facilities while enjoying a location within the protected European market. A consequence of this type of new employment opportunity was an unprecedented decline in Northern Ireland's unemployment rate to less than 7 percent in the late 1990s. With the equivalent of full employment now enjoyed by the Protestant majority, employers in Northern Ireland were forced to turn to Catholic workers previously excluded from any form of continuing employment due to discrimination in hiring.

Prior to the economic boom of the late 1990s, most Protestant politicians in Northern Ireland perceived their major role as confirming a very limited amount of economic advantages to their own Protestant constituency. Continued political affiliation with the United Kingdom was considered to be indispensable to the maintenance of their current level of economic well-being and the continuation of their political careers. The Republic of Ireland was regarded as a backward, church-dominated, hopelessly rural nation with no prospects for economic advancement. It was also viewed as offering no real advantage to Northern Ireland in terms of economic and political contacts.

The meteoric rise of the Republic of Ireland's economy suddenly altered that perception. Beginning in 1995, the Republic achieved seven consecutive years of economic growth at the fastest rate in Europe for each of those seven years. By the beginning of the new century, its citizens enjoyed an annual gross national product (GNP) per individual that exceeded the average. This continued throughout the membership of the very prosperous European Union. Also, the Republic's business leaders had become key players in all areas of European industry and commerce. This was in stark contrast to their counterparts in Northern Ireland, who, despite their own impressive gains, remained marginal players within a United Kingdom from which they were geographically separated and from which they received only very limited flexibility in overall economic decision making.

In this context, the reunification of Northern Ireland with the Republic of Ireland, in some sort of phased sharing of political and economic decision making, became an attractive goal for many business leaders in Northern Ireland. In theory, of course, the United Kingdom might someday enjoy the remarkable economic boom occurring in the Republic of Ireland. But even if this unlikely event were to occur, Northern Ireland's business leaders knew that, as a division of the United Kingdom, they, and their political leaders, would be forced to share any economic boom with other divisions of the United Kingdom. That type of sharing, over which they would have little or no control in terms of their limited population, would be a perpetual drag on their own advancement, both bureaucratically and politically.

Unification with the Republic, achieved through a democratic process rather than the violence espoused by the IRA, has been a goal of the major Catholic political party in Northern Ireland. This party is the Social Democratic and Labor Party (SDLP) and has been led by John Hume in recent decades (Coogan, 1996). IRA leaders traditionally had refrained from providing substantial support for that party because they believed that its leadership was hopelessly idealistic regarding the possibility of political reunification. For most of the three decades of the Troubles, the IRA turned to the Sinn Fein Party as the instrument for its announcements regarding IRA actions, strategy, and policy.

The agreement arranged between the IRA and the British government in 1994 dramatically altered the role of Sinn Fein in Northern Ireland's political system. That party was once ridiculed as a mere mouthpiece for a paramilitary group. It achieved a new level of legitimacy when British authorities accepted it and its basic IRA leadership as permanent participants in all future peace negotiations. The promise of Sinn Fein's participation at the top level of negotiations began a slow but steady increase in its membership and in its performance at local-level elections. Political acceptance also meant that IRA terrorists with a long record of violence could look forward to playing the role of respected politicians. They would be competing for seats in a future legislative body with real power over the political and economic future of Northern Ireland. Sein Fein's political membership has subsequently advanced to include 10 percent of all voters in Northern Ireland.

By U.S. standards, a party with only 10 percent of the popular vote is relegated to third-party status with extremely limited opportunity for political impact. Northern Ireland, however, will not in the immediate future have a two-party political system in the U.S. pattern. Sinn Fein, in a divided, multiparty legislature, could become a significant political player under leaders characterized by both the Protestant and the Catholic communities as former, and possibly future, terrorists.

Sinn Fein's advance in political power has come at the expense of the older and long-established Catholic political party, namely Hume's SDLP. Gerry Adams was once an active IRA leader and is still believed to participate in IRA deliberations. Adams now overshadows Hume as a political spokesman, by reason of his post as leader of Sinn Fein. Both Catholic political parties, the older SDLP of Hume and the Sinn Fein of Adams, represent 40 percent of the voters of Northern Ireland. Two Protestant parties, the mainline UUP, led by David Trimble, and the smaller Democratic Unionist Party, can count on a combined Protestant vote representing 60 percent of the population.

American readers somewhat confused by the multiplicity of players and issues in violence-prone Northern Ireland may find help from an analogy to the American political process. Imagine for a moment that the Democratic Party is an out-of-power, exclusively Catholic-supported political party with a small military force at its immediate disposal. Similarly, the Republican Party is an in-power, exclusively Protestant party that also has a military force at its disposal. In this imaginary scenario, the streets of America's major cities are patrolled and secured by Mexican military forces who live in barracks that they have built at key control points. The Mexican military and the Mexican government want to withdraw from this onerous task because it is very expensive. Also, their soldiers constantly are being ridiculed and fired upon, often with deadly results, by the very small but very efficient military forces maintained by the Democratic and the Republican Parties.

Again, in this scenario, the Canadians on the northern border have a solution to the problem of three decades of constant civil strife within the United States. For the last seven consecutive years the Canadian economy has advanced at the fastest growth rate of any industrialized nation in the world. The result is a standard of living in Canada that is far superior to that being experienced in the United States. The United States, as a division of the Mexican Empire, will forever be limited in its growth rate because the Mexican Empire has many domestic problems. It gives precedence to these problems over all United States–related issues. The Canadians, however, have a labor shortage that will soon impede the future economic growth that they crave. The Canadians make a proposal to the people of the United States: Join us and forget the Mexicans, since they really want to forget you.

There is a problem. The heads of the Democratic Party and the Republican Party have told their respective paramilitary groups to cease their violent actions. In the meantime the party leaders and their party members discuss the Canadian offer. The top leaders of the paramilitary groups agree that there should be a cessation of violence. Unfortunately, however, they have no control over splinter groups within their respective paramilitary groups.

The Catholic-based Democratic Party is very enthusiastic over the possibility of union with Canada. But the Protestant-based Republican Party fears a loss of political power and a future subordinate status in all-Catholic Canada. In response, the Democrats and the Canadians promise equality to Protestants in an advanced economy infrastructure where everyone benefits on the basis of a skilled labor force. They also promise that a long line of multinational firms wants to expand their industrial bases within this very successful common market, as Canada is their most promising global location.

The above scenario may appear to be very unrealistic. But, for over thirty years, Northern Ireland appears to be an unreal land where senseless violence and meaningless injuries, deliberately directed at innocent people, have become routine. In one sense, the Good Friday Agreement of April 10, 1998, achieved by marathon negotiations brokered by a U.S. chairman (Senator George Mitchell) acting on behalf of President Clinton, represents an attempt to return to reality (Smith, 1999). That 1998 agreement directly confronted the issues of structured economic inequality and flagrant political discrimination. For over thirty years these issues have been the driving forces behind the continued acts of violence within Northern Ireland (Cairns and Darby, 1998).

The 1998 Good Friday Agreement called for the establishment of an alternative set of political institutions that would reverse the sophisticated gerrymandering of voting districts and the voting procedures discriminating against Catholics. Also established were commissions designed to bring reform to four areas believed to be the keys to ending violence: (1) a sharing of political power at all levels of government, (2) a scheduled withdrawal of all British troops from Northern Ireland, (3) an end to Protestant bias in all future hiring of police officers by mandating a future 50-50 split in hiring between Protestant and Catholic candidates, and (4) disarmament by all paramilitary forces.

The agreement subsequently was ratified by 71 percent of the total electorate in Northern Ireland. However, polls indicate this approval rate occurred on the basis of an almost-total approval by Catholic voters, with only a bare majority of Protestants voting approval. A major provision of the agreement was the establishment of a Northern Ireland Assembly with a proportional voting system. This system assured the inclusion of the Catholic minority in both the legislature and the executive positions designed to serve as the administrative offices for implementation of legislation.

A total of 108 representatives were elected to the first assembly in 1998.

The agreement mandated that the position of prime minister be held by the political party with the largest number of elected representatives. The position of deputy prime minister was to be determined by the largest minority party. This agreement resulted in a Protestant leader, Trimble of the UUP, being selected as first prime minister. The Catholic Seamus Mallon was elected to serve as deputy prime minister. The voting process brought to the assembly the leadership of the IRA, now acting as elected representatives of the Sinn Fein Party. IRA leaders technically acting as Sinn Fein representatives gained two out of the ten executive positions of the assembly.

As indicated earlier, the Good Friday Agreement assigned to the assembly the responsibility for resolving the fundamental problems dividing the Protestant and Catholic communities. They would do this on the basis of reports prepared by assembly-directed commissions. The most difficult of these fundamental problems is the disarmament of paramilitaries. IRA forces have opened their extensive weapon depots to inspection by selected international representatives. However, in keeping with a long-established practice, the IRA has discussed at length the elimination of its weapons without taking any specific or verifiable action in this regard (MacGinty, 2000). This IRA policy has infuriated Protestant leaders. These leaders maintain that the Protestant community has negotiated away many of its long-standing privileges, while Catholic paramilitaries have stonewalled on the key issue of ending violence by eliminating the tools of violence.

The IRA appears to believe that time is on its side in the gradual evolution of Northern Ireland into a democratic society with a full range of legal protections for the Catholic minority. Its Sinn Fein Party, however, does not yet possess the voting power to determine the direction of reform legislature, even when allied with the Catholic-supported SDLP. In this context, the documented possession of guns and explosives provides, in the IRA estimation, a type of political leverage not otherwise available.

The Protestant community and a majority of the Catholic community perceive IRA resistance to disarmament as the major threat to continuation of the peace process. IRA leaders respond by citing their seven-year record of maintaining a cease-fire, broken only by the sporadic violence of its splinter paramilitaries. The IRA denounces their actions and affirms its non-involvement in what widely is perceived as a steady decline in violence. This decline has been linked to splinter Catholic paramilitary groups.

Protestant leaders have expressed privately concern that eventual control of Northern Ireland is destined to pass to Catholic voters within a twenty-year period, due to demographic trends. For the last three decades Catholic fertility rates have been almost 50 percent higher than Protestant rates. A continuation of this trend could conceivably result in parity between the Protestant and the Catholic population in the 2020s. In turn, it also could lead to a Catholic majority in the voting population in the following decade.

Catholic politicians have suggested that their political power inevitably will grow as a result of a birth rate advantage. It is thought that with this growth will come an end to the old order of political and social subordination of Catholics. However, fundamental changes in Northern Ireland may not require a twenty-year wait for a parity in voting blocks that definitively would end the discrimination against Catholics. This is the discrimination that triggered the beginning of the Troubles and three decades of internal violence. It is extremely unlikely that the next generation of Catholic workers, now about to enter a job market with a projected long-term labor shortage, will ever encounter the 25-percent unemployment rate experienced year after year by the previous generation. Nor is it likely that this new generation of young Catholic workers will be impeded methodically in economic and social advancement. This is a region that clearly is destined to become a legally integrated part of a multinationally supported European Union.

At the beginning of the Troubles, both Northern Ireland and the Republic of Ireland were backwater regions with stagnant economies. They were forced to endure an incredibly high migration of their young to foreign lands in search of employment (O'Donoghue, 2002). During the years of the Troubles, however, the Republic of Ireland has advanced economically. This advancement occurred to the point that the Republic now desperately sends search parties to other industrialized nations to find people to help relieve the severe shortage of workers in Irish firms and Ireland-based multinationals. Fortunately, economic development in Northern Ireland finally is beginning to follow the pattern of the Republic of Ireland. This is a pattern in which a legally enforced equality of opportunity in hiring and promotions, plus a police system that is subject to open review in law enforcement, has provided a growth base for what is now respectively termed the "Celtic Tiger" of global business. It can be anticipated that thirty-two years of paramilitary violence and retaliatory violence will end if a pattern of justice-based economic development can occur in Northern Ireland.

REFERENCES

Alonso, R. (2001). The modernization in Irish Republican thinking toward the utility of violence. *Studies in Conflict and Terrorism, 24*, 131–144.

Birnie, J.E., and Hitchens, D.M. (1999). *The Northern Ireland economy: Problems, prospects, and policies.* Ashgate, England: Aldershot.

Bloomfield, K. (1998). *We will remember them: Report of the Northern Ireland violence commission.* Belfast, Northern Ireland: Northern Ireland Assembly.

Brewer, J.D., Lockhart, B., and Rodgers, P. (1998). Informal social control and crime management in Belfast. *British Journal of Sociology, 49,* 570–585.

Cairns, E., and Darby, J. (1998). The conflict in Northern Ireland: Causes, consequences, and controls. *American Psychologist, 53,* 754–760.

Coogan, T. (1996). *The troubles: Ireland's ordeal 1966–1996.* London, England: Arrow.

Crafts, N.E. (1999). Some comparative aspects of Ireland's economic transformation. *Irish Banking Review, 22,* 39–51.

Crotty, W. (2000). The changing faces of Ireland, *Policy Studies Journal, 28,* 779–784.

Darby, J. (1997). *Scorpions in a bottle: Conflicting cultures in Northern Ireland.* London, England: Minority Rights Group.

Dunn, S. (1995). *Facets of the conflict in Northern Ireland.* London, England: Macmillan.

Gallagher, T. (2001). The Northern Ireland conflict: Prospects and possibilities. In D. Chirot and M.E.P. Seligman (Eds.), *Ethnopolitical warfare: Causes, consequences, and possible solutions* (Vol. 17, pp. 205–214). Washington, DC: American Psychological Association.

Getso, R. (2001). More violence expected in Northern Ireland. *Peace Review, 13,* 97–101.

MacGinty, R. (2000). Hate crimes in deeply divided societies: The case of Northern Ireland. *New Political Science, 22,* 49–61.

McAllister, R.J. (2000). Religious identity and the future of Northern Ireland. *Policy Studies Journal, 28,* 843–858.

McGarry, J., and O'Leary, B. (1995). *Explaining Northern Ireland.* Oxford, England: Blackwell.

Mulcahy, A. (1999). Visions of normality: Peace and the reconstruction of policy in Northern Ireland. *Social & Legal Studies, 8,* 277–295.

Northern Ireland Statistics and Research Agency (NISRA). (2001). *Research & Statistical Bulletin, 3,* 1–14.

O'Donoghue, J. (2002). Emigration from Ireland to the United States. In L.L. Adler and U.P. Gielen, (Eds.), *Migration: Immigration & emigration in international perspective,* Westport, CT: Greenwood.

O'Donoghue, M., and O'Donoghue, J. (1981). Conflict in Northern Ireland. *International Journal of Group Tensions, 11,* 119–125.

Reynolds, A. (2000). A constitutional pied piper: The Northern Ireland Good Friday agreement. *Political Science Quarterly, 114,* 613–638.

Rose, P. (1999). *How the troubles came to Ireland.* New York: St. Martin's Press.

Ruane, J., and Todd, J. (1996). *The dynamics of conflict in Northern Ireland: Power, conflict, and emancipation.* Cambridge, England: Cambridge University Press.

Smith, M.L.R. (1999). The intellectual internment of a conflict: The forgotten war in Northern Ireland. *International Affairs, 75,* 77–98.

Smith, M.L.R., and von Tanzen, M. (2000). War by other means: The problem of political control in Irish Republican strategy. *Armed Forces & Society, 27,* 79–105.

Wilson, A.J. (2000). The Ulster Unionist Party and the U.S. role in the Northern Ireland peace process, 1994–2000. *Policy Studies Journal, 28,* 858–875.

8

Violence in Israel

Noach A. Milgram

NEWS ITEMS ON A TYPICAL DAY (APRIL 29, 2001) IN *MAARIV*, A MAJOR DAILY NEWSPAPER

"An Israeli was shot to death on a major highway traffic intersection in the center of Israel by Palestinian terrorists." (pp. 1–2)

"Five teen-age boys were injured, one seriously, when an artillery shell fired from Gaza by the PLO [Palestine Liberation Organization] hit their clubhouse." (p. 3)

"Rifle shots penetrated the home of a family in the community of Zur Yigal, less than a mile from the home of the former prime minister of Israel, Ehud Barak." (p. 9)

"A 19-year-old Palestinian boarded a cab and repeatedly stabbed a passenger; another passenger prevented the assassin from killing the victim." (p. 9)

"A 5½-year-old boy was beaten with a broomstick by his mother's live-in male friend because the boy couldn't solve problems in arithmetic. The mother, separated from the father, first stated that her friend was responsible, and later changed her testimony and said to the police that the husband's family was responsible." (p. 16)

"A frustrated suitor stabbed the present male friend of a divorced woman and held the woman captive against her will for five hours. (p. 16)

"A 20-year-old man pretended to be a policeman and persuaded preteen girls (eight or more victims) to accompany him to a secluded place, where he performed indecent acts upon them and videotaped his actions." (p. 18)

"A 33-year-old man offered a ride to a young foreign worker, tied her with chains, raped and beat her, and drove away; he was apprehended several hours later. (p. 18)

"A 17-year-old tourist was raped by two young security guards from a nearby Arab village; the guards were apprehended." (p. 20)

"Tomorrow [April 30] sentence will be passed on a former senior minister in the Israeli government who was convicted of performing indecent acts with force on two women working under his authority." (p. 20)

"A 60-year-old man was found stabbed to death in an Arab village in the Galillee. (p. 20)

"A 45-year-old man was stabbed to death in a drunken brawl." (p. 20)

"A young Beduin soldier shot to death his mother and sister after learning that his father was forced to leave the home because the mother and sister complained to the authorities about the father's physical violence. He afterward offered a second explanation for his actions. His mother and sister argued with him and did not automatically submit to his will on a family matter. (p. 23)

> *Violence* in Hebrew (*alimut*) has the same root as the terms *silence* or *non-communication*. The significance of the common root of *violence* and *silence*, according to Martin Buber (cited in Shoham et al., 1995, ii), is that when communication ceases, verbal and physical violence occur. By implication, the antidote to violence is reasoned communication.

INTRODUCTION

Definition of Violence

Violence has many definitions and is often considered synonymous with *aggression*. *Violence* is defined as actions, generally antisocial or criminal in nature, that are designed to harm people and/or the property of individuals, groups, or society as a whole (Cohen, 1984; Horowitz, 2000). Violence has been investigated from many perspectives, including the motives of the perpetrators, the settings in which violent acts occur, the characteristics of the victims, and the consequences of these acts. Violence stems from a state of hyperarousal, uncontrollable impulse, or severe psychiatric disorder or from planned actions in the service of revenge or other goals of the perpetrator (Hunt, 1993). It takes place everywhere, in the home, the schools, the workplace, and public settings. Particular groups of people are more likely to be the victims of violence than others. For example, the very young, the very elderly, the poor, and girls and women are often the victims of violence.

The following types of violence in Israeli society will be examined in this chapter:

a. Physical violence (e.g., pushing, hitting, stabbing, shooting) and verbal violence (e.g., insults, curses, threats): The incidence of physical violence in Israeli society is affected by the prevalence of verbal violence. Specifically, verbal violence may trigger physical violence in all social groups. Verbal acts of violence (such as cursing at and insulting others) are highly prevalent in Israeli society, and are far more common than are acts of physical violence.

b. Criminal and non-criminal acts of violence: Criminal acts of violence (such as armed robbery and mugging, physical and/or sexual assault, and murder) fall within the jurisdiction of the law enforcement agencies and courts. In contrast, teenage violence in schools or in the community is often treated as a non-criminal offense.

c. Criminal violence committed by family members or friends: Some men batter their wives and children, or may even murder them. Others assault and rape the women they are dating.

d. The violence of war and terrorist attack: Prior to 2001, discussions of violence in Western countries did not include these topics. However, Israel has been at war or under terrorist attack by Arab nations for over a century. At the time this was written (May 2001), all Israeli citizens are potential targets of terrorist attack by the Palestinian Authority. Terrorist attacks are the indiscriminate efforts to maim or kill non-combatants—men, women, and children—as well as soldiers. During the past year there have been thousands of rocks and bullets, dozens of explosive devices, fire bombs, and mortar shells directed against individuals and communities. Bombs were exploded in public places from a distance and by terrorist suicide bombers. Over seventy people have been killed and several thousands injured. The constant threat of war and terrorist attack in Israel justifies adding this topic to the more conventional ones of violence in the home, school, and community.

THE INTERDISCIPLINARY NATURE OF VIOLENCE IN SOCIETY

The study of various forms of violence, their incidence in Israeli society, and the features in Israeli society that effect the occurance or intensity of these kinds of violence is necessarily interdisciplinary in nature. Theories, research studies, and statistical surveys drawn from many relevant fields (e.g., biology, criminology, economics, history, political science, psychology, and sociology) all contribute to our understanding of the past and present and enhance our ability to intervene and to affect the future. Length restrictions dictate that the author be highly selective in the scope and depth of the material presented. Apologies are offered in advance to readers who find that material they consider highly relevant to the topic is treated scantily or omitted entirely.

Shoham and his associates (Shoham, Rahav, and Addad, 1987; Shoham et al., 1995) have formulated a comprehensive, eclectic theory of crime and violence. They attribute the predisposition toward violence to genetic, biological, psychological, and sociological factors. The specific triggers that elicit violent behavior are identified as features of the specific situation preceding the outburst of violence that correspond to features of the pre-disposition. This theory provides a structure for identifying and investi-gating the psychological, sociological, and situational factors that account for the particular forms of violence that are prevalent in Israeli society. Some of these factors—immigration, war, and schismatic trends—are dis-cussed below.

Immigration, Crime, and Violence

Social and behavioral scientists have been studying the relationship be-tween immigration and stress reactions in Israel for over half a century (Kolker & Ahmed, 1980; Milgram, 1998). An authoritative Israeli text on criminology (Shoham, Rahav, and Addad, 1987) cites the phenomenon of immigration as contributing to crime in general and to violence in partic-ular. The major waves of immigration to Israel occurred in 1933–1939 (300,000: Germany and western Europe), 1948–1951 (700,000: Western Eu-rope, eastern Europe, northern Africa, and Asia Minor), 1955–1963 (400,000: northern Africa and Asia Minor), and 1967–1972 (100,000: North and South America, and Western Europe) and after 1970 (800,000: Russia and eastern Europe). No other country has ever permitted, much less en-couraged, so many people, relative to the size of the native population, to immigrate to their shores. Many social scientists (Eisenstadt, 1954, 1967; Shoham, Rahav, and Addad, 1987) documented the culture clashes that occurred in each of these periods both between newcomers and estab-lished residents and between different groups of immigrants. They pointed to the higher incidence of crime and violence among the new-comers, particularly in those who came to Israel from Arab-speaking countries in North Africa and the Middle East after 1948. These immi-grants, the Sephardi Jews, lost economic and social status in the process and had to contend with the condescending, if not contemptuous, atti-tudes of the civil bureaucracy who hailed from a European background (the Ashkenazi Jews).

Marx (1976), an eminent sociologist, concluded from his studies of lower-class Sephardi immigrants that violence serves a number of goals. Violence may be coercive (to gain resources immigrants believe they lack). It may be a form of appeal (for public attention and subsequent change of policy). It may be private and directed against other family members, pos-sibly out of the frustrations felt by many immigrants when their efforts to gain needed resources are unsuccessful. One consequence of their frustra-tions and their economically marginal status might be to resort to violence and to crime when their demands are not met. However, when new immi-grants live in their own cohesive small communities, they create and maintain social and cultural norms that restrain violence and crime (Shoham, Rahav, and Addad, 1987). When they move to the large cities, however, and are surrounded by people from other backgrounds, they become susceptible to social and psychological forces—subsumed under the headings of urbanization, secularization, and modernization—that undermine their stability.

War and Violence

Solomon (1993), a major researcher of combat stress reactions in Israeli soldiers, documents the enduring toll of war on the well-being of soldiers, their families, and the society as a whole. Nearly 20,000 soldiers died in combat in the past half century, and ten times that number were injured physically. The number who returned to civilian life with permanent psychiatric injury is unknown. Other researchers (e.g., Ayalon and Soskis, 1986) have documented the suffering of children and adults who survived terrorist hostage situations and terrorist attacks. It is reasonable to assume that war and terrorist attacks on civilians victimizes people no less than rapists, muggers, or brutal husbands do. It is also reasonable to ask whether the cumulative effect of war-related stress has lowered the threshold for violent reactions in Israeli society. Fishman (1983) examined the postwar homicide rate with respect to two wars, the 1967 war (Six Day War) and the 1973 war (Yom Kippur War). He found no rise in violence after the first, but a tenfold increase in crimes against persons in general and a more modest, but impressive, rise (58%) in homicide and attempted homicide following the second. He attributed this rise to the possible devaluation of life following the high loss of life (3,000 soldiers) in the Yom Kippur War and to the greater opportunity during that war to acquire skill in using lethal weapons. He acknowledged, however, that the many variables that change following a war of this magnitude did not permit a simple explanation. He also commented on the overall low annual rate of homicide during the 1960s and 1970s in Israel, a country that fought four wars following World War II, in comparison to the higher rates of homicide in other Western countries that were not at war during this period.

Violence and Schismatic Trends in Israeli Society

The modern State of Israel was founded in the midst of controversy, not only with the Arab world in general, but also within Israel itself. There were bitter arguments between the socialist, universalist Left that established the state and the capitalist, nationalist Right that came to power some thirty years later. There were also bitter controversies within the Left itself, between communist and socialist groups. These ideological divisions and the acrimony to which they gave rise are still evident in Israeli life today. The following overlapping divisions in Israeli society also have given rise to verbal as well as physical violence:

a. the division between Sephardi and Ashkenazi Jews discussed above

b. the division between those who wish to emphasize Jewish religious and cultural traditions and those who wish to emancipate themselves and the Jewish state from these traditions

c. the division between the newcomers who have fewer economic resources and less political power (the classic have nots) and the established residents who wish to retain their economic, political, and cultural dominance (the haves)

Many attribute the widespread verbal violence in Israeli society and the physical violence that it elicits to the divisive controversies that are generated by these groups. Avigdor Kahalani (Gur, 1999, 8–12), a former minister of police, decried the hatred expressed by some leaders of various political parties in parliament against their rivals. He argued that the verbal violence that characterizes many deliberations in the Israeli Parliament serves as a model for verbal violence in society as a whole, and that attitudes and behaviors practiced by leaders are adopted by citizens at large and are generalized to other areas of contention in Israeli life.

Popular theories designed to account for the prevalence of violence in Israeli society also have been discussed:

Scarcity

The economic austerity that characterized Israeli society until the 1970s lead to the expectation that there were not enough of any one particular item or commodity for everybody, so it was imperative to jump the line in order to get one's share. However, if an individual decided to push ahead, those who waited their turns could retaliate, and violent altercations could result.

Rejection of the Diaspora or Jewish Exile

Before the founding of the state, Jews who lived in countries other than Palestine (as Israel was known before 1948) were seen as a frightened, insecure minority that cultivated good manners so as not to offend the majority, their non-Jewish neighbors. Hence, the Israeli, or new Zionist, Jew eschewed good manners that were adopted out of fear or insecurity. As a result, these individuals became the very opposite: confident, self-centered iconoclasts, aggressive, noble savages, or Sabras. The term *sabra* literally translates to "the cactus fruit prickly on the outside and sweet on the inside," and is also the term used for all native-born Israelis.

Never a Chump

A common motto in Israeli life is, "I will never let anybody make a chump out of me." Therefore, one must never be a sucker or permit others to take advantage of him or her. This kind of moral imperative and associated hypervigilance also may contribute to violence.

Closing of the Frontier

Israelis used to regard their country as a Wild West, or frontier society, with a "you can do whatever you want as long as I can do whatever I want" philosophy. This rule may have been feasible when there were fewer people and more open space. However, this sense of freedom has been threatened by a tenfold population increase and by legislation restricting the actions of the individual. These restrictions have increased over the past half century and have elicited violent reactions by those who are no longer able to exercise the three freedoms that are hallowed in Israeli society: to do *what* you want, *when* you want, and *where* you want.

SURVEY OF THE VARIOUS CATEGORIES OF VIOLENCE IN ISRAEL

Violent Crime in Israel: An Overall Comparative Analysis

Surveys of crime in Western countries indicate that the incidence of crime in Israel is approximately equal to that of other industrialized countries (Rahav, 1998). Of the twelve countries compared in 1994, Israel was eleventh in regard to murder and robbery, but had a higher rate of other crime incidences (e.g., burglary and auto theft). Consequently, Israel had a moderate overall crime rate. Rahav compared the 1994 Israeli data with data collected in the 1960s and 1970s, and concluded that robbery, burglary, and murder increased sharply between 1960 and 1980 and remained at a plateau or slightly declined thereafter. However, these statistics do not provide a precise picture for two reasons. First, the number of violent incidents became inflated when rock throwing by Palestinians was included in the tabulation of acts of violence in 1980. This form of violence was included because some Israelis had been severely injured or killed when struck by rocks. Second, the actual number of persons injured or killed was underestimated because the number of incidents, rather than number of victims, were tabulated, and terrorist incidents often involve more than one victim.

Another source of data on the incidence of violence is a survey of victimization in which a representative sample of citizens were asked whether they were the victims of violence during the previous year (Rahav, 1998). This survey revealed that about one in four Israeli households in 1990 were being victimized, mostly due to burglary and auto theft, with slightly less than one in twenty-five households reporting an offense against persons. Recent data suggests that crime in general plateaued in

Israel in 1999, following annual increases of 15 to 25 percent in the pre-ceding three years. A plateau also was noted in violent crime (murder, rape, sexual molestation, and mugging) in that year.

Rahav (in press) provided the latest comprehensive study (in manu-script form) on criminal violence in Israel. In this report, he highlighted the methodological problems that plague epidemiological research in this field in Israel. He was able to confirm, cautiously, many of the overall con-clusions of his earlier research and those of other investigators cited else-where in this chapter. Specifically, he found that men are more likely to be both the perpetrators and the victims of criminal violence than are women. Criminal violence, as contrasted with milder forms of violence, is rare in earlier adolescence, becomes more prominent in middle adoles-cence, and reaches a peak in the midtwenties. The incidence of homicide and intended homicide has risen in recent years among Israeli males and even more so among Arab males. Arab males perpetrated twice as many violent acts against persons per 100,000 people (6) than Israeli males (3) in 1994.

Violence in the Family

The police opened 22,540 cases of violence between couples in 1999, which corresponds to 375 offenses per every 100,000 persons. The break-down was physical assault (54%), threats (26%), and other transgressions (20%). Only 18% of these cases involved incarceration for any period of time (Israel Police, 2000). Many more violent acts occur within the family but are never reported. Others, such as the murder of one's spouse or com-panion or of one's children, cannot be concealed. These crimes are rare (15–27 cases in a given year of the last decade). Their heinous nature, how-ever, has aroused public indignation to the point that a government agency (Authority for the Advancement of the Status of Women) was es-tablished in the mid-1990s within the Office of the Prime Minister to deal with all forms of violence against women. A national women's organi-zation (Na'amat), which maintains day-care settings throughout Israel for preschool children, also has established a Department for the Prevention of Violence in the Family. This department distributes to women pam-phlets identifying the warning signs of potential violence on the part of their husbands and provides counseling to women who find themselves victimized in this manner (Lev-Ari, 2000).

Police statistics, based entirely on cases that come to the officers' atten-tion, are only the tip of the iceberg. According to an authoritative report by Haj-Yahia (cited in Gur, 1999, 15–19), there are as many as 200,000 women in Israeli society who are subjected to repeated beatings by their husbands or male friends. At the same time, there are only eleven to twelve shelters in Israel for battered women, and each shelter can hold a maximum of only 200–250 women and children. While there is a public awareness of the problem and considerable discussion about formulating laws and constructing programs to combat this social ill, little is actually done. The agencies that are formally responsible for executing these programs claim they do not have the funds to do what needs to be done.

Contrary to expectation, the new groups of immigrants, Russians and Ethiopians, do not contribute any more than the rest of the population does to the number of spousal homicides or other categories of violence. The Russian immigrants tend to be better educated than native-born Israelis. Their cultural background and their large numbers (over 800,000) have allowed them to establish their own newspapers, radio commentary, political parties, and businesses. However, there were no self-support criteria for entry into Israel, and no efforts to identify criminal elements among the Russian immigrants were made. As a consequence, new phenomena appeared in Israeli life (Rattner, 1997):highly organized gang activity and systematic extortion; importation of prostitutes and the establishment of vice rings; alcoholics and drug addicts, alone and without family, who wander the streets and constitute most of the "homeless" population in the cities. In spite of this, the extent of these phenomena is small. The Ethiopian immigrants, on the other hand, reside in self-segregated areas and tend to live traditional lives. As a group they are not disproportionately represented as either perpetrators or victims of violence.

Murder by family members of Israeli Arabs is not necessarily higher than expected, given their proportion of the population (approximately 20%). When it occurs, it serves a purpose unique to Arabs. The code of "family honor" dictates that a woman who is not chaste before marriage or gives the appearance of being promiscuous before or during marriage must be killed by a male member of her own family (Rahav, 2001a; Schneider, 1971). These incidents are few in number, not necessarily because the code has lost its hold, but because Arab women tend to live very traditional lives, wear modest garb and headdress, and are aware of the dire consequences of sexual transgressions.

Gender and Physical Violence

According to Haj-Yahia (cited in Gur, 1999, 15–19), there are a number of reasons for physical violence against women. Israel is a modern, Western-oriented country, but in some respects it has remained a very traditional, patriarchal society. Israeli society condones and even fosters the dominance of men over women. It socializes young men to assume masculine superiority and dominance, and hereby justifies the violent coercive response of men to women when their dominance is challenged. It fosters an exaggerated form of masculine ("macho") behavior and, in so doing, encourages contempt for more considerate, gentle, cooperative "feminine" behavior. Men in patriarchal societies may come to regard their wives or female friends not as persons in their own right, but as their personal property. Under highly stressful circumstances (e.g., unrequited love, suspicion of unfaithfulness, willful defiance of the man's wishes), violence, even deadly violence, may erupt against the woman and even against children (hers or theirs). Wife beating is even more common among Israeli Arabs. According to Haj-Yahia (2000), 54 percent of Arab women reported at least one instance of physical abuse in the previous twelve months.

Why do women remain with men who dominate and beat them? According to major researchers in the field (Ayalon, 1983; Eisikovits and Buchbinder, 1999; Hah-Yahia, 1998; Ron, 1983):

1. Israeli society assumes that a woman is not a woman unless she is married and raising children, and the responsibility for child-rearing is placed wholly on them.

2. Israeli society does not provide every women with alternatives to maternal child-care. Women are not guaranteed comparable pay and advancement in the workplace. The reality of gender-related economic inequality dooms some women to remain subservient to men because they cannot adequately support themselves and their children.

3. The society strongly dictates that a child must have two parents, not just a mother. This statement implies that battered women should remain with their husbands out of concern for their children's welfare.

4. Battered women are frequently subject to rejection, insult, or indifference when they turn to the authorities for help, and they are admonished that they must be lenient and understanding when their husbands behave violently since they work so hard (Shoham, 2000).

Efforts are being made to deal with violent husbands. Hartaf and Bar-On (2000) describe their experiences with a project for violent family men. As a part of the project, men reside in a residential setting for three months, but go to work each morning. Three hundred ninety men were referred from 1996 to 1999. Of these, seventy-nine were accepted, while the others were rejected because of mental illness, drug abuse, or outright refusal to enter the home. Of those accepted into the program, sixty-five were treated. The others dropped out due to incompatibility or family pressure. Immediate follow-up after discharge from the program was positive, with changed behavior at home and at work. Although half these men divorced, all maintained better behavior with their children. The apparent success of the program is encouraging, but this success was achieved only with mentally healthy, drug-free men, willing to enter the program. Moreover, this program served sixty-five men, an infinitesimal fraction of the estimated 200,000 who are responsible for spouse abuse and child abuse.

Violence against minors is also disheartening. Nearly 7,000 cases were opened in 1999 for crimes against minors: physical assault (54%), sexual molestation (37%), and repeated physical victimization (9%). Of these reported cases, more than a quarter took place within the family. The offenders were almost invariably male, and the victims more frequently tended to be female (Israel Police, 2000).

Violence against elderly people by strangers or by family members is becoming more common in Western society (Council of Europe, 1992). The family, once the bastion of protection of the elderly from victimization and infirmity, now has become a major source of violence for them. The breakdown of both the extended family (3 or more generations in close physical and psychological contact) and the nuclear family (parents and their adult offspring) has made elderly people more vulnerable in Israeli society than they ever had been before. However, while there are occasional reports of negligence or cruelty to elderly family members in Israel, the phenomenon is not as widespread because the extended family is more intact here than in many Western countries.

Sexual Harassment and Rape

Sexual harassment has been a very common phenomenon in the past, both in the army and in the workplace. Compulsory military service for women created countless situations in which young women just out of high school worked in close quarters, away from home, under the command of older men. Many of the liaisons that developed were not consensual, but if the woman complained, she tended to suffer more punitive consequences than did the male officer. This situation has changed drastically in the last few years. A candidate for prime minister, the highest elected office in Israel, recently was convicted of forcible indecent acts during his illustrious military career. The next area of sexual harassment was in the workplace, where male employers are becoming far more their circumspect about their sexual advances to women employees.

The rape of and forcible indecent acts against Jewish girls and women are not uncommon in Israel, with 690 and 584 cases reported in 1998 and 1999, respectively. These figures reflect a 16 percent decline from the previous year, but it is too early to draw any conclusions about the trend (Israel Police, 2000). Survey data of Western countries indicated that many more women are raped than are accounted for by police statistics. A recent survey of U.S. naval recruits (N = 3776) reported that 45 percent of the female recruits had been victims of attempted rape (9%) or completed rape (35%) before entering the navy; of the male recruits, 15 percent admitted to attempting rape or to actual rape. Only a small proportion of these cases was ever reported to the authorities. However one attempts to attribute these frightening statistics to the idiosyncrasies of the sample (i.e., naval recruits), one cannot avoid the conclusion that rape is endemic in the United States, that more cases are not reported than are reported, and that male offenders are at high risk for repeating their behavior. One can assume safely that many Israeli girls and women choose not to report rape to the authorities. The same applies to men, who are even more reluctant to report sexual attacks upon their person.

There have been periods in which serial rapists initiated a reign of terror among women in the greater metropolitan area of Tel Aviv. In most instances these men were apprehended and convicted. Nevertheless, rape continues unabated for the same reasons that it is prevalent in the United States.

1. Victims are reluctant to report what has happened because of the social stigma associated with rape. They often receive unsympathetic treatment from the authorities when they report what has happened. They are not comfortable testifying because defense attorneys will attempt to establish that the victims were not raped at all, but engaged in concentual sex, even rough sex in which they suffered injury.

2. The rate of convictions is a function of the physical injuries suffered by the victim. A woman who does not resist out of fear for her life has no injuries to show. Thus, conviction is less likely, and if convicted, the rapist will receive a light sentence.

3. Many male judges administer relatively light sentences, especially for nongenital rape, because of their inability to comprehend the anguish and suffering experienced by female victims. They may not know of the long-term consequences of rape for many victims.

4. The judges may empathize more with the male defendant who expresses remorse than for the depressed or bitter victim who demands that the rapist be punished for the suffering inflicted upon her.

There are many adverse consequences associated with post-traumatic stress reactions to rape, such as the reexperience of the rape, avoidance of stimuli associated with the event, hyperarousal, and disturbance in social or sexual functioning. Additional consequences include loss of self-confidence, fear that it will happen again, and belief that the victim herself will be unable to protect herself (Herman, 1992; Swink and Leveille, 1986). Rape prior to their military service accounted for half of the cases of post-traumatic stress disorder (PTSD) reported by women on active duty in the navy and Marine Corps and explains in part why PTSD is found five times more frequently in the women than in the men in the sample (Hourani and Yuan, 1999). However, while victims of sexual assault are at high risk for developing somatic and/or psychological problems that require professional treatment, many, if not most, rape victims do not receive treatment (Merrill et al., 1998).

Teenage Violence in the Schools and the Community

Minors are not only the victims of violence, but also the perpetrators of violence. One way to examine teenage violence is in the context of the overall violence reported in Israel. When the proportion of teenage violence (9% of homicides, 6% of serious assaults, and 12% of robberies) was compared with the corresponding percentages of other Western countries in 1995, Israel ranked relatively high on homicides and low on assaults and robberies (Rahav, 2001a). However, most of the violence that is committed by children and youth does not come to the attention of the authorities at all.

A major setting in which unreported teen violence occurs is in the schools. Violence in the high schools of the United States has been rising steadily in the last forty years and has now become an endemic problem high up on the national agenda (Heller, 1996). A recent report estimated that 5,000 teenagers are the victims of violent crime in the United States (Raia, 1999). Israel is subject to the same sociological and psychological trends that affect the United States and is usually a decade or two behind it. It is not surprising, therefore, that violence in the schools has drawn the attention of Israeli educational authorities in the last twenty years.

Major surveys of teenage violence in Israel are summarized briefly here. The first major study of this phenomenon (Horowitz and Amir, 1981) identified the following main forms of violence in the schools: theft, break-in, and vandalism. Violence may take the form of student-student, teacher-student, student-teacher, and parent-student attacks. They described several kinds of environmental factors that contribute to violence:

1. *Characteristics of the community in which the schools are situated.* Neighborhoods characterized by poverty, crime, and social alienation are afflicted with more teen violence than are other neighborhoods.

2. *Administrative faults in the schools.* The schools themselves bear some responsibility for the high incidence of violence within their walls. Schools that are characterized by violence lack trained personnel and regulatory structures to monitor student behavior in and out of the classroom. They place too many poor learners in a single classroom and do not have staff and the curricula to work with weak students. They have a high tolerance for disruptive behavior and react only after violence escalates to the point that it can no longer be ignored. Then, and only then, are the authorities informed.

3. *Professional faults.* The schools do not have adequate intervention programs for disruptive students or student dropouts. They expel disruptive students as a last resort and do not provide an alternative educational setting for them. This was confirmed in a recent newspaper report (*Maariv*, April 29, 2001, p. 21) that 30,000 youngsters, 10 percent of the age 15–17 group, are not in school and are not employed gainfully. Lack of funds from the Ministry of Education has handicapped efforts by the local communities to reach out to these young people and provide them with educational and/or occupa-

tional challenges. The situation is even worse among Israeli Arab youngsters. Administrators are reluctant, and even afraid, to acknowledge serious
problems and to take steps to solve them because they will be held account-
able for future violence and for failing to prevent it.

A second survey (Horowitz, Frenkel, and Yinon, 1990) of this phenomenon was of 4,500 Israeli youth and also showed that alarming proportions
of children and adolescents were perpetrators, victims, or both, and that
these proportions increased during the 1970s and early 1980s. Most of the
cases that were reported to the authorities were closed with no provision
of therapeutic or judicial intervention. These investigators found that violence was not confined to any one place. It was found on sports fields and
in pubs, discos, and the neighborhoods. Some settings are more likely to
trigger violence than others. For example, violent acts were more likely to
occur at hotly contested sports events and places where intoxicated young
people gather. Violence was more common in students enrolled in trade
schools than in those enrolled in college-oriented high school programs.
Alienated youth and youth from economically impoverished backgrounds
had less respect for the law than their peers, and were, therefore, more
likely to break it. Nevertheless, violent acts, including murder, also were
perpetrated by middle-class youth from so-called good homes. This survey documented that groups at risk for engaging in violent acts hold to a
code of behavior and values that justifies the use of violence in response to
frustration, insult, and other forms of interpersonal friction that could be
resolved by non-violent means.

A third survey of violence in youth, conducted by Dgani and Dgani
(1990), was of children in grades 5, 7, 8, and 10 in Tel Aviv public schools
and confirmed the prevalence of physical violence in public schools.
Nearly half the students reported that they had been beaten by their
schoolmates during the school year, and one in six were injured during
these beatings. A recent survey (Harel, Kani, and Rahav, 1997) based on
7,637 students in grades 6–12 in the public schools confirmed the disturbing trends of the earlier surveys. The investigators point out that Israeli
school children are exposed to high levels of interpersonal violence, both
verbal as well as physical, in Israeli society as a whole. If, indeed, adult Israeli society promotes interpersonal violence, it follows that Israeli children and youth learn to behave in a similar fashion in and out of school.
These investigators found that more than half the students had been the
victims of bullying, physical hazing, or physical attack in the course of the
school year. Thirteen percent of the boys and four percent of the girls suffered injury as a consequence of bullying or physical attack. The finding
that 22.6 percent of boys and 6.6 percent of girls carried a weapon to
school—usually a knife, club, or brass knuckles, though occasionally a
gun—is evidence of the violent atmosphere there. Some students carried

weapons to school to frighten or bully others; some of those and others also carried weapons to defend themselves against attack.

A nationwide study (Benvenishti, Astor, and Zeira, 1998) of 15,000 students provided similar findings. The majority of students considered violence in school a serious problem. Well over half reported verbal insults and cursing to be extremely common. More than half of the students in the primary grades were hit or pushed during the month prior to the study (57%), but fewer reported hitting or pushing in junior high (48%), and still fewer in senior high school (28%). The lawless atmosphere was a factor in some children being absent from school. At least once during the year, 6.8 percent of students in the primary grades and 4.5 percent of students in junior high stayed home out of fear that they would be attacked at school. Some students also reported that the professional staff in their schools insulted or mocked them, especially in the lower grades (22%), with a decline in junior high and high school (10% and 5%, respectively).

Rahav (2001a) compared teen violence in Israel to that of other countries. He found that bullying in school is higher than average in Israel, as compared to twenty-two other Western countries, with boys and girls combined ranking eighth, and boys alone ranking fifth. Across all countries, boys were more violent than girls and were more likely to be the victims of violence than girls. Children were found to be more violent between the ages of 11 and 13 than they were at later ages. The apparent drop in violence with age may be explained by maturation, which leads to greater self-regulation and management of anger. It also may be due to the fact that the more violent adolescents are expelled from school or drop out on their own.

Comparisons of groups within Israel provided the following conclusions: Israeli Arab youth are more violent than Israeli Jews by a factor of two or greater—probably due to cultural, social, and economic differences—and Sephardi (African/Asian background) youth also are perceived as engaging in more violent acts than Ashkenazi (European/American background). However, the official statistics do not provide sufficient information to reach a definitive conclusion. Nevertheless, Sephardi youth have higher levels of macho values, justify the use of violent response in altercations, are exposed to more violence, and participate more frequently in violent acts. These findings are consistent with higher rates of criminal violence (Horowitz, Frenkel, and Yinon, 1990).

The Effect of War on Israeli Children

War is not healthy for growing children or for grownups, but it is less damaging if the children reside in homes and in intact families based in communities with strong ideological convictions (Hobfoll et al., 1991; Milgram, 1993b; Zuckerman-Bareli, 1982). Under these conditions, children experience less personal anxiety and fewer behavioral disturbances. However, they may become sensitized to future situations that resemble the anxiety-provoking experiences of wartime (Kristal, 1978). A theme that runs through many clinical studies concerns the adverse reactions of children to the deaths of their fathers in Israel's wars. Studies document the grief reactions and the short-term deleterious effects of the loss, including lack of attention and concentration in school, poorer grades, mood swings, and depressive episodes. Boys were more likely than girls to manifest behavior problems in the months following the loss of the father. Conversely, girls were called upon to exercise greater responsibilities in their personal and family life and, in fact, did so. Boys who were seen as similar to the deceased father and saw themselves in this light appear to do better (Milgram, 1982).

The Gulf War—A Case in Point

The Gulf War (1990–1991) was brief, but its effects, like those of other Arab-Israeli wars, were not confined to the duration of the hostilities. The objective damage to property and persons was large in scale. The loss of life and damage to property caused by the thirty-nine missiles launched from Iraq against Israel was enormous, especially considering the geographical size of Israel. Given that the ratio of the population of the United States to Israel is 50:1, the comparable amount of loss of life and damage in the United States would come to 450 people killed directly by the attacks, 3,000 would die from indirect causes, 11,000 would be injured, 16,000 would have severe stress reactions, and a half a million dwellings would be damaged or destroyed (Bleich, Dycian, Koslowsky, Solomon, and Weiner, 1992). Numerous studies (summarized in Milgram 1993a, 1994) documented the rise and gradual decline in anxiety and other stress reactions exhibited by children during the missile attacks on Israel cities. They found that toddlers were more apparently upset than infants. On the other hand, younger children in the 8–16 age range reported a higher frequency of behavior problems, more intense stress reactions, and more somatic complaints than did older children. They also reported a higher frequency of post-traumatic stress reactions three weeks after the war. A thirty-month follow-up study of children who were 3–5 years old during the Iraqi missile attacks reported that children who were displaced from their homes because of missile strikes reported more post-traumatic stress symptoms than did non-displaced children. The children's symptoms were strongly accounted for by their mothers' general psychopathological reaction.

The psychological effects of this war were influenced by its unique features:

a. death, injury, and damage to property were confined to the civilian sector;

b. adults in general, and men in particular, were unable to play their customary protective wartime roles and were accordingly upset;

c. all family members sat wearing gas masks in sealed rooms during air raids, but were unable to do anything about the air raids themselves.

As a consequence, there developed a collective sense of learned helplessness (Seligman, 1975) that affected individuals both during and after the war. People's sense of well-being and their attitudes about their collective and personal security were lowered because of feelings of uncertainty. The end of the war did not dispel the fears of future missile attacks and their potential effects (chemical or biological) or the uncertainty about the Israeli Defense Force's ability to predict and avert such attacks in the future (Milgram, 1994).

To emphasize the enduring consequence of this relatively minor war in Israel's history, it is suggested that the reader substitute the term *rape* for *war* with reference to these consequences and read the above paragraph again.

Adult Victims of War and Terrorist Attacks

Solomon's comprehensive analysis (1993) of thousands of Israeli veterans leads to sobering conclusions. Soldiers who were exposed to threats to life and limb, suffered injury and/or witnessed the injury and/or death of their comrades in arms, are never the same again. They may exhibit acute stress reactions that become chronic conditions which impair the quality of their lives at work, at play, and at home with their loved ones. They may relive their traumatic experiences because of involuntary intrusions of these experiences into their awareness and by efforts to avoid situations that return them to these experiences. It is as if they try to run but cannot escape because the experience is within them. They may appear to be symptom free until they return to military service to fulfill their reserve duty requirements (until age 43) and are again exposed to difficult combat experiences. They may become disturbed later in civilian life when difficult experiences (e.g., illness, unemployment, the death of loved ones) place an intolerable level of strain on their weakened ability to cope with their prior traumatic exposure. The prevalence of lifetime impaired functioning in combat soldiers is extraordinarily high (Solomon, 1993).

Terrorism is a form of warfare whose psychological and psychiatric effects on the civilian population are far greater than the physical damage that these acts cause (Friedland and Merari, 1986). Civilian victims of terrorist attack are in some respects more vulnerable to psychiatric disturbance than are soldiers, because the traumatic episode is sudden, unpredictable, and uncontrollable, and civilians are ill prepared to deal with it. When these acts do occur, civilians do not have the training or the support of comrades-in-arms to thwart them or to bring other victims to a safe haven for respite and treatment. Long-term follow-up studies document the adverse consequences of highly stressful and prolonged terrorist hostage experiences (Desilviya, Gal, and Ayalon, 1996), and professional and volunteer organizations have emerged to help the victims of terrorist attacks cope in the aftermath (Ayalon and Lahad, 1990; Israel Support Center for Victims of National Psychotrauma, 2000, 2001).

CLOSING COMMENTS

One may come away from this exposition with the impression that Israeli citizens may be characterized as belonging to one of two groups: those who are already traumatized by one kind of violence or another and those who are on a constant vigil to ward off traumatizing situations. There are many features of Israeli life that (a) insulate citizens from the deleterious effects of violence, (b) mitigate the effects of the violence that does take place, and (c) provide rehabilitation opportunities for those who have suffered psychic injury. The nuclear family and the extended family are relatively intact institutions in Israeli life, and, although divorce is becoming more common, both parents are available to their children. People derive some degree of security during wars and terrorist attacks from their trust in the Israeli Defense Force. Victims of all kinds—battered wives and children, raped girls and women, bereaved families—all receive sympathy and social support from appropriate sources (e.g., neighbors, volunteer and professional organizations). These forms of support help to assuage the effects of acts or violence inflicted on people in Israeli society. Many of these supports are derived from classical Jewish religious customs and cultural traditions of social concern for the weak and the unfortunate. There is a quotation that is often repeated by Israelis:

> If I don't look out for myself, who can be expected to look out for me? And if I look out only for myself, what kind of a person am I? And if I do not act now [in behalf of others] then when [will I do so]? (*Ethics of the Fathers* 1:14).

REFERENCES

Appreciation is expressed to colleagues who provided me with research materials: Professor Giora Rahav, Department of Sociology and Anthropology, Tel Aviv University; Ms. Mali Schori, doctoral student, Department of Criminology, Bar-llan University; and Ms. Ronit Lev-Ari, director, Department for the Prevention of Violence in the Family, Tel Aviv University.

Ayalon, O. (1983). *The delicate balance: Coping with stress in the family*. Tel Aviv: Sifriat Hapoalim. [Hebrew]

Ayalon, O., and Lahad, S. (1990). *Life on the border*. Haifa: Nord Publications. [Hebrew]

Ayalon, O., and Soskis, D. (1986). Survivors of terrorist victimization: A follow-up study. In N.A. Milgram (Ed.), *Stress and coping in time of war: Generalizations from the Israeli experience* (pp. 257–274). Washington, DC: Brunner/Mazel.

Benvenishti, R., Astor, R., and Zeira, E. (1998). *Violence in the educational system*. Jerusalem: School of Social Work, Hebrew University. [Hebrew]

Bleich, A., Dycian, A., Koslowsky, M., Solomon, Z., and Weiner, M. (1992). Psychiatric implications of missile attacks on a civilian population. *Journal of the American Medical Association, 268*, 613–615.

Cohen, S. (1984). Sociological approaches to vandalism. In C. Levy-Leboyer (Ed.), *Vandalism: Behavior and motivation*. Amsterdam, The Netherlands: North-Holland.

Council of Europe. (1992). *Violence against elderly people*. Strasbourg, Germany: Author.

Desilviya, H.S., Gal, R., and Ayalon, O. (1996). Extent of victimization, traumatic stress symptoms, and adjustment of terrorist assault survivors: A long-term follow-up. *Journal of Traumatic Stress, 9*, 881–889.

Dgani, A., and Dgani, R. (1990). *Violence within the school walls: A phenomenon and its dimensions in the educational system and the social-urban setting of Tel-Aviv Jaffa*. Tel Aviv: Geocartographia. [Hebrew]

Eisenstadt, S.N. (1954). *The absorption of immigrants*. London: Routledge & Kegan Paul.

Eisenstadt, S.N. (1967). *Israeli society*. Jerusalem: Magnes Publishing.

Eisikovits, Z., and Buchbinder, E. (1999). Talking control: Metaphors used by battered women. *Violence against Women, 5*, 845–868.

Fishman, G. (1983). On war and crime. In S. Breznitz (Ed.), *Stress in Israel* (pp. 165–180). New York: Van Nostrand Reinhold.

Friedland, N., and Merari, A. (1986). The psychological impact of terrorism on society. A two-edged sword. In N.A. Milgram (Ed.), *Stress and coping in time of war: Generalizations from the Israeli experience* (pp. 243–256). New York: Brunner/Mazel.

Gur, S. (1999). *Violence in Israeli Society* (Conference). Van Leer Institute, Jerusalem: December 23. [Hebrew]

Haj-Yahia, M.M. (1998). Perceptions of abusive and violent husbands by engaged Arab men in Israel. *Journal of Social Psychology, 138*, 772–786.

Haj-Yahia, M.M. (2000). Implications of wife abuse and battering for self esteem, depression, and anxiety as revealed by the Second Palestinian National Survey of Violence against Women. *Journal of Family Issues, 21*, 435–463.

Harel, Y., Kani, D., and Rahav, G. (1997). *Israeli youth: Social welfare, health and risk behaviors from an international perspective*. Jerusalem: The Joint-Brookdale Institute and the Department of the Sociology of Health, Bar-Ilan University. [Hebrew]

Hartaf, H., and Bar-On, N. (2000). *Pleasant home: A New direction for violent men*. Jerusalem: Office of Service Development, National Insurance Institute. [Hebrew]

Heller, G. (1996). Changing the school to reduce school violence: What works. *National Association of Secondary School Principals Bulletin, 80*, 1–11.

Herman, J.I. (1992). *Trauma and recovery*. New York: Basic Books.

Hobfoll, S.E., Spielberger, C.D., Breznitz, S., Figley, C., Folkman, S., Lepper-Green, B., Meichenbaum, D., Milgram, N.A., Sarason, I.G., and van der Kolk, B. (1991). War-related stress: Addressing the stress of war and traumatic events. *American Psychologist, 46*, 848–855.

Horowitz, T. (2000). *Violence as an antisocial phenomenon: Theory and practice.* Jerusalem: Henrietta Szold Institute. [Hebrew]

Horowitz, T., and Amir, M. (1981). *The coping patterns of the educational system with reference to the problem of violence*. Jerusalem: Henrietta Szold Institute. [Hebrew]

Horowitz, T., Frenkel, E., and Yinon, Y. (1990). *Categories of violence in youth* (Research Rep. No. 239). Jerusalem: Henrietta Szold Institute. [Hebrew]

Hourani, L.L., and Yuan, H. (1999). The mental health status of women in the navy and the Marine Corps: Preliminary findings from the perception of wellness and readiness assessment. *Military Medicine, 164*, 174–181.

Hunt, R. (1993). Neurobiological patterns of aggression. *Journal of Emotional and Behavioral Problems, 2*, 14–20.

Israel Police. (2000). *Annual Report*. Jerusalem: Author. [Hebrew]

Israel Support Center for Victims of National Psychotrauma. (2000). A nation under stress. *With Regard to Feelings* (No. 1). Tel Aviv: Author. December. [Hebrew]

Israel Support Center for Victims of National Psychotrauma. (2001). Life in the shadow of events. *With Regard to Feelings* (No. 2). Tel Aviv: Author. April. [Hebrew]

Kolker, A., and Ahmed, P.I. (1980). Integration of immigrants: The Israeli case. In G.V. Coelho and P.I. Ahmed (Eds.), *Uprooting and development* (pp. 479–496). New York: Plenum.

Kristal, L. (1978). Bruxism: An anxiety response to environmental stress. In C.D. Spielberger and I.G. Sarason (Eds.), *Stress and anxiety* (Vol. 5, pp. 45–59). Washington, DC: Hemisphere.

Lev-Ari, R. (2000). *Before the blow: Identifying the red lights that predict violence in couples*. Tel Aviv: Na'amat, in cooperation with the Municipality of Tel Aviv, the Department of Welfare, and the Ministry of Labor and Welfare. [Hebrew]

Marx, E. (1976). *The social context of violent behavior*. London: Routledge & Kegan Paul.

Merrill, L.L., Newell, C.E., Milner, J.S., Koss, M.P., Hervig, L.K., Gold, S.R., Rossowork, S.G., and Thornton, S.R. (1998). Prevalence of premilitary sexual victimization and aggression in a navy recruit sample. *Military Medicine, 163*, 209–212.

Milgram, N.A. (1982). War related stress in Israeli children. In L. Goldberg and S. Breznitz (Eds.), *Handbook of stress: Theoretical and clinical aspects* (pp. 656–676). New York: Free Press.

Milgram, N.A. (1993a). Stress and coping in Israel during the Gulf War. *Journal of Social Issues, 49*, 103–123.

Milgram, N.A. (1993b). War-related trauma and victimization: Principles of traumatic stress prevention in Israel. In J.P. Wilson and B. Raphael (Eds.), *International handbook of traumatic stress syndromes* (pp. 811–820). New York: Plenum.

Milgram, N.A. (1994). The effect of the Gulf War on Israel. *Anxiety, Stress and Coping*, 7, 205–215.

Milgram, N.A. (1998). *Immigration and emigration: Unique patterns in Israel*. Tel Aviv University and the Academic College of Judea and Samaria.

Rahav, G. (1998). Criminal statistics. In R.R. Friedmann (Ed.), *Crime and criminal justice in Israel* (pp. 65–78). New York: New York University Press.

Rahav, G. (2001). Israel. In A.M. Hoffman and R.W. Summers (Eds.), *Teen violence: A global view* (pp. 59–71). Westport CT: Greenwood Press.

Rahav, G. (in press). *Violent assault*. Department of Sociology and Anthropology, Tel Aviv University. [Hebrew]

Raia, J.A. (1999). Treatment of children and adolescents exposed to community violence. *Clinical Quarterly of the National Center for Post-Traumatic Stress Disorder*, 8(56), 58–60.

Rattner, A. (1997). Crime and Russian immigration: Socialization or importation? The Israeli case. *International Journal of Comparative Sociology*, 38, 235–248.

Ron, S. (1983). *Violence in the family*. Jerusalem: Welfare Services for the Individual and the Family, Ministry of Labor and Welfare. [Hebrew]

Schneider, J. (1971). Of vigilance and virgins: Honor, shame, and access to resources in Mediterranean societies. *Ethnology*, 10, 1–24.

Seligman, M.E.P. (1975). *Helplessness: On depression, development and death*. San Francisco: Freeman.

Shoham, E. (2000). The battered wife's perception of the characteristics of her encounter with the police. *International Journal of Offender, Therapy, and Comparative Criminology*, 44, 242–257.

Shoham, S.G., Ashkenazy, J.J.M., Rahav, G., Chard, F., Addi, A., and Addad, M. (1995). *Violence: An integrated multivariate study of human aggression*. Aldershot, England: Dartmouth Publishing.

Shoham, S.G., Rahav, G., and Addad, M. (1987). *Criminology: Theories, research and application*. Jerusalem: Shocken.

Solomon, Z. (1993). *Combat stress reaction: The enduring toll of war*. New York: Plenum.

Swink, K.K., and Leveille, A.E. (1986). From victim to survivor: A new look at the issues and recovery process for adult incest survivors. *Women and Therapy*, 5, 119–141.

Zuckerman-Bareli, C. (1982). The effect of border tension on the adjustment of kibbutzim and moshavim on the northern border of Israel. In C.D. Spielberger and I.G. Sarason (Eds.) and N.A. Milgram, *Stress and anxiety* (Vol. 8, pp. 81–92). Washington, DC: Hemisphere.

9

Violence in Japan

Seisoh Sukemune

THE PRESENT AUTHOR'S DESTINY IN 1945

World War II ended with Japan's total defeat on August 15, 1945. The single cataclysmic event that led to Japan's surrender occurred on August 6, when the city of Hiroshima was first A-bombed by the U.S. Air Force. It was followed by a second nuclear attack on the city of Nagasaki on August 9. Both cities were devastated completely and leveled to the ground. Tens of thousands of civilians were killed instantly, and many thousands more died later from the nuclear fallout.

The present author escaped this mass destruction by a hair's breadth on that fateful day. He was a 16-year-old student at the Hiroshima Normal School at that time. Most students even at that young age, were either drafted as service men or mobilized to work at the ammunition plants or barracks around the city. Students stayed on the campus, but classes no longer were given. Instead, they were conscripted to work as laborers at plants and railheads. In addition, they were equipped with a bamboo spear, and required to receive unsparing military training. A first-hand account of the critical days before the tragic day of August 6, 1945, follows.

On August 3, students were told by teachers that one half of each class was to remain in the city to continue working while the other half had to leave the city to engage in needed work outside the city. Students were asked to choose either stay in the city or leave the city. In those days, Japanese people expected to be given orders by the authorities and carried them out without choice or preference. Therefore, the students were pleased to be given a choice between either staying or leaving. The present author, without any hesitation, chose to stay and was admitted in the staying group. In one of the unexplainable moments of life, an unshakeable thought came to him on the early morning of August 4. He went to his teacher and said, "I want to leave the city." The teacher denied his request and did not permit the changeover at this late hour. However, the present author persevered until the teacher listened to his entreaties. Finally, he was given permission to join the leaving group. The present author to this day is not aware why he suddenly changed his mind. Many students who stayed did not survive the nuclear terror. Many students in the staying group died not knowing what democracy is.

The new constitution of Japan was established on November 3, 1946, under the occupation policies required by the Allied General Headquarter in Tokyo. The Japanese Empire was no more, and the emperor was shifted from being regarded as a living God to a human being and became a symbol under the new constitution. Japan became a country with its sovereignty resting with the people.

People eagerly studied democracy, the responsibilities of freedom, and their new roles and political obligations. The women's suffrage was given and the young were delighted to be able to choose their marriage partners. The Fundamental Law of Education also was established and the 6-3-3 school system was introduced following the American system.

The new constitution, promulgated in 1947, renounces the sovereign right of the country to use war as a means to settle international disputes. This does not mean, however, that Japan has renounced the right of the country to defend itself. Japan has self-defense armed forces in the army, navy, and air force.

POSTWAR DEVELOPMENTS

In 1951, Japan concluded a peace treaty with all the allied countries except the Soviet Union. Security was assured with the presence of U.S. forces. Young people were not required to undergo military training. Okinawa was returned to Japan in 1972, fulfilling a long-awaited desire. However, the northern territorial claim involving several islands has not been resolved with Russia, despite very frequent negotiations between the two countries for many years.

Since World War II ended, the rate of higher education has advanced dramatically. Japan's postwar economy also has grown remarkably, and the standard of living has improved accordingly. Like in the West, family size has shrunk, families are more nuclear, and information technology has developed rapidly. In terms of economic development and affluence, Japan became second only to the United States.

POST–BUBBLE ECONOMY BURST

Recently, in the past decade, Japan's bubble economy has burst into recession. Many corporations went into bankruptcy. Most banks hold bad loans and have to be supported by public debt and capital. Many banks merged to survive. The unemployment rate is risen to an unprecedented high of about 5 percent. The plazas in most cities are crowded with not shoppers but job hunters who have lost or were forced to quit their jobs. It is difficult for students to get jobs to support their education and even harder to find new employment upon graduation. Japan's high-education industry—made up of numerous junior colleges, colleges, and universities—are also in crisis, as enrollment has declined drastically. The economic state of Japan remains depressed, with no sign of recovery.

CRIME AND VIOLENCE AS SOCIAL PROBLEMS IN MODERN JAPAN

Japan has been regarded for the past fifty years as a peaceful country with great respect for law and order. That sense of internal security within Japan soon may change. New social problems similar to those in the West are evident. The birthrate is very low, declining to less than 1.8. Together with having the highest longevity in the world, Japan has become a country with an aging people and zero population growth. Violence is on the rise among the young and criminal organizations, and so is public fear of this threat to personal security.

It is interesting that American friends visiting the present author in Hiroshima thirty years ago never locked their car doors. It was simply not necessary. Today people lock their cars wherever they are parked. Auto theft is common even at home, and stolen cars are sold off in major cities. According to recent television news, over 10,000 new model cars were stolen and sold off in the city of Osaka alone per year. Daily organized and random crime has made Osaka (incl., neighboring Kobe, where the present author currently resides) Japan's capital of crime. Theft, kidnapping, bombing, hijacking, corruption, narcotics, and gang wars are common. First on the list is murder and homicide. The prime-time news by NHK television channel every morning announces "murder cases in the community," "family murder and violence," and "school murder and violence."

SCHOOL VIOLENCE AND DEATHS

With the introduction of American cinema, Japanese people were exposed to the idea of school violence as an every day occurrence. Everyone was shocked at the idea, but no one then, even in their wildest dreams, could foresee such violence in Japanese schools. However, the nightmare of children being attacked, maimed, and killed in school is a reality today. Yet few people seem to show any interest to resolve school-related violence. This problem is surely one pathological symptom of a much wider

Table 9.1
Frequency and Percent of Both In-School and Out-School Violence
in Public Schools, 1997

School	Total number of schools	Number of schools in which violence occurred		Frequency of both in-school and out-school violence		
		in-school	out-school	in-school	out-school	total
Elementary School	24,051	557 (2.3%)	117 (0.5%)	1,528	178	1,706
Junior High School	10,497	3,599 (34.3%)	2,001 (19.1%)	22,991	3,792	26,783
Senior High School	4,160	1,809 (43.5%)	1,032 (24.8%)	5,152	1,591	6,743

Source: Tokyo Metropolitan Government Office, 1998.

problem in modern society reflected in the place where we educate our children. World, as well as internal, peace is today's greatest challenge facing human societies everywhere. The world must be a safer place and schools also must be safe for children. Conflict and violence must be replaced with peace and harmonious living.

Child resilience, or a calm and peaceful self-concept, is no longer a personal issue but society's responsibility. An attitude of violence and destruction is a social problem that requires all of societies' resolve and resources to overcome. What is helpful is the commitment of disciplines such as psychology, education, social welfare, and health and other child-related professions. Research in clinical education and educational psychology and resilience would contribute toward the improvement of student attitude and behavior to make violent behavior unnecessary. In practice, the role of the community in the campaign for peace and peace building must be greatly expanded.

Table 9.2
Frequency of Violence to Teachers of Both In-School and Out-School Violence in Public Schools, 1997

School	In-school				Out-school				Total		
	a	b	c	d	e	f	g	h	i	j	k
Elementary School	103	192	137	144	2	3	5	3	195	142	147
Junior High School	1,286	3,629	3,080	3,226	53	62	61	72	3,691	3,141	3,298
Senior High School	395	577	595	587	9	11	15	10	588	610	597

a & e: number of schools where violence occurred
b & f: number of violent incidents that occurred
c & g: number of students who attacked
d & h: number of teachers who were attacked
i: total number of occurrences
j: total number of students who attacked
k: total number of teachers who were attacked
Source: Tokyo Metropolitan Government Office, 1998.

Table 9.3
Frequency of In-School and Out-School Violence among Students in Public Schools, 1997

School	In-school				Out-school				Total		
	a	b	c	d	e	f	g	h	i	j	k
Elementary School	328	728	742	799	84	134	169	143	862	911	942
Junior High School	2,575	10,655	13,479	11,223	1,412	2,564	5,126	3,281	13,219	18,605	14,504
Senior High School	1,480	3,333	5,305	3,562	703	974	1,933	1,090	4,307	7,238	4,652

a & e: number of schools where violence occurred
b & f: number of violent incidents that occurred
c & g: number of students who attacked
d & h: number of teachers who were attacked
i: total number of occurrences
j: total number of students who attacked
k: total number of teachers who were attacked
Source: Tokyo Metropolitan Government Office, 1998.

Table 9.4
Frequency of In-School Violence toward Furniture and Building Damage in Public Schools, 1997

School	Number of schools in which violence occurred	Number of occurrences	Number of students who attacked	Cost of damage (unit: JPY 10.000)	Cost equivalent in U.S. dollars
Elementary School	268	578	681	801	$ 6.65
Junior High School	1,793	8,603	7,041	18,231	$151.37
Senior High School	522	1,196	985	3,945	$ 32.75

Source: Tokyo Metropolitan Government Office, 1998.

Table 9.5
Frequency of In-School Violence Recorded by Police in Public Schools, 1997

	Total	Junior high school students	Senior high school students
Total number of cases	661	624	37
violence cases against teachers	446	434	12
Total number of students taken into protective custody	1,208	1,093	115
violence cases against teachers	569	554	15
Total number of persons damaged	884	831	53
violence cases against teachers	588	570	18

Source: Tokyo Metropolitan Government Office, 1998.

Table 9.6
Rate of Children's Violence Directed toward Family (Lineal) Relations

	Total number	Father	Mother	Sibling	Grandparents	Furniture	Other
Frequency	1,000	107	553	50	121	158	1
Percent	100.0	10.7	55.3	5.0	12.1	15.8	1.1

Source: Tokyo Metropolitan Government Office, 1998.

FAMILY VIOLENCE

Children's family violence in Japan increasingly becomes one of multiple-based attacks on parents, siblings, and other extended family members, such as grandparents. Children's violence also is directed toward home furniture. Table 9.6 shows the rate of children's violence against their parents and others. The frequency and percentage rate of family violence per 1,000 cases are shown in this table.

Several varieties of child-initiated violence are centered in the school. Children's in-school and out-school violence is the most representative violence, as briefly shown above. Children not only target other children, but also their teachers. Before the end of World War II, most Japanese children had deep respect for their teachers. Violence against teachers was unheard-of. Today circumstances around children and teachers have changed drastically. In addition, child-initiated violence directed at parents is devastating Japanese society. This is increasing as family violence, or domestic violence, between parents is also on the rise. One of the most serious social problems is domestic violence.

Discipline and corporal punishment was an accepted practice in schools prior to and during World War II in Japan. Most schoolteachers were very stern in terms of school discipline. Many students in those days meekly accepted the corporal punishment in school. Parents also believed in strong discipline at home, though it was a matter of degree. However, circumstances around school and home have changed dramatically since democracy came to Japan from the West. Today, most teachers and parents are very lenient with their students and with children in general. However, some adults who are caregivers or educators are not positive role models. They may show pathological behaviors and attitudes. In their roles as teachers or parents, they commit violence against students and children. Male teachers, for example, develop sexual relationships with their students. In other words, teachers force students into indecent behavior, and this behavior is followed by violence, and sometimes by mur-

Table 9.7
Frequency and Percent of Spousal Abuse as Reported by Wives

	Very frequent	A few times	None	No response
Mental violence n=1183	15.7	40.2	40.8	3.2
Physical violence n=1183	6.9	26.1	63.7	3.3
Sexual violence n=1183	3.7	17.2	75.7	3.3

Source: Tokyo Metropolitan Government Office, 1998.

der. Parents' violence against children generally is viewed as child abuse. In extreme cases, there is incest, extreme violence, and murder.

DOMESTIC VIOLENCE

Husbands' violence against their wives, which is today regarded as "domestic violence," should be named *family violence*, but the present author follows precedent.

Domestic violence increases currently. Table 9.7 shows the frequency and rate of spousal abuse, as reported by wives.

Table 9.8 shows the comparison of the rates of family violence perpetrated by husbands in Japan and Canada in 1993. As seen in Table 9.8, the top five violence categories in Tokyo Metropolis are almost the same as those in Canada.

FINAL REMARKS

Violence and acts of aggression in all forms must be condemned. The present author referred to school violence and domestic violence in contemporary Japan involving children and families. The perpetrator may be an adolescent who feels victimized or a deranged adult, even a teacher. Threats and assaults with weapons on peers and teachers in school are not new, but such violence has accelerated. School is no longer a safe place for children or teachers. The biggest murder case in schools occurred in the summer of 2001 in the city of Osaka. A man armed with a dagger entered an elementary school attached to the Osaka University of Education. He stabbed to death first graders and teachers one by one. Today, walls and heightened security in schools cannot effectively stop such attacks or prevent violence from spilling over from the community. It is not uncommon for children to be kidnapped or attacked, or for young people to assault homeless elderly in public. Violence within families is

Table 9.8
Comparison of Rate of Family Violence Perpetrated by Husbands
in Japan and Canada, 1993

Violence categories	Tokyo Metropolis n=1183*	All over Canada n=2652*
Husband pushes wife, grasps, pinches, and pokes himself against wife	20%	25%
Husband strikes wife with the palm of his hand	18%	15%
Husband threatens, pretending to strike wife with his fist	17%	19%
Husband kicks, bites, and strikes wife with his fist	15%	11%
Husband flings dangerous things against wife	12%	11%

*N equals number of women reporting.
Source: Hada and Hirakawa, 1998.

just as problematic. Family violence can be domestic violence, that is, a husband's attack on his wife. It also can be perpetrated by adolescents on their parents or grandparents. Investigations on sexual violence in schools and sexual harassment in the workplace also have attracted much attention in Japan.

Violence is associated with school pathological acts, family stability, and community disorganization. As economic and community tensions heighten in contemporary Japan, so do problems of dismissal, unemployment, depression, domestic violence, immorality, family separation, and so on. Further research on the family itself is needed to understand its relation to violence. More research on how society contributes to violence is needed from the interdisciplinary and cultural points of view. Violence has become endemic, to the degree that society fails to live in peace.

The terrorist attacks in the United States that occurred on September 11, 2001, are sad and tragic. People everywhere in the world are traumatized by this tragedy. International terrorism is despicable, totally unacceptable, and evil, and it should be regarded as the biggest kind of violence in the world. Can we prevent future violence on such a scale from occurring? As a person who survived the Hiroshima A-bomb violence and as a psychologist, the present author knows there is a solution to resolve interpersonal and ideological conflict without resorting to violence. Our efforts must deal with the roots of human conflict through peace building, starting from within oneself—learning to be peaceful and to live in peace.

REFERENCES

The present author is deeply grateful to Dr. Chok C. Hiew for his kind edit of this manuscript.

Hada, A., and Hirakawa, K. (1998). *Shelter: To escape from violence: Women's escape from husbands' or partners' violence.* Tokyo: Aoki-shoten.

Management and Coordination Agency. (2000). *The youth white paper (1999).* Japanese Government.

Tokyo Metropolitan Government Office. (1998). *Survey report on "violence against women."* Tokyo: Author.

10

Peace and Violence: A Comparison of Buddhist Ladakh and the United States

Uwe P. Gielen

In traditional Ladakh, aggression of any sort is exceptionally rare: rare
enough to say that it is virtually nonexistent. . . . I have hardly seen
anything more than mild disagreement in the traditional villages.

—Norberg-Hodge

Violence is as American as apple pie.

—Carmichael

Not only does democracy make every man forget his ancestors, but it
hides his descendants and separates his contemporaries from him; it
throws him back forever upon himself alone, and threatens in the end
to confine him entirely within the solitude of his own heart.

—de Tocqueville

Psychologists such as Bonta (1997), Fromm (1973), and Gielen and
Chirico-Rosenberg (1993) and the anthropologists Briggs (1970), Howell
and Willis (1989), Montagu (1978), and Sponsel and Gregor (1994) have
studied the nature of small-scale, traditional, nonviolent societies located
in various parts of the globe. Examples of reputedly nonviolent societies
include the Semai Senoi of Malaysia (Robarchek, 1977), certain Zapotec
communities in Mexico (Fry, 1992), a group of Inuits (Eskimos) in Canada
(Briggs, 1970), and the Zuñi Pueblo Indians of New Mexico (Benedict,
1934/1959; see Bonta, 1993, 1997, for more information on peaceful societies). Students of these societies have tended to focus on worldviews,
value systems, cognitive scripts, cooperative attitudes, the control of
anger, and child-rearing practices, holding various combinations of these
responsible for the prevailing low rates of violent behavior.

Although some of the claims regarding the absence or near absence of violence in these societies have turned out to be premature (Edgerton, 1992; Eibl-Eibesfeldt, 1979; Fox, 1975), there remains little doubt that overall levels of violence vary dramatically from society to society. This is as true for nonliterate and folk societies as it is for nation-states. Whereas, for instance, among the fierce Yanomamö of southern Venezuela and northern Brazil, up to one-third of all males die by the hands of other males (Chagnon, 1983, 1992), the chances for such a death are minuscule among the peaceful Ladakhis described below. Similarly, Japan's prevalence rates for homicide, assault, robbery, and many other forms of antisocial behavior remain far below those of the United States. The same holds true for other relatively harmonious, nonviolent nations, such as Denmark, Netherlands, New Zealand, Norway, and Switzerland (Kinloch, 1990).

The anthropological study of peaceful societies took as one of its origins Ruth Benedict's famous book, *Patterns of Culture* (1934/1959). In it, Benedict contrasted the peaceful way of life of the Zuñi Pueblo Indians with the status- and power-oriented ethos of the Kwakiutl Indians on the U.S. northwest coast and the prevailing attitudes of mistrust, paranoia, and treachery among the Dobu of Melanesia. Benedict's book became a monument to cultural relativism, that is, the idea that value systems, moralities, and worldviews differ radically from society to society. The book had a strong impact on the anthropological profession: Cultural relativism became the reigning ideology of American anthropology under the influence of Franz Boas, Benedict, Melville Herskovits, and Margaret Mead, while also importantly influencing cross-cultural psychology (e.g., Segall, Dasen, Berry, and Poortinga, 1990). Benedict's book shaped the imagination of countless college students and of the educated public, with more than one million copies being sold over the years.

Benedict's book played an important role in the battle of the cultural anthropologists, behaviorists, and social learning theorists against the "instinctivists." Instinctivists such as the psychoanalyst Sigmund Freud, the hormic psychologist William McDougall, and the ethologist Konrad Lorenz have claimed that there exists an innate, universal core of human characteristics among which aggression, hostility, readiness for anger, and self-seeking tendencies are prominent. By showing that peaceful societies do exist, the anthropologists sought to demonstrate that there are no universal and innate aggressive drives or instincts. Although hardly conclusive, this argument was advanced forcefully by Montagu in his edited book, *Learning Non-Aggression: The Experience of Non-Literate Societies* (1978). Similar but less ideologically oriented collections by Howell and Willis (1989) and by Sponsel and Gregor (1994) also contain studies of peaceful societies. The studies are based on the premise that sociality rather than aggression is the psychological basis upon which humans have built their societies and created satisfying religious and moral frameworks for living. However, neither Montagu nor Howell and Willis are fully prepared to recognize the contradictory nature of human beings, in whose souls opposing impulses and needs for selfishness and altruism, dominance and surrender, cooperation and resistance, and aggression and nonviolence have always lived side by side. Potentialities for such impulses and needs are part of human nature, although societies differentially channel, shape and reshape, reinforce, suppress, and sidetrack universal inclinations.

Although psychologists have conducted numerous studies dealing with the prosocial, altruistic, and cooperative behavior of individuals, they have played only a limited role in the study of peaceful societies. One important exception is Fromm's (1973) survey of thirty "primitive" (nonliterate) tribes, which he divided into life-affirmative, nondestructive-aggressive, and destructive societies. Among the life-affirmative societies he placed the Zuñi Indians, the Mountain Arapesh, the Aranda, the Semangs, the Todas, the Polar Eskimos, and the Mbuti Pygmies. Relying on evidence collected by anthropologists, he claimed that, in these societies, "there is a minimum of hostility, violence, or cruelty among people, no harsh punishment, hardly any crime, and the institution of war is absent or plays an exceedingly small role. Children are treated with kindness, . . . [and] there is little envy, covetousness, greed, and exploitativeness. There is also little competition, . . . a general attitude of trust and confidence . . . ; a general prevalence of good humor, and a relative absence of depressive moods" (Fromm, 1973, 194).

This chapter investigates how well Fromm's generalizations apply to the society of Ladakh, a mostly Tibetan society located in northwest India which, until some decades ago, was relatively isolated from Western contact. The chapter centers on the nonviolent ethos and worldview of traditional Ladakh, an ethos based on Buddhist conceptions of "no-self," religious merit and demerit, karma, compassion with all sentient beings, and the undesirability of mental poisons such as greed, anger and hate, jealousy, envy, and spiritual ignorance. The nonviolent ethos of Ladakh culminates in the ideal of the *bodhisattva*, a religious-savior figure embodying the ideals of compassion, altruism, nonviolence, and karmic interconnectedness. Our interviews suggest that most Ladakhis have internalized deeply the Buddhist "ethos of peace."

Subsequently, the chapter compares the ethos of Buddhist Ladakh to the worldview and competitive ethos of the modern United States. The argument advanced is that the aggressive and expressive forms of individualism prevailing in the United States stand in stark contrast to the restrained, synergistic, cooperative forms of social interaction found in Ladakh and other peaceful societies. It also is argued that because modern psychology is a manifestation of individualism, it unwittingly contributes to the forces of fragmentation that undermine American society, leading to social disorganization and violent behavior.

BUDDHIST LADAKH

Ladakh is located in the northwestern area of India and forms a part of the state of Jammu and Kashmir. About half as large as England, it has approximately 135,000 inhabitants. More than 99 percent of the land is a high-altitude, mountainous desert, but barley, buckwheat, potatoes, turnips, and walnut and apricot trees are planted in the valleys. Ladakh borders Pakistan and Tibet, the latter now forming part of China. There is one town, Leh, that currently has more than 20,000 inhabitants. The other Ladakhis live in villages, but some nomadic pastoralists roam the higher, more remote areas. Most Ladakhis are farmers, craftsmen, small-business owners, government officials, or members of the Buddhist clergy. They speak Ladakhi, a Tibetan language. Hindi, Urdu, "standard Tibetan," and English are spoken by some Ladakhis in business or government transactions or by the Buddhist clergy. Literacy levels vary greatly by region, social class, gender, and age, but the large majority of children in Leh and surrounding villages are now attending at least primary school.

The upper Indus valley forms the cultural center of Buddhist Ladakh. Many of the monasteries that traditionally have dominated the spiritual life of Buddhist Ladakh are located here. The monasteries belong to a variety of Tibetan lineages, such as the Gelugpa ("Yellow Hat"), the Kargyupa (including Digunkpa and Dukpa), the Nyingmapa, and the Sakyapa.

Close to 60 percent of Ladakh's population professes the Buddhist faith, while most other inhabitants of Ladakh belong to the Sunni and Shia traditions of Islam. Among the Muslims are Baltis and Ladakhis. The Baltis share their culture, language, and religion with the Baltis of neighboring Baltistan, a province of Pakistan.[1] Pervasive cultural differences and certain political tensions separate the Baltis from the Buddhist Ladakhis. In contrast, the Muslim Ladakhis are often rather similar in their cultural habits and personality traits to the Buddhist Ladakhis, although the two groups differ in their religion. The present chapter confines itself to the Buddhist population and is based on interviews that were conducted with seventy-two Buddhist children, men, women, and monks during 1980–1981. The findings of this study cannot necessarily be extended to other Tibetan societies, since many of them follow a less peaceful way of life than Ladakh. In addition, Ladakh has undergone many sociocultural and economic changes during recent decades, which will not be discussed in this essay (see Gielen, 1993, 2001, for additional information on this point).

METHOD

Sample

The sample of seventy-two respondents included eight boys and eight girls, ages 10–12; eight boys and eight girls, ages 14–16; ten men and ten women, ages 25–73; and twenty monks, ages 20–72. All respondents were Buddhists and came from Leh and surrounding villages. The twenty monks were affiliated with a wide variety of monasteries throughout Ladakh. Their educational attainments and ranks within their monastic communities varied considerably, and some of the monks had, in the past, gone to Tibet for higher religious studies. Four *rinpoches* (abbots) were included in the sample. A large majority of the interviewees spoke little or no English. They came from a considerable variety of backgrounds and included farmers, village workers, shopkeepers, small-government officials, and their wives and children. Some prominent citizens from Leh also were included in the interviews. Educational levels of respondents varied from no schooling at all to college education.

The sample included a highly varied cross section of Ladakhis from Leh and its surrounding areas, but, compared to the rest of Ladakh, the sample was better educated, had been more influenced by exposure to the "modern world," and included a smaller percentage of farmers.

Questionnaire and Interview Procedure

The questionnaire included two moral decision stories taken from Colby and Kohlberg (1987) and two social reasoning dilemmas taken from Selman (1979). The author presented his Ladakhi informant—Nawang Tsering Shakspo, J & K Cultural Academy, Leh—with a selection of moral and social decision stories and asked him to select those stories that appeared to him to be especially appropriate for Ladakhi settings. The stories were translated into Ladakhi and some of their details, such as names, were changed. Each of the four stories described a hypothetical dilemma in which the actions and expectations of the fictitious adults and children clashed with one another. The following is an example of a dilemma:

> Should desperately poor Stobdan steal *dakjun* (a difficult-to-attain, traditional-type medicine) from a doctor-druggist in order to save his deathly ill wife? (Heinz story, adapted from Colby and Kohlberg, 1987, vol. 2, p. 1)

The four vignettes were followed by an extensive series of standard questions that attempted to elicit the reasoning behind the interviewee's decisions. The questions were designed to raise issues such as the value of life, property, theft, mutual role-taking, interpersonal expectations and duties, punishment, guilt, promise and trust, conceptions of the subjective nature of persons (thoughts, feelings, motives), self-awareness and self-reflection, personality traits, self-esteem, dyadic relationships, anger, and friendship. Depending on a person's answers to these issues, numerous other questions were introduced.

In addition to the decision stories described above, three new dilemmas were constructed with the help of Wangchuk Shalipa. Sixteen of the interviews included the three new dilemmas. The three stories described a son who wanted to become a monk against the wishes of his mother, a young couple who had been married against the determined opposition of the husband's parents, and a woman who felt cheated after buying a shawl from a Kashmiri shopkeeper. Thirty-eight respondents were given an abbreviated version of Fowler's (1981) faith interview. In this interview, a person was asked about his/her life story, the meaning of life, the nature of his/her religious commitments, and various values and attitudes that constituted his/her faith. The faith interview included a wide variety of broad, open-ended questions that were used to elicit a person's overall outlook on life.

The interviews took place in schools, monasteries, the author's guesthouse and hotel, and, occasionally, in the fields. They usually lasted ninety minutes to three hours and were tape-recorded. Several interpreters were used throughout the research. More details about the research procedures and findings may be found in Gielen and Chirico-Rosenberg (1983).

Constructing the Ethos of Ladakh

Based on the interviews with seventy-two Ladakhis; the author's daily interactions with Ladakhis over a time period of six months; his participation in religious festivals; and a review of sacred writings, mythology, folk songs, and poetry, themes that were felt to reflect the prevailing ethos of traditional Ladakh were identified. The term *ethos* is used here to signify the characteristic spirit or "genius" of a people. This includes characteristic value systems, forms of moral reasoning, attitudes, and overall worldview. If intact, the ethos of a people makes its life meaningful and shapes basic attitudes toward existence and social life.

The author's observations were condensed into an "ideal-type" (Max Weber) representation of Ladakh's Buddhist ethos, which, in a coherent, but purified and exaggerated way, sums up the guiding spirit of Ladakh's traditional culture. The ideal-type representation of Ladakh's ethos then is contrasted with an equally purified and exaggerated representation of the culturally dominant ethos of modern, liberal America. By contrasting the worldviews, moral conceptions, and guiding spirits of such highly different societies, the inner coherence and spiritual beauty of Ladakh's ethos are highlighted. The comparison also points to the enormous psychological and spiritual distance that separates the Buddhist vision of inner and outer peace from the competitive, individualistic, assertive-aggressive vision of self-actualization that shapes life in modern capitalist America.

In Ladakh, the Buddhist vision of human nature, the situation of humans and other sentient beings in the illusory realm of suffering (*dukkha*), and the way to overcome suffering are frequently depicted in the form of the Wheel of Life. By understanding the symbolic messages encoded in the Wheel of Life, the reader will gain a preliminary understanding of the worldview that prevails among the Buddhists of Ladakh.

THE BUDDHIST WHEEL OF LIFE

Close to the entrance door of every large Ladakhi monastery, one finds a painting of the Wheel of Life, or Wheel of Becoming (*bhavacakra*), which, in a concrete, easily understandable form, sums up the worldview of Tibetan (Vajrayana) Buddhism, the religion that helps to shape the worldview and ethos of Ladakh. The author often has seen simple farmers standing in front of the Wheel of Life, paying special attention to those parts of the painting that depict humans suffering in the Buddhist version of hell or purgatory.

The wheel shows various beings in the six zones of existence, which together make up *samsara*, the realm of illusion, reincarnation, and suffering. Shinje (Yama), Lord of Death, holds the wheel in his claws and teeth, symbolizing that the attachment to *samsara* represents a kind of spiritual death. Fortunately, every sentient being is born with the possibility of reaching enlightenment or Buddhahood in this or a future lifetime, thus escaping the Wheel of Suffering.

At the hub of the wheel one can see three theriomorphic symbols representing "mental poisons." These are said to turn over the wheel (and thereby all existence) again and again, repeating forever the karmic stages of birth, death, and reincarnation. The three poisons are symbolized by a pig, a rooster or cock, and a snake. The pig symbolizes ignorance and illusion, the cock greed for life and lust, and the snake hate, aggression, envy, and jealousy. The three animals bite one another's tails, reflecting intrinsic links between the basic manifestations of evil/sin/mental poisons. The symbolic nature of the three animals is understood easily, since they represent a kind of "Buddhist id." Similar to Freud's theory, a combination of blind, sexual (cock), and aggressive (snake) impulses, together with ignorance (pig) or repression, forms the core of raw, unreconstructed human nature. But, unlike orthodox psychoanalysis, Tibetan Buddhism teaches that one can overcome the basic impulses of greed, hate, and attachment to egoistic goals by striving simultaneously for one's own liberation and the liberation of all other sentient beings. This can be accomplished by following the basic teachings (dharma) of Buddhism: meditation, empathy for the suffering of others, nonattachment to the illusions of this world, and the fundamental insight that the self is a steadily shifting mixture of karmic factors no more solid in substance than the ever-shifting clouds that drift across the endless Tibetan sky. All life is transitory, and attachment to the goods of this world chains a person to *samsara* and the steadily turning Wheel of Life. Actions motivated by greed, anger, hate, illicit lust, envy, jealousy, egoism, and ignorance make up the basic links of the chain.

Because human beings are ignorant, they need models of perfection. In Vajrayana Buddhism, the savior figure of the *bodhisattva* serves as such a model. *Bodhisattvas* are enlightened beings who, out of compassion for all sentient creatures, forgo their chance to enter the blissful, timeless state of nirvana that would take them out of the Wheel of Life. Instead, *bodhisattvas* descend to the earthly realm, where they are incarnated in *tulkus* and *rinpoches*, including the Dalai Lama and some of the abbots of Ladakh's monasteries. The Dalai Lama is considered to be a reincarnation of Avalokitesvara (Chenrezig), patron deity of Tibet and manifestation of the principle of compassion, a principle that pervades the teachings of Vajrayana Buddhism. In daily life, the principle helps to soften relationships between people and serves as an emotional glue, binding them together. Harsh self-assertion, insistence upon one's rights, and the expression of aggressive impulses are unlikely to occur as long as the principle of compassion holds sway.

Although certain details of the Wheel of Life can be understood by only the theologically trained monks, the interview results strongly suggest that the average Ladakhi has deeply internalized the basic interpretation of human nature and human destiny underlying the Wheel of Life.

INTERVIEW RESULTS AND THE OBSERVATION OF DAILY BEHAVIOR

The results of the interviews are summarized in Table 10.1, where they are contrasted with the ethos and goals of life prevailing among many modern, well-educated, liberal Americans. When inspecting Table 10.1, the reader is asked to keep the ideal-type nature of the constructions of the two visions of life in mind.

In their interviews the Ladakhi respondents emphasized their faith in the Buddhist religion, the pervasiveness of karma, the importance of acquiring religious merit while avoiding religious demerit (sin), and the desire for a good reincarnation. These themes were emphasized especially by the older respondents, who tended to show a stronger orientation toward religious concerns than the younger respondents did.

Table 10.1

Comparison of the Worldviews, Ethos, and Personality Characteristics of Traditional Ladakhis and Modern Liberal Americans

	Traditional Ladakhis	Modern Liberal Americans
ULTIMATE MEANING OF LIFE AND ROLE OF RELIGION IN PROVIDING MEANING:	Religion is accepted universally. There are no coincidences or chance events; everything is meaningful and ruled by karma. Life means suffering, but is only a kind of dream. Death is relative, not final. Not harming others leads to good reincarnation. Meaning exists objectively and has been revealed. *Why* questions and doubt are rare. Mystic contemplation leads to ultimate truth beyond all conceptualization, but systematic meditation is practiced only by some religious specialists.	The role of religion is limited and subject to debate. Death often is seen as the final tragedy. The meaning of life is chosen subjectively and never final (existentialism). Doubt frequent and *why* questions are encouraged. Life in this world is the only provable reality. Mysticism is seen as avoidance of the struggle of life.
NATURE OF MORALITY:	Morality is an objective system of prescriptions revealed to *rinpoche*, saints, etc. It is part of an impersonal system of retribution (*karma*) and reincarnation and is embedded in religion. Central emphasis is on not causing people and animals to suffer. Moral relativism, self-consciousness, and ideological reflection on ethical systems are rare (the latter is now increasing because of political-religious "competition").	Morality is a personal choice of competitive values that must be justified to one's self and others. Morality is more or less separate from religion. Aggressive and sexual feelings must be channeled constructively, but not denied.

	Traditional Ladakhis	**Modern Liberal Americans**
GUILT AND SHAME FEELINGS:	There is an unclear conception of guilt. Guilt feelings are rare or deeply submerged. There is limited self-blame, but strong feelings of shame and moral fear when breaking interpersonal norms or especially religious prescriptions. There is considerable tolerance for other people and worldviews.	Guilt feelings commonly are recognized and often strong. There is a strong ambivalence about the desirability of guilt feelings, and about tolerance. There is frequent self-blame and blame of others.
CONSCIENCE AND SENSE OF RESPONSI-BILITY:	There is an unclear or no conception of conscience. Correctly analyzed actions rather than conscience are emphasized. There is strong but not rigid sense of moral responsibility.	There is an inner voice that guides and checks antisocial desires and produces guilt feelings.
EXPRESSION OF DRIVES:	Expression of drives is muted. Greed, selfishness, lust, and ignorance are considered the basic causes of suffering, leading to bad reincarnation. Conflicts between id and super-ego are fairly low.	Acquisition, sexual assertiveness, strivings for pleasure, and toughness are necessary for personal happiness and self-actualization, although they create intrapersonal and interpersonal conflicts. There are intense conflicts between id and superego.

	Traditional Ladakhis	Modern Liberal Americans
EMOTIONALITY, ASSERTIVENESS, DEFENSIVENESS:	Generally emotionality, assertiveness, and defensiveness are found in low levels. There is emphasis on quiet dignity, detachment, serenity, inner quietness, and emptiness. Impatience, being high-strung, tense, and driven are uncommon. Assertiveness, aggressiveness, impulsivity, inner restlessness, emotional expressivity are all considered undesirable and uncommon. Introversion, shyness and timidity are fairly common.	There are high levels of emotionality, assertiveness, and defensiveness. Emotional expressivity in the service of personal goals is valued. Persons leading exciting and richly varied lives are often admired and emulated, even if they commit morally dubious actions.
CONCRETE LIFE GOALS:	Long life, health, reasonable prosperity, happiness, and acceptance from and convivial relationships with others are life goals.	Long life, health, monetary success, achievement, good relationships and a happy family life are life goals.
SYNERGY, COMPETITIVENESS, AND STRIVINGS FOR SUCCESS	There is a high level of synergy: Altruism leads to merit and better reincarnation (limited by pragmatic concern for immediate self-interests. Little competitiveness exists. Strivings for success are muted.	There is a low level of synergy. Competition and competitiveness are considered very important. Life often is seen as approaching zero-sum game. Strivings for success, fame, and achievement are widely admired.
SELF AND SELF-ESTEEM:	There is little focus on self. Self-esteem is seen as selfish and undesirable pride. Self is embedded in society. There are few basic identity conflicts. There is a limited awareness of inner feelings and inner conflicts and of inner personality change.	There is extreme individualism and emphasis on self's autonomy and self-esteem. Self-esteem is precarious, but the key to happiness. Frequent redefinitions of self are accompanied by identity conflicts.

	Traditional Ladakhis	Modern Liberal Americans
INDIVIDUALISM AND INDIVIDUAL CHOICE:	Individualism and individual choice are not emphasized.	Individualism and individual choice are emphasized very strongly.
INTERPERSONAL RELATIONSHIPS, ROMANTIC LOVE, DEPENDENCE FEELINGS, AND RELATIONSHIP TO AUTHORITY:	Concrete reciprocity and obedience are emphasized. Ambivalence is rare or not recognized. There is little emphasis on intimacy and romantic love in husband-wife relationships. Dependence on religious leaders easily is expressed. There is a nonhostile belief in authority.	Ambivalence in relationships is frequent. Relationships are romanticized with strong emotional expectations that may not be met. Obedience is seen as inhibiting self-actualization. Dependence feelings are seen as weakness and debilitating. There is a distrust of authority and very high divorce rates and family instability.
GENDER ROLES AND DIFFERENCES	Gender roles are seen as part of the natural order. There is moderate emphasis on gender differences.	Gender roles are contested and perceived as societal constructions subject to negotiation and personal choice.
HAPPINESS:	Happiness is frequent, though life is hard; feelings of depression and tragic conceptions of life are uncommon.	Happiness is rather difficult to achieve; feelings of depression, emptiness, futility are rather common against a background of general optimism.
FAITH, TRUST, TRUTHFULNESS:	There is a very strong faith and considerable interpersonal trust. "Naive" honesty and "innocence" is combined with an inability to manipulate others systematically.	Faith, trust, and truthfulness are variable; faith and trust are often uncertain; manipulation of others may be perceived as being necessary.

	Traditional Ladakhis	**Modern Liberal Americans**
IDEAL MODEL OF PERFECTION:	This is a compassionate saint (e.g., Tibetan Saint Milarepa), who has conquered his selfish passions (greed, envy, anger, hate, lust) and fears. Such figures are known through hagiographies, *jakata* (stories that describe events said to have taken place during the numerous previous lives of the Buddha), but perfection is considered unattainable by most.	The ideal model of perfection is a well-adjusted and self-actualized person who leads a full life, achieves much, and is admired by others.
ANOMIE AND DEVIANCE:	There are very low levels of anomie and deviance.	There are moderate levels of anomie and very high levels of deviance.
PROPENSITY TOWARD VIOLENCE:	Propensity is very low.	Propensity is very high.

The traditional (Buddhist) Ladakhi lives in a world where the Buddhist religion is accepted widely and provides a convincing explanation for human suffering. Karma, as an impersonal, objective system of moral retribution and reincarnation, is felt to connect all sentient beings. By showing compassion for the suffering of others (including animals), a person can acquire religious merit while experiencing a feeling of karmic interconnectedness with the web of life. This feeling undercuts natural tendencies toward self-assertion, selfishness, and acquisitiveness. Instead, conflicts between people are reduced and cooperation and interpersonal trust are emphasized. Vajrayana Buddhism creates situations of synergy, that is, situations in which the individual perceives that his or her goals merge with the goals of others. Benefiting other sentient beings is seen as also benefiting the self, because through such actions the individual advances on the path toward religious liberation and salvation. Selfishness is not abolished; rather, it is fused with altruism. In addition, the self is submerged in a network of concrete interpersonal obligations and reciprocal relationships, which may have a rather utilitarian character, but, nevertheless, stabilize the person's role in society (Heber and Heber, 1978). Thus, both concrete reciprocal relationships as well as religious sentiments shaped by synergetic conceptions hold Ladakh's society together.

The Ladakhi admires emotional restraint, quiet dignity, serenity, a certain detachment from the affairs of the world, honesty, discretion in human relationships, and religious piety. In husband-wife relationships, little emphasis is placed on intimacy or romantic love, since romantic love is based on the principle of emotion-driven individualism. Physical aggressiveness is extremely rare and confined to the occasional, usually harmless fight between young men under the influence of the local beer, Chang. Capital crimes are almost unknown (Norberg-Hodge, 1991). Feelings of envy do sometimes surface and then are externalized and projected in an unconscious process of ego-defense onto outsiders, witches, demons, ghosts, and neighbors with "the evil eye." In addition, fear of the "mouth of the people" (what other people will say) is rather common, especially among women. On the whole, however, Ladakhis are remarkably cheerful and good-humored in the face of harsh living conditions and troublesome situations. Diffuse feelings of depression are uncommon, although, in the interviews, a few girls and women expressed concrete feelings of unhappiness about extreme poverty, ill-treatment by stepparents, and misbehaving husbands.

While the Buddhist metaphysical doctrine of "no-self" is not understood fully by many of Ladakh's villagers, the doctrine is accepted widely on the psychological level. In the interviews, there was little focus on the self, and only limited awareness of inner feelings, conflicts, and systematic personality change over time. When asked to explain the meaning of *self-esteem*, only a very few Ladakhis fully grasped the question. Instead, most respondents equated self-esteem with undesirable pride and selfishness. They saw little place for people with "big egos" in their village communities.

Because competition is downplayed, competitive sports events rarely are held in the villages, with the exception of some archery "competitions" and polo games. The archery competitions turn out to be amiable affairs during which much beer is consumed, frequent laughter is heard, and many goals are missed by the arrow. Similarly, the traditional dances held during the competitions or on other occasions tend to be quiet and stately, rather than emotional and exciting.

Traditional child-rearing practices in Ladakh support the development of children and youngsters who are well suited to function in a noncompetitive, peaceful, and hardworking, though relaxed society. Norberg-Hodge and Russell (1994) conducted in 1980 a study of birth and child-rearing practices in the very traditional Zangskar area of Ladakh. They report that the parents they observed and interviewed generally took a calm, patient, relaxed, good-humored, and loving approach to the tasks of child-rearing. The young children only very rarely were pressured or punished, and few restraints were placed upon them. Having reached the age of 5 or 6, the children were introduced step-by-step to household tasks and were expected to take care of younger siblings in a nurturing, responsible way.

Tibetan societies such as Ladakh traditionally have assigned a relatively high status to women, especially when compared to their lower and more restricted positions in the neighboring societies of Muslim Kashmir and Pakistan, Hindu India, and Confucian China (Gielen, 1985, 1993). Traditional Ladakh was—and, to a much lesser extent, still is—a center of fraternal polyandry, a system of marriage in which a wife is married to two or more brothers. Such a system is simply unthinkable in the neighboring Muslim societies, since it assigns to the wife a central if delicate position in the web of family life. Relationships between Ladakh's men and women always have been more relaxed, open, cheerful, flexible, and egalitarian than corresponding relationships in other traditional peasant societies. This is not to say that there exists true equality between Ladakh's men and women, a situation that is, at any rate, unknown in the world of peasantry.

NONVIOLENT LADAKH IN LIGHT OF FROMM'S THEORIES

Our results show considerable agreement with Fromm's previously cited generalizations concerning the nature of peaceful, small-scale societies. As predicted by Fromm (1974), we find among the people of Ladakh "a minimum of hostility" and violence: very few serious crimes: a quiet but persistent disapproval of greed, covetousness, and exploitiveness: little competition and individualism: a good deal of interpersonal trust and cooperation based on synergistic religious sentiments, as well as concrete notions of reciprocity: "a general prevalence of cheerfulness and good humor": "a relative absence of depressive moods": a fairly easygoing attitude toward sex (this is discussed more fully in Gielen, 1993): a loving approach to child-rearing: and comparatively high levels of equality between the sexes. While Fromm's investigation focused predominantly on nonliterate societies, the present study extends his findings to a semiliterate society with an upper stratum of highly trained monks, government officials, and educators. It should be added that the results of the interviews are in agreement with the observations of long-term residents of Ladakh, including anthropologists (Kaplanian, 2001) and development experts (Norberg-Hodge, 1991). There also exists convincing historical evidence that Ladakh has been an internally peaceful society for many years (Friedl, 1984).

While there is considerable agreement between Fromm's descriptive generalizations and the findings of the present study, this does not mean that Fromm's overall interpretation of anthropological findings is correct. Fromm's work is based on a secondary analysis of observations by Benedict (1934/1959), Briggs (1970), Mead (1935), Montagu (1968, 1976), Turnbull, and others, that may be partially invalid (Fox, 1975; Freeman, 1983). Above all, Fromm and the anthropologists cited above do not sufficiently distinguish between surface behavior and the world of inner, invisible impulses, fantasies, preoccupations, and fears. In a given society, very low rates of violent behavior may perhaps coexist with a cultural world filled with violent imagery. Modern Japan represents a striking case in point. It has the lowest homicide and assault rates of any industrialized country, but the popular world of Japanese comics (*manga*) is saturated with sadomasochistic imagery of the most explicit kind.

In Ladakh, the calm, nonviolent world of everyday behavior is accompanied by a religious imagination that emphasizes a central tension between serenity and a kind of "frozen inner terror." The tension is expressed in the contrast between statues of calmly meditating Buddhas and vivid religious paintings filled with monsters, skulls, and corpses. This world of religious-artistic imagination symbolically expresses just those contradictory aspects of recalcitrant human nature that cultural relativists such as Benedict, Montagu, Mead, and socialization theorists such as Fromm have neglected in their search for unitary but reductionist sociocultural explanations of human behavior. While society exerts a pervasive influence on human nature, so does our evolutionary heritage. Human nature is not "empty," as the cultural relativists implicitly or explicitly would have us believe.

In contrast to Benedict, Fromm, Mead, and Montagu, Tibetan Buddhism does assume that greed, hate, envy, jealousy, and so on, are inherent in human nature. At the same time, it teaches that these tendencies can be channeled and ultimately overcome through the constant practice of compassion, disciplined meditation, and spiritual insight into the "empty" nature of the self. At a more concrete level, religious merit may be acquired through actions such as prayer, circumambulation of sacred places and buildings, giving to the *sangha* (monks and nuns), acts of charity, saving the lives of animals, and blessings from high-ranking lamas.

According to Tibetan Buddhism, beneath the magic-like forms of the phenomenal world there is only *tongpanyi*, that is, emptiness or the void. The ultimate goal of the human journey through life is the recognition that one's own true mind, *tongpanyi*, and nirvana are one and the same. This insight, to be sure, is difficult to realize at the experiential level, but once it is achieved, violence and greed vanish—not only in theory, but (often) also in practice. In contrast, modern psychology has been remarkably unsuccessful in reducing violence, greed, and self-centeredness. Why this is so will be discussed in the next sections, which compare the peaceful ethos of Ladakh to the much more violent and individualistic ethos of the United States, of which modern psychology is a partial manifestation. In the tradition of cross-cultural psychology, the Buddhist ethos of peace is held up as a mirror, in which to see in stark outline the American ethos of expansive individualism. The comparison underlines the potential for violence that always has been inherent in the American ethos, but that, in recent decades, has manifested itself in especially virulent forms.

AMERICAN HABITS OF THE HEART

As Table 10.1 makes clear, the ethos of Ladakh presents a striking contrast to the ethos of modern America. Given its capitalistic and highly competitive economic order, we find in American society a consistent endorsement of goals and tendencies such as profit seeking, material success, high consumption levels, status striving, self-directed achievement, and competitive assertive individualism. These economically inspired tendencies are often accompanied by more psychologically motivated strivings emphasizing the desirability of high self-esteem, self-actualization, self-expression, and the search for rich, varied experience as ultimate "psychological goods." Inherent contradictions between the widely endorsed, yet abstract moral goal of equality and the search for unfettered individual freedom, have in recent decades led to widespread family instability and disorganization, child abuse, criminal activities, sexual self-assertion, sexual deviance and pornography, and a variety of narcissistic, antisocial and depressive disorders. Among the most important of these ordinary practices of life or "habits of the heart" suggested by conditions of equality is individualism: "In ages of equality . . . everyman seeks for his opinions within himself . . . in the same ages, all his feelings are turned towards himself alone. . . . Individualism, at first, only saps the virtues of public life; but, in the long run, it attacks and destroys all others, and is at length absorbed in downright selfishness" (de Tocqueville, 1835–1840/1964, 173).

In a more recent book, *Habits of the Heart: Individualism and Commitment in American Life*, Bellah, Madsen, Sullivan, Swidler, and Tipton (1985) suggest that de Tocqueville's prophecies may have come true in recent years, and that after individualism's long march through America's history it has now grown malignant and self-destructive. They argue their point well, basing their conclusions on interviews with over 200 white, middle-class respondents as well as on their wide-ranging readings in sociology, social philosophy, religious studies, and history.

Habits of the Heart should not be taken merely as one of the many recent books deploring the new "me generation," "the culture of narcissism," "being your own best friend," "looking out for No. 1," and so on. For Bellah, Madsen, Sullivan, Swidler, and Tipton, individualism does not necessarily denote mere selfishness. At its best, it may stand for "our highest and noblest aspirations, not only for ourselves, but for those we care about, for our society and for the world" (Bellah et al., 1985, p. 142). Individualism, then, forms the very core of American identity. Americans cannot give up individualism, since this would lead them to abandon their deepest identity. Yet, at the same time, individualism in recent years has grown rancid. As the self has grown autonomous and free, seemingly unencumbered by heteronomous obligations and duties, it also has grown empty. It is no wonder that people encounter more and more difficulties in "finding themselves."

The authors of *Habits of the Heart* (Bellah et al., 1985) distinguish between four strands of individualism: biblical, civic, utilitarian, and expressive. Biblical individualism came to America when the first Puritans landed on its shores, and it celebrates the moral freedom derived from a direct, personal covenant between God and man. Civic individualism may be seen in Thomas Jefferson's republican ideal of a self-governing society of relative equals. Citizens participate in the polity because of self-interest and civic virtue, which are seen as being intertwined closely. Utilitarian individualism was made popular by Benjamin Franklin. Franklin's emphasis on hard work, effectiveness, and rational calculation survives in contemporary cost-benefit analysis, B.F. Skinner's behaviorism, social psychological exchange theory, and the cool calculations of the many young men and, nowadays, women who set out every year with the goal of "making it." Expressive individualism holds that each person has a unique inner self, a core of feeling or intuition that should be developed and expressed. Today, humanistic psychology and modern psychotherapy speak the romantic language of expressive individualism.

But, while the older forms of biblical and civic individualism connect the self to society, the newer forms of utilitarian and expressive individualism drive a wedge between the self and society. Biblical and civic forms of individualism connect the self to a community of memory. The self becomes embedded in a network of obligations and interdependent persons who participate in discussion and decision making against a background of vivid memories of the community's past. Modern expressive individualism merely creates lifestyle enclaves, groups of people who express their identities through shared patterns of appearance, consumption, and leisure activities. Members share, for the time being, a common lifestyle. These enclaves, however, do not create true interdependence between their members, nor do they reflect common histories across generations.

These enclaves have become the staging ground for a new self and a new, culturally dominant attitude toward life: the therapeutic attitude. The therapeutic attitude both derives from and drastically redefines the traditional American individualism. It celebrates a changing, "authentic," rather nebulous, inner self that has become the sole arbiter of all values and commitments. Through an act of intuition or cool calculation, the therapeutic self chooses actions and commitments because they feel good, because they get desired results, or because they increase feelings of self-worth. Conventional moral expectations are now perceived as authoritarian impositions that, because they come from outside the self, are claimed to be irrational and illegitimate. The therapeutic self has grown fluid and provisional, moving in and out of social roles without ever fully identifying with any of them.

To the therapeutic self, self-insight and self-acceptance are crucial yet precarious, and commitments are always temporary. Morality has become thoroughly relativistic, though the person must demand honesty from himself/herself and others. Honesty functions as a crucial virtue because it is needed to distinguish the demands of the subtle, inner voice of the "true self" from the cacophony of other, spurious selves that were imposed externally during the necessary, but deeply suspect, process of socialization. Bonds with parents are weakened because the parents too easily are experienced as jailers of the nascent self. Interpersonal relationships rest upon an underlying, temporary social contract, which constantly has to be renegotiated as the self changes. This situation destabilizes long-term relationships and undercuts the possibility of a stable family life.

Psychotherapy, with its search for the true self, has become the model for many other social relationships. It is a thoroughly flawed model, speaking the radical language of individualistic self-expression and moral relativism, but failing to ground the self in wider communities of memory. At the same time and at the societal level, the American community of memory is threatened with fragmentation because the partial voices of ethnic self-assertion undermine a cohesive commitment to the overriding goals of the republic.

AMERICAN HABITS OF THE HEART IN BUDDHIST PERSPECTIVE

From the Buddhist point of view, many of the individualistic goals propagated in postmodern America and by psychologists serve only to chain people more tightly to the revolving Wheel of Life, thereby keeping them in a state of spiritual ignorance, emotional restlessness, self-centeredness, dissatisfaction, and self-induced suffering.

While the idea of nonviolence forms the center of Ladakh's traditional way of life, it has been marginal to the American way of life, which instead emphasizes mastery over nature and energetic competition with others. While this vision has sent some Americans to the moon, it sends others to their graves and to the overflowing prisons. In contrast to Buddhism, which favors quiet contemplation and tries to extinguish the burning fever of the craving for life, the culturally dominant vision in America underlines the desirability of success, rich experience, and an energetically led life. Whereas the Buddhist teachings emphasize an introverted approach to self-mastery—hopefully leading to the evaporation of the restless, selfish ego—the American vision stresses self-control as a prerequisite for the extroverted mastery of life, tasks, and fulfillment of goals, needs, and desires.

Americans who are under the threat of being entirely confined within the solitude of their own hearts frequently end up in the offices of those reluctant modern soul-doctors, the psychologists. Their therapeutic attitude centers the attention of their clients on the vagaries of their personal histories, thereby reinforcing just those aspects of personality that, according to Buddhism, continue to imprison them in the narrow confines of their own egos.

While Buddhist doctrine has identified greed, hate, aggression, lust, envy, jealousy, pride, and spiritual ignorance as the ultimate sources of human unhappiness, modern American society has been ambivalent about the acceptability of these mental poisons, frequently rejecting them on the surface, but accepting them in practice. In return, it has paid a high price for this ambivalence. Among all fully industrialized nations, the United States places the greatest emphasis on competitive individualism and individual choice and, consequently, has the weakest family system; the highest rates of homicide, assault, and rape; the most serious drug problem; the highest rate of litigation; and the horrendous problem of child abuse.

Violence has always been close to the center of the American way of life, but in recent decades it has grown malignant because it feeds on the forces set free by the weakening of family life. More and more children grow up in fatherless households and poverty, conditions that invariably lead to high rates of delinquent behavior during adolescence and early adulthood (Bernard, 1993). The United States is the only major country that allows its citizens to buy a wide variety of weapons. It worships the gun, as depicted in numerous movies and television series. Modern American culture emphasizes self-expression and individual choice to such an extent that competing values of restraint, sobriety, tranquility, and responsibility have lost their guiding force among major segments of the population.

The emphasis on individual choice is just as prevalent among liberal segments of the population as among conservative ones. While there exist, of course, many "softer" areas in American society, the corrosive influences of unchecked individualism steadily have been eating away at the fabric of communal and civilized life. These influences are most visible among the ruins of inner cities, where a lack of visible success induces the marginal and the poor to desperate acts of self-destruction and violence against others. The corrosive influences remain more hidden among the middle classes and the wealthy, but nevertheless surface in the form of divorce, abandonment of families by fathers, abuse of children and spouses, alcoholism, depression, and narcissistic personality disorders.

CONCLUSION

In 1934, when Benedict published her book, *Patterns of Culture*, she meant to be scientifically neutral about the basic values of the three societies she described. But this is not what many of her readers concluded, since they correctly perceived that Benedict's own value preferences leaked through her seemingly objective comparisons. Benedict, as well as many of her readers, preferred the peaceful lifestyle of the Zuñi Indians over the power-oriented lifestyle of the Kwakiutl and the fear-driven treachery of the Dobus.

In contrast to Benedict, this author makes no pretense at being value-neutral. In his opinion, the peaceful ethos of the Ladakhis has much to teach modern Americans, whose comparatively violent way of life is morally suspect. The comparison between the Ladakhi and the American ethos suggests that the American ethos is inherently flawed. These flaws cannot be remedied by the currently popular prescriptions of liberal American psychology and social science. More multiculturalism; more freedom of choice for everybody; more autonomy for women; greater freedom to express one's sexual preferences; more tolerance for alternate lifestyles; greater emphasis on self-esteem and feeling good about oneself; more psychotherapy for lawbreakers, the confused, and the anxious; and a push for laws augmenting the rights of the individual at the expense of the group—whatever the moral justifications for these prescriptions, following them will do little to stop the social disorganization and violence proneness of modern American society. It may well make the situation worse. This is so because the prescriptions themselves reflect the excessive emphasis on freedom of choice and individualism that constitutes a root cause of social disorganization (Wallach and Wallach, 1983). The prescriptions are part of the problem, not part of the solution. Without being aware of it and without meaning to, psychologists share an indirect responsibility for the bloody tears that rend the fabric of American society. This ironic, deeply disturbing conclusion is bound to displease the many who look to psychology and the social sciences for solutions to pressing social problems; however, the important questions to ask are: Are psychologists willing to confront their complicity in the violent society of today, and will they be able to incorporate lessons learned from peaceful societies, such as Ladakh, in their search for a better tomorrow?

NOTE

1. This chapter compares the ethos of a small, slow-changing, traditional, agriculture-based society with that of a large, rapidly changing, modern, postindustrial society. It does not discuss the interplay between economic-technological forces and the "superstructure" of belief systems in the two societies. Anthropolo-

gists and Marxists frequently emphasize that the belief systems and personality structures of individuals in a given society reflect the adaptation of that society to ecological and economic factors. Such a reductionist argument cannot account for the peaceful ethos of Buddhist Ladakh: In the Suru Valley of Ladakh and in neighboring Baltistan (Pakistan), there live the Baltis, who must adapt to the same ecology as the Buddhists of Ladakh. Nevertheless, there exist striking differences in culture, worldview, and psychological makeup between the Shias of Baltistan and the Suru Valley on one hand, and the Buddhists of Ladakh on the other hand. "It is clear to even the casual observer that life sits heavy on the people" of Muslim Kargil in Ladakh (Rizvi, 1989, 155). The dour but emotional Shia distrust strangers, see themselves as perennial victims of the outside world, assign an inferior place to women, and preach a puritanical, emotional, often fanatic form of religion that is directed against drinking, dancing, and having fun. All this stands in stark contrast to the cheerful, easygoing tolerance of Buddhist life in Ladakh. The passions of the Shia are aroused more easily than those of the Buddhist Ladakhis, resulting in their greater readiness for violent action. The Baltis were converted, more or less forcibly, from Buddhism to Islam during the sixteenth and seventeenth centuries, suggesting that they may have been similar to the Buddhist Ladakhis prior to that time. They continue to speak a Tibetan language. It would be fascinating to do comparative psychological research in Baltistan and Buddhist Ladakh, since the overall situation resembles that of a natural experiment: Whereas the ecological and early historical circumstances are similar for the two peoples, their modern psychological and cultural adaptations are quite different.

REFERENCES

The author is grateful to the many Ladakhis who so patiently responded to difficult questions, to Donna Chirico-Rosenberg who conducted some of the interviews, and to Wangchuk Shalipa who served as interpreter. The author also wishes to express his appreciation to the University Seminars at Columbia University for assistance in the preparation of the manuscript for publication. Material drawn from this work was presented to the University Seminar on Moral Education. This chapter builds upon an article previously published by Gielen and Chirico-Rosenberg (1983).

Bellah, R.N., Madsen, R., Sullivan, W.M., Swidler, A., and Tipton, S.M. (1985). *Habits of the heart: Individualism and commitment in American life*. Berkeley, CA: University of California Press.

Benedict, R. (1959). *Patterns of culture*. Boston, MA: Houghton Mifflin. (Original published in 1934).

Bernard, P. (1993). *The psychological development of boys in father absent homes*. Unpublished B.A. thesis, St. Francis College, Brooklyn, NY.

Bonta, B.D. (1993). *Peaceful peoples: An annotated bibliography*. Metuchen, NJ: Scarecrow Press.

Bonta, B.D. (1997). Cooperation and competition in peaceful societies. *Psychological Bulletin, 121*(2), 299–320.

Briggs, J.L. (1970). *Never in anger: Portrait of an Eskimo family.* Cambridge, MA: Harvard University Press.

Carmichael, S. [Ture, K.], and Hamilton, C.V. (1992). *Black power: The politics of liberation.* Vancouver, WA: Vintage (reissue ed.).

Chagnon, N.A. (1983). *Yanomamö: The fierce people* (3rd ed.). New York, NY: Holt, Rinehart and Winston.

Chagnon, N.A. (1992). *Yanomamö: The last days of Eden.* San Diego, CA: Harcourt Brace Jovanovich.

Colby, A., and Kohlberg, L., with collaborators. (1987). *The measurement of moral judgment* (Vols. 1–2). Cambridge, GB: Cambridge University Press.

de Tocqueville, A. (1964). *Democracy in America* (H. Reeve, Trans.). New York, NY: Washington Square Press. (Original work published 1835–1840).

Edgerton, R. (1992). *Sick societies: Challenging the myth of primitive harmony.* New York, NY: Free Press.

Eibl-Eibesfeldt, I. (1979). *The biology of peace and war.* London, GB: Thames and Hudson.

Fowler, J. (1981). *Stages of faith: The psychology of human development and the quest for meaning.* San Francisco, CA: Harper and Row.

Fox, R. (1975). *Encounter with anthropology.* Harmondsworth, GB: Penguin.

Freeman, D. (1983). *Margaret Mead and Samoa: The making and unmaking of an anthropological myth.* Cambridge, MA: Harvard University Press.

Friedl, W. (1984). *Die Kultur Ladakhs erstellt anhand der Berichte und Publikationen der Herrnhuter Missionare aus der Zeit von 1853–1914.* (The culture Ladahks according to the reports and publication of the internment of missionaries from the years 1853–1914). Unpublished doctoral dissertation. Universität Wien, Vienna, Austria.

Fromm, E. (1973). *The anatomy of human destructiveness.* Greenwich, CT: Fawcett.

Fry, D.P. (1992). "Respect for the rights of others is peace": Learning aggression versus nonaggression among the Zapotec. *American Anthropologist, 94*(3), 621–639.

Gielen, U.P. (1985). Women in traditional Tibetan societies. *International Psychologist, 27*(3), 17–20.

Gielen, U.P. (1993). Traditional Tibetan societies. In L.L. Adler (Ed.), *International handbook on gender roles* (pp. 413–437). Westport, CT: Greenwood.

Gielen, U.P. (2001). Some themes in the ethos of traditional Buddhist Ladakh. In P. Kaplanian (Ed.), *Ladakh, Himalaya occidental: Ethnologie écologie* (rev. ed., pp. 114–126). Pau, France: Université de Pau.

Gielen, U.P., and Chirico-Rosenberg, D. (1983). Traditional Buddhist Ladakh and the ethos of peace. *International Journal of Group Tensions, 23*(1), 5–23.

Heber, A.R., and Heber, K.M. (1978). *Himalayan Tibet and Ladakh.* New Delhi, India: Ess Ess Publications. (Original work published 1903)

Howell, S., and Willis, R. (1989). *Societies at peace: Anthropological perspectives.* London, GB: Routledge.

Kaplanian, P. (2001). Réponse à la première version d'Uwe Gielen [Response to the first version of Uwe Gielen). In P. Kaplanian (Ed.), *Ladakh, Himalaya Occidental: Ethnologie écologie* (rev. ed., pp. 127–130). Pau, France: Université de Pau.

Kinloch, G.C. (1990). A comparative study of relatively open, harmonious societies. *International Journal of Group Tensions, 20*(2), 167–177.

Mead, M. (1936). *Sex and temperament in three primitive societies.* New York: William Morrow.

Montagu, A. (Ed). (1968). *Man and aggression.* London: Oxford University Press.

Montagu, A. (Ed.). (1978). *Learning non-aggression: The experience of non-literate societies.* New York, NY: Oxford University Press.

Norberg-Hodge, H. (1991). *Ancient futures: Learning from Ladakh.* San Francisco, CA: Sierra Club Books.

Norberg-Hodge, H., and Russell, H. (1994). Birth and childrearing in Zangskar. In J. Crook and H. Osmaston (Eds.), *Himalayan Buddhist villages: Environment resources, society and religious life in Zangskar, Ladakh* (pp. 519–532). Bristol, GB: University of Bristol.

Rizvi, J. (1989). *Ladakh: Crossroads of High Asia.* Delhi, India: Oxford University Press.

Rorbarchek, C.A. (1977). *Semai nonviolence: A systems approach to understanding.* Unpublished doctoral dissertation, University of California, Riverside.

Segall, M.H., Dasen, P.R., Berry, J.W., and Poortinga, Y.H. (1990). *Human Behavior in global perspective: An introduction to cross-cultural psychology.* Boston, MA: Allyn and Bacon.

Selman, R. (1979). *Assessing interpersonal understanding.* Cambridge, MA: Harvard—Judge Baker Social Reasoning Project.

Sponsel, L.E., and Gregor, T. (Eds.). (1994). *The anthropology of peace and nonviolence.* Boulder, CO: Lynne Rienner.

Thomas, E. (1958). *The harmless people.* New York, NY: Random House.

Turnbull, C. (1963). *The forest people: A study of the Pygmies of the Congo.* New York: Simon & Schuster.

Wallach, M., and Wallach, L. (1983). *Psychology's sanction for selfishness: The error of egoism in therapy and theory.* New York, NY: W.H. Freeman.

11

Violence against Women in Africa: Impact of Culture on Womanhood

Wilhelmina J. Kalu

INTRODUCTION

Throughout the world, violence is on the rise. The increase is described as unprecedented, with millions of people affected by various degrees of economic, political, military, ethnic, religious, and cultural violence. *Violence* is defined as harsh conduct, mistreatment, or unlawful use of force that is intense and vehement. Basically, most forms of violence occur as the results of either power confrontations or violations of human rights and dignity. Violence can be perceptible or invisible and subtle. It can be occasional or nurtured within organizational structures. It can slip easily into an adaptable, pervasive, tenacious, and brutal mode.

Violence is a harsh element in human relationships. It is destructive and has long-term negative consequences that can last a lifetime. Without intervention it could become self-perpetuating, breeding a vicious cycle in subsequent generations. This is partly what is observed in the African setting. A major focus of this chapter is violence against women. Women are often targets and victims of violence both in relationships with men and in social, economic, political, and other areas of society. Compound effects are noticeable, and, therefore, violence against women has been described a major public health problem for the world (Ram, 1999).

Africa presents a rich spectrum of ethnic and cultural lifestyles, with traditions that are life affirming and supportive, as well as those that are life denying, negative, and traumatic. In many parts of Africa, violence against women is a common phenomenon, occurring in various forms and often engraved in the psyche of women as an inevitable part of womanhood. Until about a decade ago, women were virtually voiceless. The occasional protests were ignored, quieted down, or covered by silence. This chapter is a discussion of the dimensions of violence during the life span of the female in Africa. It focuses on the interplay of ethnic traditions (culture and religion) and modern development (economy and governmental structures). The discussion is in three broad phases of girl child, adolescent girl, and adult female in order to highlight principal features of violence. The discussion draws, for the most part, on the Nigerian experience. Emergent patterns in violence against women which are gender related are also examined.

GIRL CHILD

In Africa, culture determines the concepts of maleness and femaleness. A girl child is born into the predetermined low status of a female and is socialized to accept male domination. A girl's status is that of a helper in the household or one who facilitates the care of all persons. In the Nigerian experience the firstborn female child occupies a special position that enables her to have some measure of impact on family and communal decisions. She therefore enjoys a great deal of closeness to parents as part of her training. Subsequent girls are resigned more or less to the helper category. From the early age of 5, the girl child can help carry or look after a new baby. As she grows up her play period is reduced with the increased allocation of household chores and by being confined to the food or meal preparation area. Admittedly, the cultural contexts have been contested in recent times by the educational policies of various modern African states. The school enrollment of girl children has increased recently in most of Africa as part of the Universal Basic Education programs. This is a vast improvement from the education of girl children a decade and a half ago (Etta, 1994; UNICEF, 1995).

However, at every stage of education, from primary to tertiary, the proportion of female enrollment is on the decline. One explanation is the socialization process (Etta, 1994). Girls are socialized into prioritizing service to the male, family, and community. The pursuance of her interest is discouraged. The combination of this mindset with the pressure of household chores underlies poor school attendance and performance deficiencies. Studies show that girls perform poorly in school subjects that require greater study time and practice and that carry more assignments. Examples abound in the physical sciences (Obanya, 1981). Parents are more likely to encourage the male child than the female child to study. Boys are released from the ordeal of time-consuming house chores. Thus, unless someone else is responsible for housework, the only time a girl could do any reasonable schoolwork is in school itself. It is, therefore, understandable that female enrollment in the physical sciences and related professional courses such as engineering remained low until the 1980s. Indeed, female enrollment in engineering and agriculture was a rarity as late as the 1970s in many Nigerian universities (NUC, 1992).

The greater likelihood of poor schooling is not the only injustice experienced by girls. They also serve as a debt payer in families. When a family is unable to pay a debt, a daughter is sent to live and serve the person and family owed until the debt is repaid. Such a debt could be owed to a shrine or deity for services rendered to the family through its priest or priestess. Where a debt is not paid, she becomes the property of the debtors, and so lives in the premises of the shrine with the priest (Kalu, 2003). In this position she often is exposed to physical or sexual abuse, as she becomes the target of venting frustration and of blame when chores are not well executed, especially because of immaturity. Girls from poor families are specially recruited into harrowing experiences as household helpers for families in urban centers, in exchange for their education or skill training (Kalu, 2000).

Within the last decade, the collapse of many African economies threw many families into the grips of poverty and destitution. As a result, the girls have been sent out as child labor to sell items on the street and in motor parks to supplement family income. Sometimes they wash mountains of dirty dishes and pots at local restaurants in order to obtain food to eat or leftovers to take home to their families (Women's Rights Monitor, 1995). In such situations, their expectations of life are reduced to unwanted pregnancies, the sex trade, or early marriage.

Girls are often victims of incest or rape by relatives. This occurrence is shrouded in secrecy to protect the family image from the stain of abomination or family disorder. Manipulation and threats of dire consequences enforce the secrecy of these incidents. Society refuses to acknowledge and face this situation. The harmful effects of these events, such as shame, extreme anxiety, self-accusation, guilt, and sometimes diagnosis of sexually transmitted diseases can persist into adulthood. Mothers and guardians often fail to protect the girl child because they are concerned predominantly with protecting the status of the father and the male offender. With disclosure, the girl child is caught in a web of accusation, pain, shame, and stigma. The African Network for Protection and Prevention against Child Abuse and Neglect (ANPPCAN) has set up monitoring centers in Nigeria where such cases can be reported (Kalu, 1996).

Beyond psychological violence, the girls are subjected to strict surveillance and supervision. This leads to frequent beating and physical violence from parents, older sibling, and teachers, since cultural norms prescribe beating as a form of disciplining children. The rod, as means of correction, has not been challenged. Thus, no conscience is trammeled by the cry of the child. Much to the contrary, neighbors blame the misdemeanors of a child on the parents who spare the rod. Adults, especially male adults assert their superiority based on either age or gender by easy resort to physical abuse on those younger than they, especially girls (Kalu, 1999).

ADOLESCENT GIRL

For the female child, the period of adolescence is a period of intense harassment. She becomes a target for a traditional but violent act of ritual
sacrifice that often requires a virgin or removal of bodily organs. In addition, there has been a recent upsurge of rape of young secondary-school
girls and female undergraduate students. There also has been an increase
in the number of secondary-school girls and female undergraduates who
are enticed into entering sexual partnerships with older men for monetary
gain. In many parts of Africa there is increased violence in schools among
male youth, in the form of gangs, secret societies, and confraternities,
whose targets are mostly young women (Kalu, 2000). Last, in some parts
of Africa, and amongst several ethnic groups in Nigeria, the period of
adolescence is the phase for early marriages, marriage preparation, and
initiation, which involves female circumcision

Within the last couple of years the abduction, sacrifices, and foiled abduction and attempted abductions of young girls who are considered to be
virgins and who are intended to be used in sacrifices has been a focus of
intense discussions in Nigerian news media and church and community
groups. However, in traditional African religions, some celebrations (such
as the coronation or burial of a king or the productions of powerful
charms) involve the sacrifice of young maidens. Traditional religion,
therefore, provides a cover that encourages silence and provokes the fear
of evil personal and family repercussions should information on such
plans or activities be disclosed.

Abduction for ritual sacrifices is common in urban and rural areas
(Women's Rights Monitor, 1995). Abductors may be shopkeepers who lure
young girls into the inner rooms of shops in search of commodities for
purchase or they may be the drivers of the taxis or buses in which the girls
travel with the other passengers, who tend to be part of the abductor's
group. Apprehended abductors sometimes have changed the vehicle's
destinations and have suffered mob justice, lynching, and severe beating,
before rescued by the police. Sometimes the shrine, which is the destina-
tion of the abductors, is traced and set on fire.

Haynes (1996) has drawn attention to the resurgence of ethnicity and religion into the current African political arena. A certain manifestation of
this in Africa is the implosion of cultism into the modern space. It has
been dubbed as the "villigization" of the modern political space, as people
use religious means from their villages to compete for resources in the
modern marketplace. This phenomenon may be due to the collapse of the
economy and the softness of the African state. It is true that increased violence is a signal of a broken social order. When this occurs, there is a noticeable tendency to resort to old coping mechanisms. Due to their
cultural background and traditional African socialization practices that

emphasize virginity before marriage for both genders, young girls are at the receiving end of violent actions. Shrines usually demand these.

Another cause of increased social violence is that by the time young boys move from secondary to tertiary educational institutions, their moral beliefs may be distorted severely. Boys learn to accept rape as a means of taming shrews or girls who reject their demands. This occurs in the context of a culture in which rape brings shame on both the individual and the family, and crushing guilt, fear, and humiliation on victims. Rape of young girls has escalated in Nigerian universities to a major form of violence against women. A study on patterns of campus violence in Nigerian universities found that rape and assault of women together was the third most common crime (13%), after armed robbery and extortion together (14%), and drugs and acid attacks together (19%). Religious riots and intimidation had a low incidence rate of 1.2 percent and 1.4 percent, respectively (Kalu, 1996). Rapes usually occur at night in parks, cars, and offices, or men's dormitories where girls are visiting people they know. Cases of rape occur predominantly in the southern university campuses where there is widespread cult-gangsterism among students. Cult boys target both married and unmarried female students as part of their membership exploits or as means to "tame" certain girls. The poor state of campus security and the police force, as well as poor street lighting and frequent blackouts from power failures help to enable this situation. Moreover, corruption allows some of those apprehended, especially those from wealthy families, to buy their freedom and escape legal consequences. There are cases in which the female victims are accused of encouraging the male perpetrator by their behavior and their attire. This is a common cultural ploy used to discourage women from appearing in public. The cultural prescription is for young girls to stay at home. University campuses located in northern Nigeria with predominantly Muslim populations exhibit a different pattern of social violence against women based on fundamentalist religious convictions. Namely, Muslim youth assault Muslim females who date Christian males (Kalu, 1996).

Early marriages are prescribed and enforced culturally. Studies have investigated the massive forms of violence enacted against these young women in their marriages. The deference system demands absolute obedience to husbands and *purdah*, or seclusion. These demands are enforced, physically. Educated women suffer more because of a higher tendency to rebel.

In most countries, commentators have noted an increasing moral decline. Long, drawn civil wars, drought, migration to urban centers, and other disruptive forces have attacked traditional value systems and have created values that breed anomie, obliterate restrictive and punitive social controls, and leave the young in confusion. Young girls in secondary schools are enticed with money and expensive gifts into relationships with men the age of their fathers. They are collected from boarding schools, where supervision is lax, to attend social functions in hotels. Poor communication between parents and children help to cover up these practices until a school disciplinary action, teenage pregnancy, or abortion complication results (Kalu, 2001). Rural communities as well as the urban poor suffer the most. They tend to have high birth rates and families with limited incomes. The educational opportunities and life goals of these young girls are limited, and many young girls accept a lifestyle of promiscuity. In urban areas, marriage is a means to acquiring wardrobes and luxury items that improve the appearance and self-image of young girls. Some use marriage as a means to finance their education or generate income for other members of the family. However, this constitutes a high-risk lifestyle that poses great health hazards for young lives. Young girls have little information on contraceptive methods and limited availability to birth control. Thus, unsafe contraception and abortion are rife among young girls. Many are exposed to sexually transmitted diseases early in life (Kalu, 2000).

Moral laxity and prostitution are not the only threats to young women's health in Africa. Early marriages occur for religious, sociocultural, and economic reasons as well. Traditional culture frowns on young girls having children outside of wedlock. When it occurs, it invariably closes the door to getting suitors or married. The repercussions also extend to other female members of such a family. The fear of this leads many families to arrange early marriages for young daughters. A household survey of married Muslim women found about 14 percent married at the age of 12 or below, and 58 percent married at 13 and 14 years old. Over 54 percent of females had their first pregnancy between 15 to 16 years of age (Kisekka, 1990a). For most married young women this means the end of their education and career plans. In order to keep within *purdah* regulations, women must attend solely to the job of raising a family and refrain from unnecessary public exposure. Not surprisingly, Kisekka's (1990a) study found that 86 percent of the women were illiterate. Harrison (1990) found that impoverished women who became pregnant in their early teens suffered high rates of miscarriage, eclampsia, anemia, and obstructed labor. Young girls in early marriage also suffered vesico vaginal fistula (VVF), a condition of chronic incontinence that is linked with frequent pregnancies. To make matters worse, these women often are abandoned by their husbands because of their unpleasant health conditions and the costs of medical treatment.

Female genital mutilation, which recently has attracted much international attention and debate, is practiced in many areas of Africa, especially in Muslim areas. It is performed by traditional circumcisors, or birth attendants, who charge fees for their services. The instruments used are knives and blades, which rarely are sterilized and often are infected from the previous use. The operations are performed without anesthesia. All this is without regard to the fact that the exercise occurs in ethnic groups that by tradition and religion practice polygamous marriages, with the man having several wives. There are three types of female circumcision. One involves the cutting of the vagina. This is considered the mildest form of female genital mutilation. The second involves the cutting of the clitoris and all or part of the labia minora. The third version is infibulation. This is considered the worst form of circumcision. It consists of the cutting of clitoris, labia minora, the anterior two-thirds and some of the medial part of the labia majora. The sides of the wound are then sewn together leaving a small opening. This brutal surgery takes a long time to heal and is prone to infection. On the wedding night a husband is demanded by tradition to have prolonged sex so that blood must flow in the genitals to confirm the bride's virginity. Young brides are exposed to infection including sexual diseases and AIDS (Hosken, 1987). Female genital mutilation encouraged by tradition plunges many young African girls and women into trauma and a harrowing life and marital experience. The upsurge of modern violence of sexual harassment combines with traditional violence in the lives of many young girls.

ADULT FEMALE

The African woman experiences in adulthood a full impact of the woman-marriage-inheritance cultural package and its associated status. The traditional gender hierarchy and its attendant power relationships have designated women to a low status. In some cases, traditional practices that discriminate against women have been incorporated into the legal system. For example, many of the northern states of Nigeria, whose populations are predominantly Muslim, have adopted *Sha'ria*, traditional Islamic law based on an interpretation of the Koran. The *Sha'ria* violates the rights of women in four ways. First, it permits men to punish their wives so long as he does not cause her grievous bodily harm. In some areas, this has been interpreted as meaning a husband can injure or maim his wife without censure, so long as he does not kill her outright. Second, it prohibits women from appearing in public without being accompanied by her husband or another male relative. Third, women are not allowed to be in the company of any men who are not their husbands or their male relatives at any time. Fourth, women are required to keep their hair and bodies covered. A failure to comply with these laws leads to severe punishment (Falobi, 2001).

This status can be elevated only to some extent by marriage, ritual position, and old age. Old women in the community whose compatriots are already dead attain "manhood" and are admitted into membership of the council of elders. Recent attempts to explain the political importance of

Igbo women from the southeastern part of Nigeria, have merely shown that there are specific functions that can be taken up by women, often through manipulation. The arguments fail to show that Igbo and most African women are not marginalized and dominated by men folk in traditional politics (Anyanwu and Agunwa, 1993). Women cannot, for instance, hold *Ofo*, the Igbo ancestral symbol of authority, right conduct, justice, and affirmation of the relationship between the living and the dead. The *Ofo* holding is only for men, who are the inheritors of the ancestors and the authority figures as heads of family, clan, compound, and village. Men, therefore, own and control the supernatural (Anyanwu and Aguwa, 1993). Women cannot own land and so have a propertyless status. There are some mitigating influences embedded in religious ideologies, such as the emphasis on the role of first daughter, known as the *umuada*. This is part of the covenant made by the fathers and the ancients, with deities to set these women apart for their service as daughters of the land. They, therefore, can hold titles associated with this position, such as *queen* or *omu*. This is an elite position in which women serve as custodians and enforcers of rituals for the benefit of the fathers. Their domain of operation is largely women's affairs in the community.

Marriage Practices

The Igbo worldview sees women as helpmates to be protected, controlled, and guided in public affairs. This is typical of the Nigerian and African view. Women appear and speak in male discussion forums by invitation. Women often receive derogatory names and titles like *Adaanyinwanyi* (our daughter–our child–our woman, in Ibo language), and *Yoo* (which means consent, in the Ga language of Ghana). Women therefore continue to receive messages that they occupy inferior positions and have low status. The payment of bride price, which the groom's family may have to bid down, ushers women into marriage as a purchased commodity in the eyes of the groom and his family. This often makes the married woman an object of blame for the discharge of frustrations, especially when the extended family structure is weakened. For instance, most marital counseling problems revolve around the husband's relatives and siblings' intense hostilities toward the wife. These relatives consider the reduction of finances and of other forms of assistance from a married male relation to be caused by the wife (Kalu, 1999). Accusations mount from all sides, leading to devastating marital and psychological stress. Often, the appeals for intervention by other parties, such as elders or heads of the family, end with an admonition for the woman to be subject to the husband or be blamed for insubordination. This leaves many women even more confused and anguished.

Marital Violence

Within Nigerian society, physical aggression is used freely to settle issues in interpersonal relationships. Physical and verbal fights are common at all ages. This spills over into the marital relationship. The issue of battered wives or domestic violence is not considered important. Husbands or cohabiting partners do not consider wife-beating to be an assault. In a society that emphasizes male leadership, dominance, and female submission, many women are too ashamed to disclose information about abuse. It is more important to preserve the family image. But, more often, the abuse is ultimately blamed on the woman's failure to be submissive, or submissive enough, to her husband. Some come to accept the beatings as an inevitable part of marriage and women's status in society. A woman's role and value are related to her ability to give, serve, and satisfy the needs of others.

While tradition sanctions the practice of wife-beating, obnoxious as it may be, there is a fine line drawn between this and the vicious physical abuse many women suffer, which is sometimes accompanied by the restriction from the money needed for food and general welfare. UNICEF (1995) considers violence against women as the greatest abuse. A study by Kalu (1993) identified some characteristics of families in which the wives are battered. Over 10 percent of these incidents occurred in monogamous marriages, compared to the 29 percent that occurred in polygamous marriages. Some of the reasons the men gave for wife-beatings included maltreatment or inability of the wife to take care of the needs of the husband (33%), poor cooking (11%), misuse of money (22%), and giving birth to baby girls only (25%). Some of the reasons the women gave for why they were beaten include confrontations related to family neglect and cruelty by husband (42%), his provision of food money (13%), infidelity (22%), and drunkenness (11%). For many working women, the pressure of economic changes in the society (which resulted in the need for a dual income), combined with the strain of taking care of extended family members and the practices of separate spending by spouses and sole control of income by husbands created an environment of domestic violence.

High Fertility and Women's Health

African society emphasizes large-sized families. Reproduction is a social, cultural, and religious duty. There is a plethora of female and fertility deities who require carefully maintained rituals and practices for their blessings on the land and people. Women are showered with praise for bearing children and are socialized to feel incomplete without marriage and children. Childlessness is considered a reproach and many women without children face humiliating healing rituals, suffer abuses, or made vulnerable to exploitation by prayer houses and the male priesthood and healers. The average number of children desired by Nigerian families has remained around six for over four decades (Oppong, 1983; Kalu, 1987). Women expect to spend at least twenty years of their reproductive lives bearing a child every second, third, or fourth year. In many ethnic groups women who bear ten children are celebrated and receive gifts from the community. Married women between the ages of 20 and 45, a period of frequent childbearing are, saddled with the burden of balancing the demands and stresses associated with homemaking and income generating. It is common to find women who are pregnant or with newborn babies among undergraduate students in the universities (Kalu, 1989a).

Several studies show a high infant mortality rate in sub-Saharan Africa and that children are more likely to die if they are born less than two years after the mother's last delivery or to a very young or relatively older woman (Pebley and Millman, 1987; Omran, 1987). Thus, high fertility places infants as well as mothers at risk. It is estimated that 75,000 Nigerian women die during pregnancy and childbirth every year, which is about one death every ten minutes. For every woman who dies, 20 more are disabled or health impaired as a result of childbirth. An estimate of 1.5 million women are affected in total. A Nigerian woman, therefore, has one-in-twenty chance of dying during pregnancy and faces this situation about six or seven times in her life. In comparison, such chances are about one in 10,000 for a woman in Europe or North America (Kisekka, 1990a, 1990c). When the woman in Nigeria is illiterate, malnourished, poor, and has had more than four births rapidly, the chances of death and deformity are greater. Where she is under 18 or over 35 years old, these chances are higher (Kisekka, 1990c; Harrison, 1990).

Health practices related to childbearing women are fraught with violations of human rights and dignity. Midwives, traditional birth attendant clinics, and hospitals are ill equipped for effective and immediate treatment or operative intervention in the event of complications during the delivery or postnatal care process (Harrison, 1990). Traditional maternal health practices; the use of herbs, charms, and traditional chemicals; and pronouncements of healing phrases by priests and birth attendants are practiced widely in the population. Where there are medical facilities like hospitals, some women prefer to combine these with traditional services. There is evidence that traditional birth attendants often use rusted, unsterilized instruments. They cannot recognize symptoms of pregnancy complications until they are severe. For instance, they do not associate edema with blood pressure or eclamptic fits but, instead, attribute this condition to bad blood or bad water or see it as an indication of a big baby or a baby's gender. However, these diagnoses are reassuring to women, who therefore prefer traditional treatments for pregnancy ailments over formal care. Traditional treatments include the appeasement of the gods; the use of a particular leaf juice in the eyes, nostrils, and mouth or on the legs; and special herb drinks and baths. Thus, there is room for exploitation of vulnerable pregnant women through traditional treatment. By the time their health deteriorates and they are transferred to hospitals, it is already too late to benefit from formal medical assistance (Kalu, 2001).

The choice regarding the use of formal or traditional health practices is often relegated to the husband. A husband's permission is needed to change services or go to a hospital, even when complications arise. This permission often is delayed because husbands are traditionally not present at the delivery (Kalu, 2001). The choice and use of birth control, the observance of a traditional two-year postpartum abstinence period, and the long periods of lactation in breast feeding infants (between 14 and 20 months) are also dependent on cooperation of husbands. The degree of conjugal authority experienced by women is limited (Kalu, W.J., 1987; Kalu, 1989b). Women therefore are deprived of control over their reproductive lives.

Hospitals and clinics, especially in urban areas, tend to give women necessary information on hygiene, lifestyle changes, nutrition, and personal and baby health care. This information facilitates maternal health. Prenatal care has been associated with a twenty-two–fold decrease in the maternal mortality rate in Nigerian women (Harrison, 1990). However, overcrowding conditions in hospital and clinics lend to harsh treatment when there are not enough chairs. Payment may be demanded before certain services and supplies (soap, dressings, infusion sets, and gloves) are provided.

Sociocultural demands for male heirs and the inheritance of property put pressure on many women to have male children. Many African women want more than one son. It has been found that women's complicity in high fertility can come from the knowledge that a man can get a second wife and children outside the marriage, and competition among co-wives in polygamous marriages is fierce (Kisekka, 1990b). Thus, women with an average life span of 50 may expect to spend the majority of the years between ages 15 and 50 conceiving, carrying, delivering, and suckling infants (Ware, 1983). Studies have found a relationship between women's mental health and pregnancy (Kisekka, 1990c). Women who attend prenatal clinics attempt to discuss their domestic and social problems even when no questions are asked. About 24 percent of these women displayed psychiatric disturbance, mainly of the psychogenic type as they had suffered traumatic deliveries like caesarean sections, still births, or difficult labor (Kisekka, 1990c). Traditional and socioeconomic factors therefore nurture the persistence of unsafe maternal health practices and expose women to the brunt of cultural, gender, psychological, marital, and physical violence.

Labor Force

The role of African women in the labor force hardly is recognized. Government computations ignore women's contributions to the productive labor force. The recognition of women's role as a server and a helper in the family and home limits their role in the workforce to domestic activities, although they also are involved in subsistence agricultural activities. In the urban areas, a woman is likely to gain wage-labor or salaried employment if she is educated sufficiently or involved in a market-oriented labor force. The former category puts her in the public sector of employment, such as business firms and government institutions. The latter is in the informal sector and involves self-employment, producer cooperatives, trading, and marketing from home.

Time use surveys on total labor force have brought forth interesting information about African women. For instance, domestic activities constitute a minimum of 25 percent of the total labor expenditure of women. This includes meal preparation and the care of children, the home, clothing, and the health of household members. When activities like water collection, firewood collection, and food processing for household consumption are added, domestic activities form 45 percent of total labor time. Firewood collection accounts for 8.4 percent of gross output value of subsistence production. Evaluation of women subsistence activities, not including domestic ones amount to 54 to 70 percent of total household income in rural Africa. Domestic activities of women contribute another 30 percent of household income (Goldschmidt-Clermont, 1986).

Women also handle about 70 percent of the agricultural labor. According to the above survey, they handle 27 percent of the field preparation, 66 to 70 percent of planting and harvesting, and 95 to 100 percent of weeding, processing, and storage. These are the more time-consuming tasks that are handled on a daily basis. Men tend to limit themselves to 73 percent of field preparation and 30 percent of planting and harvesting, with hardly any involvement in weeding, processing, and storage (Goldschmidt-Clermont, 1986). Women's strength and energy is taxed and their contributions are unrewarding and unacknowledged. This is an abuse of women's health and a form of economic violence.

The urban labor force reflects an increasing participation of women in professional employment, from positions as sales workers to administrative executives (Fapohunda, 1983). Limited education and high levels of illiteracy amongst women effect access to employment opportunities in the modern sector. About 64 percent of women and 41 percent of men in sub-Saharan Africa are still illiterate. Despite this, women traders swell the Nigerian labor force and they constitute over one-half of the economically active female population in West Africa (Fapohunda, 1983). Women's response to economic hardships such as those experienced under structural adjustment programs is to take on more work, such as producing processed and cooked food items for sales. They also sell a whole range of commodities. Young children, especially girls, provide assistance. Girls work as apprentices to learn skills in exchange for basic education. They are more involved in selling on the street than boys are (Women's Right's Monitor, 1995). This creates a scenario in which women inadvertently become engaged in violence against younger women.

Economic changes therefore assist in the extension of women's multiple roles. The coexistence of high fertility; childbearing and care functions; increased economic, domestic, employment, family, and sociocultural obligations; and education or self-improving activities, leaves many women exhausted at the end of the day and unable to discharge many of these functions effectively. Nigerian women employed in the public services find that relational conflict with live-in relatives and the lack of adequate child care for infants under 6 months age, are particular areas of difficulties in the care of the home (Kalu, W.J., 1987). Although they recognized the health hazards to which infants were exposed, they were not prepared to take a temporal leave of absence from employment. Rather, they offered suggestions for governments and employers to assist working mothers through policy changes, provision of professional substitute care arrangement for children, and loans for the purchase of personal transport that would enable trips home to be made during break periods at work, for adequate supervision of the home. Employment and education are some of the few avenues that give these women a measure of autonomy, self-esteem, achievement, and fulfillment. They are also mitigating influences on the somewhat harsh experiences in which they are involved. Thus, in several ways, their experiences with labor force participation constitute economic, physical, and psychological violence against women.

Widowhood Practices

Widowhood practices in Africa denote the most excruciating form of psychological violence against women. Widowhood is a sudden change in the status of a married woman because of the death of her husband. It is a major life crisis, as the woman is faced with new experiences, including final separation from a life partner or companion, end of conjugal relationships, and the sudden thrust into the task of decision making, which often have far-reaching effects. It is a period of great personal pain, grief, and mourning. A support network and an environment of understanding are needed to facilitate the adjustment process for the bereaved family, and extended family members and friends often serve in this manner (Kalu, 1989b; Kalu, 1990). Most people who come to the home of a bereaved person also seek to aid in this adjustment. However, the traditional authority that guides the network of relationships in Africa often works against the lending of help to a widow.

According to African tradition, death is an important family and communal celebration because it marks a departure from the world of flesh, to that of the ancestors and spirits. The cultural worldview here holds a cyclical perception of time. Those living in the flesh depart at death to join the ancestors, who live as spirit beings. These ancestors may decide to return to the flesh state through reincarnation (Kalu, O.U., 1987). Both the ancestors and those living in the flesh continue to operate and influence life on earth through different modalities. Ancestors are worshipped and considered protectors of their descendants and mediators with the gods. Death is thus an opportunity for a kin group and community to celebrate their ancestors. The activities surrounding burial and funerals are entirely the affair of the extended family, or clan. The nucleus family unit and the widow are merely instructed in their roles, which, according to tradition, are often marginal ones. Most of the information on requirements is given in piecemeal fashion according to the dictate of customs and tradition.

The cultural practices associated with mourning, bereavement, and widowhood are varied and are often harrowing experiences for widows. The bereavement practices commence immediately after the death of the spouse with the gathering in the household of the extended kin, who organize and supervise all pre- and post-burial arrangements. Mourning often starts immediately after the internment of the corpse, beginning with a period of required confinement to the house. Confinement lasts a specific length of time, perhaps a year, and begins and ends with particular rituals. For example, the woman's head is shaved at the beginning of this period, and her mourning clothes are burned at the end. The widowhood period often accompanies the mourning period, but is longer in duration and punctuated by its own practices. Some of these practices comprised of harsh violation of rights and human dignity and have been described as scourge and a cultural tragedy (Okoye, 1995).

There is an interesting cultural twist, where female groups are invited to join the activities of male dominance and enforce obnoxious cultural beliefs and practices on widows. Okoye's (1995, 2000) studies have provided extensive coverage of these practices among Nigerian ethnic groups. She identified eleven practices that could be categorized as moral, political, psychological, physical, economic, spiritual, sexual, and/or criminal violence against women in the course of widowhood rites. These are:

1. *Defacement*: The widow's hair is shaved off, and she is made to sit covered in ash or soot from ritual fire in her place of confinement, or she may be denied a bath for some weeks until given a ritual bath.

2. *Dethronement*: The widow is not allowed to sit on a chair, which is a symbol of the elevated status conferred on her by marriage. She is dethroned by the death of the husband and therefore made to sit on the bare floor for some days or weeks.

3. *Confinement*: A widow is put through a compulsory period of total and/or partial seclusion and cannot appear in public or at social gatherings. Her movement is restricted, and she must stay in one room for some length of time without talking to anyone. She must wear a designated mourning dress at all times, and is regarded as unclean and as a contaminant while she is so attired. As a result, she does not shake hands, and people are not allowed to eat with her from the common dish. Sometimes utensils used for preparation of her meals must not be used for that of others.

4. *Routinized crying*: A widow is forced to cry in a routine: either everyday in the morning, afternoon, and evening, or every few days. It serves as a mark of respect to the husband. A dry-eyed widow is the subject of stories that make the rounds.

5. *Disinheritance*: By tradition, everything in the home belongs to the deceased husband. Unless a dead husband left a will, a widow is left out of the inheritance of property. If her sons are minors then property is held for them until they attain manhood. The widow may be involved in this. However, if there are only daughters, then nothing is allocated and therefore remains with her as what is given to to her by the dead husband. This practice is backed by cultural laws that deny women the right to inherit. If the woman does not have a sympathetic kin group or adult male children, the property is handled entirely by the brothers and uncles of the deceased husband, and household items, bank accounts, and financial entitlements are collected and distributed among male relatives. In several situations male relatives even have contested property allocations made through a will in courts of law. This can be a prolonged and costly process, which a widow may be unable to afford (Kalu, 1989b). In addition, it creates more stress and puts more pressure on her, as it results in socially unpleasant interactions, harassment, accusation of foul play in the death of the husband, insults, and isolation from the extended family group, something with which very few women can cope. In addition, it may prolong feelings of grief and escalate them to a pathological level. Female passivity is enforced in these situations. The sudden dispossession of personal property and the reorga-nization of the household are thus a major form of psychological and economic violence against the widow.

6. *Ostracism*: Widows are ostracized during the period of seclusion and are not allowed to buy or sell at the open markets. They can only trade among themselves in a secluded area designated for this purpose. Widows are not allowed in social settings for merriment or at happy celebrations, like weddings, while they are still in mourning clothes.

7. *Ritual cleansing*: Widows are escorted naked, sometimes by a man to a ritual bath in the dead of night. Where men take sexual advantage of the naked widow, it traditionally is considered to be *iwalu ya nku* or "breaking firewood" for her. A widow may be refused this bath, which is described as the "washing off of widowhood," if she fails to satisfy the conditions of widowhood. She thus remains "socially dead."

8. *Leviration*: There is a practice whereby a widow is required to marry a brother of her husband. This actually is considered remarriage, since the

traditional marriage rites fulfilled with the deceased husband made her "our wife," that is, a wife of the brothers. She, therefore, is inherited alongside the other belongings of the husband.

9. *Prohibition from seeing husband's corpse*: A widow is denied a parting look at her deceased husband. It is believed that any man who later has sexual relations with a widow who saw her husband's body will die. This practice was therefore meant to protect men, specifically, future husbands.

10. *Drinking of corpse water*: When a widow is accused of complicity in the husband's death, she is required to take an oath to prove her innocence. She is forced to drink the water used to wash the corpse of the late husband, irrespective of all health and sanitary hazards.

11. *Severing sexual relations with husband*: A widow is stripped naked, except for a tiny cloth around her waist, and made to walk around the husband's corpse several times. She then is forced to lie alongside the corpse in a macabrish head-to-foot direction, in the presence of others, for some time, perhaps all through the night and into the next morning. This is considered a last sexual act with the dead husband.

It is necessary to point out that prolonged grief is imposed culturally on women as widows, but not on men as widowers (Amadiume, 1987). Men as widowers are not expected to participate in all these rites. Widowers, for instance, may shave their heads after the burial of the deceased wife and are expected to receive sympathizers and mourners for a brief period. Widowers are allowed to cut down the mourning period and find it easier to remarry whomever they want shortly after the death of their wives (Kalu, 1989b).

While not all widows go through these practices, it should be observed that each practice entails a traumatic and dehumanizing experience. Many of them are old customs that should be discarded. However, they persist in some version and are enforced with a sense of exploitation of the vulnerability of the widow. Confrontation by the widow or others on her behalf creates antagonism and serves only to complicate issues, as it leads to prolonged widowhood, additional fines, and harsh measures. The burial itself may be interrupted or refused if the widow does not honor the requirements for the appropriate recognition of the enforcers of widowhood practices. Most of the enforcers are women. Among the Igbos, enforcers are the *umuada*, the first daughters of the lineage who are in charge of women's affairs. They are diligent and swift in enforcing these traditional customs and widowhood practices. Widowhood is therefore a load whose weight causes too many women to be crushed physically, spiritually, and psychologically. It is the epitome of violence against African women.

Separation and Divorce

Separation and divorce are instruments of psychological and economic terror to a married woman. Women in African society are socialized to get married and to stay married. A woman's marital status enables her to join certain social groups and to be accorded respect in the society. A woman's dignity, therefore, is linked to the institution of marriage. Staying married is described in the vernacular as staying within "the grips of a man," or, in other words, not being promiscuous. A woman who is not married is considered to be the opposite and is accorded a derogatory status. A woman's fidelity, her ability to prioritize service to the husband, care for him, and feed him adequately preserves her marriage. When domestic conflicts or violence occur, the arbiters and counselors give the man's perspective. The woman stands accused and with less sympathy. While women must struggle to exist in their marriages, the tradition of polygamy allows the man to operate outside the marriage and transform marital infidelity into several other marriages, many of which are outside the wife's knowledge.

In many African groups, traditional marriages are legal contracts. Children born outside marriages formerly were considered illegitimate, but, through changes in national constitutions, they now are allowed to share in the inheritance of their biological father's property. Thus, a woman may struggle to preserve a marriage and to help in the husband's achievements in order to ensure an inheritance for her children, only to receive a rude disappointment at his death. Other children, referred to in the vernacular as "children of the woods," emerge from where they have been kept by their mothers. This is their opportunity to be recognized publicly by national and traditional laws. However, it is an additional shock and a painful experience for the widow and her children. Thus, many women are vigilant and suspicious of the husband's movements outside the home. This creates a psychological duress.

Separation serves as a convenient relief period in which the marriage remains intact. However, elders and the society as a whole have a stake in keeping a marriage together. They participate as veritable witnesses in the traditional marriage rites. Thus, in situations of acknowledged physical violence and maltreatment of the woman, they work to shorten the period of separation and sojourn outside the marital home. Several women, therefore have been exposed to a continuous ordeal of physical violence where the origin of the problem is not addressed. In addition, it is difficult for men to accept marital therapy and counseling. Tradition helps them to exonerate themselves and see women as the cause of marital problems and as the ones in need of counseling.

Divorce means a return of the bride price and the performance of certain rites. It is literally a return of the woman to the father's house, where she is considered to be no longer married. This is an undignified position to be in and is considered a threat to other marriages in the family. Divorce generally occurs on the grounds of proven infidelity, cruelty, continuous insubordination, waywardness, infertility, and financial impropriety (Oppong, 1983; Oduyoye, 1997). However, current trends in psychosocial counseling indicate a frequent termination of long-standing marriages of twenty-six to over thirty years so that the husband may marry a younger woman. While men in rural areas are likely to take advantage of the tradition of polygamy and marry a young girl who is accorded more favor than the older wives, among the educated and those who practice monogamy, the older wife is set aside through divorce. She, therefore, suddenly is thrown into turmoil, deprived of a stable life and a marital home she had worked hard to build. This also creates hostility between middle-aged married women and young girls in the workplace, where older women may be unwilling to mentor young women. This situation also presents a new wave of economic, marital, and psychological violence against married women in their advancing years. A major problem for women who are divorced or separated is not her children's custody, but their humiliation, the children's education, and maintenance. This is a source of great distress and is on the increase in social work case records (Kalu, 1993).

AIDS and Sexually Transmitted Diseases

There is a worldwide concern on the rapid spread of the AIDS virus. It has reached epidemic proportions in many African nations and has become a form of violence against women. Some governments are embarrassed and outraged about the association of their nations with AIDS, and therefore do not pay attention to accurate compilation of figures. AIDS affects the African woman in three major ways. First, unlike in Europe and the United States, where the spread of AIDS is associated with homosexual men and intravenous drug users, AIDS in Africa is spread primarily through unprotected heterosexual intercourse (Edemikpong, 1990). Where tradition and religion endorse and encourage polygamy, women in multiple-wife marriages are at risk. Their subordinate position and the existence of co-wives make them unable to insist on protected sexual intercourse. In addition, men are generally resistant to family control practices and tend to reject the use of condoms (Oppong and Abu 1987; Kisekka, 1990b). An infected husband easily spreads AIDS in his wives and other sexual partners. There have been incidents of sexual violence against women who suspected that their partners were infected and who refused to engage in sexual relations with them. Second, AIDS is transmitted through the exchange of body fluids, especially blood. Thus, the practice of female circumcision in itself, as well as the bleeding that occurs during the sexual relations of those circumcised, also exposes such women to AIDS infection. Third, inadequate maternal health care practices, birth complications due to frequent pregnancies, anemia, and malnutrition may either expose women to AIDS through transfusions of unscreened blood, or may weaken women's bodies and enable the AIDS virus to thrive. This also adds to the perinatal transmission of the virus to infants. Moreover, it is likely that the African desire to immortalize his/herself and his/her name also encourages infected individuals to reproduce, in order to leave a survivor (Kisekka, 1990a). This is a trap filled with dangers for women and their unborn babies.

The spread of ethnic violence and wars in Africa make women vulnerable to the high incidence of war rapes and sexual harassment from men and soldiers. This also assists in the spread of sexually transmitted diseases in females of all ages. Kisekka, (1990b) observes that AIDS has increased African women's burdens, as they care for the terminally ill without adequate protection against infection or assistance with the provisions needed to care for the infected person. Moreover, the shift of interest to the control of AIDS often has meant diverting scarce medical resources, personnel, funds, and drugs from other areas—such as the treatment of sexually transmitted diseases, malaria, and prenatal care where women are the beneficiaries. Once again, violence is displayed against the body, reproductive rights, and health of the woman.

SOME EMERGENT PATTERNS IN VIOLENCE AGAINST WOMEN

Culture, accompanied by traditional and religious practices, form a background to the various expressions of violence against women in Africa. There are three broad emergent patterns of violence against women. The first is the men-on-women violence. This is a declaration, an exploitation, and an abuse of the patriarchal and male-dominant position against women, and it constitutes the most widespread version of violence against women. It is found in practices that stifle the education of the girl child and in the abduction of young girls for ritual murder. It forms the basis for perpetuating the excruciating practice of female circumcision, which is a result of the desire to control females' sexual behavior for the benefit of men and to reduce their experience of sexual pleasure. Men, use tradition and religion to exploit women as sex objects. Early marriage of young girls to older men and the enticement of young girls into sexual partnership to the detriment of their health and education are means to fulfilling the sexual desires of men. Rape and proliferation of sexual partners occur under the cover of polygamy. Maternal mortality is largely a result of male control of reproductive rights and men's own resistance to the use of condoms and birth control, as well as their will and authority to insist on their wives' frequent childbearing despite inadequate health practices. Marital violence is made acceptable as part of the enforcement of the submission of women. Widowhood practices are deliberate means of increasing the suffering of bereaved women. There are no equivalent practices for men.

The second expression of violence against women is women-on-women violence. This is found in female circumcision, maternal health care practices, girl child domestic-help abuse, and widowhood practices. Women who serve as traditional birth attendants perform female circumcisions. Maternal health care in ill-equipped, unhygienic clinics of traditional birth attendants and midwives contribute to the increase in maternal mortality and disabilities in women. The economic pressure faced by women lends to the need of help in the organization of the household. Many women prefer the girl child for this service. She is often exploited in the performance of domestic chores, the production of items for sale, and street trading. This is at the cost of her safety, education, and general welfare. Similarly, women, such as the Igbo *umuada* enforce widowhood practice. Such women's groups have a traditional-religious position, and their realm of operation is limited to women's issues. The exercise of their sense of duty is exploited to cover activities that are cruel and that reflect vengeance or vindictiveness. Widowhood serves as a period in which women who have been aggrieved about the behavior of the wife of a male relative during his lifetime take the opportunity to settle the score. The bereaved woman who is no longer enjoying the protection of the husband is vulnerable. She is forced into submission and to accept her punishment in the form of widowhood rites.

A third pattern in the expression of violence against women can be found in the weak governmental structures. The government is silent on issues such as women's status in inheritance practices, the role of men in spread of HIV/AIDS, the negligible participation of men in family planning, and male control of the reproductive rights of women. These positions help the persistence of violence against women. The government's inability to provide accurate figures on the spread of AIDS, other sexually transmitted and other diseases that adversely impact women's health helps to keep women vulnerable to health hazards. Governments also lack policies that clearly promote education or that provide supportive services for women who carry heavy burdens in labor activities of the agricultural and informal sectors of the economy. Many government measures taken in response to women's appeals are palliative, superficial, and endorse practices of injustice and violence against women.

CONCLUSION

This discussion is not exhaustive. There are several limitations. The attempt is to examine some areas of African cultural activities relevant to women and point out the dangers.

African traditions continue to change, and it is expected that several practices that violate human rights will receive urgent attention. The discussions highlight violations of the rights of African women under many cultural practices. Violence is observed at every phase and stage of the life of women, from childhood to adulthood. There is great damage done to the person, and these layers of damage are ignored. There is, instead, an attempt to normalize, explain, or retain an expression of violence against women.

Traditional male and religious perspectives are dominant. The concept of questioning violence is absent in these circumstances. Power given to males by tradition often is used to assert their rights to possess women, their bodies, labor, and their services. Several traditional practices encourage perspectives that reflect insensitivity to women, their lifestyles, and their disadvantaged positions. The more prominent forms of violence are sexual, physiological, economic, and mental.

These practices need to be exposed and made untenable. Some need to be eradicated and replaced with those that affirm the worth of human life and dignity of women. Awareness should be raised about the existing laws, which make several forms of violence against women legal offenses. Legal and counseling services need to be set up to encourage women to tell their stories and to offer them appropriate help. There should be education, cultural confrontation, and transformation. For instance, human rights, especially rights of women and children should be taught as part of social and general studies courses in schools and universities. It is expected that such changes will add to the richness of African culture and encourage the resourcefulness of African women to impact on their nations and economy in rewarding and effective ways.

REFERENCES

Amadiume, I. (1987). *Male daughters, female husbands: Gender and sex in an African Society*. London: Zed Books.

Anyanwu, U.D., and Aguwa, J.C.U. (1993). *The Igbo and the tradition of politics*. Enugu: Fourth Dimension.

Edemikpong, N.B. (1990). Women and AIDS. In E.D. Rothblum and E. Cole (Eds.), *Women's mental health in Africa* (pp. 25–34). New York: Haworth.

Etta, F.E. (1994). Gender issues in contemporary African education. *Africa Development*, 19(4), 57–84.

Falobi, O. (2001, June/July). Cruel and unusual. *Ms.*, 22–23

Fapohunda, E. (1983). Female and male work profits. In C. Oppong (Ed.), *Female and male in West Africa*, (pp. 32–53). London: George Allen & Unwin.

Goldschmidt-Clermont, L. (1986). *Economic evaluations of unpaid household work: Africa, Asia, Latin America & Oceania*. Geneva: International Labor Office (ILO).

Harrison, K.A. (1990). *Maternal mortality in Nigeria*. Paper presented at the International Conference of the Society of Gynecology and Obstetrics of Nigeria (SOGON), Abuja, Nigeria.

Haynes, J. (1996). *Religion and politics in Africa.* London: Zed Press.

Hosken, F. (1987). Female circumcision. *Women's International Network (WIN) News,* 46.

Kalu, O.U. (1987). Precarious vision: The African's perception of his world. In O.U. Kalu (Ed.), *Readings in African humanities: African cultural development.* Enugu: Fourth Dimension.

Kalu, O.U. (1996). *Silent victims: Violence against women in tertiary institutions of Nigeria.* Unpublished Manuscript.

Kalu, W.J. (1987). Child bearing experiences of contemporary Nigerian working mothers. *Women's Studies International Forum, 10*(2), 141–156.

Kalu, W.J. (1989a). *Motherhood role strains in married female undergraduate students. Counseling and Development, 4,* 106–113.

Kalu, W.J. (1989b). Widowhood and its process in contemporary African society: A psychosocial study. *Counseling Psychology Quarterly 2*(2), 143–152.

Kalu, W.J. (1990). Bereavement and stress in career women. *Women and Therapy, 10*(3), 25–87.

Kalu, W.J. (1993). Battered spouses as a social concern in work with families in two semi-rural communities of Nigeria. *Journal of Family Violence, 8*(4), 361–373.

Kalu, W.J. (1999). Concerns in marital relationships and counseling needs: Nigerian experience. *International Journal of Women Studies, 1*(2), 81–89.

Kalu, W.J. (2000). Change and the family: The Nigerian experience 1960–1999. In A.M. Koschorke (Ed.), *Documentation for International Congress on Forces Impacting Relationship* (pp. 201–212). Berlin, Germany: Np.

Kalu, W.J. (2001). Human dignity for youth and women: Reproductive health care practices in Nigeria. *Society for Intercultural Pastoral Care and Counseling (SIPCC), 8,* 25–33.

Kalu, W.J. (2003). The covenant child: Influence of the worship of deities on children. *Proceedings on the 6th International Congress of the International Council Pastoral Care and Counseling (ICPCC)* (1999). Accra, Ghana.

Kisekka, M.N. (1990a). *Social inequality, health and safe motherhood.* Paper presented at the International Conference of the Society of Gynecology and Obstetrics of Nigeria (SOGON), Abuja, Nigeria.

Kisekka, M.N. (1990b). AIDS in Uganda as a gender issue. In E.D. Rothblum and E. Cole (Eds.), *Women's mental health in Africa* (pp. 35–53). New York: Haworth.

Kisekka, M.N. (1990c). Gender and mental health in Africa. In E.D. Rothblum and E. Cole (Eds.), *Women's mental health in Africa* (pp. 1–13). New York: Haworth.

National Universities Commission (NUC). (1992). *Statistics on enrollment in Nigerian universities.* Lagos: National Universities Commission.

Obanya, P. (1981). A longitudinal study of school subject preferences of a group of Nigerian adolescents. *Ilorin Journal of Education, 1*(1), 111–115.

Oduyoye, M.A. (1997). *Daughters of Anowa: African women patriarchy.* Maryknoll, New York: Orbis Books.

Okoye, P.U. (1995). *Widowhood: A natural or cultural tragedy.* Enugu: Nucik.

Okoye, P.U. (2000). *Harmful widowhood practices in Anambra state: The new millennium strategies for education.* Enugu: Nucik.

Omran, A.R. (1987). Health aspects of family planning: The evidence from Africa. In A.R. Omran, J. Martin, and B. Hamza (Eds.), *High risk mothers and newborns: Detection management and prevention* (pp. 203–210). Thun: Ott Verlag.

Oppong, Amma C. (1989). Healers in transition. *Social Science & Medicine, 28*(6), 605–612.

Oppong, C. (Ed.). (1983). *Female and male in West Africa*. London: George Allen & Unwin.

Oppong, C., and Abu, K. (1987). *Seven roles of women: Impact of education' migration and employment on Ghanaian mothers*. Geneva: International Labor Office (ILO).

Pebley, A.R. and Milman, S. (1987). Birth spacing and child survival. *International Family Perspectives, 12*(3), 71–79.

Ram, E. (1999). NGOs can bolster health by promoting human rights. *Together: A Journal of the World Vision Partnership, 63*, 1–6.

United Nations Children's Fund (UNICEF). (1995). *The state of the world's children*. London: Oxford University Press.

Ware, H. (1983). Female and male life-cycles. In C. Oppong (Ed.), *Female and male in West Africa*. London: George Allen & Unwin.

Women's Rights Monitor. (1995). Any future for the Nigerian girl? *Journal of Women Justice Program, 1*(4), 13–16.

12

Domestic Violence against Women and Children in the Philippines: Sociocultural Factors

Elena L. Samonte-Hinckley

INTRODUCTION

The Philippines is a developing country. The majority of its 76.5 million inhabitants are Christian. Women comprise 49 percent of the population and children up to 14 years old comprise 38 percent of the population (National Statistics Office, 2001). Children are valued in this culture and women enjoy a relatively higher status than those in the neighboring countries. Given these positive attitudes toward women and children and the fact that the Philippines is a Christian country, one would expect them to be respected and treated well. Unfortunately, this does not seem to be the case.

This chapter reviews the studies on violence against women and children, the sociocultural variables that may help explain this phenomenon, and the services that address this issue.

PROBLEMS REGARDING DEFINITION

One of the difficulties that is found in the literature on violence is the varying definitions and usage of the term by different disciplines. This has implications for obtaining statistics on "domestic violence" (Walker, 1999). The American Psychological Association (APA) Task Force on Violence and the Family (APA, 1996, cited in Walker, 1999) has defined *domestic violence* as a pattern of abusive behaviors including a wide range of physical, sexual and psychological maltreatment used by one person in an intimate relationship against another to gain power unfairly or maintain that person's misuse of power, control, and authority.

Some studies use the term *violence* when referring to maltreatment of women, but use the term *abuse* when referring to the same types of physical, sexual, and psychological abuse against children (ibid.). The general and broad legal definition of terms such as *child abuse* also overlaps with other categories of abuse. Another term, *children in especially difficult circumstances* (CEDC) includes a subcategory, "children subject to abuse and neglect." Thus, in documenting cases of child abuse, institutions in the Philippines, like the Department of Social Work and Development, use categories that other groups may not (Protacio-Marcelino, de la Cruz, Balanon, Camacho, and Yacat, 2000).

Categories of violence also have changed over the years. For example, from 1975 to 1985, statistics from the Philippines National Police show the use of categories like "crime vs. person" and "crime vs. chastity." However, the "crime vs. chastity" category was removed from statistics from 1990 to 1999. The category of "crime vs. person" (which includes homicide, physical injury, and rape) remained (Philippine National Police, 1975–1985, 1990–1999; Paid, 2000).

Sometimes categories are further subdivided into more specific categories. Statistics on crimes against children are divided into three subcategories for rape: rape, incest rape, and attempted rape (Ibid.).

Moreover, there are also different definitions of the subjects themselves. For example, the "children" category is defined differently by various agencies or groups. The literature on child labor shows the use of various age groupings such as 10–17, 5–17, or under 15 years old. Most of the literature on child labor uses the category "under 15 years old," which is in keeping with the legal provision prohibiting employment of children under 15 years old. Those between 15 and 18 years old may be employed, but only in nonhazardous occupations (Gatchalian et al., 1986).

These differences in categorization make it difficult to make statistical comparisons over the years and across institutions/groups.

TYPES OF VIOLENCE

The Department of Social Work and Development has ten categories of child abuse. These ten categories are: sexual abuse, physical abuse and maltreatment, sexual exploitation, neglect, child labor exploitation, illegal recruitment, missing children and other victims of trafficking, emotional abuse, children in situations of armed conflict, and street children (Protacio-Marcelino, de la Cruz, Balanon, Camacho, and Yacat, 2000). The most vulnerable among Filipino children are those who live in difficult circumstances, such as the street children (Torres, 1996; Triviño, 2000), children forced into prostitution (Gonzalez-Fernando, 2000; Laguisma-Sison, 2000), and other children living in especially difficult circumstances (Araneta-de Leon, 2000; Puente, 2000; Protacio-Marcelino, de la Cruz, Balanon, Camacho, and Yacat, 2000).

A wealth of information on child abuse in the Philippines is included in the literature review and annotated bibliography by Protacio-Marcelino, de la Cruz, Balanon, Camacho, and Yacat, (2000). In their collection of 189 materials, they categorize the types of abuses as: sexual abuse, physical abuse, sexual exploitation, neglect, child labor exploitation, missing children and victims of trafficking, emotional abuse, and street children. They added "youth offenders" and "the girl child" categories to the list of the Department of Social Welfare and Development.

The United Nations Declaration on the Elimination of Violence against Women defined violence against women as

> Any act of gender-based violence that results in, or is likely to result in, physical, sexual or psychological harm or suffering to women, including threats of such acts, coercion or arbitrary deprivation of liberty, whether occurring in public or in private life. (Rivera, Quizon, Urmatam, 1997, 8)

Thus, it is "any violation of a woman's personhood, mental and physical integrity or freedom of movement" (Monares, 1996, 141). It includes domestic violence, institutional violence, occupational discrimination, violence in the media, and public sexual abuse.

A review of studies on domestic violence (Guerrero et al., 1997); Women's Health Concerns, 1998; Rivera, Quizon, and Urmatam, 1997) revealed four types of violence: physical abuse, sexual abuse, psychological/emotional abuse, and economic abuse.

A study that analyzed 1000 documented cases from 1994 to the first quarter of 1996 found that the most frequently occurring type of abuse was physical assault accompanied by verbal and economic abuse (Guerrero et al., 1997). This occurred in one out of three cases. It was also noted that the abused women experienced not just one, but several types of abuse (73% reported experiencing at least three types). Moreover, the abuse they suffered increased in frequency and severity over time.

In another study, this one conducted by the Bureau of Family and Community Welfare (Baseline Study on Domestic Violence, n.d.), the most frequently cited type of violence as recorded by institutions and by the courts was psychological, emotional (56%). This refers to "actions which hurt and damage self-esteem and cause fear and confusion" (ibid. 11). The most prevalent forms of this type of violence recorded by institutions were abandonment and neglect, while for those documented by the court the most prevalent cases were those of bigamy and concubinage.

PRECIPITATING FACTORS

The precipitating factors of domestic violence are "problems in marital relationships, ineffective parenting, and vices. These account for 74 percent of the cases. The other cases attribute domestic violence to poverty (13%) and parental absence (10%) (ibid., 14–15).

A study of 200 wives and 200 husbands in rural communities in the south of the Philippines compared husbands and wives' perspectives regarding wife battering. When asked when wife battering occurs, wives gave the following circumstances: when the husband gets drunk or is jealous; when the wife refuses sex, goes out without asking permission, shouts back, is unable to prepare food on time, or is pregnant; and when they quarrel over money or children (Sanchez and Sobrevega-Chan, 1997). The husbands beat their wives when they are drunk, and cited the following reasons for beating them: the wife is nagging, jealous or bad/arrogant; the wife gambles, uses aggressive behavior, puts the husband to shame, refuses sex, goes out too much, does not answer when spoken to, or gets pregnant; or there are financial problems or quarrels (ibid.).

A study on murder, an indicator of social violence, showed that most murders (75%) were due to disputes. The rest were "for motives such as financial or material profit or related to other crimes" (ibid., 46).

The extensive literature on child abuse shows both macro and micro factors contributing to child abuse. On the macrolevel, "poverty, urbanization and family disintegration" contribute to child abuse (Protacio-Marcelino, de la Cruz, Balanon, Camacho, and Yacat, 2000, 25).

PROFILE OF PERPETRATORS AND VICTIMS

Victims of domestic violence are mostly children and married women. They are usually literate and employed in the service sector (sewers, vendors, receptionists, carpenters, bakers, laundrywomen, masons, and construction workers). The perpetrators are fathers, husbands, or relatives of the victims. Those cases brought to the court usually involve male perpetrators, though half of the perpetrators documented by institutions were women or mothers who abandoned or neglected their children.

Profiles of abused women show that they are an average of 23 years old, educated (almost half reach high school), and usually not gainfully employed. The abused children comprise one-third of the victims, and their average age is 11 years. The abusers are usually spouses or partners of the victim and are, on average, 35 years old, educated, and employed (Guerrero et al., 1997).

Documentation of incest indicates that most of these cases involve the father raping his daughter (Women's Crisis Center, 1989–1992). Studies on rape (Candaliza and Zarco, 1995) also underscore the fact that most of the cases involve families belonging to the lower class, with the victim and perpetrator coming from the same socioeconomic class. Rape was found to be a premeditated act by a person known to the victim (88%). Most of the victims were young, with more than half of them under 18 years of age. Assailants were twice as old as their victims, with a mean age of 30 years old.

In another study of child abuse, this one involving cases handled by the Child Protection Unit (CPU) of the University of the Philippines General Hospital (UP-PGH) Department of Pediatrics, data shows that the victims in the 123 cases were mostly females, with a mean age of 6.5 to 7.3. In the majority of the cases, abusers were close relatives or immediate family members, mostly unemployed and with low educational attainment.

Seventy-one percent of the incest cases were repeated abuses. Intimidation and threats were used by the offenders. More than half of the attackers in rape cases used weapons or other devices (Candaliza and Zarco, 1995).

Although the majority of the victims tried to put up a fight, it took a while before they reported the abuse. Reasons cited were fear, ignorance of the process, fear of losing economic support, and lack of awareness of what constitutes sexual abuse (Guerrero-Manalo, 1998; Guerrero et al., 1997). Those who did seek help asked for medical care, police protection, legal assistance, and temporary shelter. Childhood incest survivors who did not file charges against their fathers often felt fear, shame, and guilt; those who did file did not receive support from their mothers (Women's Crisis Center, 1989–1992.)

As far as rape cases are concerned, it was found that the closer the relationship between the victim and offender, the longer the interval between the rape and the filing of a police report. Sometimes the delay took as long as five years from the date of abuse. Rapes typically took place in an environment familiar to either the victim or offender or both. More than half of the perpetrators used weapons or other devices to intimidate their victims (Candaliza and Zarco, 1995).

Most of the battered wives did not seek help either. The few who went back to their family's home or asked friends for help did not get the emotional support they sought. A few did try shouting at their husbands or hitting back. Husbands corroborated this passive response of wives in that the women just kept to themselves, kept silent, or cried themselves to sleep. In some cases, wives talked things over with their husbands. Husbands claimed it was easy to woo back their wives (Sanchez and Sobrevega-Chan, 1997).

SOCIOCULTURAL FACTORS IN VIOLENCE

Sociocultural variables that may offer some explanation of the phenomenon of violence are seen in various studies: in Japan, the authoritarian and hierarchical family structure, corporal punishment, and attitudes toward sex (Kozu, 1999); in Russia, roles of women and legal double standards (Horne, 1999); in Mexico, societal and community norms and lack of supportive mechanisms for victims of violence (Fawcett, Heise, Isita-Espejel, and Pick, 1999); in Chile, cultural factors such as machismo, alcoholism, and social permissiveness of family violence, and political factors (state-sponsored violence and use of torture to extract information from women and children during the dictatorship) and legal factors (civil code that states that the wife must be obedient to the husband and that the husband has authority over the wife's possessions and person; illegality of divorce) (McWhirter, 1999). In Nicaragua, women also are expected to deal with machismo as a given. The use of violence by husbands against wives as a type of punishment is accepted widely (Ellsberg, Caldera Herrera, Winkuist, and Killgren, 1999).

In the Philippines, some of the sociocultural factors to be considered include child rearing and gender socialization, authoritarian family structure, marital power structure, attitudes toward sex, consequences of migration, broken families, violence in the media, value of children, and the concept of work by children.

Child Rearing and Gender Socialization

The family is the primary socialization agent in the Philippines. The literature shows that Filipino parents rigidly adhere to "societal prescriptions," especially those regarding the different behaviors required of Filipino girls and boys. There are separate sexual and behavioral standards for girls and boys, be this at play or at work. Girls engage in play that resembles housework (*bahay-bahayan*, or playing house, and *lutu-lutuan*, or cooking) and in quiet games (Lim-Yuson, 1982, cited in Liwag, de la Cruz, and Macapagal, 1999) and activities that are not rough (Sobritchea, 1990). Girls are socialized to be feminine, modest, refined, and demure, while boys are taught to be masculine, strong, brawny, and healthy (Liwag, de la Cruz, and Macapagal, 1999). Although girls are trained for their roles as wives and mothers, boys do not seem to be trained adequately for their role as breadwinners.

Filipino boys tend to be pampered and spoiled by their mothers (Lapuz, 1977). They also are given more freedom than girls (Quiambao, 1965, Mendez and Jocano, 1979a, cited in Liwag, de la Cruz, and Macapagal, 1999; Razon, 1981), who are expected to stay home more (de la Cruz et al., 1971, cited in Liwag, de la Cruz, and Macapagal, 1999). Such permissiveness is seen also in the greater tolerance of male aggression (Razon, 1981). Although the boy child is warned not to get into fights, he also is taught to defend himself and his family's honor (Macalandong et al., 1977, Mangawit, 1981, cited in Liwag, de la Cruz, and Macapagal, 1999).

Corporal punishment is "the most common and considered the most effective method used by parents to instill discipline" (Medina, 1991, 201). However, parental strictness is dependent on the site, occasion, and birth order (Mendez et al., 1984, cited in Medina, 1991). Parents are stricter if the behavior or place is "hazardous to the child's health and safety" (p. 203). They are more tolerant with the youngest and eldest children.

Authoritarian Family Structure

Deference to older people is seen not only in parent-child relationships, but also in sibling relationships. Children are expected to follow and obey their parents, but, among children, there is also a ladder-type of authority whereby the older children acquire quasi-parent status and even have the authority "to punish younger siblings for misbehavior" (Medina, 1991, 24). This authoritarian structure is seen also in the nomenclature to indicate birth order among siblings. "Headship of the household is automatically assumed by the oldest male" (ibid.).

Marital Power Structure

Although Filipino society is said to be egalitarian (Fox, 1961, Gonzales and Hollnsteiner, 1976, Mendez et al., 1984, cited in Medina, 1991), statistics and other studies show otherwise (Samonte-Hinckley, 1989; Contado, 1991). For Filipino families, there is still a predominance of male-headed households (Medina, 1995). Although there are social scientists who claim that the *padre de familia* (head of the family) is still the male, there are also those who say that this is a myth (Illo, 1989) and that decision making is shared. Medina (1991) claims "it is difficult to pinpoint precisely the real position of the Filipina wife in the power structure" (p. 223) Studies seem to point to the greater burden put on Filipino wives, in terms of the double burden and the double standard of morality. In a study of Filipino rural families by Contado (1991), the majority of husbands and wives said that the authority figure in the household was the husband, as he was the stronger one and the family breadwinner. However, this power seems to be based on the family life cycle. "The wife's dominance in the decision making process seems to peak at the child-rearing and child-leaving stage and tends to decline at the empty-fold stage" (ibid., 159).

Filipino husbands take on the traditional role of being the breadwinner and are not expected to help in household chores (Sevilla, 1982, cited in Medina, 1991). Husbands still prefer that their wives take on the traditional role of being homemaker rather than being a working wife (Jimenez, 1981, cited in Medina, 1991). The most significant predictor of labor force participation of married women is husband approval (ibid.).

However, despite the clear delineation of marital roles, studies on nullifying marriage show more women petitioners whose husbands are psychologically incapable of fulfilling their obligations in their marriage (Vancio, 1980; Jacob, 1994). There were also more female petitioners who gave more than one reason for filing for nullity of marriage, and more who complained about their extremely angry, demeaning, and violent spouses (Samonte-Hinckley and Dayan, 1998). In terms of reasons for filing for nullity of marriage, there were more female petitioners than male petitioners who said they were physically/sexually abused.

This emotional dependency and male inadequacy, particularly in the role/function of providing emotional and financial support, was described by Lapuz (1977) as some of the types of marital crises experienced by Filipino couples. In a study by de Arana (1980), six psychological factors were identified as contributing to marital discord: (1) emotional instability, (2) loss of sense of responsibility, (3) poor interpersonal roles, (4) lack of self confidence, (5) emotional immaturity, and (6) sexual conflict. Another study, by Vancio (1980), on the causes of marital discord between Filipino couples listed nine major causes of marital distress. In decreasing proportion, the top four are (1) infidelity, (2) incompatible personalities, (3) financial problems, and (4) spouse immaturity and insecurity.

Dayan, Magno, and Tarroja (1995), in their study of sixty petitioners of nullity of marriage, found that there were multiple reasons for filing for nullity of marriage, including (1)adultery, (2) desertion, (3) substance abuse, (4) spouse/child abuse, (5) immaturity, (6) psychoses, (7) personality disorders, (8) conflict about in-laws, (9) financial pressures, and (10) sexual dysfunction. They found significantly more females than males complaining about substance abuse and immaturity of their husbands in their petitions.

Jacob (1994) identified the following traits of respondent husbands to be the ones appreciated by the court as constituting psychological incapacity: (1) absence/lack of financial support, (2) inability to hold on to a job, (3) abandonment of spouse/family, (4) inability to copulate, (5) abnormal or inconsiderate demands for sex, (6) homosexual behavior, (7) staying out late, and (8) refusal to seek professional help to solve marital problems. These traits were grouped into five clusters: (1) inability to function as family breadwinner, (2) social deviance, (3) sexual deviance, (4) erroneous/defective conceptual grasp of marriage, and (5) personality defects and disorders.

Attitudes Toward Sex

Adultery or the so-called *querida* system (having a mistress), is a reality in the Philippines (Alano, 1995). Despite the Catholic Church's condemnation of extramarital affairs, marital infidelity is one of the leading causes of marital breakup among Filipino couples. Alano's study showed greater disapproval of adulterous women than of adulterous men. Differential tolerance is seen also in the Filipino men having the prerogative to give into polygamous tendencies, while women are given the heavier burden to make the husband happy and keep the family intact. The study also showed that unfaithful husbands believe that "sex outside of marriage is appropriate and extramarital relations are okay should one be able to afford it and/or provided the material needs of the legitimate family are met" (Alano, 1994, 85). They see it less as a reasonable cause for separation. Causes of affairs point to "deficits" in the marital/familial situation such as neglect of kids/household duties, neglect of the spouse, negative personality traits of the spouse, and not having legitimate children. Ironically, "adulterous men oppose affairs for women" (ibid., 88).

The 2001 Young Adult Baseline Survey, which was administered to 430 college students between the ages of 15 and 24 from Metro Manila, also showed prevailing traditional attitudes. For most of the respondents, virginity is still an important consideration in choice of a spouse, although it is more acceptable for men to have more experience in that regard. A little over half were aware of a movement that advocates equality between the sexes, but less than 10 percent were involved in such organizations. Most agreed that it is the male partner who makes the decisions in a relationship.

Broken Families

A profile of boy child prostitutes shows that many of them have lost a parent, either through death, marital separation, or abandonment (Laguisma-Sison, 2000). In their stepfamily or in the care of their extended family, they were physically abused by their caretakers. They then left home, having been subjected either to physical or verbal abuse or to neglect. Consequently, in order to survive on the streets, they resorted to various ways of earning a living, one of which was prostitution. In-depth interviews of the girl child prostitute also revealed a notable lack of mothering during their childhood (Gonzalez-Fernando, 2000). Of the eight girls who were interviewed, six had lost their mothers either through death or abandonment, while the two who still had their mothers were physically and verbally abused by them. Lamberte's study of 700 street children (1995) also revealed a history of disagreements with and abuse by family members. These experiences were cited as reasons for their escape from their living situation.

Consequences of Migration

In an effort to improve their lives, Filipinos have gone abroad to work as contract workers (Samonte-Hinckley, 1991; Cariño, 1998). However, although there are economic gains, there are also adverse effects not only on family relationships but also on the children. Some reports show that these children "are often rowdy, disruptive in class, troublesome, and get into fights frequently" (Battistella and Gastardo-Conaco, 1996, p. 153). Newspaper accounts also relate cases of incest that occurs when the mother is absent. There are also cases of physical abuse and violence when children are left to the care of surrogate parents (Aganon, 1995).

Violence in Media

The impact of violence in the media on children is underscored by the fact that attitudes toward violence and aggression are formed through exposure to programs containing violence (Murray, 1997; de Leon, 2000).

A study conducted by the Philippine Children's Television Foundation of 10 percent of a composite week of 728 programs showed that 50 percent of the programs contain violence, averaging 6.2 violent incidents per hour. Given that the average length of viewing time that 2 to 12-year-old children spend watching television is 2.18 hours, this would mean about thirteen violent incidents are viewed daily. Sixty percent of violent programs are intended for adult viewers, 40 percent are intended for children. Other statistics show implications for learning aggressive behavior: 50 percent of violent acts are rewarded while 30 percent are not, 44.7 percent of the violent shows do not show any negative effects on the perpetrator, 57 percent of violent incidents are portrayed realistically, and 82 percent of violent incidents are graphic.

Value of Children

Filipinos view their children in terms of economic utility and psychological security (Palejo, 1992, cited in Liwag, de la Cruz, and Macapagal, 1998), someone who can take care of them in their old age. This is bolstered by the value of daughters, who are seen as an important resource since they can help in the household (Licuanan, 1979, Castiglioni, 1982, cited in Liwag, de la Cruz, and Macapagal, 1998) and also be responsible for nurturance. It is little wonder that the labor and migration literature is replete with stories of women who work in order to support their parents and siblings (Samonte-Hinckley, 1998; Tacoli, 1996).

Concept of Work by Children

In a study by Torres (1996) of 308 street children in six different Philippine cities (Manila, Quezon City, Pasay, Caloocan, Olongapo, and Davao), it was found that there are certain dynamics that lead to children working: (1) There is a common perception on the part of the child and his/her family that the family desperately needs more money. This comes from the realization that the present household income is barely enough to meet the family's needs. (2) The economic requirements are largely unmet because (a) a large proportion of the family members are minors, students, and unemployed adults, and (b) employed members tend to be underemployed. Moreover, the families and households are fairly large in size. (3) The presence of several minors in a household increases the risk that one or several of them will become wage earners. This is especially true when only one or two adults are working. (4) Children's work can make a substantial difference in family/household income, whatever the source may be: work similar to what adults do, like vending, scavenging, or engaging in services, or marginal jobs like begging. (5) Both children and adults believe in fulfilling familial obligations. It seems that this sense of mutual obligation justifies the decision of minors to work. These children willingly give their earnings to their parents, and parents consider it to be the child's responsibility to contribute to the family's finances. (6) Parents and children face no social stigma when minors go to work. (7) Children are highly influenced by their peers in their decision to work. There is a thin line separating play and work, and the world of work easily becomes a world of games. (8) Part of the attraction of work for the children is the self-efficacy that they are able to experience, particularly in a world where they could be rendered helpless given their background of poverty. This translates into money for school projects, food, and other basic needs. It is instrumental to their goals, such as completing their studies. (9) There are no alternative solutions, even though there has been legislation and social policy, and even action programs within the communities.

Torres (1995, 18–19) thus argues that "dependency relations in marginalized families living below the poverty threshold . . . could mean the need by children for continuing psychological and emotional security . . . Clearly poverty situations lead to the expectation that children and adults alike will help provide for the family's needs. Children's participation in the economic life of a poor household becomes part of the socialization and expectations from among its members."

SERVICES

There are various services available for abused women and children. These are offered by private groups, nongovernmental organizations (NGOs) as well as government agencies. Services come in a variety of forms, ranging from rescue operations to more long-term interventions such as training and legal assistance.

An example of a private group is the Bantay Bata Call Center (Bantay-bata 163, 2001), which operates in Manila twenty-four hours a day and in Iloilo (Western Visayas) twelve hours a day to respond to reports of child abuse through rescue operations. The call centers also offer online counseling concerning child-family relationships. They provide immediate protective custody by giving rescued children the needed physical and psychological rehabilitation.

Child abuse cases are documented on print and video and used as educational materials to educate and empower other families on how to prevent and eradicate child abuse. Social workers visit abused children in their homes and provide the whole family with intensive counseling. On weekends, information on children's rights and responsible parenthood is disseminated in various communities, and every Saturday, volunteer lawyers offer free legal counseling concerning issues on child abuse to indigent clients.

Some examples of NGOs are the Child Savers Foundation Philippines, Children's Rehabilitation Center, and Rotary's Crusade against Child Abuse. There are center-based services, street-based services, and community-based services (Protacío-Marcelino, de la Cruz, Ma., Balanon, Camacho, and Yacat, 2000).

For abused women, there are crisis centers set up by NGOs such as the Women's Crisis Center, the Third World Movement against the Exploitation of Women (WMAEW), GABRIELA, BATIS, Asian Women Human Rights Council, Women's Legal Bureau, KALAKASAN, and Congressional Research and Training Services (Monares, 1996; Unas, 1992). They offer various programs such as counseling services, women's desks, information campaigns, gender and development trainings and other interventions.

CHALLENGES TO THE PSYCHOLOGISTS

Clearly there are many gaps in the theoretical as well as practical arenas that psychologists can address. In terms of the research agenda, the following topics require investigation: how child rearing in the Philippines can explain how gender stereotypes or differences came to be; the dynamics of child rearing in dysfunctional families; the role of peer socialization, school, church, and media in strengthening or modifying the effects of family socialization (Liwag, de la Cruz, and Macapagal, 1998); the impact on children and women of exposure to violence, including the factors that may play a role, such as the age of the child, frequency, and type of violence exposure, the amount and quality of support given by caregivers and other significant adults, and familiarity with the victim or perpetrator (Osofsky and Fenichel, 1997).

In terms of the more practical aspects, there is also a need to work with perpetrators of violence and the sociocultural, political predictors of violence. Researchers and practitioners would do well to learn from the models used in South America (Corsi, 1999) and Greece (Antonopolou, 1999) and to look at the broader picture of social transformation (Decenteceo, 1997) as well as the discourse of the child (Protacio, de la Cruz, Balanon, Camacho, and Yacat, 2000). No doubt, capability building both on the individual and structural levels are wanting. Psychologists could look into the factors and methods that facilitate this development. For example, phenomenological-clinical approaches have been used to study children in especially difficult circumstances (Bautista, 2000; Laguisma-Sison, 2000; Gonzalez-Fernando, 2000; Araneta-de Leon, 2000; Triviño, 2000). This is in response to the need for an approach that can make a difference and highlights the role of the clinician as researcher-innovator-communicator (Carandang, 2000).

REFERENCES

Aganon, M.E. (1995). Migrant labor and the Filipino family. In A.E. Perez (Ed.), *The Filipino family* (pp. 79–96). Quezon City: Office of Research Coordination, University of the Philippines.

Alano, M. (1995). *Pambansang samahan sa Sikolohiyang Pilipino* (Infidelity: The dynamics of the querida system in the Philippines). A dissertation. Faculty of the Graduate School, Ateno de Manila University.

Antonopolou, C. (1999). Domestic violence in Greece. *American Psychologist, 54*(1), 63–64.

Araneta-de Leon, R.C. (2000). Makasalanan o kapus-palad: A phenomenological study of children in conflict with the law. *Philippine Journal of Psychology, 33*(1), 92–110.

Bantaybata 163. (2001). <http://www.abs-cbn.com>.

Battistella, G., and Gastardo-Conaco, Ma. C. (1996). *Impact of labor migration on the children left behind*. Manila: National Secretariat for Social Action, Justice and Peace.

Bautista, V. (2000). Developing a method for understanding the resiliency of abused children. *Philippine Journal of Psychology, 33*(1), 27–42.

Candaliza, F.A. and Zarco, R.M. (1995). An analysis of rape incidents in Metro Manila. *Philippine Social Sciences Review, 52*(1–4), 99–124.

Carandang, Ma. L.A. (2000). The clinician as researcher, innovator and communicator. *Philippine Journal of Psychology, 33*(1), 1–10.

Cariño, B.V. (Ed.). (1998). *Filipino workers on the move: Trends, dilemmas and policy options*. Quezon City: Philippine Migration Research Network, and Philippine Social Science Council.

Contado, M.E. (1991). Power dynamics of rural families. In B.T. Medina (Ed.), *The Filipino family: A text with selected readings*. Quezon City: University of the Philippines Press.

Corsi, J. (1999). Treatment for men who batter women in Latin America. *American Psychologist, 54*(1), 64.

Dayan, N., Magno, E., and Tarroja, C. (1995). Psychosocial and personality factors in sixty petitioners for marriage nullity: An exploratory study. Unpublished paper.

de Arana, R.O. (1980). Psychological factors in marital discord. Unpublished doctoral dissertation, University of the Philippines, Quezon City.

Decenteceo, E.T. (1997). *Rehab: Psychosocial rehabilitation for social transformation*. Manila: Bukal.

de Leon, C.A. (2000, December 2). Impact of TV violence on children. *Philippine News and Features*, 17.

Ellsberg, M., Caldera T., Herrera, A.W., Winkuist, Killgren, G. (1999). Domestic violence and emotional distress among Nicaraguan women: Results from a population-based study. *American Psychologist*, 54(1), 30–36.

Fawcett, G.M., Heise, L.L., Isita-Espejel, L., and Pick, S. (1999). Changing community responses to wife abuse: A research and demonstration project in Iztacalco, Mexico. *American Psychologist*, 54(1), 41–49.

Gatchalian, J., Baltazar, J., Estrella, D., and Valencia, L. (1986). Child labor: The Philippine case. *Philippine Journal of Industrial Relations*, 8(1), 2–23.

Gonzalez-Fernando, P. (2000). Self-concept, womanhood, and sexuality: A phenomenological study of the inner world of the girl child prostitute. *Philippine Journal of Psychology*, 33(1), 67–91.

Guerrero-Manalo, S. (1998). A closer look at child abuse. In *Women's health concerns: A research brief on family violence*, 8–9.

Guerrero, S.H., Sobritchea, C.I., Caragay, J.T., Cayabyab, M.M., Feliciano, M.S., Peñano-Ho, L., Israel, L.Q., Guerrero-Manalo, S., Patron, M.C., and Vasquez, M.S.C. (1997). *Breaking the silence: The realities of family violence in the Philippines and recommendations for change*. Manila: United Nations Children's Fund, and University of the Philippines, Center for Women's Studies, Foundation.

Horne, S. (1999). Domestic violence in Russia. *American Psychologist*, 54(1), 55–61.

Illo, J.F. (1989). Who heads the household? Women in the Philippines. In A.T. Torres (Ed.), *The Filipino women in focus* (pp. 113–120). Bangkok: United Nations Educational, Scientific, and Cultural Organization.

Jacob, F.P. (1994). Psychological incapacity as a ground for marriage nullity: Definitions, issues, directions. Unpublished master's thesis, Ateneo de Manila University, Quezon City.

Kozu, J. (1999). Domestic violence in Japan. *American Psychologist*, 54(1), 50–54.

Laguisma-Sison, B.A. (2000). The inner world of the boy-child prostitute: A phenomenological and in-depth clinical study. *Philippine Journal of Psychology*, 33(1), 43–66.

Lamberte, E. (1995). Family relationships and street children. *Social Science Information*, 23(1–2), 21–22, 34.

Lapuz, L.V. (1977). *Filipino marriages in crisis*. Quezon City: New Day Publishers.

Liwag, Ma. E.C.D., de la Cruz, A.S., and Macapagal, Ma. E. (1998). How we raise our daughters and sons: Child-rearing and gender socialization in the Philippines. *Philippine Journal of Psychology*, 31, 1–46.

Liwag, Ma. E.C.D., de la Cruz, A.S., and Macapagal, Ma. E. (1999). *How we raise our daughters and sons: Child-rearing and gender socialization in the Philippines*. Manila: United Nations Children's Fund, and Ateneo Wellness Center.

McWhirter, P.T. (1999). La violencia privada: Domestic violence in Chile. *American Psychologist*, 54(1), 37–40.

Medina, B.T. (1991). *The Filipino family: A text with selected readings*. Quezon City: University of the Philippines Press.

Medina, B.T. (1995). Issues relating to Filipino marriage and family. In A.E. Perez (Ed.), *The Filipino family* (pp. 27–39). Quezon City: Office of Research Coordination, University of the Philippines.

Monares, Ma. D.A. (1996). Violence against women: The Philippine context. In R. Pineda-Ofreneo et al., (Eds.), *A woman's work is never done: A review of literature on women 1986–1996*. Quezon City: Human Development Network Philippines.

Murray, J.P. (1997). Children and youth violence: An overview of the issues. In J.D. Osofsky (Ed.), *Children in a violent society* (pp. 3–8). New York: Guilford Press.

Murray, J.P. (1997b). Media violence and youth. In J.D. Osofsky (Ed.), *Children in a violent society* (pp. 72–96). New York: Guilford Press.

National Statistics Office. (2001). *Gender quickstat: Population quickstat*. <http://www.census.gov.ph>.

Osofsky, J., and Fenichel, F. (1996). *Islands of Safety*. Washington, DC: National Center for Infants, Toddlers, and Families.

Paid, R.S. (2000). *Crime trends CY 2000*. <http://www.pnp.info.com.ph>.

Philippine National Police. (1975–1985, 1986–1995, 1990–1999). *National Crime Volume*. Manila: Author.

Philippine National Police (1993–1997). *Cases handled by PNP Women's and Children's Desk*. Manila: Author.

Philippine National Police (1998). *Youth offenders*. Manila: Author.

Philippine National Police (1999a, First quarter). *Crimes against children*. Manila: Author.

Philippine National Police (1999b, January–December). *Violence against women case monitoring system: January–December 1998*. Manila: Author.

Protacio-Marcelino, E., de la Cruz, Ma. T.C., Balanon, F.A.G., Camacho, A.Z.V., and Yacat, J.A. (2000). *Child abuse in the Philippines: An integrated literature review and annotated bibliography*. Quezon City: University of the Philippines, Center for Integrative and Development Studies.

Puente, M.K.B.N. (2000). Re-visiting the children of Smokey mountain: The past still speaks for the present. *Philippine Journal of Psychology*, 33(1), 1–25.

Razon, P.G. (1981). Child rearing practices of Filipino urban mothers: Relationship to children's cognitive development. *Philippine Journal of Psychology*, 14(1–2), 8–15.

Rivera, R.L.K., Quizon, J.J.R., and Urmatam, M. (1997). *Action against VAW*. Quezon City: Arugaan ng Kalakasan.

Samonte, E.L., (1991). Filipino migrant workers in Japan: In search of a better life: The price of a dream. *Philippine Journal of Industrial Relations*, 13(1–2), 75–122.

Samonte, E.L., (1998). Filipino migrant workers: Cost benefit analysis of their sojourn and its implications. In A.B.I. Bernardo, N.A. Dayan, and A.A. Tan (Eds.), *Understanding behavior bridging cultures: Readings on an emerging global psychology* (pp. 77–99). Manila: De La Salle University Press.

Samonte, E.L., and Dayan, N.A. (1998). Sources of marital dissatisfaction among Filipino petitioners seeking nullity of marriage. Paper presented at *The 4th Conference of the Afro-Asian Psychological Association* and *35th Annual Convention of the Psychological Association of the Philippines*, University of the Philippines, Diliman, Quezon City, July 23–26.

Sanchez, R.D., and Sobrevega-Chan, L.S. (1997). *Women and men's perspectives on fertility regulation and other reproductive health issues*. Unpublished manuscript. Ateneo SRO and University of the Philippines Center for Women Studies, Quezon City.

Sobritchea, C.I. (1990). The ideology of female domesticity: Its impact on the states of Filipino women. *Review of Women's Studies, 1*, 26–41.

Tacoli, C. (1996). Migrating "for the sake of the family?": Gender life course and intra-household regulations. *Philippine Sociological Review, 44*(1–4), 12–32.

Torres, A.T. (1996). *Profiles of disadvantaged children: Street children in six Philippine cities*. Quezon City: University of the Philippines, Office of Research Coordination.

Triviño, Ma. L.P. (2000). Minding the minds of the sexually abused street children: A look into their cognitive functioning. *Philippine Journal of Psychology, 33*(1), 146–155.

Unas, R. (1992). Violence against women in the Philippines. *Asia Pacific Women's Studies Journal, 1*(3), 5–11.

Vancio, J. (1980). The realities of marriage: The urban Filipino women. *Philippine Studies, 28*(2), 11–15.

Walker, L.E. (1999). Psychology and domestic violence around the world. *American Psychologist, 54*(1), 21–29.

Women's Crisis Center. (1989–1992). Partial report from case files on incest. Unpublished raw data.

13

The Roots of Violence in Modern Russia: A Psychocriminological Analysis

Sergei V. Tsytsarev and Yakov Gilinsky

INTRODUCTION

As a whole, humans have very aggressive and violent ancestors. Indeed, it was necessary to be aggressive and violent in order to survive while surrounded by even more aggressive neighbors: predators and competitors. The entire human evolution is comprised of a history of war, elimination of enemies, torture, rape, and other expressions of violence. There are plentiful examples of culturally approved expressions of extreme violence. For instance, rape during wars has not been viewed as a crime until very recently. Vigorous fights between men have been documented as thrilling experiences for crowds of people since the time of ancient Rome. Until the nineteenth century, public executions were an enthralling sight in most European countries and in the United States. Today, violent movies, television shows, and video games are the most sellable kinds of entertainment for millions of people around the world. Wherever guns are available, they are used to destroy, to hurt, to punish, and to humiliate others. Thus, violence has been and still remains an inextricable part of a variety of cultures around the world.

In the nineteenth and twentieth centuries, educated people in Europe and America made a few attempts to stop violence by introducing more progressive laws, drawing public attention to the consequences of violence, and developing alternative strategies to rehabilitate overly aggressive and violent individuals. Interestingly, these endeavors always made exceptions for certain groups. Some people have always been viewed as "enemies," toward whom the use of violence and aggression is justifiable. Among these groups were political and military rivals, slaves, ethnic minorities, unfaithful spouses, homosexuals, mental patients, drug addicts, and criminals.

The proliferation of violence during the twentieth century, including the physical extermination of more than 150 million people during two world wars and the massive genocide that occurred in Russia, China, Germany, Cambodia, Africa, and Latin American countries, made some scholars believe that, despite the advances of civilization, it is totally impossible to stop some forms of violence in contemporary societies. Indeed, the statistics are scary. According to Kressel (1996), 61,911,000 people were killed in the USSR from 1917 to 1987, 45,311,000 were killed in China from 1928 to 1987, and 20,946,000 people were killed in Germany from 1934 to 1945.

The past twenty years have been characterized as another major period of violence around the world. This pessimistic perspective has made the entire field of research on violence quite unattractive for many scholars, and has consequently hampered scientific investigations in this area.

Despite their violent pasts, many nations have developed ways to channel aggressive behavior and have created clear limits for violence. Aggression has been taken under the control of societies, and violence is no longer reinforced. Contrary to some theoretical assumptions, a number of peaceful societies emerged in the latter quarter of the twentieth century. However, there are very few rigorous studies in which cross-cultural aspects of aggression and violence have been elucidated.

A brilliant study of this subject was recently published by Bonta (1997). In contrast to nearly all societies, there are cultures in which aggression is significantly less common than in most others. Bonta (1997) reported that in at least twenty-six cultures worldwide the incidence of violence and aggression is rare. He attributed the low rate of aggression among these peoples to the collectivistic, cooperative nature of their societies.

Cooperation and aggression appear to be negatively correlated, whereas competition and aggression are strongly positively correlated. In most competitive cultures, aggression and violence are facilitated by the media, some professions, the educational system, and various social institutions.

Thus, in order to understand the roots of violence in any given society or country, one should try to analyze the interaction of historical, economic, social, political, and psychological factors.

In this chapter empirical and theoretical perspectives on violence in Russia will be presented, with an emphasis on its roots and origin. We will try to elucidate the present situation as well as the trends that are likely to determine the future of this country.

THE HISTORICAL PERSPECTIVE

Russia has always been a country surrounded by enormous empty lands that allowed the inhabitants of ancient Russia to live quite peacefully. It was not necessary for them to fight for territory to survive (as was the custom in Europe), since land could be taken at a very low cost. According to anthropologists, the Slavs, who once populated the present territory of Russia, were not initially aggressive or violent, but rather cooperative and peaceful. It took them hundreds of years to develop the aggressive habits and violent patterns of behavior demonstrated in the bloody internal wars in which a number of other nations were involved. The country finally was unified on the basis of suppression of the smaller counties and neutralization of those who were against the unification. It would be logical to hypothesize that the nontraditional forms of violence seen in the modern history of Russia stemmed from the lack of necessity and skills to deal with competitors in the ancient times. More civilized forms of struggle for power, resources, and money have not been developed fully. It is helpful to examine violence in Russia using a historic perspective.

The Byzantine Heritage

In 988, Prince Vladimir had selected the Greek Orthodox variation of Christianity as the official religion of Russia. Although it was an important step toward the Westernization of the country, some negative aspects of the "christening of Russia" must be recognized. For example, the Greek clergy insisted that the death penalty be adopted to punish robbers. It was documented that Vladimir tried to resist the use of the death penalty by saying "I am afraid killing is a sin," but the bishops convinced him by replying, "You are blessed by God to execute evil people." This historic tradition has continued, and even today, the Russian Orthodox Church regularly blesses tanks, missiles, cannons, and troops going to the war in Chechnya.

The Russian Tradition

Russia has never been a state whose existence and functioning was based on the law. Instead, it was based on the absolute power of tsars (emperors) and, during the first three quarters of the twentieth century, the general secretaries of the Communist Party. Individuals always had been defenseless and helpless against the tsar, the state, or the bureaucracy. The "progressive" reforms issued by Peter the Great in the beginning of eighteenth century are an example of the cruel coercion of hundreds of thousands of people to adopt Western customs. Coercion was followed by the physical elimination of peasants, clergy, and nobility who did not accept the reforms. The city of St. Petersburg, often called "a beautiful Venice of the North," literally was built on the blood and bones of thousands of people who were forced to participate in that megalomaniac project in the beginning of eighteenth century. The cost of Peter's reforms was the lives of millions of citizens and slaves, yet he remains the most revered Russian leader.

The communist reforms enacted between 1917 and 1920 were conducted by the extremely violent physical elimination of the nobility, the intellectuals, the most competent and successful farmers, and others who simply did not support the new rulers. In the 1930s Stalin, who was preoccupied with the idea of the purity of communist ideology, initiated a massive act of genocide against all groups of people and executed millions of his former supporters. The numerical data still require clarification, but a few million people disappeared into concentration camps and were executed. As a consequence, Russians developed an intense fear of the state, of authority figures, and of their neighbors, who potentially could have been reporters for the secret police. This fear was an inextricable element of the Soviet mentality for three generations. The people "learned" from the government that the only way to resolve a conflict was to get rid of one's counterpart. As Stalin used to say, "If there is no man, there is no problem."

The Soviet Constitution of 1936 was one of the most democratic constitutions ever adopted in Europe. However, Stalin and his political allies never intended to follow or enforce their own laws. The laws were written only to make a positive impression on other countries. As a result, the use of coercion and violence to achieve political goals was justified in terms of enmification (see next section), and the unconstitutional persecution of millions of people, viewed as political rivals ("enemies of the nation"), had become a routine practice of the law enforcement agencies. The court system was reduced to the "triads," which were administrative units consisting of three individuals who usually decided each case within an hour. In most cases, the sentencing was "10 years in prison with no right to correspond," which was actually a euphemism for immediate execution. Not surprisingly, the recent attempts to modify this system by allowing attorneys to protect the civil rights of defendants enraged many law enforcement bosses who are used to exercising unlimited power upon their "clients."

In sum, during the past 300 years, all Russian governments have been engaged in a war against their own people. Any substantial changes in society have been achieved primarily by the use of terror (political, economic, or psychological); deception of the masses ("nice" slogans and brainwashing used to reach the selfish goals of the bureaucracy, be it feudal, communist, or criminal); humiliation of individuals, nations, or any other social group; and development of the false concept of self-sacrifice for the sake of either "faith, motherhood, and tsar," "bright communist future," or, currently, "democracy and free market."

Once the government was weakened, revenge immediately was taken by the masses who were led by revolutionaries. Basic mistrust of the government, in conjunction with feeling of being "fooled again," provided a ready source for frustration, hostility, anger, and aggressive behavior.

THE CULTURAL PERSPECTIVE

One of the most effective strategies that facilitated the development of the Russian economy and society was the formation of the "image of enemy." Enmification (Rieber and Kelly, 1991) was used effectively to foster anger and aggression. In his famous novel *1984*, Orwell (1984) showed the extent to which the "lessons of hatred" could be used to unify people. Although this phenomenon characterizes the mentality of many nations, it has been used consistently by the Russian leaders. An *enemy* has been defined as a threat to humanity, peace, independence, national values, socialist motherland, and, more recently, to democracy, the free market, or a ruler of the country. Enmification unites groups of people universally; however, it also easily leads to violence toward those who are perceived as enemies and enemy sympathizers.

There is a long list of individuals and groups of people who have been hated in Russia over the past century, ranging from the enemies of the tsar and motherland before the 1917 revolution, to the enemies of communism (1917–1985), and, lately, to the enemies of the free market and democracy (1985–2000). For instance, people of "Caucasian nationality" (a term that is used widely but doesn't make any sense, since there are dozens of nationalities populating the Caucasus area) are the current objects of hate because of their association with the international terrorists from Chechnya. The Russian pattern of enmification is a ready source of and a potential trigger for expressions of anger and aggressive and violent behavior.

In Soviet Russia (1917–1985), the level of cooperation (as reported in Bonta's 1997 study on cooperation versus competition) was always high because of the collectivistic nature of Russian society and the Russian Orthodox Church, as well as their communist ideology (despite their fundamental ideological differences). In addition, in a communist society where most people experienced a shortage of all kinds of consumer goods and where protectionism (support of relatives and friends) was a necessity, cooperation was a common trend and a true cultural attribute.

After the decline of communism in 1985–1991, individualistic values constantly were imposed and indeed showed a dramatic rise. The loss of a sense of security in conjunction with new materialistic opportunities led many people to extreme forms of individualism that, generally, had been unknown in the West. "Wild capitalism" and chaotic and unlawful privatization of the national property was followed by the "deideologization" of society and the adoption of a "jungle" ideology, in which any means were good for survival. The loss of collectivistic rights and values led to the destruction of the basic structure of society, since the most significant cultural attributes were challenged and then discredited.

Violent behavior has been glorified in the mass media. The most violent American and Asian action movies have been shown continuously on Russian television channels. In addition, *bratki* ("brothers" who are members of the local organized criminal groups) occupying positions of power and authority in most high places of business and political power have become the heroes of many domestic television shows. It has become very common for youngsters to imitate the offensive behaviors, poses, gestures, and criminal slang of these individuals.

Violence Reinforcing Culture

As described in previous publications (Tsytsarev and Callahan, 1995), the following two types of cultures can be distinguished using the operant learning perspective: violence reinforcing and violence repressing cultures. Violence reinforcing cultures provide multiple reinforcements for various types of aggression and violence. In such cultures, even law enforcement activities, which are also frequently violent, could be considered reinforcers that maintain a very high incidence of aggressive behavior and violence. Violence repressing cultures provide consistent reinforcement for nonviolent problem-solving behaviors and virtually no reinforcement for aggression in everyday life. There are several good examples of violence repressing cultures, including contemporary Japan, a highly collectivistic society that has the lowest crime rate among industrialized nations.

Social psychology provides a comprehensive database on the cause-and-effect relationships between attitudes toward aggression and aggressive behavior. Permissive attitudes seem to be the consequence rather than the cause of aggressive behavior. Most authors maintain that aggression and violence usually are learned through classical, operant, and vicarious conditioning and that attitudes serving aggression are very likely to develop *post factum* (Berkowitz, 1993; Averill, 1983). However, the literature on attitudes is rich with controversy, and it is not uncommon to find discrepancies between attitudes and behaviors.

Contemporary Russian culture falls under the category of violence expressive cultures, which are characterized by the reinforcement of aggression and the use of violence as acceptable means of solving interpersonal, social, and political problems. Numerous instances of aggression in the business, politics, industry, and everyday life of Russian citizens illustrate the proliferation and perpetuation of anger and aggression. In the next sections, specific examples of violence used to resolve problems are cited.

In addition, Russian people traditionally have had a tendency to over-dramatize and exaggerate their stressors. In the Russian language two of the most commonly used words are *uzhasno* (horrible) and *koshmar* (nightmare, horror). These words are applied to a number of situations. The use of those words causes angry outbursts followed by aggression, quite probably due to the lowered threshold of emotional excitement (Kassinove and Sukhodolsky, 1995).

THE ECONOMIC PERSPECTIVE

Poverty is one of the factors that universally leads to aggression and violence. The overwhelming majority of people in Russia always have been extremely poor, and starvation always has been an element of the everyday life of millions of Russians. Outbursts of anger and aggressive behavior displayed by starving people have been as common as manifestations of their social anxiety. Numerous generations of Russians have learned that, in order to survive, any means will justify the goals. Extremely violent revolts of various poor groups followed by even more violent ways of suppressing them can be found during any historical period in Russian history.

What is happening now in Russia is what some observers call a "permanent economic crisis." The crisis currently is manifested as a catastrophic stratification of the society into two polar classes: a superrich and powerful minority and an impoverished majority.

The ratio between the income of the most affluent 10 percent and the poorest 10 percent has reached fifteen, and a score of 10:1 is considered to be a critical score. However, in the study conducted under the auspices of the United Nations, this coefficient was estimated to be 25:1 (Russian Federation, 1999).

At the end of 1998, 43.3 million people, or 29.5 percent of the Russian population, were earning less than the minimal living standards and therefore were not able to provide enough to ensure their physical survival. For a number of years the "symbolic" (extremely low) monthly salary of 400 rubles (about $15) was not paid at all. Outside of private businesses, people still do not have incentives to work hard, to save, to buy property, and so on.

The aforementioned economic difficulties contribute to the feelings of hopelessness, chronic frustration, worthlessness, anger, and depression. The unemployment rate in the country has been skyrocketing. The official unemployment rate in Russia was 4.8 percent in 1992 and 13.3 percent in 1998 and is still going up. In the city of St. Petersburg alone, there are nearly 500,000 unemployed adult individuals who seem to be unable to find any job.

CRIMINOLOGICAL PERSPECTIVE

The crime rate in modern Russia has been on the rise since 1985. During the first three years of Mikhail Gorbachev's perestroika (1985–1988), the rate of registered crime had decreased, perhaps due to the enforced alcohol prohibition policy as well as the feeling of hope that increased the overall optimism of people. However, between 1987 and 1999, the crime rate rose dramatically from 817 to 1,863 per 100,000 people and, after a short decrease in 1996–1997, has increased again to 2,027 in 1999 and 2,028 in 2000 (Gilinsky, 2000).

The statistics for murder are even more staggering. The 350% increase over twelve years, noted in Table 13.1, (6.3 in 1987 and 21.1 in 1999) is quite depressing. However, these numbers do not reflect fully the tragedy that has unfolded in Russia, as the government officials consistently have decreased these numbers. According to the less-biased World Health Organization (2001), the murder rate was 32.6 per 100,000 in 1994, and has been steadily increasing, as is noted in Table 13.2. As of 2002, the murder rate in Russia is the second highest in the world (21.8) after Colombia (over 78 per 100,000).

Between sixty-two and seventy-five thousand people are murdered because of acts of criminal violence ever year. In addition, 25,000 people are declared missing and are never found. In the military, 5,000 to 6,000 of those who *do not participate in wars* die every year. Most of them die due to violent "uncommissioned relationships" (*dedovshina*, the abuse of power by the older soldiers that often takes sadistic forms), accidents related to military service, and suicide. In the past, military service was viewed as a positive experience for young men, but now it is perceived as a variation of imprisonment and as yet another source of violence.

In addition to violent crimes such as murder and assault, other criminal activities are associated closely with the use of violence. For instance, in the climate of wild capitalism, violence is viewed as an acceptable, and often *the only*, means to solving problems between business competitors. Private corporations, including large firms and commercial banks, tend to hire criminals to ensure their personal safety and business security, to assist in acquiring property and financial resources, to aid in the collection of debts, and to establish control over various sectors of the local and central economy. Practically all private companies are associated with local gangsters (called *krysha*, meaning the "roof" or "cover") for protection in their struggle against competitors and in order to achieve their own business goals. All the aforementioned activities would be considered to be illegal in the West but have become quite conventional in modern Russia. In many ways, the organized criminal groups have replaced some institutes of justice, such as arbitration, enforcement of ruling, private security, insurance, and so on.

Table 13.1
Rate (per 100,000 Inhabitants) of Severe Violent Crimes in Russia and in the City of St. Petersburg, 1985–2000

	1985	1986	1987	1988	1989	1990	1991	1992	1993	1994	1995	1996	1997	1998	1999	2000
Premeditated murder (including assault)																
Russia	8,5	6,6	6,3	7,2	9,2	10,5	10,9	15,5	19,6	21,8	21,4	19,9	19,9	20,1	21,1	21,8
St.Petersburg	5,1	3,9	3,4	4,9	4,9	5,8	7,7	11,2	17,7	20,4	19,5	17,5	16,2	19,3	19,2	18,4
Severe bodily injuries																
Russia	19,9	14,7	13,9	18,2	25,0	27,7	27,8	36,2	45,1	45,7	41,7	36,2	31,4	30,8	32,4	34,1
St.Petersburg	12,4	10,4	8,2	12,6	16,7	17,7	20,2	34,4	43,5	40,8	36,0	26,4	24,0	23,3	22,4	21,3

Table 13.2
The Mortality Rate (per 100,000) Due to Homicide in Various Countries, 1984–1995

	1984	1985	1986	1987	1988	1989	1990	1991	1992	1993	1994	1995
Australia				1,9	2,4	1,8	2,2	2,5	1,6	1,8	1,8	
Austria				1,3	1,2	1,1	1,6		1,5	1,3		1,0
Argentina	4,5	4,9		5,4			5,0	4,3	4,6	4,4		
Hungary				2,5	2,7	2,9	3,1		4,0	4,5	3,5	3,5
Germany				1,1	1,1	1,0		1,1	1,2	1,2	1,2	1,1
Denmark			1,2	1,0	1,3	1,2	1,0		1,3	1,2	1,3	1,2
Israel			1,8	1,3			1,7	1,2	1,4	2,3	2,7	1,4
Spain	0,9	1,0	1,0	1,2			0,9	0,9	1,2	0,9	0,9	
Italy	1,6	1,5	1,3	1,6	1,9	2,1	2,6	2,8	2,2	1,7		
Canada			2,0	2,2				2,3	2,1	1,8	1,7	1,6
Columbia	33,3							89,5	88,5	88,5	78,7	
Mexico		18,6	19,4					17,5	18,8	17,8	17,7	17,1
Netherlands			1,0	0,9	0,9	0,9		1,2	1,3	1,2	1,1	1,2
Norway			1,5	1,4	1,1	1,3		1,5	1,1	0,9	0,8	
Poland			1,7		1,7	2,1	2,9		2,9	2,7	2,9	2,8
Russia					9,7	12,6	14,3	15,2	22,9	30,6	32,6	30,8
USA		8,2	8,9	8,5	8,9		9,9	10,4	9,8	9,9	9,1	
Finland				3,1	2,8	3,2			3,4	3,3	3,2	2,9
France			1,2	1,1	1,0	1,1		1,1	1,0	1,1	1,1	
Switzerland				1,2	1,2	1,3	1,5		1,5	1,5	1,3	
Sweden			1,4	1,2	1,4		1,3	1,4	1,3	1,3	1,2	0,9
Japan				0,7	0,7	0,6	0,6		0,6	0,6	0,6	

The practice of paid assassination has been extremely widespread during the era of privatization and redistribution of property between 1993 and 2000. Between 500 and 600 bankers, business executives, owners of private companies, and government officials have been murdered every year over the past ten years (Gall et al., 1996). A few political leaders in Moscow and St. Petersburg were killed within the past two years. During the same time, the "enforcers" have become heroes of novels, movies, and news media.

Professor Alexander Yuriev, a psychologist and political consultant, was attacked in his own apartment: Acid was thrown on his face and chest by unknown assailants. As a result, he was severely injured and his life was in jeopardy. Of course, the attempted assassins have not been found.

This way of resolving business disputes in modern Russia is quite similar to Stalin's idea of "there is no man—there is no problem." Despite significant ideological differences between the communist regime of the past and the present government, many methods of solving problems remain quite similar. The expression of violence seems to be transforming from one type to another.

An example of the role of the local criminal groups in the proliferation of violence is found in the disputes over car accidents. Once a road accident takes place, the owners of fancy cars would rather call *bratki* than the local police. Under the threat of physical punishment, the driver whose car collided with an expensive car is forced to either pay the damages in cash on the spot (which is usually impossible) or the gangsters will seize his property, including his car, apartment, or house. Not infrequently, the fear of being killed leads these drivers to sign away their own property by officially "donating" it to one of the gangsters.

Crimes of passion (Tsytsarev, 1997) are sometimes described as a "Russian way of crime." An accumulation of tension (jealousy, anger, frustration) followed by an uncontrollable outburst of anger and brutal aggressive behavior has been well researched in Russian forensic psychiatry and psychology due to its high prevalence in the society. Family violence often is fostered by the consistent use of alcohol that is a true national catastrophe in Russia.

The alcoholism rate in Russia is the highest in Europe and the highest in the modern history of Russia. Even though it is very hard to obtain reliable statistics on alcohol consumption in Russia, several estimates have been presented in literature. In the early 1990s the official figure of alcohol consumption was around six liters of pure alcohol per capita per year, whereas the indirect estimates based on the number of the alcohol-related deaths yielded figures as high as thirteen to fifteen liters of pure alcohol per capita (Nemtsov, 2001). If these figures are accurate, Russia occupies the leading position on alcohol consumption in the world and is nearing a level of alcohol consumption that could paralyze the national economy, to say nothing about the many physical and psychological consequences related to drinking.

Unemployment and alcoholism paired together almost universally lead to very high levels of violent criminal activities in various forms. Frustration commonly leads to aggressive behavior and, unfortunately, family members frequently become the victims. Besides the data presented above, the rate of family violence in Russia seems to be increasing quite rapidly. In Western countries, physical abuse of spouses, wife battering, and marital rape currently are perceived as serious manifestations of violence. In Russia, these acts are often viewed as acceptable, especially among poorly educated and alcohol-abusing families. According to Shestakov (2000), nearly 12,000 murders in Russia are committed every year by blood relatives, usually members of the nuclear family. This accounts for 40 percent of all murders in Russia. Sixty-five percent of them are committed by spouses, which accounts for 25 percent of the total number of murders in the country (Shestakov, 2000). As indicated by these figures, the family appears to be an institute of violence in Russia.

Sexual violence always has been a serious problem in Russia. Fifteen thousand, six hundred and twenty incidents of rape were registered in 1997. However, this statistic must be interpreted with caution, since many sex crimes (rape, sexual assaults, and sexual harassment) go unreported. The violent ways of intimidating the rape victims frequently make them withdraw their litigations. As a result of such intimidation, the rate of reported sex crimes has declined during the past fifteen years. In 1987 the rate was 7.5 per 100,000. It was 9.9 in 1989, 9.5 in 1991, 9.7 in 1993, 8.5 in 1995, 6.3 in 1997, 5.7 in 1999, and 5.4 in 2000.

Law Enforcement and Violence

Police brutality and corruption has reached outrageous proportions. It starts with the small bribes of the traffic inspectors and goes to the extremely violent ways of getting a defendant's confession. Physical abuse of citizens by police officers is commonplace in the everyday life of the Russian people. The numbers are staggering. In 1994, police officers were arrested for 3,088 criminal acts. This figure rose to 3,603 in 1995, 3,868 in 1996, 3,605 in 1997, 3,869 in 1998, and 3,523 in 1999. Taking into consideration the data on corruption in the police force, these numbers appear to be very high. Torture is used widely in the prison system, special "pressing rooms" exist in the detention houses, and various methods of coercion reportedly have been developed there (Agruzov, 1994).

It is important to recognize that Russia consistently has occupied first place in the world on the relative number of police officers. In 1998, there were 1,360 officers per 100,000 people. To compare Russia with other countries, Singapore has 1,074, Uruguay 831, Austria 367, United States 300, and Japan 207 (*Global Report of Crime and Justice*, 1999). However, instead of protecting people, the police officers often pose a direct threat to their well-being. The corruption of the entire law enforcement system makes it impossible for the citizens to appeal if an act of police brutality takes place. A typical complaint about the police is that "they beat you up first and then ask for your ID." In one of the surveys conducted by Russian sociologists, residents in St. Petersburg admitted that they were more afraid of their own police than they were of foreign invaders.

Prison System and Violence

A tragic and quite hopeless problem appears to be the Russian penitentiary system. There are over 740 prison inmates per 100,000 people. This is the highest number in the world. Only the United States has a comparable index of 650, whereas all other countries fall into the 200 to 300 range. The overcrowding of jails and prisons in conjunction with the timeworn facilities and the crucial role played within the prison system by organized criminal groups create an atmosphere of unfailing violence against the majority of inmates, leading them to experience intense fear and humiliation. It is very difficult to obtain any numerical data on brutality and abuse of power within the penitentiary system.

The prison system in Russia produces numerous social deviations, including various sorts of physical abuse and coercive sexual relationships. Prison is likely to help those who are prone to violence to become professional criminals. The criminal/prison slang is extremely widespread in modern Russia. This is an indirect indicator of the fact that criminal types of relationships have penetrated all segments of Russian society.

PSYCHOLOGICAL PERSPECTIVE

Psychological explanations of violent behaviors among Russians today could be based on the model that was developed in previous publications (Tsytsarev and Grodnitsky, 1995). In fact, this model originally was linked to the Russian way of violent crime and to the addictive nature of violent behavior that could be observed in the former Soviet Union.

Within this model, the ultimate goal of the psychological study of violent behavior is the investigation of various psychological mechanisms involved in the development of violence as well as the basic frustrated needs underlying cravings and related motivations. The previous sections presented a number of ways that the frustrated needs of people could be pseudo-satisfied with the use of violent behavior. One must therefore evaluate the subjective and objective meanings of violent behavior and how they derive from needs that are satisfied by violent conduct. Kon (1988) suggested the use of a similar model to analyze sexual behavior. From this perspective, Tsytsarev and Callahan (1995) considered violent behavior in the following ways:

a. As a means of *tension reduction*: Anger and violence are elicited by inner impulses that demand to be discharged by any means. Violent behavior is just one possibility.

b. As a means of the temporary *self-esteem growth*: Violence toward others may provide a strong feeling of self-confidence, even omnipotence and grandiosity.

c. As a means of *emotional state transformation* and *sensation seeking*: The use of violence offers an unusual affective experience and escape from emotional emptiness and boredom.

d. As a means of *compensation* or *substitution*: A profound frustration of any basic need (e.g., the need for love, affiliation, power, or social achievement, as well as some basic security needs) results in excessive motivational tension and anger which can be directed toward others, or rarely, at the subject himself/herself.

e. As a means of *communication*: Violence is an integral part of certain specific subcultures (e.g., criminals, drug and alcohol abusers, etc.), wherein violent behavior serves as a sign of affiliation with the group and as a means to establishing a hierarchy of interpersonal relations. Moreover, violent and aggressive behaviors substantially simplify the complex emotional relationships within these groups. Physical or psychological violence commonly is employed as a means to manipulate others and is aimed at achieving goals that are otherwise unattainable.

When analyzing different types of violent behavior, it is important to bear in mind that, initially, some kind of motivation (i.e., one of the basic frustrated needs), leads to a psychological predisposition toward violence and facilitates its behavioral manifestations. But later, if the need is not satisfied, it may become progressively stronger and result in more intense aggressive or destructive motivations and expressions. Moreover, the individual who becomes accustomed to using violence to "satisfy" one of a need subsequently may employ the same mode of gratification to satisfy his/her previously frustrated needs. Thus, violent behavior may become a "process addiction." Compulsive craving with massive denial as a prevalent defense mechanism, confusion, self-centeredness, dishonesty, perfectionism, "frozen feelings," and ethical deterioration may predominate. Other significant features may be present as well, including crisis orientation, depression, stress, abnormal thinking processes, forgetfulness, dependency, negativism, defensiveness, projection, tunnel vision, and fear (Schaef and Fassel, 1988).

There is a need to study the types of objects that are sufficient for normal need-gratification (fulfillment) but that are unavailable for subjects displaying violent behavior. There are three common avenues available to different cultures to provide their members with goal objects to satisfy their needs and normal cravings. The first is well known and widely used in free societies and grants individuals access to the choices and opportunities to search for and find appropriate goal objects, allowing them to fulfill their lives. The second commonly is observed in so-called addicted societies (Shaef and Fassel, 1988), where various opportunities are replaced by some form of "harmless" substitute—such as gambling, excessive work, and so on—that pseudo-satisfies individuals' needs. The third avenue is related directly to anger and aggressive behavior and occurs when the society is unable to offer any socially acceptable way to satisfy people's needs, but allows them to resolve their conflicts and problems from positions of power. The information presented in the previous sections of this chapter is sufficient to conclude that a lot of normal avenues to cope with frustration are blocked for many Russian people.

Unfortunately, the specific data on the prevalence of various types of motivation to commit violent acts in Russia is not yet available. It would be interesting to carry out a cross-cultural study in the future to elucidate how, exactly, different motives lead to various types of violence in different cultural contexts. The current Russian cultural context provides too many reasons and motives for violence and therefore it must be compared with other cultures. However, it is quite clear that all aforementioned factors continue to lead millions of Russian people to use violence in their everyday life: to solve business-related, personal, family, and other problems. The Pandora's box was opened, and aggression is not only not suppressed, but also largely reinforced in the climate of a wild capitalism. Solving problems from the position of power is a usual and everyday practice. If no positive changes take place within the Russian economy, culture, and law enforcement systems in the near future, all mechanisms leading to violence and aggression will lead to a society in which nonviolent ways of behaving would be perceived as really strange.

In a cross-cultural study of anger and aggression in Russia and America conducted by Kassinove, Tsytsarev, Sukhodolsky, and Solovyova (1997), very few differences in the experiences and expressions of anger between the two cultures were found. The incidence, intensity, frequency, and duration of anger episodes were very similar among both Russian and American groups. On the other hand, the data on violent resolutions to all kinds of problems in real life presented above apparently shows the greater prevalence of aggression and violence in Russia than in America. It leads us to an additional interpretation of violence as a form of social behavior that is not essentially connected with emotions or, specifically, with the expression of anger. Violent aggressive behavior appears to be a learned social behavior that reflects societal (or cultural) norms and standards that provide consistent reinforcement for various forms of violence in the society. Unless these norms change, violent behavior (whether criminal or not) is likely to persist.

REFERENCES

Agruzov, I. et al. (1994). *The White Book of Russia*. Frankfurt am Mein: International Society of Human Rights [Internationale Gesselschaft fur Menschen-rechte—IGFM] (in German).

Averill, J.R. (1983). Studies on anger and aggression: Implications for theories of emotion. *American Psychologist*, *38*(11), 1145–1160.

Berkowitz, L. (1993). *Aggression: Its causes, consequences and control*. New York: McGraw-Hill.

Bonta, B. (1997). Cooperation and competition in peaceful societies. *Psychological Bulletin*, *121*(2), 299–320.

Gilinsky, Y. (2000). *Crime and deviance: State from Russia*. St. Petersburg: Baltic University of Ecology, Politics, Law. (in Russian). *Global report of crime and justice* (1999). New York: Plenum.

Kassinove, H. and Sukhodolsky, D. (1995). Anger disorders: Basic science and practice issues. *Issues in Comprehensive Pediatric Nursing*, *18*(3), 173–205.

Kassinove, H., Tsytsarev, S.V., Sukhodolsky, D., and Solovyova, S. (1997). Self-reported constructions of anger episodes in Russia and in America. *Journal of Social Behavior and Personality*, *17*(1), 1–24.

Kon, I. (1988). *Introduction to sexology*. Moscow: Medicina (in Russian).

Kressel, N. (1996). *Mass hate: The global rise of genocide and terror*. New York: Plenum Press.

Nemtsov, A. (2001). *Alcohol-related morbidity in Russia in 1980–1990s*. Moscow: Moscow Research Institute for Psychiatry. (in Russian).

Orwell, G. (1984). *Nineteen Eighty Four*. Oxford: Clarendon Press; New York: Oxford University Press.

Rieber, R.W., and Kelly, R.J. (1991). Substance and shadow: Images of the enemy. In R.W. Rieber (Ed.), *The Psychology of war and peace* (pp. 3–39). New York: Plenum Press.

Russian Foundation. (1999). *Human Development Report*. New York: United Nations Development Program.

Schaef, A.W., and Fassel, D. (1998). *The addictive organization*. San Francisco: HarperCollins.

Shestakov, D. (2000). The crisis of the family and criminality. In H. Kassinove (Ed.), *Criminology in the 20th century* (pp. 494–514). St. Petersburg: Law Center Press (in Russian).

Tsytsarev, S.V. (1997). Pathological anger in "crimes of passion." *Security Journal*, *9*, 203–204.

Tsytsarev, S.V. and Callahan, C. (1995). Motivational approach to violent behavior: A cross-cultural perspective. In L. Adler and F. Denmark (Eds.), *Violence and prevention of violence* (pp. 3–10). Westport, CT: Praeger.

Tsytsarev, S.V. and Grodnitsky, G. (1995) Anger and criminality. In H. Kassinove (Ed.), *Anger disorders: Definition, diagnosis, and treatment* (pp. 91–108). Washington, D.C.: Taylor and Francis.

United Nations Development Program. (1999). *Report on the Development of the Human Resources in Russia*. New York: UNDP.

World Health Organization. (2001). *World Health Statistics: Annual Report*. Geneva: Author.

14

Manifestations of Violence in South Africa

André J. Pelser and Chris P. de Kock

INTRODUCTION

The perception that South Africa suffers from a pervasive culture of violence—some would even typify the country as *the* most violent society in the world—has gained considerable momentum over the past few years. A legacy of violence has indeed characterized South African society over many decades of repression and resistance. During the struggle for and against apartheid, structural, political, and social violence dominated the South African scene, while various other manifestations of violence continued backstage.

Contrary to expectations, however, the demise of apartheid and the advent of democracy did not result in an overall decrease in violence. In fact, since the rise of a new sociopolitical dispensation in 1994, South Africa has been caught up in an escalating and unprecedented spiral of violence, and of violent crime in particular. Many South Africans indeed have come to accept crime and violence as normal and ordinary realities of their daily existence. Surveys conducted by various organizations reflect the public's growing perception that the police have lost control and are unable to protect them from crime. This perception has not only contributed to the rise of vigilante groups, but also resulted in many South Africans leaving the country, stating an uncontrollable wave of crime and violence as one of the most important reasons for their decision. In addition, international investments, business confidence, and development programs all have been impeded to some extent by the tide of crime and violence.

On scanning various reports on violence, it seems that the violence and crime that characterized South Africa before the first democratic elections in 1994, have moved from serving a political agenda to being purely unbridled acts of violence and crime that prey on the seeming absence of social-control mechanisms. Politically related violence—waning, though not yet eradicated—has largely made way for criminal violence, taxi violence, and violence perpetrated by vigilante groups. This chapter will profile the dynamics of these four typologies of violence in South Africa and their impact on South African society and will suggest possible strategies for the prevention of violence in South Africa. Since the nature and dynamics of violence in South Africa have changed profoundly since 1994, a comparison of trends and profiles of the pre- and post-1994 eras is imperative for understanding the bigger picture. However, it is important to bear in mind that the categories to be discussed are by far not the only manifestations of violence in South Africa. Violence instigated by labor militancy, prison uprisings, and campus students are not uncommon incidents to most South Africans. The latter manifestations are, however, more likely to assume a sporadic character, compared with the (current) more continuous nature of the former.

POLITICAL VIOLENCE

The root causes of political violence in South Africa are located within the social matrix and the long history of sociopolitical oppression, exploitation, and poverty in the country. This can be traced back to the cradle of the previous dispensation in 1948, when the apartheid government denied the majority of its citizens access to central political structures and thereby entrenched racially based social inequality. The state used various forms of vertical institutional violence (detentions without trial, convictions, banning of opposition groups, suppression of protest marches by the security forces, sanctioned assassinations, etc.) to maintain this inequality, racial superiority, and social control. Consequently, opposing political groups resorted to an "armed struggle" as they reviewed the benefits of violence in pursuing their own ideological and political objectives. This reactive violence, met by continued repressive violence by the state, resulted in an exponential growth of political violence over the next four decades, culminating in the intensified violence of the late 1980s and early 1990s. With the implementation of two successive states of emergency in 1985 and 1986 (renewed annually until 1990) and the consequent clampdown on open political activity, events such as funerals, strikes, consumer boycotts, and protest marches became rallying occasions for mobilizing communities against the state. On many occasions this led to violent confrontations between township residents and the security forces. On both sides of the political boundary violence was sanctioned and legitimized as a means of either maintaining the status quo or of achieving change. The intensity of this violent nexus—as expressed in the annual number of deaths emanating from acts of political violence—is depicted in Table 14.1.

Table 14.1
Political Fatalities in South Africa, 1987–1997

Year	Total
1987	661
1988	1149
1989	1409
1990	3699
1991	2706
1992	3347
1993	3794
1994	2476
1995	1044
1996	683
1997	470
Cumulative Total (10 year period)	21,438

Sources: Pelser and Botes, 1992; South African Institute of Race Relations, 1998

Because apartheid permeated all aspects of South Africans' lives, the violence in the political arena inevitably spread to the social and civic arena—so much so that, by the 1990s, the term *culture of violence* frequently was used to describe the conflict endemic to South African society. A comparison between Northern Ireland, where 2, 847 people have died as a result of political violence in the past twenty-one years, and South Africa, where more than 21,000 were killed between 1987 and 1997, serves as an indication of the intensity of political violence during the past decade or more in South Africa (Breytenbach, 1999; see Table 14.1). The period 1989 to 1990, in particular, was marked by unprecedented incidents of inter- and intracommunity violence. Hamber (1998) observes quite correctly that political and criminal violence started escalating precisely at the point of peaceful negotiations toward political change (i.e., 1987 to 1997; see Table 14.1). This, however, is not an uncommon trend in societies going through a process of political transformation. In fact, the history of societal transformation cautions that social and political reform always go hand in hand with violence or the imminent likelihood of violence (Pelser, 1993). Political violence is the customary way in which deprived groups draw attention to their grievances and demands for reform, and South African society proved to be no exception in this regard.

Several other factors also triggered and sustained violence during the transition period. Among these were the competition within impoverished communities over access to scarce resources and the fact that various political role-players fueled violence to achieve their own ends and to strengthen their hand at the negotiating table. Of particular importance was the manipulation of "ethnic identity" as a recruitment tool to further political agendas. As pointed out by de Kock and Schutte (1998), this can develop into ethnic or racial violence, especially where party boundaries coincide with ethnic or racial boundaries. Once mobilized, groups that were formed on the basis of ethnicity were generally volatile, defensive, and very difficult to demobilize. These factors led to unprecedented levels of inter- and intra-community conflict in the years preceding the first democratic elections in 1994. Hamber (1998: 354) refers to this phenomenon as "horizontal conflict," that is, conflict between communities that are themselves the objects of vertical state aggression.

In contrast to the situation in the 1980s, the conflict and violence in South Africa during the 1990s occurred between political interest groups, largely to the exclusion of the security forces (Minnaar, Pretorius, and Wentzel, 1998). For instance, there were indiscriminate massacres, political assassinations, revenge attacks by migrant laborers in hostels, attacks on train commuters, and minibus taxi "wars," among other violent acts. However, statistics on political fatalities tell only part of the effects of the violence. In addition to the fatalities, thousands of women and children became internal refugees, education was severely disrupted, numerous employment opportunities were lost, and a good deal of psychological trauma occurred.

In the days running up to the 1994 elections, political violence occurred not only among the black population, but also among the (white) right wing of the political spectrum. Sympathizers of right-wing resistance movements instigated a series of racial attacks and killings, bomb explosions, and violent disruptions of public meetings and political negotiations. Although some observers (Coetzer, 1993) cautioned against a major violent onslaught from the right wing, others (Pelser, 1993) pointed out that the right-wing movement would lack the necessary legitimacy and ability to mobilize resources—both vital prerequisites for the success of such a movement. The later indeed turned out to be the case, as white right-wing resistance quickly waned after 1994.

The 1994 elections in South Africa heralded the so-called miracle transi-

Table 14.2
Political Fatalities in KwaZulu-Natal, 1994–1997

Year	Total	Proportion of Total Fatalities
1994	1 464	59.1%
1995	684	65.5%
1996	347	50.8%
1997	226	48.1%
Cumulative Total/Average %	2,721	55.9%

Source: South African Institute of Race Relations, 1998 (adapted)

tion to democracy. Although political violence decreased significantly, other types of violence, particularly violent crime, showed a sharp increase. Political violence also continued, albeit at lower levels than before the elections (see Table 14.1). In 1997 political fatalities dropped to the lowest level since 1985, showing a 31 percent decrease as compared with 1996 (see table 14.1). A significant proportion of the total number of political unrest–related deaths after 1994 occurred in the province of KwaZulu-Natal and appeared to be linked closely to local and regional political dynamics (see Table 14.2). In the ten years preceding the country's first democratic elections, more than 10,000 people died in political rivalry between the African National Congress (ANC) and the Inkatha Freedom Party (IFP)—the two dominant parties engaged in a power struggle for authority in KwaZulu-Natal.

Since the elections in April 1994, more than 2,000 people have been killed in political conflict in KwaZulu-Natal. It is believed that these killings are related to the fact that the IFP is primarily an ethnic-based party, which draws most of its support from the some 80 percent isiZulu-speaking inhabitants of the province. Although the violence was triggered initially by political party competition between the IFP and the ANC, there is little doubt that it has assumed significant ethnic dimensions since 1994. Numerous examples from elsewhere in the world prove that it is much more difficult to achieve a negotiated settlement on demographic attributes like language, religion, and ethnicity than on political party policy or ideology. Political tension, accompanied by episodes of violence—

Table 14.3
Taxi Violence in South Africa, 1993–1997

Year	No. of incidents	No. of injuries	No. of deaths
1993	162	300	181
1994	225	346	212
1995	269	247	175
1996	577	586	285
1997	339	335	218
Total	1572	1814	1071

Sources: Minnaar and Pretorius (1997); South African Institute of Race Relations, 1998 (adapted)

especially in KwaZulu-Natal—is therefore likely to continue for the foreseeable future.

VIOLENCE AND CONFLICT IN THE TAXI INDUSTRY

While political violence in South Africa in general has declined since 1994, violence in the minibus taxi industry exhibited just the opposite trend, although statistics do point to a decline since 1996. The continuation of killings, assassinations, and conflict between rival taxi organizations are symptomatic of deeply entrenched antagonisms and unresolved underlying problems. Some of the problems include accusations of corruption, false licenses, fraudulent permits, pirate vehicles, overtrading in existing markets, competition for routes, and a range of other factors, which all threaten the viability of the taxi industry (Minnaar and Pretorius, 1997). As the various taxi organizations compete for the large yet limited market, many operators resort to random violence to assert functional control over routes and ranks. In the process, commuters, the pillar of the industry, often become the real victims. The full extent of the taxi-related violence can be gauged from Table 14.3, which reports the number of violent taxi incidents and the number of people injured and killed for the period ranging from 1993–1997.

Taxi violence and killings have become a stark monument to overwhelming greed. Too often, disagreements over specific routes and ranks, which are regarded as the exclusive domain of a selected group of operators, are settled by armed violence. An underlying cause of the violence is no doubt the intolerance and mistrust taxi associations have for one another, fueled by an ongoing rivalry over control of passengers. In some cases buses have been set on fire by taxi drivers attempting to discourage commuters from using them. In such cases, taxi operators claim that the buses are poaching commuters from taxi ranks and that buses should be allowed to pick up passengers only at designated bus stops.

The larger economic environment of the taxi industry probably lies at the root of the problem. The tremendous growth of the industry was not planned, and, as a result, operators who wanted to enter the industry found themselves in a nonregulated environment, competing for scarce resources (Patel, 1997). The past decade or more also has seen a general economic decline, which has led to a reduction in the profitability of individual operators. According to Minnaar and Pretorius (1997), disputes over ranks, routes, and commuters became increasingly common during the 1990s, especially as severe overtrading and market saturation occurred in more and more areas. Many operators have refused to accept the fact that economically uncompetitive taxis should be allowed to wither away through the natural market processes of nonprofitability and bankruptcy. Instead, most of them attempt to swing the odds in their favor by resorting to illegal methods such as violence, elimination, intimidation, and bribery.

By the end of 1994, there were an estimated 70,000 legal (with permits) taxis and 40,000 illegal (without permits) taxis operating in South Africa. Accusations of high-level corruption were made, as it was claimed that some of the legal taxis were operating either with forged or with bribed permits. It also was claimed that some prominent traffic officers and police officers had a stake in the industry, which led to their favoring or even victimizing certain taxi association to further their own interests.

Among the measures called for to address the situation is legislation to empower provincial governments to withdraw the permits of taxi owners who have broken the law. The need has been expressed also for a sound policy for passenger transport in its broadest form and for the implementation of regulatory and control mechanisms for the taxi industry at the level of the central government.

VIOLENT CRIME

Although the figures in Tables 14.1 and 14.2 are alarming, the number of deaths from political violence is overshadowed dramatically by the high levels of violent crime in South Africa. A comparison with international case studies (in Namibia, eastern Europe, Soviet Union) suggests that this is not uncommon during a period of social and political transformation (Hamber, 1998). In the four-year period prior to the elections in 1994, violent crime (i.e., murder, rape, public violence, aggravated assault,

Table 14.4
Violent Crimes to the Person, 1990–1998

Year	Assault*	Murder	Rape	Robbery**
1990	124,030	15,109	20,321	61,132
1991	129,626	14,693	22,761	69,936
1992	136,322	16,067	24,360	78,644
1993	144,504	19,583	27,037	87,102
1994	210,250	26,832	42,429	117,323
1995	220,990	26,637	47,506	120,952
1996	230,425	25,782	50,481	118,755
1997	234,554	24,588	52,160	122,371
1998	234,056	24,875	49,280	150,430

* With intent to inflict serious bodily harm (excluding common assault)

** Including robbery with aggravating circumstances

Sources: South African Institute of Race Relations, 1998 (adapted); CIAC, 1999

and aggravated robbery) increased at a greater rate than less serious categories of crime. Table 14.4 illustrates the incidence of violent crimes committed against people that were reported to the police during the period 1990–1998.

Many of the news reports of violence and crime in South Africa reach the international media and influence the perceptions that people, including potential investors and tourists, have of the country. There can be no doubt that the negative portrayals of South Africa need to be addressed. However, any attempt to change these perceptions must be accompanied by a real decrease in crime, and particularly in violent crime.

Violent Crime Figures and Trends

Table 14.5 reports crime ratios by comparing the number of crimes per 100,000 people that occurred during the 1994 and 1999, and Table 14.6 indicates the annual frequencies for reported crime for the period 1994 to 1998.

A comparison of the ratios, figures, and trends in Tables 14.5 and 14.6 with those of 113 Interpol member countries (1996), reveals that in 1996 South Africa was:

Table 14.5
A Comparison of Crime Ratios (per 100,000 of the Population) Related to Specific Crime Categories, 1994–1999

	1994	1995	1996	1997	1998	1999	
Violent crimes							
Murder	34.3	30.6	30.1	27.6	27.2	26.7	↓
Attempted Murder	34.6	32.9	34.2	32.4	32.9	31.6	↓
Robbery with Aggravating Circumstances	103.4	102.8	83.5	77.0	94.7	108.1	↑
Rape	48.7	54.6	60.2	60.2	55.5	55.6	←→
Assault (serious)	251.8	262.4	273.4	268.2	262.1	274.3	↑
Common Assault	234.9	251.7	252.5	237.5	228.4	244.9	←→
Property-related crimes							
Housebreaking – Residential	286.0	302.0	313.1	297.9	303.0	303.3	↑
Housebreaking – Business	115.4	109.2	108.7	106.0	107.7	109.2	←→
Other Robbery	38.6	39.6	63.2	58.5	66.4	77.4	↑
Theft-Motor Vehicle	129.4	133.8	116.9	115.8	123.9	119.8	←→
Theft – Out of/from Vehicles	225.0	237.8	230.6	207.8	213.6	218.7	←→
Other Thefts	481.5	488.4	481.2	455.9	486.1	542.4	↑
Violence aimed at property							
Arson	14.4	11.3	11.3	11.0	11.2	10.4	↓
Malicious Damage to Property	151.6	152.5	155.6	148.4	143.1	147.2	←→
Total	2 149.6	2 209.6	2 214.5	2 104.2	2 155.8	2 269.6	↑

KEY	
Increased	↑
Stabilized	←→
Decreased	↓

Source: CIAC, 1999 (adapted)

Table 14.6
Violent Crime in the Republic of South Africa, January to December 1994–1998

CRIME CATEGORY	CASES REPORTED: JAN – DEC					RATIO PER 100 000 OF THE POPULATION					% DIFFERENCE IN CASES REPORTED				
	1994	1995	1996	1997	1998	1994	1995	1996	1997	1996	1995/94	1996/95	1997/96	1998/97	1998/94
Murder	26 832	26 637	25 782	24 588	24 875	69.3	67.2	63.5	59.2	58.5	-0.7%	-3.2%	-4.6%	1.2%	-7.3%
Attempted murder	27 300	26 512	28 516	28 148	29 418	70.5	66.9	70.3	67.7	69.2	-2.9%	7.6%	-1.3%	4.5%	7.8%
Robbery with aggravating circumstances*	84 900	80 071	67 249	69 691	88 319	219.2	202.0	165.7	167.7	207.6	-5.7%	-16.0%	3.6%	26.7%	4.0%
Other robbery	32 423	40 881	51 506	52 678	62 111	83.7	103.1	126.9	126.8	146.0	26.1%	26.0%	2.3%	17.9%	91.6%
Public violence	1 223	992	907	1 043	1 093	3.2	2.5	2.2	2.5	2.6	-18.9%	-8.6%	15.0%	4.8%-	-10.6%
Rape and attempted rape	42 429	47 506	50 481	52 159	49 280	109.6	119.8	124.4	125.5	115.8	12.0%	6.3%	3.3%	5.5%	16.1%
Indecent assault	3 874	4 873	5 220	5 053	4 851	10.0	12.3	12.9	12.2	11.4	25.8%	7.1%	-3.2%	-4.0%	25.2%
Kidnapping	3 984	4 167	4 156	4 035	4 196	10.3	10.5	10.2	9.7	9.9	4.6%	0.3%	-2.9%	4.0%	5.3%
Abduction	2 808	2 299	2 019	2 705	3 090	7.3	5.8	5.0	6.5	7.3	18.1%	-12.2%	34.0%	14.2%	10.0%
Assault with the intend to inflict grievous bodily harm	210 250	220 990	230 425	234 554	234 056	542.9	557.4	567.8	564.5	550.2	5.1%	4.3%	1.8%	-0.2%	11.3%
Common assault	193 764	205 101	205 333	201 863	199 313	500.3	517.4	506.0	485.8	468.5	5.9%	0.1%	-1.7%	-1.3%	2.9%
Burglary – business premises (including attempts)	89 058	86 379	87 863	88 610	94 102	230.0	217.9	216.5	213.3	221.2	-3.0%	1.7%	0.9%	6.2%	5.7%
Burglary – residential premises (including attempts)	228 021	244 063	246 438	249 375	266 817	588.8	615.6	607.2	600.2	627.2	7.0%	1.0%	1.2%	7.0%	17.0%
Theft of motor vehicles and motorcycles	104 302	101 056	96 715	100 637	107 513	269.3	254.9	238.3	242.2	252.7	-3.1%	-4.3%	4.1%	6.8%	3.1%
Theft out of or from motor vehicles and motorcycles	182 624	189 811	180 229	176 254	188 438	471.5	478.8	444.1	424.2	443.0	3.9%	-5.0%	-2.2%	6.9%	3.2%
Arson	11 357	9 761	10 064	9 830	10 130	29.3	24.6	24.8	23.7	23.8	-14.1%	3.1%	-2.3%	3.1%	-10.8%
Malicious damage to property	122 598	128 393	130 313	127 004	127 590	316.6	323.9	321.1	305.7	299.9	4.7%	1.5%	-2.5%	05.%	4.1%
Illegal possession of firearms and ammunition	11 136	11 866	12 886	12 877	14 463	28.8	30.0	31.8	31.0	34.0	6.7%	8.4%	-0.1%	12.3%	29.9%

* Including hijacking of motor vehicles and trucks, bank robbery, and robbery of cash in transit
† Table 14.6 depicts a selection of violent crimes or crimes that are likely to induce violence. Crimes that usually are associated with nonviolent behavior (shoplifting, forgery, embezzlements, stock-theft, etc.) do not appear in the list. An exception is the illegal possession of firearms and ammunition. The figures for this crime have been listed, since the use of firearms is associated closely with some of the more serious violent crimes

Source: CIAC, 1999 (adapted)

- first in regard to murder, rape, robbery, and violent theft;
- fourth in regard to serious assault; and
- in a somewhat more favorable situation in regard to property-related crimes. For example, South Africa ranked in the thirty-second and twenty-first positions in regard to burglary and the theft of motor vehicles respectively. In these two property-related crime categories, South Africa is in a better position than countries like Canada, Australia, and New Zealand.

International comparisons are, however, always a very risky undertaking. This is because such things as the definitions/descriptions of crime, the counting rules, the sophistication of crime information systems, and the level of underreporting (the so-called dark figure) may differ from one country to another, which may create great differences between countries. Nevertheless, the fact remains that South Africa has particularly high levels of violent crimes against the person. From Table 14.5 it is furthermore clear that, while there was an improvement (decreases and stabilization) in the crime situation during 1996 and 1997, the socioeconomic deterioration in 1998—especially in the second half of 1998—has had a negative effect (increasing trends) on crime in 1998 and 1999. Currently (July 1999) there are increases in the following categories: aggravated robbery, aggravated assault, residential housebreaking, other robbery (mostly unarmed street robbery), and other thefts.

Overall there was an increase of 16.7 percent in serious crime between the first half of 1994 and the first half of 1999 and an increase of 8.4 percent between the first half of 1998 and the first half of 1999. These statistics indicate that since 1998, South Africa again has been in a crisis situation, as far as crime in general and violent crime in particular are concerned. The 8.3 percent increase during the four years between 1994 and 1998 coincides with a population growth rate of 2.2 percent, but the 8.4 percent increase between 1998 and 1999 is far above that expected by the population growth rate. According to Table 14.5, murder, attempted murder, and arson show a decrease between 1998 and 1999. It is, however, noteworthy that, in the case of murder, attempted murder, and (to a lesser extent) arson, these decreases are not at all as significant when compared with those categories that show an increase. The decrease in murder and attempted murder since 1998 can be seen just as readily as a stabilization trend.

The remaining serious crime trends have stabilized since 1994, but it is also clear that, in the majority of crimes, there was upward pressure if one were to compare 1999 to 1998. Examples of this are common assault, housebreaking (business), theft out of/from vehicles, and malicious damage to property. What especially warrants attention is the 16.7 percent increase in robbery with aggravating circumstances between the first half of 1998 and the first half of 1999, and the increases in certain subcategories of violent crime (i.e., hijacking, house and business robberies, and attacks on police officers and farmers), together with the very high levels of violent crime against the person, compared with other Interpol countries.

The Generators of Violent Crime in South Africa

If the crime figures/ratios in Table 14.5 and 14.6 are seen as a crime "scoreboard," the question can be asked: Which factors or generators contribute proportionately to the crime rate? An answer to this question is essential to fight crime effectively in South Africa. However, various problems have been encountered in the attempt to answer this question. A first problem is the fact that the existing crime code list that is used to register all crimes in South Africa was not compiled for use in research. The crime code reporting system was developed as a docket registration and tracking system. Thus, the crimes are registered in broad categories like murder, robbery with aggravated circumstances, and rape. Robbery with aggravated circumstances may include anything from a single person being robbed of a small sum of money at knifepoint outside a neighborhood bar to the theft of large sums during a highway heist of cash in transit, in which six security guards are killed. Likewise, murder may be anything from a single person being killed accidentally in a bar fight to a political massacre of ten people, killed execution style, in a village in KwaZulu-Natal.

A second major problem in analyzing crime data is the lack of explanatory variables on police databases. In other words, crime statistics are not associated with socioeconomic, demographic, or policing (logistical and human resources) data, so it is impossible to test the relationships between crime types and some of these factors. Despite this, analyses of the crime problem have been conducted, especially since 1994. Before 1994, most social scientists in South Africa focused their attention on political transition, instability, and political violence. Soon after 1994, however, it became clear that crime, and violent crime in particular, was the highest priority in South Africa. Consequently, an increasing amount of scientific attention was paid to the subject. For example, a nongovernmental organization (NGO), the Institute for Defense Policy, changed its name to the Institute for Security Studies (ISS), and started to focus on crime and policing. Other NGOs, like the Center for the Study of Violence and Reconciliation and the Institute for Strategic Studies (University of Pretoria), also redirected a substantial amount of their energy to studies of crime, especially violent and organized crime. At the same time, the South African Police Service (SAPS) also started to refocus its energy from the old political security issues to the crime security issue. In fact, the new Department of Safety and Security currently has three sections involved in crime analysis and policing research. The largest of these three sections is the Crime Information Analysis Center (CIAC). Research conducted by the CIAC and other organizations has identified the following generators of crime:

(1) social/socioeconomic, (2) political and ideological, and (3) organized crime.

The Social/Socioeconomic Generator of Crime

It is accepted internationally that the urbanization of youth (especially the 15- to 29-year-old age group) and the social processes that accompany urbanization are very conducive to crime. In South Africa, the role of the almost abnormally high levels of urbanization and urban unemployment should never be underestimated as a contributor to crime. Up to 1986, the majority of black people were kept in the rural areas by influx control measures that were part of the apartheid system. In the overcrowded rural situation, the majority of people were unemployed but nevertheless could rely on the extended family (social network) and subsistence economy to fulfill at least the basic needs of food, clothes, and shelter.

When influx control was abolished in 1986, it released a massive urbanization process that would have started naturally three to five decades earlier. Suddenly, within a space of a decade, a "compacted" urbanization occurred. In reality, the end of urbanization has not yet been seen—at least 50 percent of the black population (15–29 years old) remained in rural areas in 1996. The people who migrate to the cities first are the youngsters (18–30 years), who only find massive unemployment and no extended family (social support network) or subsistence economy to support their basic needs. In the cities, the only support many of them may find is their peer group. The difference between the rich and the poor in the city is very obvious and stark. At the same time, the material possessions of the rich become the measure of success, so a strong and vicious cycle of rising expectations is created. At first the peer group may help provide basic needs, but later the new arrivals are swept away by their destitute circumstances. The inability to support basic needs, plus the vast difference between themselves and the more privileged sector of the population, *may* lead these individuals to become involved in criminal gang activities. This does not mean that all new or poor or unemployed arrivals in the city will become criminals under peer pressure. What it does mean is that the likelihood of these people becoming involved in crime is very high and that the possibility that they will become involved through gang/peer pressure is even higher.

In addition to the compacted urbanization, there is a massive and mostly illegal influx of young work-seekers to South African cities not only from neighboring countries, but also from as far afield as Nigeria, Morocco, Europe, and China. It is estimated that there are between 5 to 8 million of these illegal immigrants in the urban areas of South Africa, amounting to a staggering 10–15 percent of all people in South Africa (Pelser, 1998). The rising levels of crime and violence in South Africa are being linked increasingly to the growing number of illegal immigrants.

Often these immigrants are poverty stricken and, therefore, easily driven to crime. There was an increase of 150 percent in serious crime involving illegal immigrants during the months following the elections in 1994, compared with the same period in 1993. The SAPS has estimated that 14 percent of all crimes within South Africa involve illegal immigrants (Pelser, 1998).

Statistical analysis, victim surveys, docket analysis, and interviews with police officers and perpetrators by the CIAC during 1995–1999 has confirmed several of the aforementioned statements and arguments. The following examples point to specific social trends in violent crime:

- An analysis of an extensive sample of murder dockets in 1996 and 1997 indicates that most murders occur during the weekend, especially on Saturday afternoons or evenings after liquor outlets are closed. In most cases, the perpetrator, victim, or both are under the influence of alcohol. In a typical scenario, an argument ensues between the perpetrator and victim and leads to a common assault. The assault may then escalate into a serious assault and may possibly even end in murder. The weapons that usually are used are knives or broken bottles. Further docket analysis indicates that most murders happen in and around *shebeens* ("illegal" neighborhood taverns or bars).

- Most of the violent crimes against the person follow a definite seasonal cycle with a very high annual peak from December to January and a low from June to July. Other peaks occur over weekends, especially long weekends, and at other times on a monthly basis. These fluctuations indicate that violent crimes may be influenced by social behavior over weekends, the Christmas season, and long weekends (e.g., Easter weekend).

- Geographic crime pattern analysis at the police area level points to a very constant picture over the past few years. The police areas in the Western Cape, the Northern Cape, and, to some extent, the Eastern Cape constantly had much higher ratios of assault (common and serious), rape, and murder than police areas in other provinces. This pattern of violent crime can be related to the vineyard-growing areas of South Africa. Traditionally, the laborers on the wine farms, who were mostly colored people (people of mixed origin), were at least partly remunerated in wine (the notorious "tot system"). Although the tot system has been abolished, it seems to have left a very negative legacy on the drinking habits of future generations. In the above regions, excessive drinking and interpersonal fights are still more visible than in the northeastern regions of the country.

- Victimization surveys (cf., Louw, Shaw, Camerer, and Robertshaw, 1998; Camerer, Louw, Shaw, Artz, and Scharf, 1998; and Statistics South Africa, 1998) completed during the past two to three years indicate that violent crime against the person mostly occurs between victims and perpetrators who knew each other. An analysis of the clearance rates of case dockets also indicated that the clearance of murder (56.3% in 1996), serious assault (73.2% in 1996), and rape (65% in 1996) compare very strongly with those in many Interpol (1996) countries. This also may point to a situation of violence between people familiar to each other and where the perpetrators actually are arrested on the scene of the crime or give themselves over to the police after the crime has been committed.

As in the case of political violence, structural deprivation provides the context in which to understand the increasing levels of crime in South Africa. Apart from the explanations offered above, the increase in crime often is attributed to the destruction of social-control mechanisms, enormous social and economic disparity, unemployment and underdevelopment, and the continued perseverance of a general culture of violence in the country (Hamber, 1998). Clearly, these explanations coincide with the issues, briefly explored earlier, that shaped the period of political violence of the 1980s and 1990s.

The Political and Ideological Generator of Crime

Based on the South African experience during the 1980s and 1990s, there is also evidence that high levels of fear and insecurity may lead to crime and violence (cf., de Kock and Schutte, 1998; de Kock, 1994; and de Kock, Schutte, Rhoodie, and Ehlers, 1993). If people experience high levels of insecurity or fear because of violence, they will start to lose confidence and trust in the official security forces of the state (e.g., the police). They may even believe that the security forces are supporting the "enemy" or "criminal element" and, as a result, start to arm and organize themselves in vigilante or self-protection groups. The moment this situation evolves, the "explosives" are ready to be "ignited." Usually the trigger for vigilante action and the use of violence is a single emotional event that confirms the vigilante group's existing perception of a situation. Consequently, it is believed that action must be taken and that it is appropriate to take preemptive measures against the enemy. Once violence has started in this way, it quickly becomes a vicious cycle of revenge and counterrevenge. Such a cycle of violence is typified by (1) a growth and hardening of existing negative stereotypes, attitudes, intolerance, and dehumanization of the "opposing group"; (2) the institutionalization and internalization of the values of violence in the community and the individual; and (3) the committing of even more violent crimes, which will, in turn, exacerbate the existing feelings of insecurity and fear.

If a feeling of insecurity or fear is the only common denominator for the mobilization of vigilante groups, it probably provides a sufficient condition to resort to violence. However, if historical, ethnic, or cultural denominators such as language or religion are also present and are used as a medium for mobilization among members of the vigilante group, it may pose a much more serious threat to security and stability. All these variables indeed fostered the rise of the vigilante movement People against Gangsterism and Drugs (PAGAD) in South Africa (see next section).

The Organized Crime Generator

Another type of crime that contributes to the statistics on violent crimes is organized crime. According to several analyses by the CIAC, there are at least 500 crime syndicates operating in South Africa, many with wider African and international links. Although it is very difficult to determine the exact extent of organized crime, and even more difficult to determine its contribution to overall crime statistics, it can be said with certainty that organized crime is on the rise. The local conditions for organized crime are stimulated by South Africa's long and porous borders; the end of the country's isolation period; attractive markets of gold, diamonds, ivory, rhino horn, abalone, and so on; a lack of proper money-laundering legislation (until 1998); and unrealistic material expectations brought about by political transformation. In addition, during the years of political struggle many members of the former security forces and liberation armies were trained in guerrilla warfare skills like intelligence gathering, ambush techniques, firearm and explosives handling, and so on. Many of these combatants are now unemployed, but continue to use these skills in hijackings, house and business robberies, bank robberies, and robberies of cash in transit.

Organized crime contributes to the violent crime rate both directly and indirectly. Organized crimes can contribute to the crime rate directly, as through property crimes (e.g., motor vehicle theft and burglaries) committed on a large scale, or through armed robbery, hijacking, and bank robberies that result in violent crimes like murder, attempted murder, rape, assault, and so on. Organized crime also may contribute to violent crime in an indirect fashion. For example, illegal firearms may be supplied to members of the public, who then may use these weapons in situations of interpersonal, domestic, and/or political-ideological conflict.

Current information suggests that, contrary to popular belief, organized crime may contribute much less *directly* than *indirectly* to the crime rate, especially when it comes to violent crime. For example, it seems that the hijacking of vehicles, which is by and large an organized crime, is responsible for approximately sixty murders out of a total of 25,000 that are committed annually. This accounts for only 0.2 percent of the total number of murders. The same applies to bank robberies and robberies of cash in transit: Approximately 100 persons are killed annually in these crimes. This amounts to (only) 0.4 percent of all murders committed.

The Future Prospects of Violent Crime

The historical politicization of social, economic, and civic concerns, amidst the freedom the new dispensation has come to symbolize, has propelled expectations of material progress and has generated a "culture of entitlement" among members of historically disadvantaged and deprived communities. Although these expectations are understandable and even appropriate, there has been inadequate engagement with the residual culture of violence and a lack of anticipation as to the expectations that go with newfound freedoms (Hamber, 1998). Since large numbers of disillusioned South Africans perceived the new government to be failing in its mission to create a better life for all, the unmet expectations and relative deprivation are likely to continue to contribute significantly to violent crime and other forms of violent conflict in South Africa.

THE COMMUNITY STRIKES BACK: VIOLENCE BY VIGILANTE GROUPS

The criminal justice system's perceived inability to combat the rising tide of violent crime in South Africa has lead to the emergence of a number of vigilante groups over the past decade. The most prominent of these groups are PAGAD and the Mapoga-a-Matamaga (the colors of the tiger).

PAGAD originated in 1995 among members of the South African Muslim community as a direct response to the escalating crime and drug situation in the country in general and in the Western Cape Province in particular. PAGAD is said to represent a cross-section of people who believe that they have done all that is in their power to get the police to react to their plight, but to no avail. Thus, they feel left with little alternative but to take the law into their own hands (le Roux, 1997). Ideologically, the movement is rooted firmly in Islamic fundamentalism, and it has been speculated that the group may have ties to militant Middle Eastern Islamic fundamentalist groups such as Hizballah and Hamas.

Over the past few years, members of PAGAD have staged hundreds of marches to the homes of alleged drug dealers and gangsters and also carried out numerous acts of urban terrorism, including drive-by shootings and petrol-bomb and hand-grenade attacks. Since 1997, there also has been a gradual increase in the antigovernment content of PAGAD's message. The changing message can be ascribed to an increasing frustration with the government's inability to combat the tide of drugs and crime. Likewise, the relationship between the police and PAGAD currently is one of growing mutual frustration, as both sides accuse the other of contributing to, rather than solving, the escalating crime problem. The execution-style shooting and killing of police officers investigating PAGAD activities in early 1999 is no doubt indicative of the deterioration and tension in the relationship between the two parties.

Close on the heels of PAGAD, the Mapoga-a-Matamaga, which mainly consists of black businessmen, was formed in August 1996, following the robbery and killing of businessmen. Within a few months membership of the group increased to more than 3,000. According to reports, the group admitted to the "execution" of people whom they alleged the police had been either unwilling to arrest or incapable of arresting (South African Institute of Race Relations, 1998). In mid-1997, most of the leaders of the group were arrested on charges of assault, attempted murder, and public violence. However, by late 1999, the group had gained growing support for its cause among residents of the predominantly white neighborhoods. At the same time, the provincial government of the Northern Province started an investigation, after it had been reported that more than twenty provincial schools had called on Mapoga-a-Matamaga for protection against criminals.

Since mid-1996, several other anticrime groups fashioned after PAGAD emerged in cities such as Durban, Johannesburg, Pietermaritzburg, Port Elizabeth, and Pretoria. The authorities reacted by condemning the vigilante's acts of taking the law into their own hands and stressed the need for strategies that would prevent the spreading of vigilante action to other parts of the country. However, by late 1996, anticrime groupings from Cape Town, Johannesburg, Kimberley, and Port Elizabeth united to form a national anticrime body, People Against Drugs and Gang Violence. At the same time, the Free State Agricultural Union announced that farmers in the Northern Province and in the North West Province had set up commando-style self-defense units and had begun armed patrols in surplus armored vehicles of the South African National Defense Force. The union advised the farmers—who were the targets of successive attacks in the two provinces—to shoot to kill if their lives were threatened.

The operation of vigilante movements, despite grim warnings by the authorities, seems set to become part of South African civil society, especially considering that some 46 percent of South Africans indicated in a Nedcor survey that crime is the country's most serious problem (Hawthorne, 1996). No doubt regular media reports, and hence public perception, of an understaffed, ineffective, poorly managed, and often corrupt police force aggravate this belief.

THE IMPACT OF VIOLENCE ON SOUTH AFRICAN SOCIETY

Apart from what already has been pointed out, the spree of violence and crime has left South Africa scarred in many respects. Although this section highlights only some of the impacts of violence at the structural level (i.e., socioeconomic), it should not be forgotten that the individual consequences at the psychological and personal levels are sometimes equally detrimental to a society's development and well-being. This is particularly true concerning the impact of political violence on the lives of children in South Africa (cf., Botha, 1998; Duncan and Rock, 1997; and Lombard and Van der Merwe, 1998).

Violence is clearly undermining South Africa's already weak and vulnerable economy. A number of potential investors have been frightened off by the violence, as concern about political stability and escalating crime statistics grows on foreign financial markets. Clearly a vicious circle is in operation here: While economic investment and job creation are seen as imperative to solving the problem of violence and crime, such developments are, in themselves, inhibited and compromised by the magnitude of violence. Holtzhausen's observation (1999) that more than 70 percent of local businesses have been affected by some form of crime during the period 1997–1998, is indicative of this problem. Declines in foreign investment and aid, as well as a decline in exports and in the value of the South African currency, all have a negative effect on the trade deficit.

As far as government expenditure is concerned, more money has been allocated to the South African Police Services, the Department of Correctional Services, and the judicial system in an effort to combat crime and violence. Since 1989, the police budget has grown substantially, both in real terms and as a share of total government expenditure. The rising trend in serious crime since the early 1990s has led to growing public pressure on the government to increase the allocation of resources to the police force. By 1996, the police comprised almost 141,000 full-time personnel, compared to 80,000 in 1989 (Batchelor, 1998). In the five years following the first democratic elections in 1994, the Department of Correctional Services opened nine new prisons, with more to follow. While these changes might be interpreted as a dedicated effort on the part of the government to address the problem, the fact remains that protection services (notably the police, prisons, and courts of law) are absorbing a growing proportion of the total budget at the expense of social services such as education, health, housing, and social security. It is reported that, in terms of the medium-term expenditure framework, the government intended to increase spending on justice, police, and prisons by an average of 7.8 percent per year from 1998–1999 to 2000–2001 (South African Institute of Race Relations, 1998). This would imply an increase of 25.4 percent in government expenditure on these sectors for the period 1997–1998 to 2000–2001.

On the social front, thousands of South Africans—mostly highly skilled people—have officially left the country since 1994, citing among others the climate of violence as one of the primary reasons for their decision. In fact, between 1994 and 1997, South Africa experienced a net loss of 3,500 people per year—the longest consecutive period of net loss since the Second World War (South African Institute of Race Relations, 1998). During the same period, the tourism industry experienced a spate of cancellations in foreign bookings, as the major national newspapers headlined several incidents of violence and crime—some of which involved foreign tourists. This also has had a negative impact on the economy in general, and on the creation of new jobs in particular. As such, the causes, manifestation, and impact of violence clearly and inevitably assume a diverse and self-perpetuating life.

IN CONCLUSION: TOWARD THE REDUCTION OF VIOLENCE IN SOUTH AFRICA

Having outlined some of the dynamics and key factors responsible for the culture of violence in South Africa, the question of how to prevent such violence in the future still remains. As South Africa moves through the transition period to democracy, the legacy of political and other manifestations of violence is likely to take its toll on the social, political, and economic lives of all South Africans. In some of these areas the division between political and criminal violence has long been obscured, to the effect that the violence is dragging on and threatening to assume a life of its own—outside the political arena. Unless the root causes of the violence are addressed, it will be extremely difficult to contemplate sustainable processes of reconciliation between the diverse communities in South Africa.

What is clear from the South African context is that the causes and culture of violence are rooted deeply both in history as well as in the process of social transformation. It is of crucial importance to realize that there is no single cause of violence and crime in South Africa. Any attempt, therefore, to establish mono-causal explanations will result merely in simplistic solutions. It is only by examining each of the overlapping factors that lead to a predisposition toward violence that effective strategic planning can be achieved and interventions can be developed. At first glance, it becomes clear that the overlapping factors and possible solutions are much more intertwined—and, in some cases, even virtual images of one another—than at second glance.

Having said this, the question still remains: Can the current unacceptable levels of violence in South Africa be resolved? For various reasons the magnitude of violence can be reduced, but it is unlikely to be resolved. The reason for this belief is the fact that, up to now, violence has paid off. On the political front in particular, violence has led to results in the liberation struggle; it undoubtedly has been used as a mechanism by which parties and movements have positioned themselves and also as a demonstration of the effect of individual power bases. Such sensitivity to the possibilities and rewards of what violence can achieve, or, in other words, perceptions pertaining to the utility value of violence, will not vanish quickly from South African society (Pelser, 1993; Schlemmer, 1997).

There are also sharp inequalities between communities in South Africa, which enables people to compare their circumstances with those of others and which, of course, intensifies feelings of relative deprivation and anger. In South Africa, the underprivileged are especially inclined to evaluate their own position in relation to that of the more privileged sector of the population. A sharp competition for available resources, demands for land, and a fierce competition for jobs aggravate this situation in the transformation period. The latter, like elsewhere in the world, is typified by a vortex of shifting status and power relationships as the old establishment is making way to a new one. In this process, rising expectations for rapid and visible improvements in their circumstances are rife among members of historically deprived communities, and, if these are not fulfilled at an acceptable level, the resultant emotional fuel often explodes into violence (Pelser and Botes, 1992).

Amidst all these realities, South Africa suffers from a very high unemployment rate, combined with high levels of poverty and ultra-poverty. Statistics indicate that approximately 19 million or almost 50 percent of the South African population are currently living in poverty. Some 61 percent of the black population is considered poor (South African Institute of Race Relations, 1998). Simultaneously, the national unemployment rate is fluctuating around 30 percent escalating to almost 37 percent in the black community. In parts of the Eastern Cape Province, up to 70 percent of youths and adults are unemployed (South African Institute of Race Relations, 1998; Schlemmer, 1997). These figures simply mean that there is relatively large contingent of destitute people available to become involved in criminal activities. This does not, however, suggest that there is a direct correlation between poverty and *violent* crime. There is probably some correlation between poverty and acquisitive criminal acts such as theft, shoplifting, and burglary, but it is considerably more difficult to prove any direct link between poverty and *violent* crime. Nevertheless, the view that poverty and relative deprivation both play crucial roles in violence and crime in South Africa has given rise to the important perspective that *long-term* solutions to the problem reside in economic growth and investment, particularly in the creation of employment opportunities and work security for the unemployed.

Long-term undertakings and solutions, however, will do little to address the immediate concern of most South Africans, especially those who are falling victim to violence and crime daily. Thus, the government has introduced a number of initiatives and legislative measures to curtail violence and to demonstrate its seriousness to "take the fight to the criminals." Apart from the implementation of a National Crime Prevention Strategy in 1996, several laws were tabled to address problems in the criminal justice system. Legislation was passed to tighten up bail laws, thus making it more difficult for those accused of committing serious crimes to be granted bail. A non-parole period in the sentences of convicted criminals was introduced to ensure that they would not be considered for release too soon. In May 1997, a three-year moratorium on police recruitment was lifted, and, later the same year, the minister for safety and security announced a program aimed at reducing the proliferation of both legal and illegal firearms in South Africa.

The above measures, however, will not eradicate structural inequalities in the short term. Owing to their structural position, most of those marginalized and victimized in the past remain potential victims as well as potential perpetrators of violence. In addition, their social position of vast poverty and unemployment means that they remain structurally entangled in the cycle of violence and crime. The challenge, therefore, is to couple the process of political transformation with a broader process of social transformation. Such a transition would be characterized by directed development, programs for the prevention of physical violence, and social-awareness and violence prevention education programs. Most important, however, is the need for the resocialization of South Africans, and the younger generation in particular, to eradicate perceptions of entitlement and to foster a culture of greater acknowledgement of authority, greater tolerance, and more respect for basic human rights.

REFERENCES

Batchelor, P. (1998). Policing the provinces: A budgetary analysis. *Development Southern Africa*, *15*(2), 165–185.

Botha, M. (1998). Exposure to television violence and the development of aggression among children: Evidence from various longitudinal studies. In E. Bornman, R. van Eeden, and M. Wentzel (Eds.), *Violence in South Africa: A variety of perspectives* (pp. 287–322). Pretoria: Human Sciences Research Council.

Breytenbach, D. (1999, April). *Crime, violence and conflict in South Africa: A comparison and impact of that on development prior to the 1994 and 1999 democratic elections*. Paper presented at the biennial congress of the Development Society for Southern Africa, Johannesburg.

Camerer, L., Louw, A., Shaw, M., Artz, L., and Scharf, W. (1998). *Crime in Cape Town: Results of a city victim survey*. Johannesburg: Institute for Security Studies.

Coetzer, J.A. (1993). Die omvang van regse geweld in Suid-Afrika. *Journal for Contemporary History*, *18*(2), 152–171.

Crime Information Analysis Center (CIAC). (1999). *The incidence of serious crime: January to December 1998*. Pretoria: Author (South African Police Service).

de Kock, C.P. (1994). Political violence in South Africa: Are we putting out the fire from the top or bottom? In N.J. Rhoodie and I. Liebenberg (Eds.), *Democratic nation building in South Africa* (pp. 21–54). Pretoria: Human Sciences Research Council.

de Kock, C.P., and Schutte, C.D. (1998). Political violence with specific reference to South Africa. In E. Bornman, R. van Eeden, and M. Wentzel (Eds.), *Violence in South Africa: A variety of perspectives* (pp. 57–83). Pretoria: Human Sciences Research Council.

de Kock, C.P., Schutte, C.D., Rhoodie, N.J., and Ehlers, D. (1993). A quantitative analysis of some possible explanations for hostel's township violence. In

A. Minnaar (Ed.), *Communities in isolation: Perspectives on hostels in South Africa* (pp. 31–52). Pretoria: Human Sciences Research Council.

Duncan, N., and Rock, B. (1997). The impact of political violence on the lives of South African children. In C. de la Rey, N. Duncan, T. Shefer, and A. van Niekerk (Eds.), *Contemporary issues in Human Development* (pp. 133–158). Johannesburg: Thomson.

Hamber, B. (1998). Dr. Jekyll and Mr. Hyde: Problems of violence prevention and reconciliation in South Africa's transition to democracy. In E. Bornman, R. van Eeden, and M. Wentzel (Eds.), *Violence in South Africa: A variety of perspectives* (pp. 350–369). Pretoria: Human Sciences Research Council.

Hawthorne, P. (1996). Freedom stained by violence. *Time Australia, 36,* 53.

Holtzhausen, L. (1999, April). *Community-based rehabilitation.* Paper presented at the biennial congress of the Development Society for Southern Africa, Johannesburg.

International Criminal Police Organization (Interpol). (1996). *International Crime Statistics.* Lyons: Author.

le Roux, C.J.B. (1997). People against gangsterism and drugs (PAGAD). *Journal for Contemporary History, 22*(1), 51–80.

Lombard, S., and van der Merwe, A. (1998). Preventive programmes for schools and other institutions. In E. Bornman, R. van Eeden, and M. Wentzel (Eds.), *Violence in South Africa: A variety of perspectives* (pp. 371–398). Pretoria: Human Sciences Research Council.

Louw, A., Shaw, M., Camerer, L., and Robertshaw, R. (1998). *Crime in Johannesburg: Results of a victim survey.* Johannesburg: Institute for Security Studies.

Minnaar, A., and Pretorius, S. (1997). Minibus taxi–related violence in South Africa: A failure of peace efforts or intractable infrastructural problems? In A. Minnaar and M. Hough (Eds)., *Conflict, violence and conflict resolution: Where is South Africa heading?* (pp. 131–158). Pretoria: Human Sciences Research Council.

Minnaar, A., Pretorius, S., and Wentzel, M. (1998). Political conflict and other manifestations of violence in South Africa. In E. Bornman, R. van Eeden, and M. Wentzel (Eds.), *Violence in South Africa: A variety of perspectives* (pp. 13–53). Pretoria: Human Sciences Research Council.

Patel, D. (1997). Taxi wars in South Africa: Can there be peace? In A. Minnaar and M. Hough (Eds.), *Conflict, violence and conflict resolution: Where is South Africa heading?* (pp. 115–130). Pretoria: Human Sciences Research Council.

Pelser, A.J. (1993). The (im)probability of right-wing political violence in a future South Africa: Some indications. *Acta Criminologica, 6*(2), 16–22.

Pelser, A.J. (1998). Heading for Canaan: A reflection on illegal migration in South Africa. *Journal for Contemporary History, 23*(1), 1–14.

Pelser, A.J., and Botes, L.J.S. (1992). *Temas in die politieke sosiologie.* (Themes in political sociology). Pretoria: Academica.

Schlemmer, L. (1997). Political violence in South Africa: Can it be resolved? In A. Minnaar and M. Hough (Eds.), *Conflict, violence and conflict resolution: Where is South Africa heading?* (pp. 1–18). Pretoria: Human Sciences Research Council.

South African Institute of Race Relations. (1998). *South Africa Survey 1997/1998.* Johannesburg: Author.

Statistics South Africa. (1998). *Victims of crime survey.* Pretoria: Author.

15

Violence in the United States of America

June F. Chisholm and Alfred W. Ward

INTRODUCTION

One of the major problems facing contemporary American society is that all Americans now live in an atmosphere in which the *threat* of violence is the reality as much as the pervasiveness of violent acts in the culture is. It is a reality that has been experienced for a much longer time within certain subcultural groups and some women in this country, as well as within the international community. This chapter will present demographics of violence and types of violence, review psychological theories on violence with emphasis on those theories addressing youth, and explore intervention strategies aimed at reducing youth violence in the United States. Any intervention must address the impact on youth, for they are the adult citizens of our future.

VIOLENCE IN AMERICAN HISTORY: A COMMENTARY

The United States of America is the most violent nation in the industrialized world, and the level and types of violence occurring in the United States are comparable to violence occurring in nations in the midst of civil wars or social chaos. Some types of violent behavior have increased, while other forms have been on the decline, or are virtually nonexistent today. Some socially sanctioned behaviors of the past are considered violent by today's standards and, depending on the nature of the act, criminal (e.g., killing a slave, physical battering of a wife by her husband, sexual harassment, coerced sexual relations like date rape, and severe corporal punishment of children). The contemporary experience of violence in the United States leads some to conclude that society is becoming increasingly more violent than ever before. For example, it is true that the prison population has risen 239 percent from 1980 to 1997, from 501,886 people to 1,700,000 people; the United States of America has 4,700 prisons at an annual cost of $38 billion (Bellesiles, 1999). The occurrence of violence in the United States of America varies depending upon how and by whom it is defined, where it occurs, the ways it is documented/recorded, and how it is handled. It is beyond the scope of this chapter and the expertise of the authors to review the history of violence in the United States. Future efforts to understand the historical context of contemporary violence in the United States are necessary from a psychological standpoint in order to address violence in our society comprehensively and to develop preventive strategies from the micro-to the macrolevel, from the individual to the society at large.

In 1984, then–Surgeon General of the United States C. Everett Koop, declared that violence had become a public health issue. Within the last twenty years of the twentieth century, Americans witnessed heightened security measures to thwart acts of terrorism from international militant groups. Barricades and fences surround many of the federal, state, and local government agencies. In the past, these places were deemed "open" to the public, reflecting the Zeitgeist of the times about the form of democracy and the right of every individual to "free" access. Within the past twenty years, visiting an airport ceased to be an occasion for the family ritual of seeing a loved one travel. Years ago, anyone, not just the person traveling, could mill about in airport restaurants and lounges, even board the plane. No more! The use of commercial airplanes, fueled for long-distance travel, as armed missiles by terrorists to wreck havoc in the United States on September 11, 2001, shut down the industry and has stopped many Americans from flying, despite the increased security measures now in place.

Heightened security in the United States has taken on new meaning since September 11, 2001. Prior to that date, heightened security meant shatterproof-glass partitions shielding public servants from the "public," including the would-be perpetrator; in urban settings in particular, these partitions are now commonplace in banks, post offices, local candy/newsstands, and taxicabs. Now heightened security may involve policies and procedures that might change the American fundamental notion of civil liberties. How to establish and maintain better security for all, while preserving the constitutional civil liberties of the individual, is the question before the democracy now.

Carll (1999) captures the real tragedy in the kind of violence occurring in contemporary United States. She writes, "If there is one point that has come up again and again . . . it is the deeply troubling sense of disconnection on the part of so many perpetrators of violence from the consequences of their violent acts. It is not even that they lack remorse for what they did. It is that in so many cases . . . they seem almost totally oblivious to the loss, grief, and pain they have inflicted. The perpetrators often seem simply not to perceive others as really existing, with lives, loves, and hopes of their own. They seem to think that others exist merely for their own use and can be abused or beaten without question or even worse. A terrible loss of empathy runs throughout all segments of our society" (p. 192).

CULTURE, ETHNICITY, RACE, GENDER, SEXUAL ORIENTATION, AND VIOLENCE IN THE UNITED STATES

The society of the United States is pluralistic, consisting of individuals from all over the world representing different cultures, ethnicities, nationalities, and religions. The vitality of our nation is enhanced by continued efforts to embrace the uniqueness of diversity in the United States. Unfortunately, some forms of violence in the United States stem from conflict, prejudice, and discrimination against certain groups of people (e.g., racial minorities, women, gays, lesbians, and transgendered individuals). Any serious discussion of violence in the United States, therefore, must acknowledge the influence of culture, ethnicity, gender, race, sexual orientation, and socioeconomic status, although it is beyond the scope of this chapter to explore fully the multitudinous impact of these variables on violence in the United States.

With respect to women, Cole (1986) eloquently expresses the dilemma:

> To address our commonalities without dealing with our differences is to misunderstand and distort that which separates as well as that which binds us as women. Patriarchal oppression is not limited to women of one race, ethnic group, women in one class, women of one age group or sexual preference, women who live in one part of the country, women of any one religion, or women with certain physical abilities or disabilities. While oppression of women knows no such limitations, we cannot, therefore, conclude that the oppression of all women is identical. . . . That which women have in common must always be viewed in relation to the particularities of a group, for even when we narrow our focus to one particular group of women it is possible for differences within that group to challenge the primacy of what is shared in common. (Pp. 2, 3)

From this perspective, the view that women are more likely to be abused, violated, and subjected to acts of violence due to gender inequality (i.e., lack of power relative to men), while generally believed to be true, can overlook the vicissitudes of the abuse inherent in practices rooted in class- and gender-related and/or cultural/ethnic/racial/religious traditions. Consider, for example, the practice of female genital mutilation (FGM) (Heise, 1994).

During the late 1990s, the plight of 19-year-old Fauziya Kasinga, who sought asylum in the United States of America after fleeing Togo when she was 16 to escape having a tribal member scrape her woman parts off, drew international attention and condemnation of this type of gender abuse. Apropos of this, in 1996, legislators in several states, upon learning that the practice of FGM has been occurring in the United States of America, drafted legislation that made FGM illegal in the United States. Enforcing this law will be very difficult unless women from the effected communities reach out to the larger society for help in changing the beliefs that perpetuate the practice.

Race in the United States takes on a cultural significance as a result of the social processes that sustain majority-minority status (Pinderhughes, 1989). The subordinate status assigned to persons with given physical traits and the projections made upon them are used to justify exclusion or inclusion within the society. The responses of both those who are dominant and the victims who are subordinate have been violent at times (e.g., Ku Klux Klan lynchings and cross burnings and the race riots of the 1960s), becoming part of their cultural adaptation. The meaning assigned to class status as well as racial categorization is determined by the dynamics of stratification and stereotyping.

Subordinates can and have coped with the power imbalance between them and the dominants through "horizontal hostility" (Pharr, 1988 p. 61), that is, members of a subordinate group expressing hostility in a horizontal direction toward one's own kind. Consequently, there may be infighting among members of a subordinate group. According to Pharr (1988), "we may see people destroying their own neighborhoods, displaying violence and crime toward their own kind, while respecting the power of those that make up the norm" (p. 61). Self-hatred is often the result of the internalization of the dominant group's beliefs that those who are subordinates are substandard, defective, and inferior. The form this hatred takes varies from subordinate group to subordinate group.

While the pervasiveness of violence in American society is evident, the perception linking violence primarily with poverty, pervasive unemployment, the uneducated, and disenfranchised ethnic groups persists. The public (e.g., politicians, social-policy makers, mental health practitioners, social workers, educators, etc.) is beginning to comprehend that violence is a significant threat to everyone in our society, not just those who live in inner cities and who are poor, unemployed, uneducated, or a member of an ethnic minority. While reducing "black crime" or "inner-city crime" is vitally important, even the elimination of black/inner-city crime will not make a significant dent in the endemic nature of violence and the threat of violence in the United States.

The misperception of the relationship between nonwhite crime (including acts of violence) and violence in our society makes it virtually impossible to launch successful initiatives for social reform. As Cose (1993) indicates:

blacks account for about 45 percent of those arrested for USA's violent crimes. But it is not true that most black males are vicious. FBI statistics show, that blacks were arrested 245,437 times in 1991 for murder, forcible rape, robbery, and aggravated assault. The country's total population then was just under 249 million, including nearly 31 million blacks and roughly 15 million black males. If we assume that each arrest represents the apprehension of a separate individual, blacks arrested for violent crimes made up less than 1 percent of the black male population (less, in fact, since the aggregate figure of 245,437 includes crimes committed by females). In other words, less than one-tenth of a percent of the population—not 6 percent—is committing 45 percent of violent crimes. (P. 95)

Cose goes on to suggest that any reasonable analysis of the statistics on crime should dispel the association between violent perpetrators and "black." However, the stereotype persists and obfuscates the root causes of the problem. One can maintain the illusion of security and safety by attempting to secure the boundaries that separate racial and ethnic minority groups, the affluent from the working classes and the poor. Indeed, the trend of the affluent is to move into "gated" communities with high-tech security systems encapsulating them from the realities of those less financially secure. Violence, when it does occur and does not fit the stereotype, is perceived and often depicted in the media as an aberration, as a random, tragic incident, rather than a reflection of the American way of life gone awry.

DEMOGRAPHICS OF VIOLENCE

The U.S. Department of Justice defines acts of violence as crimes; a crime can be the violent act of murder or stealing property without injury to anyone. Criminal activity, then, involves breaking laws, hence demographers keep records of what is reported by victims or known to the police. The Federal Bureau of Investigation (FBI) compiles crime statistics according to various categories (FBI, 1999). Tables 15.1 and 15.2 present information on crime indexes and the region of the country where they occur.

MEDIA VIOLENCE

While it is commonly accepted that the media contributes to the proliferation of violence in the United States, the precise mechanism through which the media influences the impact of violence remains controversial. Psychological research has investigated such factors as observational learning, role modeling, and exposure leading to desensitization as possible mechanisms in this process. Aggression and violence in the United States seemingly have become idealized, as evidenced in television programs, films, video, and music. Clearly there are more explicit violent im-

Table 15.1
Index of Crime, 1998

Area	Population[1]	Crime Index total	Modified Crime Index total[2]	Violent crime[3]	Property crime[3]	Murder and non-negligent man-slaughter	Forcible rape	Robbery	Aggravated assault	Burglary	Larceny-theft	Motor vehicle theft	Arson[2]
United States Total	270,296,000	12,475,634		1,531,044	10,944,590	16,914	93,103	446,625	974,402	2,329,950	7,373,886	1,240,754	
Rate per 100,000 inhabitants		4,615.5		566.4	4,049.1	6.3	34.4	165.2	360.5	862.0	2,728.1	459.0	
Metropolitan Statistical Area	215,575,223												
Area actually reporting[4]	92.7%	10,119,626		1,306,087	8,813,539	14,036	71,744	416,390	803,917	1,834,598	5,868,594	1,110,347	
Estimated totals	100.0%	10,724,952		1,359,174	9,365,778	14,538	77,788	426,706	840,142	1,940,002	6,276,315	1,149,461	
Rate per 100,000 inhabitants		4,975.0		630.5	4,344.6	6.7	36.1	197.9	389.7	899.9	2,911.4	533.2	
Cities outside metropolitan area	21,991,208												
Area actually reporting[4]	77.1%	870,077		81,827	788,250	732	6,172	12,236	62,687	157,975	589,853	40,422	
Estimated totals	100.0%	1,096,760		97,708	999,052	884	7,825	14,517	74,482	194,599	755,413	49,040	
Rate per 100,000 inhabitants		4,987.3		444.3	4,543.0	4.0	35.6	66.0	338.7	884.9	3,435.1	223.0	
Rural Counties	32,729,569												
Area actually reporting[4]	76.0%	534,982		62,497	472,485	1,344	5,861	4,639	50,653	159,113	278,450	34,922	
Estimated totals	100.0%	653,922		74,162	579,760	1,492	7,490	5,402	59,778	195,349	342,158	42,253	
Rate per 100,000 inhabitants		1,998.0		226.6	1,771.4	4.6	22.9	16.5	182.6	596.9	1,045.4	129.1	

[1] Populations are Bureau of the Census provisional estimates as of July 1, 1996-1998, and are subject to change.

[2] Although arson data are included in the trend and clearance tables, sufficient data are not available to estimate totals for this offense.

[3] Violent crimes are offenses of murder, forcible rape, robbery, and aggravated assault. Property crimes are offenses of burglary, larceny-theft, and motor vehicle theft. Data are not included for the property crime of arson.

[4] The percentage representing area actually reporting will not coincide with the ratio between reported and estimated crime totals, since these data represent the sum of the calculations for individual states which have varying populations, portions reporting, and crime rates.

Complete data for 1998 were not available for the states of Illinois, Kansas, Kentucky, Montana, New Hampshire, and Wisconsin. See Offense Estimation, Appendix I, for details.

Source: *Crime in the United States, 1998: Uniform Crime Reports.* Federal Bureau of Investigation, 1999.

Table 15.2
Index of Crime, by Region, 1998

Region	Population	Crime Index total	Modified Crime Index total[1]	Violent crime[2]	Property crime[2]	Murder and non-negligent manslaughter	Forcible rape	Robbery	Aggravated assault	Burglary	Larceny-theft	Motor vehicle theft	Arson[1]
United States Total[3]	100.0	100.0		100.0	100.0	100.0	100.0	100.0	100.0	100.0	100.0	100.0	
Northeastern States	19.1	14.4		16.9	14.0	13.1	13.1	21.4	15.3	13.1	14.1	15.5	
Midwestern States	23.3	22.1		20.3	22.3	21.4	24.8	19.9	20.0	20.9	23.1	20.1	
Southern States	35.3	40.0		39.5	40.0	43.9	39.1	36.1	40.9	42.8	39.8	36.2	
Western States	22.3	23.6		23.3	23.6	21.7	22.9	22.6	23.8	23.2	23.0	28.2	

[1] Although arson data are included in the trend and clearance tables, sufficient data are not available to estimate totals for this offense.

[2] Violent crimes are offenses of murder, forcible rape, robbery, and aggravated assault. Property crimes are offenses of burglary, larceny-theft, and motor vehicle theft. Data are not included for the property crime of arson.

[3] Because of rounding, the percentages may not add to totals.

Complete data for 1998 were not available for the states of Illinois, Kansas, Kentucky, Montana, New Hampshire, and Wisconsin. See Offense Estimation, Appendix I, for details.

Source: *Crime in the United States, 1998: Uniform Crime Reports.* Federal Bureau of Investigation, 1999.

ages portrayed in the visual arts (movies, television, video games, porno-graphic magazines, etc.) and more violent themes and lyrics produced by the music industry than a generation ago. Yet, there is considerable dis-agreement about the role the media plays in creating and maintaining the climate of violence in our society. Is it simply a question of art imitating life or life imitating art? Do media violence and violent lyrics harm chil-dren? How should society respond to media violence? What action, if any, should the government take to safeguard against the portrayal of exces-sive and graphic violence in the media? In the last political campaign for president of the United States of America, Albert Gore, his wife Tipper, and his running mate Joseph Lieberman, took a firm stand, appealing to Hollywood and the media to exercise self-restraint and regulate them-selves lest the government be called in to put a stop to the promulgation of media violence. Based on findings of several empirical studies, the mass media and entertainment industries have been called to task for their "glorification of violence" and gratuitous inclusion of violence in televi-sion and movies because of evidence suggesting a casual relationship be-tween viewing and aggression/violence (Drevitch, 1994; Guthmann, 1994; Murray, 1997; *National Television Violence Study*, cited in Dudley, 1999, pp. 17–23). On the other hand, Freedman (1999) in 1995, argued be-fore the U.S. Senate Committee on Commerce, Science, and Transporta-tion that the empirical evidence does not support the claim that television violence effects aggression or crime. From the studies he reviewed, he cites a small effect at the most, indicating a minor causal relationship be-tween television violence and aggression and violence.

DOMESTIC VIOLENCE/CHILD ABUSE/ELDER ABUSE

Although in the United States husbands no longer can beat their wives legally, and although wives in the United States legally can sue their hus-bands for damages, the practice remains a reality for far too many women and their families. The U.S. Department of Justice estimates that about one woman in four will be subjected to domestic abuse during her lifetime. Approximately 20 percent of emergency room visits for trauma and 25 percent of homicides of women involve intimate partner violence (IPV). Women are about eight times more likely to be victimized by an intimate partner than are men. According to Meadows (1998), although women do assault their partners, it is more likely to be in self-defense. As will be dis-cussed in more detail later in this chapter, those family members who ex-perience violence, as well as those who witness it, are likely to experience emotional and/or physical trauma that compromises future healthy de-velopment and predisposes them to acts of violence within and outside of the family. Research indicates that early exposure to abuse increases the risk of violent behaviors in children. Girls who witness beatings in abusive relationships are 300 times more likely to be in abusive relationships when they grow up; boys who see their mothers beaten are more likely to be abusive adults (Van der Kolk, 1984, 1991).

More than 1 million confirmed cases of child abuse and neglect occur in the United States annually. Eighty percent of abused children receive their injuries from their own caretakers. Other relatives account for an additional 10 percent.

Within the past decade, researchers have identified different types of elder abuse, including physical abuse, psychological abuse, material abuse, financial abuse, violation of rights, active neglect, passive neglect, and psychological neglect. In 1984, a California study conducted by the California State Department of Social Services found that the typical elder abuse victim was female (73%) and about 78 years of age; almost two-thirds of the abused were white (65%) or unknown (17.8%), and Hispanics followed with 8.8 percent, blacks with 7.5 percent, and others with 2.2 percent (Landes, Foster, and Cessna, 1995).

VIOLENCE IN THE WORKPLACE

Violence in the workplace was rare twenty years ago; today homicide in the workplace is increasing more rapidly than homicide in any other sector of society. This type of violence occurs mostly in urban settings, and the crime can be committed by virtually anyone within the workplace (e.g., coworker, supervisor) or those having no direct relationship to the workplace or the employees (e.g., random killings and robberies at fast food restaurants). A survey of human resource managers throughout the nation and conducted by the Society for Human Resource Management in Alexandria, Virginia, found that 153 of the 479 respondents reported that acts of violence had occurred in their workplace. These most often involved employee-to-employee confrontations, followed by employee-to-supervisor and customer-to-employee confrontations (Dawson, 2001).

Some of the workplaces with the highest rates of homicide are in taxis, liquor stores, gas stations, grocery stores, jewelry stores, hotels, justice/public order establishments (e.g., courts), and eating/drinking establishments. Of the 7,600 homicide victims in the workplace during the period 1980–1989, 80 percent were male (Mantell and Albrecht, 1994).

HATE CRIMES

Hate crimes constitute a special category of violence characterized by violent acts against people, property, or organizations because of the group to which the victims belong or with whom they identify. Targeted groups include people of color (e.g., black, brown people), ethnic minorities (e.g., African American, Puerto Rican, Asian American), different religious and/or ethnic groups (e.g., Jews, Muslims, Catholics), people with different sexual orientations (e.g., gay, lesbian, bisexual, transgendered) women; and people with disabilities, to name a few (Dawson, 2001). Since 1991, the year after the passage of the Hate Crimes Statistics Act, state and federal law enforcement agencies have been compiling nationwide hate crime statistics. According to the FBI, about 85 percent of hate crimes in 1998 involved an attack against a person. The offense ranges from simple assault (i.e., no weapon) to aggravated assault, rape, and murder (FBI, 1999).

Two of the most heinous examples of hate crime in the United States took place in Jasper, Texas, and Fort Collins, Colorado, both in 1998. In Jasper, three white men with jail records offered a ride to a black man who apparently accepted and was then beaten, tied to the back of their truck, and dragged until his body was partially dismembered. In Fort Collins, Matthew Shepard, a young gay man, was beaten badly and tied to a fence by two homophobic men; he died several days later.

It is important to note that there are varying accounts on the prevalence of hate crimes because of states' differences in the way such crimes are defined and reported. Also, data on hate crimes collected by social scientists and organizations—such as the Anti-Defamation League, the National Asian Pacific American Legal Consortium, and the National Gay and Lesbian Task Force—show a higher prevalence of hate crime than do federal statistics.

YOUTH VIOLENCE

Homicide was the second leading cause of death in 15- to 24-year-olds, the third leading cause of death among elementary school children ages 5 to 14, and the leading cause of death for young African Americans during the late 1980s and early 1990s (CDC, 1992; Children's Defense Fund, 1997, Osofsky, 1997). Homicides by adolescents ages 14 to 17 rose from 16.2 per 100,000 juveniles in 1990 to 19.1 per 100,000 in 1994 (Herbert, 1996). Moreover, the number of juveniles under the age of 15 years arrested for murder increased by 50 percent from 1984 to 1992 (Greenwood, 1995). The rate was up not only among poor youths in urban areas (the rate among black youth is five times that for white youths), but also among all races, social classes, and lifestyles. Youth crime shifted from crimes against property to violent crime against people. According to the FBI, there was a 249 percent increase in gun-related murders committed by juveniles between the years 1985 and 1995. While the rate of juvenile arrests for violent crimes increased during that period, the rate peaked during 1994 and began to decline thereafter. In 1998, the rate stood just 13 percent above the 1980 or 1988 levels (see Figure 15.1). The sharp declines in the juvenile murder arrest rate from 1993 through 1998 have returned the rate to its 1987 level,

Figure 15.1
Juvenile Violent Crime Index Arrest Rate, 1980–1998

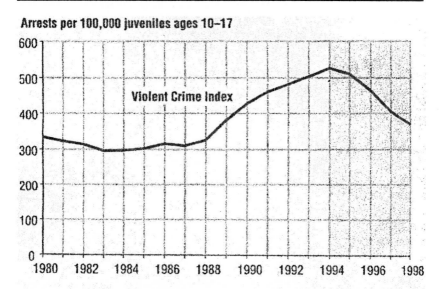

Arrests per 100,000 juveniles ages 10–17

Violent Crime Index

The growth in the juvenile violent crime arrest rate from 1988 to 1994 was largely erased by 1998, with the 1998 rate just 13% above the 1988 level.

Source: Snyder and Sickmund, 1999.

negating all of the increase that stimulated so many changes in juvenile justice policy in the 1990s (Synder, 1999).

A small percentage of youth join delinquent gangs, and few gang members engage in violence. However, in three out of four cases of murder and assault committed by youth, the perpetrators are more than likely to be gang members. Gang violence increased considerably in both level and type of violence in the United States during the 1970s and 1980s. Gangs exist in all fifty states, in suburbia as well as the inner city. A survey of thirty-five cities in 1989 reported a total of 1,439 gangs. Today the estimate has increased to about 2,000 gangs with as many as 200,000 members. Whereas in the past the weapons of choice were fists, chains, and switchblades, the shift to AK-47s or Uzis and the practice of drive-by shootings has escalated the level of destruction and violence astronomically.

Today, young people face unprecedented choices and pressures, and all too often the parental guidance they need is lacking. At a time when the role of the father in the process of parenting is changing such that many more fathers are assuming more primary care responsibilities, too many others are reneging on their parental responsibilities by emotionally and financially abandoning their children, particularly if separated or divorced. When examining incidents of familial violence along with the increase of juvenile violence, research findings indicate that children who are exposed to violence directly or indirectly are at risk for engaging in aggressive and violent tactics themselves, especially as a way of dealing with interpersonal conflicts and coping with stress (Garrett, 1997).

School Violence

Metal detectors and armed security guards are now commonplace in many inner-city school districts. Acts of school violence are now distributed across the entire spectrum of the United States and are no longer viewed as basically an inner-city phenomenon. For example, on February 14, 2001, Jeremy Getman, an 18-year-old senior at Southside High School in Elmira, New York, was arrested after a police officer found him in the school cafeteria armed with a .22 caliber semiautomatic weapon and carrying a duffel bag packed with fourteen pipe bombs, three carbon dioxide cartridge bombs filled with gunpowder, one propane bomb, and a sawed-off shotgun with several rounds of pellets. A classmate, after receiving a disturbing note from Getman, informed a teacher, who then notified school officials, who then thwarted whatever this youth was planning (*New York Times*, 2001). On December 2, 1997, it was reported in the *New York Times* that a 14-year-old boy in West Paducah, Kentucky, drew a gun and shot eight students who had just finished a prayer meeting in a high school lobby.

The present author (Chisholm) recently had lunch with an old friend who is a principal of a middle school in a middle-income neighborhood in a community on Long Island, New York. She related her experience with the emergence of gang activity among a group of 12-year-old boys and girls at her school during December 2000. An alert school coordinator noticed the signs of gang-related activity (e.g., change in style of dress, including scarves of a particular color, jackets with the word *killer* inscribed on the back, handshakes, and menacing behaviors toward other children) and brought it to her attention. She took immediate action by rounding them all up and calling in their parents for a mandatory three-hour session, about which she said, "I had to let them know who was in charge and instill the fear of God in them. Thank God their parents backed me up." What she learned was that this "gang" had been in existence for about three to four weeks; the initiation rites involved criminal acts (to that date, several had broken into cars and stolen money from other children); the majority of these children were from "good" homes with intact families. The parents in attendance were horrified at what they were hearing, apparently for the first time, and agreed to cooperate with whatever recommendations were made. When asked what she thought had prompted these children to behave in this way, she replied without hesitation, "peer pressure and parents asleep at the wheel" (Brown, 2001).

THEORETICAL PERSPECTIVES ON VIOLENCE

Theories and research on violence have explored and attempted to understand this phenomenon from different perspectives, ranging from the micro-(i.e., the psychology of the offender) to the macrolevel (i.e., a focus on society itself examining sociopolitical, economic, and cultural factors).

Lefer (1984) discusses why some individuals can restrain themselves from inflicting injury while others cannot. Depending on the strength of repression, suppression, inhibition, reaction formation, rationalization, and conscience, a violence-prone individual (VPI) may be categorized as (1) one who uses violence as a means to an end without a need for justification, (2) one who uses violence as a means to an end but must justify it to his/her conscience, (3) one who is violent only in a dissociated or drugged state, or (4) one who becomes symbiotic with another VPI and aids the other in committing violence. The dreams of VPIs often reenact the violence inflicted upon them and their intimates in childhood and youth.

The Gluecks' longitudinal research in delinquency found that the quality of the home environment distinguished between delinquent and nondelinquent boys (1950). Recent research examines the relationship between exposure to chronic community violence and various stress reactions, such as posttraumatic stress symptoms, dissociation, and antisocial behavior (including violent acts) among inner-city adolescents (Bell and Jenkins, 1993; Richters and Martinez, 1993; Cole, 1995; Hoch-Espada, 1997). It is hypothesized that the impact of exposure to chronic violence traumatizes the child or adolescent. This individual who, without treatment, may become desensitized to acts of violence, develops a habitual pattern of coping with chronic, albeit unpredictable, violence, which perpetuates the violent climate by which they were once threatened. Hoch-Espada (1997) found a relationship between exposure to violence, stress, and antisocial behavior. She speculates that youth who engage in aggressive behavior may be attempting to master their own feelings of helplessness they experienced while being traumatized. She writes, "In behavioral reenactments of the trauma, these youth play the vacillating roles of both victim and victimizer" (p. 128). These studies raise questions about the trends toward more punitive measures for dealing with violent youth. "The truant, the juvenile delinquent, and/or the disobedient adolescent son may require therapeutic intervention before and/or in place of punitive consequences. Unless violent and criminal behavior is treated differently, with attention to the underlying PTSD (Post Traumatic Stress Disorder) component, a perpetuation of violence will continue to occur" (Hoch-Espada, 1997, 131).

Juvenile delinquents are not the sole perpetrators of violence within our schools and neighborhoods. Today many young people resort to acts of violence as a means of dealing with high levels of stress, anxiety, fear, frustration, and anger. All too often, these children lack the guidance of a mature, nurturing parent in the home or an empathic teacher in the school.

It is extremely difficult to analyze the ways in which contemporary parenting attitudes and behavior among "healthy" and functional families may contribute to the level of violence the United States is now witnessing. Practices not sufficient to be classified as abuse and hence warrant sanction may nonetheless be precursors to maltreatment and/or detrimental to the healthy development of the individual. These qualitatively different disturbances in parent-child interactions are likely to be more subtle, frequent, continuous, and detrimental in their long-term effects on the family (Lyons-Ruth, Connell, Zoll, and Stahl, 1987; Chisholm, 1995).

Miller (1990) refers to those child-rearing practices that are harmful because the intent is to suppress vitality, creativity, and feeling in the child as "poisonous pedagogy." In general, parents who raise children to be obedient, compliant, "well behaved," and deferential to authority figures adhere to coercive methods consistent to Miller's view. It is a learning process that teachers power differences when it is difficult for the child to evaluate what is being taught. Miller writes, "No one ever slaps a child out of love but rather because in similar situations, when one was defenseless, one was slapped and then compelled to interpret it as a sign of love. This inner confusion prevailed for thirty or forty years and is passed on to one's own child. That's all. To purvey the confusion to the child as truth leads to new confusions that, although examined in detail by experts, are still confusions. If, on the other hand, one can admit one's errors to the child and apologize for a lack of self-control, no confusions are created" (p. 35).

VIOLENCE PREVENTION STRATEGIES

Historically, each of the models (i.e. community mental health, social action, and ecology) within psychology can be used to conceptualize prevention of violence from micro-to the macrolevel contexts (e.g., intrapersonal, interpersonal, group, behavior, setting, organization/institution, community, society). Psychologists adhering to one or more of these models have sought competency-based training programs, social advocacy, and grassroots community development as viable solutions to try to curb violence in the United States.

Grossman's (1995) application of the lessons of combat killing is instructive to the course of action necessary to control peacetime violence. He posits that the three psychological processes at work in enabling violence are classical conditioning, operant conditioning, and the observation and imitation of vicarious role models in social learning. The major difference between these processes as they operate both during combat training and in our culture is that, within the latter, the built-in stimulus discriminators that ensure that violent acts are triggered under authority are missing. That is, according to his metaphor, the United States has removed the safety catch; the mechanism to inhibit the expression of violence has been disengaged. Americans as a people are desensitized to violent behavior. Moreover, because of the influence of the media, acts of violence are linked to "entertainment." Consequently, Americans as a people have lost the capacity to empathize with the pain and suffering of others.

Primary Prevention Strategies

As with other public health concerns like tuberculosis, smoking cigarettes, and AIDS, reducing and hopefully eliminating the impact of school violence requires comprehensive, multifaceted strategies that recognize the pervasiveness of the problem. Prothrow-Stith (1991) recommends intervention strategies at the primary, secondary, and tertiary levels of prevention. A primary preventative initiative, for instance, might focus on the industries that, operating according to the profit motive, are making money by producing and marketing products that contribute to our violence-ridden society. That is to say that one needs to examine those industries that are directly or indirectly connected to the proliferation of violence. For example, the manufacture, marketing, and distribution of guns are lucrative fields. Unfortunately, the number of children who died between 1983 and 1993 because of gunfire nearly doubled, and gun crime among juveniles has risen steeply (Children's Defense Fund, 1997).

Society needs to consider why the production and sale of guns—especially handguns and assault weapons having the sole purpose to injure or cause death to the general public—are sanctioned. For those who argue that it is a constitutional right to bear arms, perhaps legislation and sanctions could be imposed on the industry to make "smart guns." As Wilson (1985) suggests, the technology exists whereby guns can be equipped with devices that render them inoperable when fired by someone other than the licensed owner.

Primary prevention strategies aimed at school reform for the elimination of gross discrepancies in the scope and quality of public education provided by the state and local municipalities for children from different socioeconomic backgrounds would lead to a reduction in a host of social ills, including the prevalence of violence among youth.

Initiatives designed to combat violence at the secondary prevention level emphasize approaches to identify youth at risk for violence, establishing programs for early detection, and implementing conflict resolution/management strategies in the school. Sarason (1982) suggests that explanations (and consequent solutions) that are based on the characteristics of individuals may contain an element of truth (and be modestly successful), but that truth is obtained at the expense of discerning regularities that transcend the individual, persisting more as a function of structure and process variables. Thus, solutions focusing on individuals (microlevel) would not necessarily prove, and indeed have not proven, to stem significantly the tide of violence in the schools. Recognizing school violence as a phenomenon existing within the culture of the schools, which in turn mirror some disturbing trends in contemporary American culture, becomes imperative.

TERRORISM

Terrorism is the use of violence and/or the threat of violence to intimidate a government and civilian population for some political agenda. Americans have witnessed acts of terrorism both overseas and within the borders of the United States, including:

- The September 11, 2001, terrorist attack, in which four commercial airliners were hijacked and used as missiles; two crashed into the World Trade Center Towers in New York City, destroying them and resulting in the deaths of 6,000 people; the third crashed into a section of the Pentagon in Washington, DC, killing 189 people; the fourth hijacked plane crashed in Pennsylvania after the passengers overpowered the terrorists, thwarting their plan to attack another U.S. target
- The terrorist bombing of the Murrah building by convicted terrorist Timothy McVeigh, which resulted in massive destruction and the deaths of 166 men, women, and children in Oklahoma City in 1995
- The bombing at the World Trade Center buildings in 1993
- The explosion of Pan Am Flight 103 and its subsequent crash over Lockerbie, Scotland, killing 270 people in 1988
- The bombing of the U.S. Marine barracks in Beirut, resulting in 241 deaths in 1983

From 1990 to 1995 the FBI (1995) reported twenty-nine incidents of terrorism in the United States. Of the twenty-nine incidents, only two were considered acts of international terrorism—the 1992 takeover of the Iranian Mission to the United Nations and the bombing of the World Trade Center in 1993. Domestic terrorists caused the other twenty-seven incidents (see Figure 15.2).

Figure 15.1
Terrorism in the United States, 1980–1995

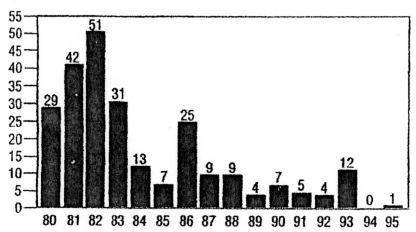

Source: *Crime in the United States, 1988: Uniform Crime Reports.* Federal Bureau of Investigation, 1999.

CONCLUSION

The American Psychological Association (APA) has recognized the complexity and scope of violence in the United States and has launched several initiatives throughout the nation in an effort to reduce violence. The present author (Chisholm) has participated in one of the APA initiatives developed in conjunction with MTV, a popular television program among youth. This past year the author has been participating in staff-development and teacher-training workshops within the high schools of New York City, talking about the warning signs of violence in an effort to curtail violence in the schools.

The motives that may generate aggression and violence result from the objective nature of events as well as the way these events are construed. According to one source, violent behavior, particularly homicide, suicide, and mass murder "is an expression of the inability to control negative emotions." Sarason's (1982) observations about the "problem of change" within the school system are apropos of our understanding about the "problem of violence" in the United States. He writes, "Far from being peculiar to schools, the problem of [violence] is the problem of every major institution in our society, and that fact alone suggests that our conceptions [about how to reduce violence] have deep roots in the nature of our society" (p. 44).

REFERENCES

Bell, C. and Jenkins, E. (1993). Community violence and children on Chicago's southside. *Psychiatry, 56*(5), 46–54.

Bellesiles, M. (Ed.). (1999). *Lethal imagination: Violence and brutality in American history*. New York: New York University Press.

Brown, D. (2001). Personal communication.

Carll, E. (1999). *Violence in our lives: Impact on workplace, home and community*. Boston: Allyn & Bacon.

Centers for Disease Control and Prevention (CDC). (1992). Homicide surveillance: 1979–1988. *Morbidity and Mortality Weekly Report. 41*, 1–33.

Children's Defense Fund. (1997). *The state of America's children yearbook*. Washington, DC: Author.

Chisholm, J.F. (1995). Violent youth: Reflections on contemporary child rearing practices in America as an antecedent cause. In L. Adler and F. Denmark (Eds.), *Violence and the prevention of violence* (pp. 47–59). New York: Praeger Press.

Cole, H. (1995). *Effects of chronic violence on inner city junior high school aged children*. Unpublished doctoral project, Pace University, New York.

Cole, J. (Ed.). (1986). *All American women: Lives that divide, ties that bind*. New York: Macmillan.

Cose, E. (1993). *The rage of a privileged class*. New York: HarperCollins.

Dawson, M. (2001). *Crime: A serious American problem: Information Plus Reference Series*. Vol. 3. Detroit: Gale Group.

Drevitch, G. (1994, February 11). Murder she saw: Violence in mass media. *Scholastic Update*, p. 12.

Dudley, W. (Ed.). (1999). *Media violence: Opposing viewpoints*. San Diego: Greenhaven Press.

Federal Bureau of Investigation (FBI). (1995). *Terrorism in the United States*. Washington, DC: U.S. Department of Justice.

Federal Bureau of Investigation (FBI). (1997). *Uniform Crime Report, 1996*. Washington, DC: U.S. Department of Justice.

Federal Bureau of Investigation (FBI). (1999). *Crime in the United States, 1998: Uniform crime reports*. Washington, DC: U.S. Department of Justice.

Freedman, J. (1999). Studies have not established a link between media violence and violence. In W. Dudley (Ed.). *Media Violence: Opposing viewpoints* (pp. 49–53). San Diego: Greenhaven Press.

Garrett, D. (1997). Conflict resolution in the African American. *Aggression and Violent Behavior, 2*(5), 25–31.

Glueck, S., and Glueck, E. (1950). *Unraveling Juvenile Delinquency*. Cambridge: Harvard University Press.

Greenwood, P. (1995). Juvenile crime and juvenile justice. In J.Q. Wilson and J. Petersilia (Eds.), *Crime* (pp. 91–117). San Francisco: ICS Press.

Grossman, D. (1995.). *On killing: The psychological cost of learning to kill in war and society*. Boston: Back Bay Books.

Guthmann, E. (1994, May 31). Mayhem sells in youth market mass culture; industry cashes in on youthful appetite for violence. *San Francisco Chronicle*, p. A1.

Heise, L. (1994). *Violence against women: The hidden health burden*. Washington, DC: World Bank.

Herbert, B. (1996, March 4). In trouble after school. *New York Times*, p. A15.

Hoch-Espada, A. (1997). *Post-traumatic stress, dissociation, and antisocial behavior in inner-city adolescents*. Unpublished doctoral project, Pace University, New York.

Landes, A., Foster, C., and Cessna, C. (Eds.). (1995). *Violent relationships: Battering and abuse among adults: The information series on current topics*. Wylie, TX: Information Plus.

Lefer, L. (1984). The fine edge of violence. *Journal of the American Academy of Psychoanalysis, 12*(2), 253–268.

Lyons-Ruth, K., Connell, D., Zoll, D., and Stahl, L. (1987). Infants at social risk: Relationships among infant maltreatment, maternal behavior, and infant attachment behavior. *Developmental Psychology, 23*(2), 223–232.

Mantell, M., and Albrecht, S. (1994). *Ticking bombs: Defusing violence in the workplace*. New York: Richard P. Irwin.

Meadows, R. (1998). *Understanding violence and victimization*. Upper Saddle River, NJ: Prentice Hall.

Miller, A. (1990). *For your own good: Hidden cruelty in child-rearing and the roots of violence*. New York: Noonday Press.

Mowing down our children. (1992, November 9). *New York Times*. p. A16.

Murray, J. (1997). Media violence and youth. In J. Osofsky (Ed.), *Children in a violent society* (pp. 107–163). New York: Guilford Press.

Osofsky, J.D. (1997). *Children in a violent society*. New York: Guilford Press.

Pharr, S. (1988). *Homophobia: A weapon of sexism*. Inverness, CA: Chardon Press.

Pillari, V. (1991). *Scapegoating in families: Intergenerational patterns of physical and emotional abuse* (pp. 107–163). New York: Brunner/Mazel.

Pinderhughes, E. (1989). *Understanding race, ethnicity, and power: The key to efficacy in clinical practice*. New York: Free Press.

Prothrow-Stith, D. (1991). *Deadly consequences*. New York: Harper Perennial.

Richters, J., and Martinez, P. (1993). The NIMH community violence project: I. Children as victims of and witnesses to violence. *Psychiatry, 56*(3), 7–21.

Sarason, S. (1982). *The culture of the school and the problem of change*. Boston: Allyn & Bacon.

Student wounds six at high school. (1992, September 12). *New York Times*, p. 8.

Snyder, H.M., and Sickmund, M. (1999, December). Juvenile offenders and victims: 1999 nationwide report. *Juvenile Justice Bulletin*. Washington, DC: U.S. Department of Justice.

Van der Kolk, B. (1984). *Posttraumatic stress disorder: Psychological and biological sequelae*. Washington, DC: American Psychiatric Press.

Van der Kolk, B. (1991). *Psychological trauma*. Washington, DC: American Psychiatric Press.

Wilson, J. (1985). *Thinking about crime*. New York: Random House.

16

Violence and American Indians: Culture—Then and Now

John Beatty

CULTURES: THEN AND NOW

Europeans, or *Anglos* (a term used by many to refer to non-aboriginal populations), are generally thought to have arrived in the New World at the time of Columbus in 1492. Archaeological evidence indicates that the first encounter with Europeans was established originally with the Vikings around the year 1000. Some would even suggest that this contact occurred earlier than this, although this theory is not accepted widely.

Whatever the original date of contact, the information we have about the Europeans and the Vikings is hundreds of years old. In addition, both cultures have doubtlessly changed dramatically since contact was first established. Writings (by both natives and immigrant populations) and archaeology have tried to supply some data, but much of this is subject to interpretations that are problematic and that are well beyond the scope of this chapter. It is important to realize at the outset that the majority of specific events were reported by Anglos who wrote a great deal more about their interactions with the original inhabitants of the country than the natives did.

We are well aware that, even in this "multicultural age" where sensitivity to other groups is preached regularly (but often ignored in practice), intercultural interactions are often fraught with problems because each of the individuals involved interprets the situation in different ways. This happens even between members of different native cultures. For instance, some time ago, an Iroquois[1] Indian traveled to Oklahoma, where he agreed to speak at a gathering of Indians from the area (Plains Indians). He reported on his return that the Indians there were very afraid of talking or listening to people who are likely to say unpleasant things about the U.S. government. He based this conclusion on the fact that, at the meeting, the local Indians did not exit their cars immediately and go to the place where he was about to speak. In fact, Plains Indians tend to sit in their cars for a while before going into a meeting because it generally is considered polite not to barge in. What the Plains Indians did as an act of politeness was interpreted by the Iroquois as fearfulness.

If such misinterpretations can occur between two currently existing groups, imagine how great the problems are with trying to look into the history of one's own culture, to say nothing of doing the same in other cultures. The interpretation by Anglos of actions taken by Indians is highly suspect. In fact, it seems clear now that much of what was "seen" (i.e., thought to be happening) was screened Western ideas about the Anglos' social position in the world, their rights to expansion, religious beliefs, and so on. Unfortunately, little remains of the complex symbolic and belief systems that permeated Indian cultures and that caused them to make similarly erroneous interpretations. However, certain things were seen accurately. For example, the Indians' perception that their land was being overcrowded and that they were being driven away from their ancestral homes, both physically and culturally, was certainly correct. At the same time, doubtless there were things that early Anglo settlers believed about Indian cultures that were also valid.

The result, however, is that much of what is known about early contact is one-sided. There are debates from both Indians and Anglos over what actually happened. Scalping is a classic case in point. Scalping is something over which Indians and Anglos still argue, debating whether the process was in fact a European invention or was practiced in precontact cultures (for examples of "assertions" and "proofs," see Mihesuah, 1996; Friederici, 1993; and esp. Axtell and Sturtevant, 1980/1986). Most Indian apologists simply deny the existence of the practice or, when evidence is irrefutable, indicate that the Europeans started it and the Indians accepted it. Why this acceptance occurred has not been discussed widely. It seems that the things of which Anglos generally disapproved were to be purged from Indian cultures, and those cultures are now made to be some perfected form (at least from an Anglo perspective). One is left with the uneasy feeling that "traditional" Indian cultures basically lived in societies that had contemporary middle-class, liberal value systems. There is no reason to attempt to resolve the question about "who started it": virtually everyone agrees it happened and that both Indians and Anglos did it. For the purposes of this chapter, regardless of who started it, it is taken as a form of violence and is examined.

It is also important to note that violence and torture were regarded differently by both sides, both then and now. Most reports of violence by Anglos against Indians describe genocidal attacks rather than interpersonal situations between individuals. Hagan (1961, 77, 107–108) reports two examples:

It is difficult to generalize on the actual process of removal of the Seminoles and their fellow Indians. The time span covers more than half a century, if the removals from Iowa and Kansas to Indian Territory are included. At their best, the migrations of the tribesmen resembled closely the pioneering experience of their white contemporaries. At their worst they approached the horrors created by the Nazi handling of subject peoples.

Black Kettle and Little Antelope reported to Fort Lyon on the upper Arkansas. Having made their peace, they retired to Sand Creek about forty miles away. Here, late in November, 1864, a column of Colorado militia commanded by Col. J.M. Chivington, a Methodist minister, caught them unawares and perpetrated the notorious Sand Creek Massacre. Disregarding the previous negotiations at Fort Lyon, which the Indians had presumed restored them to American favor, the frontiersmen showed them no mercy. Of the band of five hundred, perhaps a third, mostly women children and the aged, were killed by a surprise charge through the camp. The militia rivaled the Indians in their brutality. Eyewitnesses told of children clubbed and pregnant women disemboweled.

Claimed by General Nelson A. Miles to be the "foulest and most unjustifiable crime in the annals of America," Chivington proceeded to exhibit "a collection of one hundred scalps between acts in a local theater. Chivington was a hero and public benefactor" (Hagan, 1961, 108).

There is little doubt that Anglos were as likely to commit acts of violence against Indians and were far less repelled by such acts when they were the aggressors. The persistence of the discussion of Indian violence against Anglos, rather than vice versa is more a function of who gets to create the history than what actually happened.

INDIANS, NATIVE AMERICANS, AND OTHER LABELS

Before embarking on a journey of this magnitude, it is necessary to deal with a number of problems, several of which are definitional. In particular, the term *American Indian* needs some scrutiny. The current debate in multiculturalism, political correctness, and a number of other approaches has been critical of the term *American Indian* and has suggested *Native American* be used in its place. By and large *Indian* and *American Indian* have been terms used by "Indians" themselves. No less a figure than Russell Means, the head of the American Indian Movement (AIM), has held that the term *Native American* is a construction of the U.S. government and is quite content to use the term *Indian*. Interviews with other prominent Indians have yielded the same results. For example, when Wes Studi, the talented actor who performed in the latest rendition of *Last of the Mohicans* was asked during an interview what he wanted to be called, he responded, "*American Indian* is fine" (see www.mohicanpress.com and allthingscherokee.com).

Given the large number of individuals, groups, and political units contained under the rubric *American Indians*, it has been hard to decide just who has the right to label this group. Shifting terms to appeal to any given individual or group being addressed is almost impossible. More importantly, as some Indians have pointed out, the term itself (whatever it may be) refers largely to a Western concept and thus is of little or no interest to many who may fall under the title.

In fact, it has been pointed out that the term covers a multitude of peoples and cultures who, before European contact, shared little in common with one another, other than the fact that they all lived in the lands that became known as the Americas before the arrival of European populations. After contact, they shared another characteristic: Their political autonomy was by and large taken away and they were subject to the control of a dominant group of outsiders. This created a "shared experience," which has led to a feeling of unity on the part of these different peoples.

Even accepting the common experience of oppression as grounds for a single title, the fact remains that there are a number of people, such as Hawaiians and Samoans, who are in basically the same position, but who are not thought of as American Indians, although the term *Aboriginal American* might apply. The term *Native American* is currently more in vogue, but it is certainly more ambiguous since it does not distinguish between American citizens born in the country (as opposed to naturalized citizens) and members of indigenous groups. To argue that *Native* (with a capital *N*) Americans are to be distinguished from *native* (with a small *n*) begs the point since, in speech (and indeed at the beginning of written sentences), they are indistinguishable.

The U.S. government tends to use the term *American Indian* to refer to the native peoples of the continental United States. This term excludes Hawaiians and Samoans, who are often grouped under the category of *Asian-Pacific Islander*! Hence *Native American* refers to American Indians, Samoans, and Hawaiians, while *Indian* refers specifically to those groups in the continental Americas. This, of course, includes those indigenous populations of Central and South America, who, in popular parlance, often are excluded from the category of *Indians*. For example, a colleague recently was asked by a graduate student for information on American Indians and alcohol. One reference dealt with Mayans. The graduate student rejected it on the grounds that Indians, not Mayans, were the subjects of the study!

In the same way that labeling such a diverse group seriously violates cultural identities and diversities, it becomes close to impossible to discuss something as complex as violence among American Indians, since the experiences of each group are varied. Some groups, like the Mohawk and the Apache, have a reputation among both Anglos and some Indians for aggression and violence. The Iroquois were warriors par excellence and had a torture complex that is discussed later. The Aztec have been seen by some as rather bloodthirsty. On the other hand, the Hopi, Zuni, and Pueblo Indians are often seen as pacifistic (see, for example, Benedict, 1946, Smith, 1975). They are the prime example of Benedict's Apollonian culture type ("avoidance of extremes"). "Violence is rare among the Hopi, so that blood feuds do not occur. According to Colton, if murder should occur, it would be the duty of the family of the murdered man to kill the murderer, but actual instances of murder are very few in modern times" (Eggan, 1973, 108). Of course, such stereotypes are generally inaccurate. The Iroquois (who count the Mohawk among them) are known for their Great League and for the Great Peace that they try to maintain. *Skennenkowa* (Great Peace) is the traditional greeting among the Mohawks. In addition, the Hopi, Zuni, and Pueblo were involved in a violent revolt against the Spanish.

Violence is difficult to define and is especially difficult to discuss in other cultures since it has very negative connotations. However, it is important to note that many activities seen as violent by one culture are not seen as such by another. This is not simply a matter of deciding whether an act is violent in and of itself, even within a single society, the same act in different contexts carries different meanings. For instance, in the United States, a person grabbing someone around the legs while they are walking or running, causing them to fall, is likely to be guilty of an offense and easily could be sued. On the other hand, football players regularly do just that, but within the context of the playing field, such behavior is considered to be reasonable. Specific behaviors contextualized in certain ways lose their connotations of violence. Violence in the context of war, religion, sports, and punishment for crime are often not thought of as violent, or, at least, the violence is positively sanctioned by the society in general. Jules Henry (1963) gives the following example in a discussion of American education:

> Boris had trouble reducing 12/16 to lowest terms, and could only get as far as 6/8. The teacher asked him quietly if that was as far as he could reduce it. She suggested he "think". Much heaving up and down and waving of hands by the other children, all frantic to correct him. Boris pretty unhappy, probably mentally paralyzed. The teacher, quiet, patiently ignores the others and concentrates with look and voice on Boris. After a minute or two, she turns to the class and says "Well, who can tell Boris what the number is?" A forest of hands appears and the teacher calls Peggy. Peggy says that four may be divided into the numerator and the denominator.
>
> Boris's failure has made it possible for Peggy to succeed; his misery is the occasion for her rejoicing. This is the standard condition of the contemporary American elementary school. *To a Zuni, Hopi or Dakota Indian, Peggy's performance would seem cruel beyond belief, for competition, the wringing of success from somebody's failure, is a form of torture foreign to these noncompetitive cultures. Yet Peggy's action seems natural to us; and so it is.* (P. 151, italics mine)

In dealing with violence and American Indian cultures, one finds that these problems are intensified since intercultural misunderstandings have made Indians (and other minorities) worry a great deal about how their cultures are seen. An act that might be seen as violent in the West might not have been in the native culture. This problem exists even in looking into the past of one's own culture. For example, Westernized countries have committed many acts of violence (such as the Inquisition) that were sanctioned by authority and not seen as particularly violent at the time.

This problem is intensified in dealing with cultures that are both temporally and spatially distant from one's own. In these cases, the patterns that have been recorded in texts, paintings, and perhaps some other forms of art become inaccessible in some ways. The contexts, feelings, and general structure of the cultures' symbolic systems may long be lost, and, hence, attempts to make hypothetical reconstructions can bring about problems for the members of those cultures.

It is important to remember that, when dealing with cultures that are removed in time and space, one might find the perceptions of the world held by those cultures difficult to explain. One is put in the unpleasant position of trying to explain a different worldview from that of a given culture, which may be at odds with the other. Anthropologists in effect play the role of cultural translators, and some translations are more difficult than others. This is particularly true when dealing with a trait that is heavily value-laden in one or both cultures, especially when those values differ. In the case of *violence*, it is clear that such a value-laden term will be particularly disquieting. In many cases recorded in the early literature of the frontier, acts of violence committed against Indians were contextualized in such a way that the acts were justified. Acts of violence committed by Indians against outsiders, on the other hand, were contextualized in such a way that they could be used to show the savage nature of the Indian, and this could be used to rationalize further acts of "justified" violence against the Indians. Since the immigrant populations had much more access to writing and were able to create written records that "validated" their positions, the Indian position was ignored. We have, in fact, much less information on how the Indians felt or interpreted the acts of the incoming populations or how they justified their own.

One need only regard the debates on abortion in America to see similar problems. There is a difference of opinion about whether or not abortion is murder, but few pro-choice supporters would be in favor of infanticide. Christopher Donnan, anthropology professor at the University of California, Los Angeles, has pointed out rather dramatically that Westerners are repulsed by the idea of human sacrifice but send off hundreds or thousands of soldiers—many of whom are expected to be killed—on a regular basis without raising any of the hackles that human sacrifice raises. In effect, the sacrifice of people is legitimized in different societies in different ways.

Still another problem that must be confronted relates to any writing about a specific aspect of a given culture. The specificity of the topic inordinately tends to stress that aspect of the culture almost to the exclusion of all others. In talking of violence among Indians, one almost automatically excludes acts of gentleness, kindness, peacefulness, generosity, and the thousands of other behaviors that exist in any society. For example, it is apparent from a precontact Mississippi known as Moundville that warfare by or against the people living there was nonexistent. Only seventy-nine arrow points were found, and, of the 3,000 skulls found at the site, only two show any evidence that there may have been violence involved.

In addition, certain levels of sociocultural integration often show similar patterns regardless of where in the world they are found. Great monuments such as the Egyptian pyramids, Nara, and the Cahokia Mounds often are associated with the appearance of city-states. Human sacrifice is also typical of many places reaching certain levels of development. These obviously should not be taken as diagnostic of a specific people, but rather of a specific level of sociocultural development.

In the heyday of America's ethnic purges, the United States removed many Indians from their homelands, frequently in defiance of court orders, and engaged in wholesale slaughter of many Indians. A classic example is the Cherokee "Trail of Tears," when the United States uprooted and moved more than 60,000 Cherokee and other Southeastern peoples to Oklahoma at the cost of thousands of Indian lives (Billard, 1989). Perhaps one-fourth of the Cherokee died en route (Josephy, 1968). The Southeastern peoples were not alone. Many of the Midwestern people were moved repeatedly: The Winnebago, for example, were moved at least six times between 1829 and 1866 (Hagan, 1961). While violence is often conceived as an act directed against a single person, the massive destruction of peoples and cultures by the U.S. government constituted what can only be referred to as "violence as government policy."

It certainly appears that many acts committed by Indians were seen as violent by Europeans, but were contextualized differently by the Indians themselves. It may be that now, in some abstract sense, the acts are seen as violent because current populations are no longer willing to accept any of the acts committed by settlers or Indians as reasonable, or they may be more likely to justify the Indians' actions. Whatever the case, this chapter looks at a number of acts that, at least in the light of today's perceptions, are likely to be considered unpleasant and negatively sanctioned. In one sense, if they are approved of or seen as intelligible, it is only because one can contextualize them in that way. It is painful that any of these events happened, but they did. There are many lessons to be learned from these events that ultimately may help us understand some things about contact between cultures and intercultural communication.

Certainly no people could tolerate continuous violence within the group. Wissler (1911, 24) reports in the rather lengthy quote below a strong aversion to violence among the Blackfoot:

> Above all, the head men are expected to preserve the peace. Should a dispute arise in which members of their band are concerned, one or more of them are expected to step in as arbitrators or even as police officials if the occasion demands. When it is suspicioned that a man contemplates a crime or the taking of personal vengeance some head men go to his tipi and talk with him, endeavoring to calm him, giving much kind advice as to the proper course for the good of all concerned. If he has been wronged, they often plead for mercy toward his enemy. Again, the head men may be appealed to for redress against a fellow member of the band. In the adjustment of such cases the head men proceed by tact, persuasion, and extreme deliberation. They restrain the young men, as much as possible, after the same method. In all such functions, they are expected to succeed without resort to violence.
>
> For mild persistent misconduct, a method of formal ridicule is sometimes practiced. When the offender has failed to take hints and suggestions, the head men may take formal notice and decide to resort to discipline. Some evening when all are in their tipis, a head man will call out to a neighbor asking if he has observed the conduct of Mr. A. This starts a general conversation between the many tipis, in which all the grotesque and hideous features of Mr. A's acts are held up to general ridicule amid shrieks of laughter, the grilling continuing until far into the night. The mortification of the victim is extreme and usually drives him into temporary exile or, as formerly, upon the warpath to do desperate deeds.
>
> When there is trouble between members of different bands, the head men of each endeavor to bring about a settlement. Thus, if one of the contending party is killed, the band of the deceased sends notice to the murderer's band that a payment must be made. In the meantime, the murderer may have called upon a head man of his own band to explain the deed. The head men then discuss the matter and advise that horses and other property be sent over to the injured band at once. A crier goes about with the order and members of the band contribute.

Violence must be seen within a cultural pattern. It is far more common for people to see violence in other cultures if it occurs in contexts where it is traditionally absent in the viewer's own culture.

THE NATURE OF VIOLENCE

Having looked however briefly at the problems associated with the labels used for the indigenous populations, it becomes necessary to look at the definition of *violence*.

> **vi-o-lence** *n.* **1.** Physical force exerted for the purpose of violating, damaging, or abusing: *crimes of violence.* **2.** The act or an instance of violent action or

behavior. **3.** Intensity or severity, as in natural phenomena; untamed force: *the violence of a hurricane.* **4.** Abusive or unjust exercise of power. **5.** Abuse or injury to meaning, content, or intent: *do violence to a text.* **6.** Vehemence of feeling or expression; fervor.

Violent acts occupy much of news media. Violent crimes are perhaps dropping, but discussion of them is not. But just what does the term *violence* mean? The dictionary definition above serves as a starting point, but generally dictionary definitions are meant to indicate how the word is used in general conversation. Technical definitions are often more problematical. Even in English, the word is used in the context in which it means "sudden" or "fierce" or "explosive" in phrases like *a violent storm* or a *violent earthquake.* It has hard to imagine just what an earthquake and a crime can have in common.

The dictionary itself rather unhelpfully uses the word *violent* in its definition of violence. Violent is then defined in the *American Heritage Dictionary* (1994) as follows:

> **vi-o-lent** *adj.* **1.** Marked by, acting with, or resulting from great force: *a violent attack.* **2.** Having or showing great emotional force: *violent dislike.* **3.** Marked by intensity; extreme: *violent pain; a violent squall.* See Synonyms at **intense.** **4.** Caused by unexpected force or injury rather than by natural causes: *a violent death.* **5.** Tending to distort or injure meaning, phrasing, or intent. [Middle English, from Old French, from Latin *violentus*, from *v*ʰ*s*, vi-, force . . .]

Even with all of this, there are problems in that violence is experienced rather personally. What is violent to one person might not be violent to another. A strong punch to the arm of a boxer as a greeting might barely be noticed and not conceived of as violent. On the other hand, the exact same act perpetrated against a weak or elderly person might very well be seen as a violent act.

The problem of events and their perceptions (known as *emic-etics*) was studied in some detail by Pike (1990). The same event can have different meanings to different individuals and peoples. For example, cannibalism has been divided into endo- and exocannibalism. In the former, the person eaten is a member of the group doing the eating, whereas in exocannibalism, the victim is an outsider. Violence, like cannibalism, may be regarded differently when it occurs between members of a group, as opposed to when it occurs between outsiders and insiders. The ability to look at this distinction across the range of American Indian cultures is well beyond the scope of this chapter.

There seems little doubt that violence generally has a negative feeling attached to it. It involves great effort or force, and the results are negative to the object or person encountering the violence. Lifting a heavy weight may require great force, but it generally is not considered to be a violent action. To lift something violently implies excessive force and perhaps with damage to the object. The violent overthrow of a government would seem to imply considerable damage to the government or the state, and may imply that the user of such a phrase feels some antagonism to the fact that the government was overthrown.

As a result, there is a serious question as to whether violence can be measured objectively or not. Sports are a classic case in point. Boxers and other athletes have been killed, paralyzed, or maimed during their athletic activities (Atyeo, 1979). Hockey games are notorious for violence that occurs both within and outside the rules. Similar problems are posed by American Indian sports in which death may be expected for some of the participants. Lacrosse, a traditional Iroquois game known as "The Little Brother of War," generally has been seen by people as violent, involving "throwing sticks at other players, holding another player with sticks or hands, tripping, spearing and threatening" (Vennum, 1994, 248, see also 229–235 and 247).

WHAT IS SEEN AS VIOLENT AND BY WHOM?

In any cross-cultural analysis, there is a need to decide just how to apply a concept cross-culturally. There is always a problem with what the culture perceives as violent. In anthropology the terms *emic* and *etic* are often used to indicate the "natives' viewpoint" (emic) and the analytic viewpoint (etic). There are grounds for serious disagreements if the analyst sees some behavior as violent and the members of the culture do not. Members of animal rights groups might frown on hunting and see the use of certain traps and hunting techniques as inhumane and perhaps even violent—a view that likely would be contested by the hunters. Conflicting interpretations of data are legion, and, as an example relative to hunting, Henke (1985) cites the fact that many of the techniques used in taking seals are humane, although aesthetically unpleasant.

Much contemporary theory, largely postmodern, tends to hold that the natives viewpoint is as valid as anyone else's, and that there is no way to evaluate whose point of view is preferable. This makes it nearly impossible to judge acts of violence since one of the participants claims the act was violent, while the other claims it wasn't. Since it is impossible to discover the truth in this theoretical mode, it would seem impossible to exact penalties either. The application of such a doctrine in this context would lead, for example, to a rape victims feeling they had been raped, and the offenders feeling they had done nothing wrong. How can a rapist be punished if he perceived the act as nonviolent and voluntary? Can one really be judged because of someone else's perceptions?

VIOLENCE AND AGGRESSION

Aggression need not be violent, but violence appears to be aggressive. Acts of violence are also acts of aggression, and, to some degree, both concepts need analysis. Girard (1972/1989, 4) suggests that one aspect of violence is "its particular terror—its blind brutality, the fundamental absurdity of its manifestations."

Here the relationship is made between violence and terror. Terrorism can be seen as acts of violence, but again, the question as to whether the definition holds in the minds of both the victims and the perpetrators arises. Lately, some environmental activists, appalled at the decision of the Makah Indians to resume whaling (which they are allowed to do by treaty), have fired weapons into signs on the Makah reservation (Craig, 1998). These may be considered terrorist tactics by the Makah, while the environmentalists probably have no idea of the "fundamental absurdity" of their acts.

VIOLENCE AND ITS CONTEXTS

In all societies, acts are interpreted differently in different contexts. Cultures create contexts and then interpret acts in light of those contexts. In some contexts, a given act may be completely free of some connotations that it would have in others. For example, undressing in a locker room with strangers present is not the same thing as undressing in a public place with strangers present. Similarly, an act may be conceived of as violent in one context but not in others. Killing is frowned upon by most Americans and is illegal, except in self-defense, warfare, or when sanctioned by the state, as in executions. The penal code gives numerous classifications for the same act, depending on external factors.

VIOLENCE AND THE SACRED

Much of the violence that has come to be discussed relative to American Indian populations is in the context of religious activity or warfare.

Ritual Sacrifice and Violence

Girard (1972/1989) has discussed the close contact between violence and what is held sacred largely in terms of sacrifice. The basic premise of his work is that "society is seeking to deflect upon a relatively indifferent victim, a 'sacrificial' victim, the violence that would otherwise be vented on its own members, the people it most desires to protect" (p. 4).

Sacrifice need not be a life-or-death situation. Catholics may offer up suffering as a kind of sacrifice. Plains Indians may try to obtain some pity from the supernatural powers through subjecting themselves to suffering. The Sun Dance, which is practiced by many of the Plains Indian tribes, was outlawed by the federal government on the grounds of its featuring self-torture. The Sun Dance and related rituals involve a number of events in which skewers are inserted through various parts of the body and weights in the form of buffalo skulls and other objects are attached to the skewers in the body. The men dance and pull on the leather thongs until they pull loose from their flesh.

Whether it is reasonable for these actions to be considered violent is again a function of the basic psychological set of the person labeling the act. Many Indians were mystified at the dance being outlawed during World War I since the dance was voluntary but the people being sent to fight often were maimed or killed involuntarily.

Ritual sacrifice seems to have occurred in several areas, many in the Mississippi Valley in Hopewell-Adena-Mississippian complex. Natchez also were involved in similar sacrifices. The Northeastern groups like the Iroquois seems to have performed somewhat similar rituals, although more on prisoners than as sacrifice.

The Pawnee Morning Star sacrifice (Dorsey, 1907; Wissler and Spinden, 1916; Wedel, 1977), on the other hand, did involve the sacrifice of a maiden. This ritual reportedly was performed in the summer, when a warrior or chief had the appropriate dream, and involved the sacrifice of a young woman on a scaffold, somewhat akin to some Mexican sacrificial rites. The ceremony had a great deal of astronomical significance, and the Pawnee involvement with the heavens is considerable. Although human sacrifice is seen as a form of violence by some, one suspects that the Pawnee no more saw it that way than today's Catholics think of themselves as cannibalistic when they consume the body and blood of Christ in transubstantiated wafer and wine.

Although this chapter does not discuss Central or South American Indians in general, it should not ignore Aztec human sacrifice and possible cannibalism, especially in light of its potential relationship with Indians of North America, many of whom appear to have had some connection with these people, as the Pawnee data indicates. Aztecs were involved in the sacrifice of large numbers of captives in order to keep their gods propitiated. Although these sacrifices are well documented, there is considerable question about whether they were accompanied by cannibalistic events, which conceivably, could make the act even more violent.

WARFARE AND VIOLENCE

Most people accept the fact that warfare occurred between the various peoples of the Americas long before the arrival of the Europeans. The heavily stockaded villages noted by the Europeans who arrived early on indicate that such was the case. There are many questions about the nature and causes of the pre–European-contact warfare. The torture of prisoners of war seems to have been accepted rather widely among several groups. There is, however, considerable discussion of the use of torture of captives by Indians in eastern North America (Knowles, 1940). Early records that contain some descriptions of torture come from the East Coast and show torture of prisoners in evidence already. However, the contexts in which such acts occurred are not totally clear. Some indicate that the torture of prisoners may have been religious in nature. The evidence is somewhat scanty and has been regarded as problematic. However, Knowles (1940) mentions that a Spaniard named John Ortis, who was captured around 1527, was bound on a "raft," which was set aloft on stakes on which he was to be burned. Actually, he appears to have been saved by the intervention of a chief's daughter. A second report of torture by Indians states that it was commanded that "the Spaniards, entirely naked, should be compelled to run by turns from one extremity of the public square to the other, that at times arrows should be shot at them in order that their death might be slower, their pain more exquisite, the rejoicing more noted, and of longer duration" (Knowles, 1940, 158).

Early indications of violence in the Southwest Pueblos comes from a description of the expedition of Francisco Vásquez de Coronado, 1539–1542 (Forbes, 1964). The army of Coronado arrived among the Pueblo Indians and began acting in a high-handed manner, seizing the Indians as captives and forcibly appropriating clothing and food. When a Spanish soldier raped a native woman, the Indians rebelled. Coronado ordered his soldiers

> not to take them alive, but to make an example of them so other natives would fear the Spanish. A group of several hundred Indians surrendered after being promised pardon; however, Garcia López de Cardenas [an officer of Coronado] . . . ordered two hundred stakes to be prepared at once to burn them alive. Nobody told him anything about the peace that had been granted them, . . . not thinking it was any of their business. Then when the enemies saw that the Spaniards were binding them and beginning to roast them, about a hundred men who were in the tent began to struggle and defend themselves with what was there and with the stakes they could seize. Our men who were on foot attacked the tent on all sides . . . and then the horsemen chased those who escaped. As the country was level, not a man among them remained alive. . . . (Narrative of Pedro de Casteñeda, translated by George P. Winship in *Fourteenth Annual Report of the Bureau of American Ethnology* (Washington: U.S. Government Printing Office pp. 496–7). (Forbes, 1964, 156)

Trigger (1969) notes similar patterns for the Iroquoian-speaking Huron, although he carefully points out that not all prisoners were sacrificed.

Some were adopted, although they might be later tortured and/or killed. By and large, there seems to have been a great deal of discussion by the Huron about family and friends who had been killed by the group to whom the prisoner belonged, thereby whipping up some enthusiasm for the revenge about to be taken. Torture, and ultimately death, was accomplished by burnings and beatings carried out often, but not exclusively, by women.

There have been some anthropological attempts to explain the rationale for the violence involved, much of which revolves around the tension generated by the constant warfare that threatened the stability of life in the Northeast (Trigger, 1969). Knowles (1940) has called attention to the fact that many of the elements in the torture are related to cults that had developed in Mississippi Valley cultures (Adena, Hopewell, and especially Mississippian) and in the Mesoamerica. He points especially to features such as removal of the heart, killing on elevated platforms in view of the sun, and cooking and eating of all or a part of the body. Since the treatment of prisoners seems not to have been a part of actual cult behavior as it was in the other areas, it is included here in the context of warfare, as opposed to religion, which appears below.

Torture has been reported by Western writers as having been perceived by the Indians as a test through which warriors ultimately could prove themselves. In this sense it would have been something akin to an extraordinarily difficult initiation rite. The evidence for this lies in that fact that Indians who were being tortured were expected to sing and otherwise keep their tormentors amused. On the other hand, Fenton's (1941) studies on Iroquois Dream Guessing rituals show some tension about such torture situations. These rituals are described by Wallace (1958) as a kind of Iroquoian-Freudian dream analysis. Dreams were taken to be requests of the individual, and when a person had a dream, other members of the group would try to guess it from a kind of riddle and make it come true. For example, someone whose dream required they be given a gourd would be given one when the dream was guessed. Similarly, warriors who dreamed of being captured and tortured were seized by friends and dealt with accordingly. Fenton (1941) argues that this kind of enactment of a dream forestalled or prevented the event from happening in reality, where the consequences would have been much worse than those meted out by friends. However, regardless of the interpretation, it certainly appears that torture was evident in cultures in the eastern part of the country and was probably charged with ambivalent feelings.

On the plains, a different situation seems to have existed, where warfare mostly involved raiding for horses. "Counting coup," a kind of "winning a point," was accomplished by deeds of bravery. Stealing horses, touching an enemy, and similar events are reported as grounds for counting coup. Killing an enemy was excluded, since it appears not to have involved bravery. It was far more difficult to slip into a camp and steal horses, or to strike an enemy, than it was to kill an enemy.

However, the remains of General George Armstrong Custer's troops, who were left naked and mutilated, seem to argue for the need to distinguish between "war games" and the real thing. The degree to which the "real thing" existed before European contact may never be known.

CRIME AND VIOLENCE

Not all violence is seen as criminal and, therefore, generally may be ignored in crime statistics. Law is complex both to define and to deal with in other cultures (see, for example, Pospisil, 1978; Hoebel, 1976). Violations of law, or at least acts that can be classified as antisocial, occur in all societies, and the society as a whole often reacts with sanctions against the miscreant involved. Occasionally such sanctions may appear violent to outsiders, although from within they may appear justified and proper. Generally speaking, a society that condones executions does not count such acts as examples of violence against the people being executed. Other groups frequently do. While Americans are scandalized by violence in Middle Eastern and Communist groups, they also are enraged at organizations that hold America guilty of the same kinds of crimes. One need only look at the Abner Luima case in New York, which rocketed America onto an Amnesty International list of countries with human rights violations (Terry, 1998; Hinds, 1998). The mayor and police commissioner of New York were among many of the Americans who immediately blasted Amnesty International for doing so. Similar problems have existed in many other countries. For example, the case of Michael Fay (who performed a minor act of vandalism), whose caning in Singapore made headlines in the United States, split the country, with many feeling that a good beating was what a "criminal" deserved and that the United States should adopt similar practices. At least in that context, people who might have been against violence in general were willing to have the state perform such acts against miscreants.

There are problems in statistical approaches to the questions of criminal activity. Stern (1965, 201) points out that:

> the sizable sum derived from law enforcement was highly unusual. While the major enforcement problem in most Oregon cities of comparable size was traffic violations, Chiloquin in 1956–57 found no less than ninety-three per cent of its offenses to be felonies and misdemeanors other than traffic violations. Tribal members and other Indians, including repeaters, accounted for over seventy-two per cent of the arrests; they paid over seventy per cent of the fines and forfeited bail; and they furnished over ninety-six per cent of the trusty labor performed in the city.
>
> Aside from a few individual instances, this record does not reflect a policy

of discriminatory arrests on the part of the city administration. It does, however, mark one of the significant confrontations upon the reservation. It was conditioned in part by the special statutory position of the Klamath, for as an Indian under the federal supervision he was enjoined by law from having or using liquor and from marrying a white within the state. Until these disabilities were removed in 1951, tribal members were subject to arrest for acts not held criminal when committed by non-Indians.

EARLY DISCUSSIONS OF CRIME

Trigger (1969) points out that the Huron recognized four kinds of crime: (1) physical violence against individuals, which included murder, wounding, and injury; (2) theft; (3) witchcraft; and (4) treason. He discussed how murder led to countermurder by the relatives of the first victim. These acts could escalate into blood feuds, which would have been enormously disruptive to developing confederacies and ultimately were seen by the Huron themselves as worse than murder. However, precontact graves reveal "bodies riddled with arrows and additional skulls possibly resulting from headhunting" (p. 78).

Reports of various tribes using physical punishments for violations of law are in evidence. The Blackfeet were said to cut off a part of the nose of women who committed adultery. In some cases, they were reported to turn women who were unfaithful over to their husbands' friends in military society, where the adulterous woman would be raped as punishment:

> Chastity of the women is held in great esteem among the Blackfeet, but is practiced by scarcely more than one-third of their number. The unfaithful wife was formerly punished with great severity. The injured husband or any chosen friend might cut off her nose, her ears, or even take her life. Cut noses were very common among the women in 1833, when for the first time the whites made the close acquaintance of the nation. Since then the custom has gradually died out and seems now to be wholly discontinued. But severe as was this penalty a still greater might be inflicted upon the woman thus disgraced. Even without the sanction of her husband she might be forcibly removed from the village by the young men who then upheld the honor of her sex by making her an object of common gratification. After such an ordeal, if permitted to live, she was regarded with universal scorn. Frequently, however, the unfaithful wife was forgiven by her husband, who sought his redress from her partner in crime. It was his privilege to dispossess him of horses, arms, and in short, everything he may own, and for property thus taken there was no reclamation. Should the paramour be unmarried and without an establishment of his own then redress may be sought from his father. (Bradley, 1923, 271)

There are also examples of the reverse. Oswalt (1978, 503) says that, while divorce was rare among the polygamous Natchez, "an upper-class woman married to a common man was free to take other husbands. Furthermore, such a woman could have her husband put to death if he committed adultery."

CRIMES

Crimes and law are bound together inextricably, and both vary from society to society. Law itself has been defined from a variety of perspectives in cross-cultural analysis. Violent crime needs to be looked into from at least two perspectives: from data about Indians prior to contact (and perhaps even at initial contact), when Indians operated largely under their own legal systems, and from information gathered since the legal system was imposed on them. In some cases, precontact evidence is obtained from physical remains or from depictions of events. Mochica pottery from Peru, for example, often depicts prisoners, naked and bound, being led to sacrificial sites and executed.

MURDER

The killing of a human takes many forms. Some are permitted, some are demanded, and some are not allowed. In many societies it is permitted to kill someone who is trying to kill you; in warfare one is expected, with impunity, to kill others. Those forms often are labeled with different terms, depending on the context in which the action occurred. Homicide, manslaughter, and criminally negligent homicide are legally distinguished. Suicide also counts as a kind of murder, and, to some people, abortion also is included.

Different societies define many of these contexts differently. By and large, in America, one is not permitted to argue self-defense because someone was practicing magic against you. Consider however, a case in the Pennsylvania Dutch country, reported by Lewis (1969), in which a man was arrested, tried, and executed for killing another man, whom he believed was trying to kill him by witchcraft (much to the amusement of the press). Consider, though, the following set of postulates proposed by Hoebel (1976, 142–143) regarding killings that are religiously shaped:

Postulate I. Man is subordinate to supernatural forces and spiritual beings, *which are benevolent in nature.*

Corollary I. Individual success and tribal well being are abetted by the beneficent assistance of the supernaturals.

Postulate II. The killing of a Cheyenne by another Cheyenne pollutes the tribal fetishes and also the murderer.

Corollary 1. Bad luck will dog the tribe until the fetishes are purified.

Corollary 2. The murderer must be temporarily isolated from the social body.

Corollary 3. Violent behavior that may lead to homicide within the tribe must be avoided.

Corollary 4. Killing an enemy while in the presence of a tribal fetish is inimical to the supernaturals.

Suicide

Suicide constitutes a murder in which both the perpetrator and the victim are the same individual. Questions of "assisted suicides," as in the case of Dr. Kevorkian, or the more recent "police assisted suicides," where a person makes the police believe they are in mortal danger, and causes them to respond by shooting them, are relatively recent examples. On the other hand, distinguishing between "accidental" deaths and suicides may prove difficult. A powerful play by the Kiowa author Hanay Geiogamah deals with a train track that lies across the stage. Periodically in the course of the play, the modern Oklahoma Indians depicted freeze in their tracks, and the sound of a train is heard. Geiogamah is referring to the fact that Indians go drinking, get drunk, and walk home. On the way, they pass out on a railroad track or highway, where they are killed by a train or auto. These seem to be a kind of "assisted suicides."

Mohawk Indians, driving from New York back to the reservations after working all week on high steel, are often killed in horrendous car accidents in which the drivers, who have often drunk substantial amounts of alcohol, lose control of and wreck their cars, killing the occupants. Some of the Mohawks have regarded this overtly as suicide, saying that, since they no longer have control over their lives, they at least will have control over their deaths.

These are examples of rather violent "suicides," as opposed to some of those reported for Inuit, where elderly people used to wander off to die. This typically was explained as a way of removing a "burden" from those with whom they lived, thereby sparing them the problems of having to care for so many people. These suicides would be hard to classify as *violent*. Being driven toward suicide because of a cultural pattern is generally not seen as violent, although being driven (or forced) into it by an individual might well be.

One of the more remarkable examples of violence and aggression appears in Lorenz' (1963) book, *On Aggression*. A psychologist named Margolin (whose unpublished work is used extensively by Lorenz), holds that violence is so endemic (and genetically controlled from a kind of inbreeding) in Ute culture that the culture requires that murderers commit suicide. Unfortunately for both Margolin and Lorenz, this seems not to be the case, as suicides are rather rare in the data and unconnected to what few murders there had been (Beatty, 1968). The Ute, in fact, are certainly not thought of as particularly violent. Rightly or wrongly, that image tends to be associated far more with the League of the Iroquois in the Northeast (specifically the Seneca, Cayuga, Onondaga, Oneida, and specifically the Mohawk) and, to a lesser extent, perhaps with the Huron.

Of particular interest is the discussion of Iroquois suicides. Fenton (1941, 95) holds that "male suicides are apt to be violent," though women also have chosen violent deaths. The methods include strangling or hanging oneself, shooting oneself, drowning, and hurling oneself under a freight train or into the rapids above a waterfall. Poisoning is the only nonviolent method given. Among the motives listed are love problems, attempts to avoid enforced marriages, martyrdom, revenge, and sickness.

Homicide

Very early written records indicate that torture and killing were carried out by native populations. René Groupil, Isaac Jouges, Jean de la Lande, Antoine Daniel, Gabriel Lalemant, Jean de Brébeuf, Charles Garnier, and Noël Chabanel were all killed in the New World as the result of attacks by Indians. Although doubtful it is that the Mohawk saw this as a ritual sacrifice (at least not in Girard's terms), it would appear that the Catholic Church (and possibly the missionaries themselves) took these deaths as a sign of martyrdom. The Iroquois themselves may have seen it as a part of their warfare. Because it is difficult to contextualize the act as being either religion or warfare (although the author leans toward the latter), it is included here as a homicide.

Homicide was a possible punishment for some cases of wrongdoing within the group. While a wife might have her nose or ears cuts as a punishment for adultery, there was no standard punishment for the male, although it was possible that the husband might kill him. "There was no other recognized punishment for the male criminal, but, as occurred sometimes in civilized society, he was occasionally slain by the injured husband, who then made peace with the relatives of the victim by the customary gifts. When all the parties belonged to the same band, the matter was usually arranged without much difficulty, but when two different bands it became almost a national dispute and scenes of bloody violence were an occasional outcome" (Bradley, 1923, 271).

Similarly, Rassmussen (1927/1969) discusses the Musk Ox Eskimos' involvement in homicide. He claimed that virtually all the adult males in the fifteen families who made up the settlement had been involved as killers or accessories in homicides in which there was a quarrel over women. Since Eskimos are often thought to have a society that does not engage in war and whose major recourse to affronts are song duels in which opponents attempt to ridicule one another, this amount of involvement in homicide seems dramatic. While the Eskimo are rather liberal in terms of pre- and postmarital sexual behaviors and have engaged in wife-exchange, cultural rules are rather explicit on these things: "the Eskimo enter into continuous competition and often violent conflict for the possession of women in a struggle that takes the form of flagrant adultery and willful appropriation of other men's wives" (Hoebel, 1976, 83).

Abortion and Infanticide

Abortion and infanticide are complex concepts since they can be classified only as murder if the victim is considered human. Current violent acts centered on abortion in America indicate that there is a schism in the culture between those who approve and those who do not approve of abortion. Doctors who had performed abortions have been killed by others who maintained that killing those who perform such procedures is justified, because in the United States, one may use deadly force to prevent another from committing murder. But what of cultures that do not see newborns as "people"? A certain amount of socialization may be required before "human" status is reached. In effect, humanness is a quality that one acquires as one develops. In such cases, infanticide may be nothing more than a kind of "retroactive abortion." The infant, who is not yet human, can be killed with some impunity.

There are a number of cultures that practice infanticide for a variety of reasons (see Harris, 1974, for his discussions on the relationships between warfare and infanticide from a cultural materialist point of view). In North America, infanticide has been found in all cultural areas to different degrees, but was probably not a universal practice (Driver, 1961). Nomadic people seemed to be willing to kill deformed children who could not keep up with their lifestyle. Another reason for infanticide was scarcity of food. Under these conditions, feeding a baby might be considered to be taking food from the mouth of one who is more likely to survive. Hence, this practice is more likely to be found in arctic and subarctic areas. For some, like the Kuskowagamiut Eskimo, Oswalt (1978) reports, what is considered infanticide might occur during the first few years of life. However, "the attitude was that [since] part of the soul of a deceased individual returned to the body in the next one born, there was no real destruction of life" (p. 119).

The Natchez, a socially stratified society, are reported to have practiced funeral rituals for the Great War Chief Tattooed Serpent, the brother of the Great Sun, that included lower-class parents strangling their children to death out of respect for the dead man. By doing so, their status was raised to that of nobles (Oswalt 1978).

ASSAULT

Assault, by legal definition requires an injurious act; in American Indian culture, assault requires that members of the group find the act offensive.

This is indicated by the use of negatively charged words, such as *quarrel*, and so on. Reports of actual homicides are included here as well, since the quotes below do not make homicide/assault discriminations.

Goldfrank (1945; 1966) gives a catalogue of violent crimes for the Blood, but it must be remembered that the period under discussion here occurred well after contact.

> They [the Blood] informed us of a quarrel between the Painted Feathers band and the Cold band caused by a woman who had been debauched by the latter . . . four of the party were wounded, and the woman shot in the leg. (Henry and Thompson, 1979 cited in ibid., 572)
> He [a Blackfoot] was a notorious scoundrel, who had murdered three of his own countrymen. (Henry and Thompson, cited in ibid., 543.)

And, some twenty years later, Maximilian (1992, cited in ibid., 268) learns from an Indian whom he meets "that an Indian had run away with his sister, the wife of a third person, and they had ridden out to look for him in order to shoot him." And in another passage, he states, "He (White Buffalo) had lately shot his sister, because she kept up an intercourse with a man against whom he had advised her. A chief of the Blackfeet with whom he had a quarrel shot him through the thigh; he, however, did not lose his presence of mind, and killed his enemy, notwithstanding his wound" (Maximilian, cited in ibid., 272).

The remaining cases, taken from winter counts and recent anthropological field notes, deal specifically with the subjects of this chapter, "the vicious . . . and turbulent" blood.

CURRENT SITUATIONS AMONG AMERICAN INDIANS

Leaving historical times behind and looking at more current examples of violent criminal activity, it appears that the same contexts in which violence occurred, namely, warfare, religion, and criminal activity, still exist. Of course, what many Indians see as *warfare*, the U.S. government classifies as *criminal activity*.

Probably the most dramatic cases have had to do with Indian rights activists (for example, the American Indian Movement) who have been involved in violent altercations with the U.S. government. As is the case with criminal cases discussed below, Indians are more likely to be on the receiving end of violent actions. Although the killing of two government agents on the Pine Ridge reservation certainly can be seen as a violent act (perhaps perceived by Indians as warfare and by the government as criminal), the catastrophe that followed was far more damaging to the Indians (see Mathiessen, 1983).

The problems that have arisen over Indian sovereignty are not restricted to Pan Indian groups. The confrontations on the Mohawk reservations at both Ahkwesahsne and Kahnawake are well documented in both book and film. Here again, the confrontations clearly involved the issue of self-government and a genuine feeling that both American and Canadian governments are foreign and invading powers, while these governments tend to regard reservations as "federal land." The fractionalization within groups often allows these governments to justify their positions. Strong parallels can be made with problems in Britain with Northern Ireland.

Recently, the Department of Justice issued a report concerning criminal violence and American Indians. The report stresses Indians as victims of crime, rather than as perpetrators, something which rarely was done in earlier cases. According to the report,

> The findings reveal a disturbing picture of American Indian involvement in crime as both victims and offenders. The rate of violent victimizations estimated from responses by American Indians is well above that of other U.S. racial or ethnic subgroups and is more than twice as high as the national average. This disparity in the rates of violence affecting American Indians occurs across age groups, housing locations, income groups, and sexes.
>
> With respect to the offender, two findings are perhaps most notable: American Indians are more likely than people of other ethnic races to experience violence at the hands of someone of a different race, and the criminal victimizer is more likely to have consumed alcohol preceding the offense. However, the victim/offender relationships of American Indians parallel that of all victims of violence. (Greenfeld and Smith, 1999, 213)

SEXUAL ASSAULT

Despite the statements above about the possible treatment of adulterous women in Blackfeet society, current statistics on sexual assault indicate something quite different. The Department of Justice report reported the percentage of Indians in jail by offense (see Table 16.1) The percentage of unconvicted inmates jailed for sexual assault is "too small to estimate." For the unconvicted population as a whole, 3.8 percent were jailed for the sexual assault. Nonetheless, 7.1 percent of the incarcerated Indian population have been jailed for sexual assault, as opposed to 3 percent of the total inmate population.

It is interesting to note that American Indians are more likely to be convicted for violent assault than the general population. While 36.7 percent of the total jailed population have been charged with violent assault, only 21.7 percent of inmates have been convicted of committing such an act (a 15-point drop). However, while 26.6 percent of Indian inmates are charged with such acts, 21.9 percent are convicted. Since roughly the same percentage of convicted inmates has been found for both groups, one may suspect that juries may be more likely to convict Indians. In all cases the drop in percent is greater for the general population than it is for the Indian one.

Table 16.1
American Indian Jail Inmates, by Offense, 1999

	Unconvicted jail inmates		Convicted jail inmates	
	All Races	American Indian	All Races	American Indian
Total	100.0%	100.0%	100.0%	100.0%
Violent	36.7%	26.6%	21.7%	21.9%
Homicide	6.6	2.7	1.5	0.2
Sexual assault	3.8	—	3.0	7.1
Robbery	8.8	2.2	5.5	7.9
Assault	15.4	15.7	10.0	10.1
Other violent	2.1	5.9	1.7	1.6
Property	25.6%	27.4%	28.6%	27.0%
Burglary	7.7	11.5	8.0	8.1
Larceny	5.6	2.3	9.5	6.2
Motor vehicle theft	3.3	7.3	2.3	4.7
Other property	9.0	6.3	8.8	7.9
Drugs	20.2%	6.5%	23.7%	15.8%
Public order	17.4%	39.5%	25.6%	35.3%
Weapons	2.2	8.2	2.4	0.7
DWI	3.6	13.8	9.6	13.1
Other public order	11.6	17.5	13.6	21.5
Number	165,733	4,241	314,867	9,824

—Too small to estimate.

Greenfield and Smith, 1999.

ALCOHOL AND VIOLENCE

The question of the relationship between alcohol and crime is significant. There has been a long standing belief that violence among American Indians is caused by alcohol. There is little doubt that the consumption of both alcohol and other drugs is a problem in crime in general. However, Levy and Kuntz (1974) have pointed out that, at least in Navajo, crime rates have remained rather constant, while the level of alcoholism has increased. If alcohol were the cause of the violence and crime, then one would expect to find a rising rate in violence and crime as alcohol consumption increased, but this is not what appears to have happened. It may be that alcohol predisposes the release of repressed aggressive behavior, rather than being the direct cause of the behavior.

In this culture, alcohol is often seen as an excuse for behavior. A person who acts out of character can either blame their behavior on their drinking or repress the memory totally and claim they were too drunk to re-member what they did. However, to blame criminal acts on a high alco-holism rate ignores cross-cultural data. There are many societies in which there are high rates of alcoholism, but the crime rate is not high. Japan is a classic example. By and large Japanese who drink a great deal do not re-sort to violence.

It seems far more reasonable to argue that alcoholism and the violence associated with it stems far more from the genocidal attacks by Europeans on aboriginal cultures, which resulted in the loss of languages and cul-tural institutions, which, in turn, led to psychological problems. It seems far more rational to see violence both by and against Indians as manifes-tations of 500 years of oppressive policies, rather than the fact that Indians are often alcoholic. The fact that Indians are more likely to be attacked by outsiders than other Indians speaks less about alcoholism than the set of political relationships between the two groups.

With the exception of alcohol, American Indians overall seem to be less involved with drugs than the surrounding population. A notable excep-tion involves the use of peyote, which is listed by the federal government as a "controlled substance." However, this substance is used in the Peyote religion (Native American church). The government has held that giving a drug ritual status does not make it legal to use it, although the author knows of no examples of Christian churches being held responsible for the giving of alcohol to minors during Mass. Neither has the author been able to locate any examples of violence that occurred while under the in-fluence of peyote. This is probably the result of peyote being contextual-ized in a religious sphere; in consequence, the behavior while under the influence of peyote is also ritualized.

NOTES

1. The classification of the peoples of the world is rather complex. One method is by language, another is by cultural area, and one is by level of sociocultural in-tegration. According to the first method, American Indian languages are grouped into a number of major "phyla," such as Macro-Siouan. Within that phyla there are subdivisions, one of which is Iroquoian. This family, like Romance languages, con-tains a number of languages (Seneca, Mohawk, Cherokee, etc.).

The second approach, by cultural area, is one that looks at the kinds of similar adaptations made by peoples living in the same kind of ecological niche. Gener-ally these areas are Plains, Eastern, Southwestern, Pacific Northwest Coast, and so on.

The last indicates the level of political organization—often bands, tribes, chief-doms, and states. Several of these classifications indicate the particular interests of those making the classifications. On occasion, some political structures were com-plex enough to label specific confederations. The League of the Iroquois was a po-litical entity that originally united five separate groups: the Senecas, Cayugas,

Onondagas, Oneidas, and Mohawks. Later the Tuscaroras joined the confedera-
tion. Hence, *Iroquois* can refer to a language family or to the League of the Iroquois. For example, a Mohawk would be a member of the League and a speaker of
an Iroquoian language. A Huron would not have been a member of the League of
the Iroquois, but would be an Iroquoian speaker.

REFERENCES

Atyeo, D. (1979). *Blood and guts: Violence in sports.* New York: Paddington Press,
    Grosset and Dunlop.

Axtell, J., and Sturtevant W. (1986). The unkindest cut of all—or who invented
    scalping. In Roger L. Nichols (Ed.), *The American Indian* (pp. 47–60). New
    York: Alfred P. Knopf. Reprinted from *William and Mary Quarterly,* 1980,
    3(37), 451–472.

Beatty, J. (1968). Refuting Lorenz on the Ute. In Ashley Montagu (Ed.), *Man and ag-
    gression.* London: Oxford University Press.

Benedict, R. (1946). *Patterns of culture.* New York: Penguin Books.

Billard, J.B. (Ed.). (1989). *The world of the American Indian.* Washington, DC: Na-
    tional Geographic.

Bradley, J.H. (1923). Blackfoot war with the whites, and characteristics, habits and
    customs of the Blackfeet Indians. *Historical Society of Montana, Contribu-
    tions, 9,* 252–288.

Craig, C. (1998, mid-December). Praying for the whales and the Makah. *News from
    Indian Country,* p. 4A.

Dorsey, G.A. (1907). The Skidi rite of human sacrifice. *Proceedings of the 15th Session
    of the International Congress of Americanists, 2,* 72–77, Quebec.

Driver, H. (1961). *Indians of North America.* Chicago: University of Chicago.

Fenton, W. (1941). Iroquois suicide: A study in the stability of a cultural pattern.
    Smithsonian Institution Bureau of American Ethnology Bulletin, 128, 79–137.

Forbes, J.D. (Ed.). (1964). *The Indian in America's past.* Englewood Cliffs, NJ: Pren-
    tice Hall.

Friederici, G. (1993). Scalping in America: Annual report of the Smithsonian Insti-
    tution 1906. In W.G. Spittal (Ed.), *Scalping and torture: Warfare practices
    among North American Indians* (175–193). Montreal: Iroqrafts Ltd. Indian
    Publications.

Girard, R. (1989). *Violence and the sacred* (Patrick Gregory, Trans). Baltimore: Johns
    Hopkins University Press. (Original work published 1972)

Goldfrank, E.S. (1945; 1966). *Changing configurations in the social organization of a
    Blackfoot tribe during the reserve period (the Blood of Alberta, Canada)* (Ameri-
    can Ethnological Society Monograph No. 8). Seattle and London: Univer-
    sity of Washington Press.

Greenfeld, L.A., and Smith, S. (1999). *American Indians and crime.* Washington, DC:
    United States Department of Justice, Bureau of Statistics.

Hagan, W.T. (1961). *American Indians.* Chicago: University of Chicago Press.

Harris, M. (1974). *Cows, pigs, wars, and witches: The riddles of culture.* New York:
    Random House.

Henke, J. (1985). *Seal wars.* St. John's, Newfoundland: Breakwater Books.

Henry, J. (1963, Spring). American schoolrooms: Learning the nightmare. *Columbia University Forums*, 24–30.

Hinds, L. (1998, July 6). Safir denies it, Amnesty International confirmed it, black police groups reconfirmed police brutality. *Amsterdam News*, p. 1.

Hoebel, E.A. (1976). *The law of primitive man*. New York: Atheneum.

Josephy, A.M., Jr. (1968). *The Indian heritage of America*. New York: Alfred A. Knopf.

Knowles, N. (1940). The torture of captives by the Indians of eastern North America. *Proceedings of the American Philosophical Society, 82*(2). Philadelphia.

Levy, J., and Kuntz, E. (1974). *Indian drinking, Navajo practice and Anglo theories*. New York: Wiley.

Lewis, A.H. (1969). *Hex*. New York: Trident Press.

Lorenz, K. (1963). *On aggression*. New York: Harcourt Brace and World.

Mathiessen, P. (1983). *In the spirit of crazy horse*. New York: Viking Press.

Mihesuah, D.A. (1996). *American Indians: Stereotypes and realities*. Atlanta: Clarity.

Oswalt, W.H. (1978). *This land was theirs*. New York: John Wiley and Sons.

Pike, K.L. (1990). On the emics and etics of Pike and Harris. In Thomas N. Headland, Kenneth L. Pike, and Marvin Harris (Eds.), *Emics and Etics: The insider/outsider debate* (pp. 184–201). Newbury Park, CA: Sage.

Pospisil, L.J. (1978). *The ethnology of law*. Menlo Park, CA: Cummings Publishing.

Rassmussen, K. (1969). *Across Arctic America*. New York: Greenwood Press. (Original published in 1927)

Smith, M.E. (1975). Cultural variability in the structuring of violence. In Martin A. Nettleship, Dale Givers, and Anderson Nettleship (Eds.), *War and its causes and correlates* (pp. 599–618). The Hague: Mouton.

Stern, T. (1965). *The Klamath tribe: A people and their reservation* (American Ethnological Society Monograph No. 41). Seattle and London: University of Washington Press.

Terry, A. (1998, October 5). Abuses in America put under scrutiny: Amnesty International global effort to allege U.S. is a world leader in high tech repression. *Chicago Times*, p. 5.

Trigger, B. (1969). *The Huron farmers of the North*. New York: Holt Rinehart and Winston.

Vennum, T., Jr. (1994). *American Indian lacrosse: The little brother of war*. Washington, DC: Smithsonian Institution.

Wallace, A.F. (1958). Dreams and the wishes of the soul: A type of psychoanalytic theory among the seventeenth century Iroquois. *American Anthropologist, 60*, 234–248.

Wedel, W.R. (1977). Native astronomy and the Plains Caddoans. In Anthony Aveni (Ed.), *Native American astronomy* (pp. 131–146). Austin: University of Texas Press.

Wissler, C. (1911). The social life of the Blackfoot Indians. *American Museum of Natural History, Anthropological Papers* (Vol. 7, part 1). New York: American Museum of Natural History.

Wissler, C., and Spinden H.J. (1916). The Pawnee human sacrifice to the morning star. *American Museum Journal, 16*, 49–58.

Epilogue: Global Violence

Kay C. Greene

AN AFTERTHOUGHT AS INTRODUCTION TO THE EPILOGUE . . .

I already had arrived inside the United Nations Secretariat Building that Tuesday morning, when I remembered that I had planned to drop the manuscript of this epilogue into a mailbox. I also had forgotten my watch, and used my taxi receipt to see what time it was. The receipt read, "September 11, 2001, 8:42 A.M."—too late to go back and mail the manuscript. I proceeded quickly down the escalator toward the conference room where I was to chair a meeting. As I always do when I walk through the UN, I glanced up with semi-awareness at the CNN television monitors that hang high on the walls. I entered the conference room and began distributing materials for the meeting. We were interrupted abruptly by someone yelling that a plane had hit the World Trade Center (WTC). I raced down the hall and arrived at a CNN monitor just in time to see an explosion in Tower Two, soon determined to have been caused by a second plane. I reluctantly returned to the conference room, where only a handful of the 1,600 participants remained, the others spread along the length of the outer hallways, huddled under the television screens. Not knowing what else to do, and at the request of the few in attendance, we went through the motions of our meeting. As we closed, we were informed that a passenger plane had plowed in to the Pentagon in Washington, D.C., and that Tower Two of the WTC had collapsed.

Within minutes, everyone in the UN Secretariat Building was evacuated to the basement. Soon, all nonessential personnel were ordered out of the building, and, when I passed through the gate, the security guard told me to get as far away from the UN as possible. As I walked breathlessly downtown toward home, I could not take my eyes off the enormous black mass pounding into the air and covering up the end of our beautiful is-land called New York City. In tears, I watched Tower One sink slowly from the skyline and disappear into clouds of smoke and debris. When I arrived at the edge of my apartment complex, I encountered families of UN per-sonnel. Many were holding babies or tending children in carriages, and all were crying. They were afraid of what we all feared: the UN or our apart-ment complex—which housed the UN International School, UN Missions, and so many UN delegates—would become the next target of this pro-tracted and obvious terrorist attack. I turned to see a long line of UN staff members coming from behind me. They told us that all personnel had been evacuated and that they had been ordered not to return to the UN Building. They assured waiting family members that their loved ones would arrive home soon.

I ran quickly up the three-flight escalator to the main plaza of the com-plex. I rushed to buy food before returning to my apartment, in case a blackout shut down the elevators and forced us to walk up the stairs of the thirty-three-story building. The store, usually empty at 11:00 A.M., was very crowded, and the milk, bread, and bottled water were quickly disap-pearing. I grabbed what I needed, stood in a long line, and handed over my credit card. In the middle of the transaction, the card processing sys-tem failed, and I had to use what little cash I had left. When I got upstairs to my apartment, my telephone was not working. When I turned on the television set, many of the stations were not functioning, and my heart fell as I came to understand why. In the early 1970s, I had worked for the man who headed the team of broadcast engineers who implemented the trans-fer of all radio and television transmitter towers from the Empire State Building to the World Trade Center. I felt sickened when I realized that the engineers who worked for those stations at the very top of the WTC were likely killed in the collapse, a fact later confirmed.

Each passing moment brought a sobering realization, a new obstacle, or an urgent need. This unspeakable act of violence had robbed us of the safety and security of routine and redirected our energies. From the in-stant of the collapses, those of us living close to the scene were forced to wear masks and goggles everywhere we went. I was struck by the total de-struction of life as we had known it. Every aspect of living had changed, and performing the simplest task took a conscious awareness and concen-trated focus that, in many instances, could not be assessed.

Eerily, the epilogue I would have mailed to the editors for this book that fateful morning had predicted that the violence associated with terrorism and its resulting refugee situations would become a stronger and stronger collective focus for the world. Although I have added this opening, I barely have revised the original epilogue, which follows.

THE ORIGINAL EPILOGUE

This book illustrates the characteristics, manifestations, and challenges of violence, as well as the problems associated with it and its impact on individuals, groups, countries, and the world. The definitions provided for *violence* are many and vary between cultures. The researchers have focused on different forms and levels of violence; for example, one country is candidly discussed in terms of its public image as a violent, unstable, dangerous country; another just as honestly is portrayed as standing in contrast to its former reputation for being home to friendly and peaceful people; and another is proudly presented as a peace-loving society free of violence. Some contributors have discussed ethnic, religious, or cultural conflicts that involve terrorism, acts designed to be shocking and glaringly public, while others have placed their emphasis on domestic or family violence, acts most often perpetrated in private and hidden from view.

As I read these chapters, I wondered whether the impact of an open act of terrorism that maims or kills a large group of people within minutes is really that different from the results wrought by hidden, repeated violations of a similar number of individual women or children over time in their own homes. Each time I thought I had found the answer, I came face-to-face with another question. For example, I thought that one difference might be that witnesses to a public act of terrorism were likely to respond and follow through proactively, while those who observed domestic or family violence were much more likely to do nothing. But, as I followed that thought through time, I realized that history reveals that proactive responses are usually short-lived, and people turn their backs and go on with their lives. The relatively few exceptions include those people who devote their lives to addressing particular types of violence.

To forge a meaningful transformation in any common manifestation of violence appears to require a critical mass of some sort . . . but even then, how significant are the changes that occur? A concerted, tireless effort over time may entice more and more people to a cause, such as the widespread knowledge about female genital mutilation (FGM) that arose from the 1995 UN Fourth World Conference on Women in Beijing, China. Nonetheless, the resultant publicizing of FGM did not reduce the number of areas in which this "operation" is performed, which still stands at more than forty countries. However, some doctors in countries where the practice is not condoned, but which house immigrants who continue the "surgery," became more aware of such possibilities among their young female patients and were inspired to provide preventative education programs.

In terms of terrorism, one wonders what the critical mass could be that would make the world take proactive notice? How many people, what kind of people, and which countries have to become victims in order for the world to rise up and say "no more"? In 1999, recognizing terrorism as an emerging threat, the UN established a Terrorism Prevention Branch of its Office for Drug Control and Crime Prevention in Vienna, Austria. Its defining booklet (1999) begins, "Terrorism is a unique form of crime. In recent years, some analysts have perceived a dangerous trend towards inflicting high casualties in terrorist actions. So far, the use of weapons of mass destruction by terrorists has largely been confined to science fiction literature, but today's fiction can become tomorrow's fact if no preventative measures are take in time." The principle objectives of the Terrorism Prevention Branch involve researching all forms and manifestations of terrorism and supporting UN Member States in preventing and combating terrorism by offering technical cooperation. Based on the branch's observation that acts of terrorism "are usually preceded by less violent forms of protest and conflict," its primary goal is to "identify early warning signals of violence in order to prevent acts of terrorism."

UN Secretary-General Kofi Annan, in *The Question of Intervention* (1999), notes that in many of today's conflicts, civilians are the main targets of violence. Various UN sources put the number of civilian casualties somewhere between 75 and 90 percent of the total casualties worldwide from acts of terrorism in 2000. In terms of just the child victims of armed conflicts in the 1990s, more than 2 million were killed, 6 million seriously injured or permanently disabled, and 1 million orphaned or separated from their families. Fifteen million became refugees or were internally displaced, and an unknown number were deeply psychologically traumatized (UNICEF, 2000).

While Annan (1999) notes that most modern conflicts have occurred within the borders of sovereign states, he believes that "State frontiers should no longer be seen as a watertight protection for war criminals or mass murderers." He sounded the warning that "most internal conflicts do not stay internal for very long. They soon spill over into neighboring countries, most obviously and tragically, through the flow of refugees." However, he provides hope and encouragement by pointing out that this "spilling over" into neighboring countries also occurs through "the spread of knowledge" by way of the news media. "Human suffering on a large scale has become impossible to keep quiet," he adds. "People in far-off countries not only hear about it, but often see in on their TV screens" (Annan, 1999).

Based on trends I've studied in UN literature and discussions, I predict that terrorism will become more commonplace for people in areas where such acts usually only have been read about in newspapers or viewed on television. And if that happens, I wonder whether such widespread repeated shocks to the world's sensitivities might shake humanity into a level of consciousness from which all forms of violence might begin to be experienced as too tiring, too draining, too painful, too destructive to be allowed. Wishful thinking?

How would one build a deep, active desire for peace and freedom of violence at the level of the planet's masses? The United Nations Children's Fund (UNICEF) believes that children, teenagers, and young adults are the hope for the future. "Ensuring that adolescents participate in their communities and civil society provides a unique opportunity to break vicious, intergenerational cycles that perpetuate violence. Teenagers have a profound and direct influence on the next generation because of their roles as older siblings, heads of households, parents and members of civil society" (UNICEF, 1999). If significant changes in all forms of violence are possible at all, they most certainly would begin with children, whose bodies, minds, feelings, and spirits are the world's greatest natural resources.

REFERENCES

Annan, Kofi A. (1999, December). *The question of intervention* (UN DPI/2080). New York: United Nations.

United Nations Office for Drug Control and Crime Prevention. (1999). Vienna: Author.

United Nations Children's Fund (UNICEF). (2000). *The state of the world's children, 2000*. New York: Author.

Index

About the Editors
and Contributors

LEONORE LOEB ADLER is a professor emerita of psychology in the Department of Psychology and the director of the Institute for Cross-Cultural and Cross-Ethnic Studies, of which she is the founder, at Molloy College. She is also a member of the advisory board of the Institute for International and Cross-Cultural Psychology at St. Francis College. She is a member of the editorial board for the *International Journal of Group Tensions*. She has edited or coedited sixteen books, published about seventy-five chapters and journal articles, and presented her research reports and papers at meetings and symposia all over the world. Adler has been honored with numerous awards.

FLORENCE L. DENMARK is the Robert Scott Pace–distinguished professor emerita of psychology at Pace University and an adjunct professor at the graduate school of the City University of New York. She serves as an NGO representative to the United Nations as well as copresident of the International Organization for the Study of Group Tensions. Denmark is a fellow of the New York Academy of Sciences, the American Psychological Society, and the American Psychological Association. In addition, she is a member of the advisory board of the Institute for Cross-Cultural and Cross-Ethnic Studies, Molloy College. She has authored or edited fifteen books and over 100 articles and book chapters and has given scholarly presentations at universities in many countries. She is a member of many honor societies, and, as a past president of the American Psychological Association, the International Council of Psychologists, and Psi Chi, she has been the recipient of many awards.

CONTRIBUTORS

RAMADAN A. AHMED has degrees in both psychology and law and received his Ph.D. in cognitive psychology—specifically in the development of concepts in cross-cultural perspective—from the University of Leipzig, Germany in 1981, and has since taught in Egypt, Sudan and Kuwait. Dr. Ahmed is a professor of psychology at Menoufia University, Egypt. At present, he is on leave at Kuwait University, Kuwait.

RUBEN ARDILA is a Colombian psychologist and a professor of psychology at the National University of Colombia. Ardila has published twenty-four books and more than 150 scientific papers in journals from several countries. He is the editor of *Revista Latinoamericana de Psicologia* (*Latin American Journal of Psychology*), which he founded in 1969. He received the 2004 Distinguished International Psychologist Award from Division 52 of the APA.

JOHN BEATTY is professor emeritus of anthropology at Brooklyn College, CUNY, and author and coauthor of a half a dozen books, the most recent of which is *Intercultural Communication* (coauthored with Junichi Takahashi). He also teaches courses in ethno- and archaeoastronomy at the American Museum of Natural History.

DIANE BRETHERTON is director of the International Conflict Resolution Centre and an associate professor in the psychology department at the University of Melbourne. She is a member of the Foreign Affairs Council of Australia and chair of the Committee for the Psychological Study of Peace of the International Union of Psychological Science.

JUNE F. CHISHOLM, a clinical psychologist, is professor of psychology at Pace University and an adjunct professor at New York University Medical Center. She has been a senior psychologist in the outpatient department of Harlem Hospital Center.

CHRIS P. de KOCK is the chief director and head of the Crime Information Analysis Centre of the South African Police Service, of which he is chief research specialist. He served as a researcher at the Human Sciences Research Council and is the author or coauthor of more than ten publications or contributions to publications.

MELVIN EMBER is president of the Human Relations Area Files, editor of *Cross-Cultural Research: The Journal of Comparative Social Science*, coauthor of several books, and coeditor of various encyclopedias. He has served as president of the Society for Cross-Cultural Research and was professor of anthropology at Hunter College and the graduate school of the CUNY.

UWE P. GIELEN is a professor of psychology and the director of the Institute for International and Cross-Cultural Psychology at St. Francis College, New York City. He served as editor-in-chief of the *International Journal of Group Tensions* and has been the editor of *World Psychology*. He is coeditor/coauthor of thirteen books.

YAKOV GILINSKY is professor and director of the Center of Deviantology at the Institute of Sociology (St. Petersburg) of the Russian Academy of Science. He serves as a dean of Law School at the Baltic University of Ecology, Politics, and Law in St. Petersburg. He has conducted numerous research studies and published over 280 papers in the field of criminology, deviant behavior, and social control.

KAY C. GREENE is a clinical psychologist in private practice, and was adjunct associate professor of psychology at John Jay College of Criminal Justice, Fordham University, Pace University in New York City, and former secretary-general of the International Council of Psychologists. She is founder and president of Bridge of Change and a regional trainer for the HOPE Program.

At the United Nations, she has been an NGO representative, senior representative for the World Federation for Mental Health, and elected chair of the executive committee for the NGO section of the United Nations Department of Public Information (DPI).

WILHELMINA J. KALU is a senior lecturer in special education and educational psychology, Faculty of Education, University of Nigeria, Nsukka. Kalu developed programs for undergraduates and postgraduates in special education. She has a number of publications in the areas of child psychology, abuse, and family violence, in addition to challenges in Nigerian special education and for women.

LUDWIG F. LOWENSTEIN an honorary member of the Polish Medical Society, founded Allington Manor in 1978. He was a visiting professor at the University of Khartoum in the Sudan and in various locations in the United Kingdom.

NOACH A. MILGRAM works at the Academic College of Judea and Samaria. He is a fellow of the American Psychology Association in the divisions of clinical psychology, developmental psychology, and international psychology. He has done empirical research and published numerous studies and chapters on various kinds of stressful situations.

CLARY MILNITSKY-SAPIRO is a professor in the graduate program of social and institutional psychology, as well as at the Institute of Psychology, Federal University of Rio Grande of the South. She is currently involved in research on "adolescent autonomy." Milnitsky-Sapiro is an active writer of chapters and journal articles as well as articles in newspapers. In addition, she frequently presented her papers at conferences and conventions.

JOSEPH O'DONOGHUE is the coeditor of *The International Journal of Case Studies and Research*. He is the author of *Corporate Strategies Effective in the Control of Computer Crime*, *The World of the Japanese Worker*, and *The World of the Irish Worker*. He served two terms as editor of *The Journal of Merger and Acquisition Analysis* and has worked as a Fulbright Scholar, and has been the recipient of numerous research grants and faculty awards at CUNY and at Hofstra University, where he served as the elected speaker of the university faculty.

ANDRÉ J. PELSER is professor of sociology at the University of the Free State in Bloemfontein, South Africa, where he has lectured for the past ten years. Prior to this, he was a researcher for the then Institute for Sociological and Demographic Research at the Human Sciences Research Council in Pretoria. He has authored, coauthored, and compiled more than ninety publications, including some thirty refereed articles. He has rendered consultancy services to various national and international institutions, organizations, and agencies.

ELENA L. SAMONTE-HINCKLEY is a retired professor with the Department of Psychology, University of the Philippines Diliman and headed the Industrial-Organizational Psychology masters program. She is also a member of the American Psychological Association, International Council of Psychologists, and National Research Council of the Philippines.

She is a recipient of various scholarships/fellowships, as well as travel and research grants and the Chancellor's Best Researcher Award in the Social Sciences. She was the President of the Psychological Association of the Philippines (PAP).

SARLITO WIRAWAN SARWONO is the dean of Faculty of Psychology at the University of Indonesia (UI), as well as professor of social psychology at the School of Police Science at UI. He also is the editor of the *South Pacific Journal of Psychology* and serves on the advisory board of the Institute for Cross-Cultural and Cross-Ethnic Studies. He has published several books and articles.

SEISOH SUKEMUNE received his Ph.D. at Hiroshima University and is now a professor emeritus. He is a member of the Japanese Psychological

Association, the American Psychological Association, and the International Council of Psychologists (ICP).

SERGEI V. TSYTSAREV is professor at the Doctoral Program in School and Community Psychology at Hofstra University in Hempstead, New York. His research findings have been presented at many international conventions and summarized in two books and more than fifty articles published in Russia, Japan, the United States, Germany, Ireland, and Italy.

ALFRED W. WARD is an associate professor of psychology at Pace University in New York, New York. He is involved in test development and has developed a norm-referenced achievement test assessing Basic Skills in Spanish and Arithmetic (BASISA) for ESL grade school students. Dr. Ward is currently engaged in an ongoing research project that examines risk and protective factors that moderate the relationship between exposure to community violence and symptomatology associated with Post-Traumatic Stress Disorder among inner-city youth.